SOUTHERN BIOGRAPHY SERIES
Bertram Wyatt-Brown, Editor

BERNICE KELLY HARRIS

BERNICE KELLY HARRIS

A good life was writing

Valerie Raleigh Yow

Louisiana State University Press
Baton Rouge

Designer: Barbara Neely Bourgoyne
Typeface: Sabon
Typesetter: Coghill Composition
Printer and binder: Edwards Brothers, Inc.

Grateful acknowledgment is made to Gordon Kelley, executor of the estate of Bernice Kelly Harris, for permission to reproduce passages from Harris's novels, short stories, children's books, and plays. The author is also grateful to Alice Jo Kelley Burrows and Frank Borden Hanes for permission to quote from Harris's letters in their possession; to Stephen Burgwyn for permission to quote from correspondence of Mebane Burgwyn with Bernice Kelly Harris; and to Marguerite Stem for permission to quote from correspondence of Thad Stem Jr. with Bernice Kelly Harris. Passages from Betty A. Hodges's article in the 28 May 1967 issue of the *Durham Morning Herald* are copyright by the *Durham Morning Herald* and used with permission. The quotation from Lee Smith's short story "Tongues of Fire" is reproduced by permission of Lee Smith.

Chapter 6 was first published, in somewhat different form, as "Haunting Work: The Federal Writers' Project," in *Pembroke Magazine* (1997).

Library of Congress Cataloging-in-Publication Data

Yow, Valerie Raleigh.
    Bernice Kelly Harris : a good life was writing / Valerie Raleigh
Yow.
        p.   cm. — (Southern biography series)
    Includes index.
    ISBN 0-8071-2348-X (cloth : alk. paper)
    1. Harris, Bernice Kelly, b. 1894.   2. Feminism and literature—
North Carolina—History—20th century.   3. Women and literature—
North Carolina—History—20th century.   4. Authors, American—20th
century—Biography.   5. North Carolina—In literature.   6. North
Carolina—Biography.   I. Title.   II. Series.
PS3515.A722Z97   1999
818'.5209—dc21
    [b]   98-51111
                                                              CIP

In memory of my mother,

MAE MOORE WYATT,

a beautiful working-class woman,
a storyteller, who always wanted to write.

And for her granddaughters,

ANNE AND LAURA QUINNEY,

who are writing women.

CONTENTS

ILLUSTRATIONS

PREFACE

I offer here a chronicle of the experience of an extraordinary woman writer, living an ordinary life in the first three-quarters of the twentieth century. Often biographies present lives marked by great adventure, exotic places, and dramatic personal events. What intrigued me about Bernice Kelly Harris is that she faced the challenges of living in a conventional marriage, in a small town, within narrow prescriptions for behavior; and from this she created imaginative, compelling literature. The personal dramas in her life were those ordinary people face: failure of dreams, loss of loved individuals, loneliness. On the other hand, her passionate interest was writing, and I try to convey the joy writing gave to her.

It is often said that a biographer is an artist under oath; I have held myself to that standard. The narration is based on evidence, either written documents, oral testimony, or published sources, with the citation given. When I do not have solid evidence, I indicate this to the reader by saying "perhaps" or "possibly" or "maybe."

I give the plots of Bernice Kelly Harris's books because the novels and plays have long been out of print. Readers may not have had access to all of them but need to know something about them to follow the interpretation of the relationship of Bernice Harris's work to her life.

Biographical study encompasses both the sweeping gaze and the minutely focused stare. As an historian, I have been fascinated with the way an individual life reveals the intersection of culture, historical moment, and the particular. As a psychologist, I have been intrigued with the way emotions are interpreted by the individual in terms of culturally approved feelings. As a woman, I have been observant of the way Bernice Kelly Harris took care of the homely tasks of daily living and in the process created her own vision of a meaningful life. And so this book is in its details the narration of a particular woman's life, but I hope it partakes in a general way of the life of Every Woman.

ACKNOWLEDGMENTS

This biography had its beginnings in a casual conversation with Lu Ann Jones, historian at East Carolina University. When I said I wanted to write a biography of a writer, that I wanted to find out what a woman writer's life might have been like in the South early in the century, she suggested I read Bernice Kelly Harris's work. It was the best advice I've ever received.

All through the research, Betty Hodges, journalist and literary editor at the Durham (N.C.) *Herald-Sun* and a friend of Bernice Harris, introduced me to people who had known Mrs. Harris, listened to my questions and helped me find the answers, and kept up a running dialogue with me about my subject. Her generosity still amazes me.

Richard Shrader and John White and their staff in the Manuscripts Department, Southern Historical Collection, Wilson Library, University of North Carolina (Chapel Hill), helped me in some way nearly every day for months that stretched into several years. A travel stipend from the Archie K. Davis Fellowship, administered by H. G. Jones, enabled me to travel to other archives. Library staff at Chowan College trusted me with two file drawers of uncataloged materials. I am especially grateful for the help given me by Robin Brabham, Special Collections Librarian at the J. Murrey Atkins Library, University of North Carolina at Charlotte, and by George Stevenson, Private Manuscripts Archivist for the North Carolina State Archives.

An invaluable source was the correspondence of Mrs. Harris with her close friend Mebane Holoman Burgwyn which her son Stephen White Burgwyn entrusted to me. Mrs. Harris's nephew Gordon Kelley researched land deeds and wills to give me the specific information I needed. Her grandniece Sandra Poindexter found the early photograph of Mrs. Harris that is in this book. Her niece Alice Jo Kelley Burrows offered family albums and generously lent me photographs from them.

Mrs. Harris's friends welcomed me and let me record their memories, heightening my understanding and making the book richer than written records alone would have allowed: Ann Basnight, Clara Bond Bell, Holley Mack Bell, Elizabeth Bullock, Linda Gay Denton, John Ehle, Magdeline Faison, Ann Bradley Ford, Frank Borden Hanes, Elizabeth Harris, Betty Hodges, Henry Lewis, Betsey Bradley Merritt, Roy Parker Jr., the late George Pyne, the late Sam Ragan, Jessie Moose Stanley, Marguerite Stem, Frances Wellman, and Bruce Whitaker. William Ivey Long, Mrs. Harris's first student in playwriting, sent me his tape-recorded remembrances. Her family members Alice Jo Kelley Burrows, Gordon Kelley, Sandra Poindexter, Carey Coats, and Patricia Coats Kube recorded their reminiscences for me and thoughtfully answered my questions in personal interviews and telephone conversations. Shelby Stephenson, editor of the *Pembroke Magazine,* published an earlier version of the chapter on the Federal Writers' Project, and I wish to acknowledge both his permission to use a revised version here and his continuing interest in Bernice Kelly Harris and encouragement to me.

Busy people took time out of their days to read the manuscript. Vashti Lewis, a scholar in the field of African American literature, read the chapter on *Janey Jeems* and gave me the benefit of her excellent critic's eye. David Cecelski, historian at the Southern Oral History Program at the University of North Carolina (Chapel Hill), read selected chapters and asked questions that caused me to think more deeply about my writing on racial issues in the first draft. Mrs. Harris's friends in the North Carolina Writers Conference, John Ehle, Clara Bell, and Holley Bell, read the chapter on the Writers Conference and corrected errors. Wood Smethurst read sections dealing with Mrs. Harris's friendship with his mother, Margarette Wood Smethurst. Elizabeth Harris, a close friend of Bernice Kelly Harris in Seaboard, read sections on life there and corrected factual errors. Beverley Buehrer, my fellow writer in the original Wordwrights, read the chapter on *Hearthstones* and offered a critique at once helpful and appreciative. Joanne Napoli, language teacher and editor with precision, read many chapters and lovingly pointed out my stylistic errors. Mrs. Harris's niece Alice Jo Burrows and grandniece Patricia Coats Kube read the entire manuscript and corrected factual errors in family history. Mrs. Harris's good friends Betty Hodges and Roy Parker Jr. also read the manuscript in its entirety and gave me a thoughtful critique; Betty, with her excellent memory and wide knowledge of the North Carolina writers' scene, caught misstatements no one else could. I am especially indebted to Lu Ann Jones, historian of North Carolina's rural people, for her careful reading of the first draft and her perceptive critique which inspired me to produce a better second draft. For all these individuals' interest in Bernice Kelly Harris and for the generous way they gave me help, I am heartened and admiring.

The women in Wordwrights South, Joyce Allen, Deborah Norman, and Mary Michael, read and pondered sections of the biography over many months of our meetings—their insightful comments helped me improve the manuscript. Always their good humor and comradeship made me feel supported in this writing. Robert Anthony, curator of the North Carolina Collection in the Wilson Library, kept the vision of a published book before my eyes. And my daughter Anne Quinney and her friend Christopher Greenwald listened with a light in their eyes over many long dinners to my adventures in researching this book. Their enthusiasm matched my own.

NOTE ON CITATIONS OF MAJOR COLLECTIONS

Bernice Kelly Harris Papers, University of North Carolina

The main collection of Bernice Kelly Harris's letters and manuscripts is in the Manuscripts Department, Southern Historical Collection, Louis Round Wilson Library, University of North Carolina, Chapel Hill, North Carolina: Bernice Kelly Harris, Papers, number 3804. After the first reference, this collection is cited throughout the text as BKH, UNC, with "f" for folder. When the page or letter does not have a number or date, the first words are given to aid in identifying the document.

Oral histories, unless otherwise noted as remaining in private archives, have been deposited with the Bernice Kelly Harris Papers in the Southern Historical Collection. The location is likewise given as BKH, UNC. After the first citation, the number of the tape side is given, followed by a colon and then by the tape counter number.

Bernice Kelly Harris Papers, Chowan College

A smaller collection of Bernice Kelly Harris's letters, notes, and manuscripts is in the Whittaker Library of Chowan College in Murfreesboro, North Carolina. This collection is contained in two file drawers and has not been cataloged. The location of the document must necessarily be imprecise. In a few cases, I found documents clumped together in a packet and put a temporary identification number on them in pencil. After the first reference, the collection is cited in this text as BKH, Chowan.

Richard Gaultier Walser Papers, University of North Carolina

A collection of Mrs. Harris's letters can be found in Richard Walser's papers in the Manuscripts Department, Southern Historical Collection, Louis Round Wilson Library, University of North Carolina, Chapel Hill, North Carolina: Richard Gaultier Walser, Papers, number 4168. After the first reference, this collection is cited throughout the text as Walser, UNC, with "f" for folder.

Stephen Burgwyn Archives

The correspondence of Bernice Kelly Harris with Mebane Holoman Burgwyn is contained in the private archives of her son Stephen White Burgwyn, who resides in Jackson, North Carolina. This correspondence is rarely dated; the undated letters are identified by the first phrase. After the first reference, the collection is cited in the text as Burgwyn archives.

Federal Writers' Project Records, University of North Carolina

Documents from the Federal Writers' Project used in this text are located in the Manuscripts Department, Southern Historical Collection, Louis Round Wilson Library, University of North Carolina, Chapel Hill, North Carolina: Federal Writers' Project Records, 1936–1940, no. 3709. Life histories written by Bernice Kelly Harris are in folders 416–480. After the first reference, the collection is cited in the text as FWP, UNC, with "f" to indicate folder number.

Bernice Kelly Harris

1

A Narrow Road to Heaven: Growing Up on a North Carolina Farm

At the end of her life the novelist Bernice Kelly Harris reflected on the reasons which compelled her to write her first novel, *Purslane*: she said the lives of simple farm people she grew up among had "too much meaning to be left unrecorded."[1] What was farming life like in Piedmont North Carolina at the turn of the century? What were these people's values? How did such a life produce a writer like Bernice Kelly Harris?

At the turn of the century people, whether urban or rural, worked with their hands, lived without automobiles or electricity, and plucked their own chickens. The childhood of Bernice Kelly Harris was not so different from the experiences many of our grandparents and great-grandparents knew, but in the temperate climate of North Carolina, working the land generally meant reward—if you were among those who owned their own land, and the Kellys owned. One of Bernice Kelly Harris's favorite words in adulthood was "bounty." By it she meant the assurance that the earth would offer what was needed and would do so in abundance. She described this environment in her autobiography:

> Gooseberry bushes yielded tart purplish fruit for mouth-watering
> pies and preserves. There were currants and figs, scuppernongs and
> black grapes to enjoy at the vines and to make communion wine out of,
> white mulberries and purple damsons, black walnuts and hickory nuts,

every kind of orchard fruit, and in the nearby meadow there were black-berries and huckleberries. There were cane patches, from which came our winter supply of sorghum. The leaves of sage bushes provided savory seasoning for sausage and tea for chills and fever. Sassafras roots from the bottom, steeped in boiling water and then lightly sweetened, gave us tonic and beverage tea, a fragrant and aromatic amber drink for springtime suppers. There were plump chickens and pigs and milk cows to supply fowl and meat and dairy foods for the table. There were garden vegetables winter and summer.[2]

To claim this bounty, work was needed—and both adults and children worked hard. The Kelly family farmed in Wake County, near Raleigh, in the Piedmont section of North Carolina. Unlike the flat lowlands of the coastal plain to the east or the mountainous terrain of the western part of the state, the Piedmont is characterized by rolling hills; it is lush with vegetation and hardwoods, veined with creeks, and studded with farm ponds. In the first decade of the century, the area was on the way toward industrialization, but the vast majority of people still worked in agriculture, with cotton and tobacco the principal crops, and grains such as oats and corn secondary crops. Bernice Kelly Harris's family produced all of these. Prices were rising in the early years of the century for cotton and tobacco, so the bounty Harris recalled was not just memory's trick.

And the family was well-situated in terms of the amount of land farmed. Bernice's ancestors, both the Poole and Kelly families, had been among the first settlers in the area and had accumulated vast amounts of land. Her mother, Rosa Poole, brought land into her marriage with William Kelly (always called Bill), who already had land and continued to acquire more. In Wake County at the time, the majority of farms—two out of three—contained less than a hundred acres; Bernice's parents had 468.5 acres by 1914, which placed them near the top of the scale for farm size. They were not among the gentry, however. This group was composed of a relatively small number who owned estates of over 500 acres—although no single farm in Wake County had as much as 1,000 acres.[3] In adulthood, Bernice Kelly Harris would insinuate in her novels that the gentry are not the people who are typical of southern society or even the people to be admired. It is rather the small landowning class, the hardworking farming families, whom she would present as the interesting and admirable people.

During his lifetime, Bill Kelly bought and sold land, and so the amount fluctuated, but he always had at least one hired family living on the land and working for him; most often there were two. Sometimes his tenant farm families were black, sometimes white. Farm owners in Wake County were predominantly white (3,962), but black farm owners were a substantial minority (2,157). However, the numbers of black and white landless farmers were nearly equal: black tenant farmers numbered 1,576; white tenant farmers, 1,754.[4] The adult writer Bernice Harris portrayed the landless with compassion. Needless to say, for tenant farmers, life was not as bountiful as Bernice experienced it. The landless made the best deal they could with the landlord, given their vulnerability. As long as there were members of a family who could work and the prices for agricultural products were rising, it was possible to live. And there was enough demand for labor that many tenant families moved year after year, seeking better terms. Bill Kelly's tenants usually stayed on for years at a time.

Even though Bill Kelly had tenants working on his land, still he, his wife, and their children were in the fields when the season demanded, plowing and planting, chopping cotton, gathering the white bolls, picking tobacco leaves and stringing them up, and hoeing and weeding the garden vegetables.

The white frame house itself demanded intensive labor. It was in the form of a square, with an extension in the back. There was a central hallway with stairs leading to the second floor. In the front was the parlor, reserved for formal occasions, such as a visit from the preacher or a wedding or a wake. On the other side in front was the sitting room, with its potbellied stove, huge black overstuffed chair, chest, and several woven cane chairs as well as a bed. At the back were two bedrooms, and upstairs there were two large bedrooms running the length of the central part of the house. The extension on the back consisted of a covered passageway that led to the kitchen and dining room. (Often in the last century the kitchen was separate from the rest of a house like this one to protect the main part from fire and in summer to keep the heat of the cookstove away from the living quarters.) A porch wrapped around two sides of the house—a typical feature of a North Carolina middle-class dwelling. Children could play on the porch on a rainy day, but on a bright day they could move around the house as the sun moved over it, seeking warmth in winter, seeking the shady side in summer.[5]

All the rooms were needed as the family grew: three girls—Rachel Floyd, Pearl, and Bernice—were born, and then three boys, Elwood, Darwin, and William Olive. There were daily, year-round chores for the boys, such as the feeding of the animals, the milking, the cleaning of the animals and their space, the spreading of manure in the fields. Every day the boys had to chop wood for the cookstove and potbellied stove. Bernice and her sisters learned to can vegetables, dry fruit, churn butter, wash and iron clothes, and sew. The girls did the daily cleaning of grey film from the oil lamps, the emptying of the buckets of human waste in the mornings, the sweeping up and scouring of floors, and the washing of rounds of dishes, pumping and carrying the water from the well. They even swept the packed-dirt yard in front of the house.

But the children also played. Bernice's brother William Olive re-membered how on Saturdays the boys rose early to get their chores done so they could play baseball in the afternoon.[6] (Darwin later be-came a minor league baseball player.) The girls ventured into the dense woods in search of huge oak leaves, from which they made hats. They found tree stumps to serve as tables for tea with their dolls. When the girls—especially Bernice's big sisters Pearl and Rachel Floyd—grew older, they looked for love vines to name after their sweethearts. They left the vines hanging in sugarberry trees to seal a future. However, Bernice's favorite pastime was to be alone with her paper dolls—not purchased ones but the figures she cut out of the annual catalogs that came to the house and were discarded after a few years. With these paper dolls, she created a world of people with exciting stories about strange encounters as well as everyday happenings. The paper people talked to each other about all these things.

Bernice also acted out stories. She put herself back in Astolat, where knights and ladies of Arthurian legend had adventures. She had learned of such from elocutionary performances her teacher had given at school. Bernice would be the Lily Maid when her mood was sad—dying, she floated down the river to Lancelot. Or she would be Christi-ana from *The Pilgrim's Progress*. She felt a kind of right to this charac-ter because she had been christened at her birth in 1891 Bernice Christiana, albeit the name came from an aunt, Christiana Poole, who had died young. *The Pilgrim's Progress* was the one book besides the Bible that was always kept open in the parlor. It had fascinating pic-tures that she spent time studying. And so sometimes she was not

Christiana but Pilgrim, bolting from the City of Destruction. She transformed her ordinary daily scene: "Guano bags slung over my shoulder were my burden of sin, and the pasture bars were the wicket gate. The muddy bottom . . . was the Slough of Despond. A fence jamb was Doubting Castle. Mud puddles in the hog lot, which looked deep and mysterious and as darkly forbidding as death itself, were the river that had to be crossed into the New Jerusalem."[7]

But she also created imaginary dramatic situations. She would use the quilts hung on lines to air in the sun as stage curtains. She pretended a wooden cracker box was an organ. Sometimes she played characters she had only heard about, such as Queen Victoria. Sometimes the stage became the schoolroom and she played her music teacher—Miss Ruth Wingate—whom she loved.[8] Upstairs in her parents' house, she made a stage, and the children created and rehearsed a performance of a well-known story, "Demons in the Glass." Uncles, aunts, and cousins were invited to the performance; but they laughed when they were supposed to cry. The performers were greatly annoyed.[9]

Sometimes Bernice and her little brother William Olive and her sisters Rachel Floyd and Pearl played death. They buried dead goslings, puppies, and biddies, making headstones of rocks and wreaths from honeysuckle. They sang "Darling Nellie Gray" and cried real tears.[10]

But most often they played life. They took the roles of the grownups they observed around them. Bernice would be her mother, Rosa Poole Kelly, but the child was soon exhausted: "For to imitate her activity even for an hour came to seem too much like real work."[11] Although her mother had too many roles for anybody to even try to imitate, Bernice was learning from her all the time about how to be a caring person. Rosa Poole Kelly often ministered to sick neighbors. Indeed, both Bernice's mother and father sat up at night with family members or neighbors who had typhoid or pneumonia or malaria. When someone died, Bernice knew that her mother bathed the corpses and that her father kept the nightlong vigils for the dead. Although her parents tried to spare their children the details of these events, the children overheard whispered talk behind closed doors and learned much about adult life's tragedies.[12]

The children also "played like" they were their uncles and aunts—they learned to observe every detail of behavior and speech so that they could reproduce it. They liked to be Uncle Paschal, who would sit on his porch and tell tall tales about strange varmints. They also portrayed his wife, Aunt Henrietta, who stopped him with just one "tch-tch."[13]

Bernice and the other children's best time in family company, however, was listening to stories. Their father, Bill Kelly, was a storyteller. Bernice said he had a gift for it: "Unhurried in recital, careful with his cumulative details, versed in colorful vernacular, Papa could make a rousing climax out of nothing."[14] Many of her uncles and aunts were also storytellers. In addition, traveling salesmen came by with their wares, stayed for a meal and sometimes the night, offering stories of far-off places. Through all this listening, the children learned the use of telling detail, the building of plot, the flourish at the ending revelation.

There were also the ballads an aunt played on her guitar and sang. These were dramatic: they moved their listeners to joy or to tears. A favorite ballad was "The Baggage Coach Ahead," the story of a young father who holds his baby while his wife's body is in a box in the baggage coach ahead. The child Bernice, at the butter churn, to the rhythm of *slap-dash-slap,* sang her aunt's ballads. She said, "Many a pound of butter came to the tune of 'The Baggage Coach Ahead' or 'Marguerite' whose thwarted lover wandered down by a little babbling brook while I sloshed buttermilk."[15]

Living in such an oral culture, the children relished words, collected them, even deliberately searched for them in print. Words were powerful—some so awful they could not be spoken in the house. The children divided words into categories, like funny words, pretty words, nice words, and low-down words. The last were those that boys let slip when they wanted to act brave and rebellious. A low-down word not to be spoken in the house was "sassy." A strange word to be sought in print was "peccadillo," which they had heard the teacher say.[16] A preacher farmed (and badly, too) in the neighborhood because he had not been called to a church. He talked to his animals with words like "obstreperous" and "exuberance."[17] The children repeated these words to each other with wonder and giggles.

Bernice's father and mother valued education; indeed, they put it nearly as high on their list of priorities as religion. Somehow, although cash was not readily available in this farming way of life, they managed the school fees so that each of their children would be educated. Bernice told her biographer Richard Walser that from the time she picked up her first reader in the neighborhood school, studying became her love.[18]

When the children had gone through the few grades of the local school, they entered the academy just across from their church, Mt. Moriah Baptist. Rosa and Bill Kelly were among the supporters of Mt. Moriah Academy, which their ancestors had founded and where their children and their neighbors' children could grow in knowledge beyond just the bare essentials of reading, writing, and arithmetic. Bernice commented in later years that it had "taken the last dollars of five of our fathers once to secure certificates of stock for the Academy and then again to carry on this subscription school after public funds had been used up."[19]

Mt. Moriah Academy was a place Bernice remembered fondly. She especially loved a teacher, Miss Nina Brown, who introduced her to Scott, Dickens, and George Eliot. Bernice also studied algebra, history, Latin, physical geography, and rhetoric.[20] It was a conventional education but outstanding in its solid academic content. Bernice played the piano and sang, and this was considered appropriate training for young ladies at the time, but academic subjects were the focus at Mt. Moriah Academy.

Bernice's mother and father wanted their children to have varied experiences. They took them to the state fair in Raleigh each year, traveling by wagon. Whenever there was a crop to be sold in Raleigh, Bill Kelly took his children with him. Whenever there was the possibility of a Sunday school trip to a distant place, the Kellys made sure the children had the chance to go. On the first such excursion, the Sunday school adults and children went by train 148 miles to Morehead City so everybody could see the ocean.

When the weary travelers came back from Morehead City, they alighted from the train at Poole's Siding in the midst of a huge storm. They sought shelter wherever they could find it—some knocked on the doors of cabins along the tracks, where black families took them in. Some pressed on up the hill to get relief from the rain and wind. Bernice's family and a few others ascended the hill to reach a cousin's house. No one was home, but they found a window they could open and climbed in.

By chance, this was a house reputed to be haunted. Belief in ghosts returning from the life "on the other side" played around the edges of the Christianity of these rural people and suggested a world as intriguing and dangerous as the ocean they had just seen. The child Bernice knew the stories:

> Strange noises had been heard here ever since old people were children. Sounds as of water being poured from pails upon the floor, as of taffeta dresses rustling in the halls, as of a gate clicking and doors opening without any visible hand, all these could be heard by day as well as by night.
>
> Most persistent and undeniable was the sound of walking. Steps could be heard in the front hall, as though being made by an elderly person in low-quarter shoes moving toward the staircase and on up the stairs. The most reliable neighbors heard them. Kinfolks attested to the sound of footsteps. They were not superstitious. They considered it ignorant and wrong to hold with ghosts and witchery. Since they could not explain the strange sounds heard at the queer house, their answer to children's queries about the strangeness was, "Hush! Don't talk about it!"[21]

"Don't talk about it" invited children to imagine "it." Cuddled up to the other girls, Bernice did not sleep the night she spent there: if grown-ups did not want children to talk about it, it must be something serious and real. But the cousins who lived in the house just took it as an accepted fact that persons from the world beyond lived there from time to time; they even considered them company, like having roomers.[22]

Probably the people who lived around them were as much a subject for discovery for Bernice as any new place or person from beyond. They would make their appearances later in her novels. Cousins, aunts, uncles abounded. Cousin Eldora told each child to be "Somebody," and so at her table the children tried to be "dignified." Aunt Alie expected them to laugh and talk freely like grown-ups, and so they practiced grown-up behavior at her table. They listened to Uncle John's witty stories about traveling salesmen or county agents and animals' personalities while they popped corn at his fireplace. Aunt Edie defied the custom that prohibited married women from wearing red—the children discovered thereby that it was possible to defy. But they also surmised that defiance of custom would feel strange because it would be considered by the community as strange.

Among other family members who were so memorable that they figured in Bernice Harris's novels was Cousin Will, a professional loafer. He came and stayed until his hostess found a way to convince him to move on to the next cousin's house. He never offered to help in any way; still he demanded a hot meal every evening for his "dyspepsia." The rest of the family might be content to eat leftovers from the huge meal at noon, but not Cousin Will. He even lifted the covers of dishes *before* the blessing to see if what was inside was to his pleasure. Once, on being asked to say the blessing before the meal, he said, "Dear Lord, thank you for this food, what there is of it!" Realizing that this did not sound quite right, he added, "Well, there's plenty of it—such as it is."[23] But he had something to contribute: "He looked out of place on the wagon seat amid country produce. For however low his pocket change might be, he had an air of the stock market about him. He knew all about the steel outlook and cotton futures, and he talked knowingly about trade treaties with Japan and free silver and anti-imperialism and prosperity unlimited. It was educating to be around him."[24]

A distant relative, Kalline, fascinated Bernice so much that in adulthood she wrote her into plays and two novels. Kalline had no home and simply lived among her kin, working for one family for her keep and then for another. She was, for the children, an extraordinary presence. Small in stature, probably less than four feet tall, her eyes crossed over a beaklike nose. She was toothless and her thin grey hair was pulled back tightly in a knot at the back of her head. She came to them, wearing a black sateen dress, green-tinged with age, and a black hat so faded it looked rusty, though it still sported purple violets on one side. She carried all her earthly belongings in a cloth flour sack slung over her shoulder. Best of all, she was irreverent:

> She was headstrong and self-willed, not minding anybody's orders or advice. She blurted out vulgar words without regard to age or sex of listeners. Her irreverence was upsetting too. For her, God was Old Boss with Whom she was as chatty as with folks. Before waiting for the second table one day, we children hid our favorite pieces of chicken, knowing that the first table would leave just necks and backs. Left alone with Kalline, we asked her to say grace. "Thank Old Boss for dinner," she said and added chattily, sharing the joke with Him, "and we had it hid!"[25]

When Bernice's mother heard her telling the girls about how "nature came on them," Kalline was sent away. Kalline wept and so did Bernice.[26]

Kalline was sure that her extended family would take care of her and bury her in a family plot, but eventually they took her to the "poor house" instead, despite her wailing protests. After being there a few days, she decided she did not want to return to the rural way of life. At the "county home"—she insisted her country kin call it this—she had electric lights and indoor plumbing and was addressed as "Miss Caroline."[27]

Among other relatives outstanding in Bernice's childhood were the two grandfathers—Calvin Kelly and Calvin Poole. They were patriarchs in their families. Bernice said, "We thought of God and Grandpa [Poole] together. Sometimes we dreaded to go into the presence of either."[28] The children were given a lesson in life by their parents, who told them their grandfathers were "plain people for whom nobility was in character rather than in exploits."[29]

Calvin Poole, with his wild white hair and the open Bible on his lap, was considered something of a saint in the community. People regarded him with awe as a representative of their past, for Calvin Poole, along with his seventeen-year-old son, had fought in the Civil War, and his spoken remembrances kept this history in the immediate present. Bernice recalled that his sons and daughters and their families always had Christmas dinner at his house, and the occasion was always extraordinary:

> During dinner Grandpa told again the story of his Christmas Day in camp.
>
> "I well recollect that Christmas dinner during the War, for it was the best I ever ate," he mused. "One piece of fat meat, fat side meat—that was all we soldiers had for Christmas dinner. And it was better to us than all this ham and turkey is to you all today."
>
> I glanced at Grandpa. At that instant he was Confederate soldier more than saint. But then I thought of his favorite song, "Am I a Soldier of the Cross?" which we would sing for him around the parlor organ after dinner. And he was saint again.[30]

The other grandfather, Calvin Kelly, had not been a soldier, but whereas Calvin Poole was meek, this one was formidable. Once he came upon little Bernice crying because her two older sisters would not let her come into the barn with them. He locked the barn door, and all three girls, both inside and outside the barn, began to wail. He had only meant to teach the older girls a lesson, but soon he understood that they did not appreciate his intervention. He seemed a little humbled.[31]

Every Christmas, the families belonging to the Poole side had a feast at Grandpa Poole's, and Santa left each child a little gift there along with a most unusual item tucked into the stocking—an orange. There was always a large Christmas tree in the sitting room with real candles on it, which were lit once and only briefly, but the sight amazed the children so much they looked forward to it all year.[32]

For these Christmas celebrations, the Kelly family gathered mistletoe and holly in the woods near Rocky Branch, a small creek on the Kelly land. Rocky Branch was a favorite place for the children to play: ravines awaited exploration, the water flowed swiftly over the rocks there, and wildflowers grew along its banks. Spring and summer, there were family picnics at Rocky Branch, and fish fries in the fall.

Both Bill Kelly and Rosa Poole Kelly might be stern at moments, as parents were wont to be. Rosa might say, "Keep crying like this and I'll give you something to cry about." But in fact she understood children's ways. When Bernice got into the habit of snitching her mother's cologne from behind the clock on the mantel, dabbing and adding water to make it look like the level was as before, her mother pretended not to notice.[33]

Little luxuries such as cologne or lace for a child's collar or ribbons for pigtails were the prerogative of the women who sold butter and eggs and thus provided a small but steady source of cash for the family. This cash was necessary to keep the family going in between the large sales of cotton and tobacco harvests or the smaller sales of melons and garden vegetables in the Raleigh markets. Rosa Poole Kelly had an additional way to bring in cash. When she told a traveling salesman how much Native Herb Pills had helped her family members, he offered to sell her wholesale quantities of the pills that she could then retail to neighbors. She begged her husband to let her sell the Native Herb Pills. Bill Kelly agreed to let his wife have this little business only if she did not leave the house. And so Rosa augmented the family's cash flow with this enterprise and received many visits from neighbors, as well as provisions of pills for her own family. Whenever Bernice complained of a headache so she would not have to do something she did not want to do, she was given a Native Herb Pill and told to go right ahead with her duty.[34]

Luxuries like cologne and necessities like needles and thread were purchased from peddlers, who carried them in a huge sack on their back. Usually walking from house to house, the peddlers brought with them not only tempting goods but news from the outside world as well. This news was made more interesting for Bernice by the peddlers' saying words differently from the way her family said them. Bernice loved these visits. The sack would be opened to reveal things so lovely that she could picture them for days afterwards, and the peddler always had little presents for the children. Most often she got a tiny mirror.[35]

If the peddler was there at mealtime, he sat down to a meal with the family; sometimes he stayed the night. Although her father did not like these men who came from the outside and tempted his wife to buy trinkets, hospitality was expected behavior in this culture, and so he acquiesced.

Bernice grew up with the certain knowledge that both her mother and father were well respected in their world. Hard-working and honest, the Pooles and Kellys were ardent and consistent supporters of the Baptist church.

They were also Democrats. Bernice came home one day to find her mother crying. The child was shocked: mothers did not cry except at funerals. Her mother explained that someone had accused Grandpa Kelly of being a Republican.[36] It was akin to alliance with the Devil. The state was dominated by the Democratic Party around the turn of the century. One party aim was to disfranchise African Americans, which Democrats succeeded in doing in 1898. Historian Paul Escott has demonstrated that conservatives used the issue of white supremacy to get elected, thereby ensuring their own continuance in office.[37] Power was thus kept in the hands of the large landowners and the owners of the nascent manufactures. Later in the century, issues and party platforms changed; in adulthood Bernice Harris voted Democrat.

Bernice's family attended the Mt. Moriah Baptist Church, in which her father served as deacon. He was in the church leadership that planned the revival meetings, hired and fired preachers, entertained them and saw to their needs, brought the sinners before the congregation for public denouncing, and supervised the religious upbringing of the children. The church members expected that children reaching the age of twelve would begin to consider dedicating themselves in a formal way to Christ: this meant being "saved" in a public demonstration of walking to the altar during a revival meeting and later being baptized by immersion in a small pond near the church. Only by these formal ceremonies could the child become a member of the community.

One evening during a revival meeting, the preacher pointed out the "fleshpots of Egypt," drawing on the blackboard the narrow road to heaven and the wide road to "the bad place." Bernice was impressed, and she knew that with all her passions she was surely on the wide road. But she decided that since she was not yet eleven, she could wait a little longer to be saved.[38]

In truth, she hated even the thought of walking down the aisle by herself at a revival meeting. She had some fears about being dunked in her uncle's pond. And there were repulsive images in her mind: "I dreaded drinking wine out of the communion cup because old Mr. Mundy, who had a dirty-looking white beard, would be served ahead of us children." She agonized over what she would have to give up— like her paper dolls. But most of all, she wanted to write novels. She was reading novels by Mary Jane Holmes, for which she saved up her pennies and which she bought at seven cents each. To read a novel—let alone write one—was a sin.[39]

But the weight of her mother's and father's expectation was too heavy: she knew she could not refuse to be "saved" because that would mean she lived outside the community of good people, that her father and mother would be saddened beyond words. When she was twelve, she went down the aisle as the congregation sang "Just As I Am" and pledged to believe in Christ and live a Christian life.[40]

Before the baptism, Bernice burned her paper dolls because she considered their adventures her occasion of sinful thoughts, her fleshpots of Egypt. So much pleasure had to be sinful. As she burned them, she cried, or as she described it: "My tears fried on the hot stove into which I was thrusting so much happiness I had created."[41] She even gave up to the fire the catalog pages in which she had kept her paper people.

But she could not give up her desire to be a writer. In fact, Bernice was determined more than ever to be a writer. She had been writing poems, which she stored away in a wooden cracker box. Her mother was impressed; her father said she would outgrow poetry like knee ache. In a dramatic act that demonstrated her faith in her daughter, Rosa Poole Kelly took all her cash from selling Native Herb Pills and sent it to Chicago to have a publisher put Bernice's poem "My Home by the Sea" to music.[42] Later, when money was scarce because of the expense of a new carpet in the parlor for Rachel Floyd's wedding, a poem was *not* sent to Chicago. Bernice took this with stoic acceptance.

Bernice believed that if she wrote in her notebook each day, the pages would accumulate and she would have a book. She spent five cents on a tablet and bought pencils with whatever other pennies came her way. Her first novel, written when she was about eleven, was called "The Gypsy's Warning," inspired by a ballad she had heard an aunt sing. In the ballad, a young girl is warned by a gypsy not to trust the handsome young man who is sweet-talking her into sin. The girl refuses to heed the gypsy's warning, gets her heart broken, and drowns herself.

In the eleven-year-old Bernice's novel, the plot has a different twist. A mother deserts her family, only to return years later disguised as a young man. To get revenge for having her own heart broken in a disastrous marriage, the "man" goes around breaking the hearts of young girls. A gypsy warns the girls against trusting the romantic words of the handsome young man, but one young woman—the mother's daughter—falls in love with the mysterious stranger in spite of the gypsy's warning. Eventually, the girl learns that the handsome stranger is also the gypsy. She cannot understand how this can be. The girl feels betrayed—she drowns herself. Thus, the mother, sometimes playing the role of the heartbreaker, sometimes the gypsy-warner, unknowingly sends her own daughter to despair and death.[43]

It is a strange story for anyone to write and highly significant for a girl just entering adolescence. In the original ballad, the mother is not the heartbreaker, nor is she the gypsy. The moral in the original is simple: don't trust pretty-talking, good-looking men. Bernice changed the plot so that mother-temptor-warner are the same.

Suffice it to say that Bernice believed a mother capable of presenting an attractive enough picture of romantic love to lure her daughter to a death, while giving her warning hints all along—although the mother herself would not be fully aware of the consequences of what she was doing. Did Bernice entering adolescence begin to feel distrustful of the adult women role models available to her? Did she weigh the expectations that she would marry and find romance and happiness, against the reality of a married woman's constant hard work, which would deny her any writing time? Did she feel on some deep level that her mother's expectations of her were a kind of betrayal of her dreams for herself? Was she worried over the lack of autonomy that her mother's life demonstrated? She remembered years later, for example, that her mother had to *ask* her father for permission to sell Native Herb Pills and that he gave it only on condition that she would not leave his house.

Apparently, the question of what Bernice would do in adulthood greatly troubled her. Psychologist Carol Gilligan has shown in her research that girls at age eleven are especially conflicted in regards to society's expectations of them in adulthood versus their own desires about what they want to be.[44] For Bernice the choice seems to have been to rebel against community expectations and be a writer or to settle into the role of married woman whose concerns would be cooking, nurturing, cleaning.

Often the Bible was consulted when a decision was to be made or the future told. Especially, it was believed that if you closed your eyes, opened the Bible, placed your finger somewhere on the page, and it said, "And it came to pass," you could be sure that what you wanted would happen. She had begun to seriously wonder if she would become a writer: it was a scary prospect. She tried the customary way of discovering what was to be:

> I wanted to know for sure if I would become a bookwriter. I went to the big Bible. There I made my wish to become a writer and not a married lady like other girls. If I opened the page on "And it came to pass," then I should never need to hang up love vine in trees again. I would know my fate. Gauging the right place to open, I put my fingers between the pages.
>
> Suddenly I closed the Book without looking inside. I might turn to "And it came to pass." But oh, if I did not!
>
> I kept the dream without knowing for sure about my fate. And sometimes I went along with school mates, who expected to be married ladies one day, to look for love vine. Just in case.[45]

The prospect of being a writer was troubling because it was unknown; there were no live writers in her world. Women married and raised children and forgot such things as writing books. The world around her was a "paired order." Outside it were only strange people like the single, homeless man, Cousin Will, and the lone, homeless woman, Kalline.

Her favorite reading had been the novels of Mary Jane Holmes, a nineteenth-century American novelist whose theme consistently hammered out the message that a woman could be happy only if married and dependent. Holmes did this in thirty-nine novels, the first published in 1854 and the last in 1905. There is no evidence in Bernice's autobiographical writings that at this time or later in college she read such protest literature on women's condition in society as Margaret Fuller's *Woman in the Nineteenth Century* or expositions of rebel women's lives, like George Sand's *Histoire de ma vie,* or closer to Bernice in place and time, Kate Chopin's novel *The Awakening* (1899).

In an analysis of Mary Jane Holmes's novels, a twentieth-century critic, Lucy Brashear, concluded that Holmes's consistent theme stressed that young women must "conform to the manners and morals prescribed by society if they were to be victorious in winning the coveted title of wife." Brashear described the end result of the novels: "Although Holmes buries her advice under a thin veneer of mawkish claptrap, it is clear that a woman who follows the rules governing acceptable female decorum and trains herself for a career of marriage will be bountifully rewarded with material blessings bestowed by a rich husband, but the woman who fails to do so will be punished by poverty, the trademark of the spinster or the sign of an unfortunate alliance."[46]

It must have been clear from this kind of reading that deviance from conventional expectations was dangerous. And yet, all the imagination, keen observation, sensitivity to the nuances of words, and delight in the narrative form that make a writer were in Bernice Christiana Kelly. She had developed her gifts in a culture that provided children with little ready-made entertainment and compelled them to make creative use of materials at hand. For her, the most important materials at hand were people and words. Now this same culture discouraged the expression of her creativity.

The dilemma had to be lived with. Early on, she began to develop the habit of checking into an imaginary world when the real one was not to her liking: "There was always the Lily Maid to go back to when I felt sad and faraway," she said.[47] The ability to enter an imaginary world—which she would put to good use in her writing—would also be a saving strength in the difficult years of her adulthood.

And adult life was bearing down. Rachel Floyd married. This was a change that upset Bernice so much that before the wedding she became weak and nauseated. Her mother stole a little of the Communion wine entrusted by the church to Deacon Bill Kelly to give Bernice a drink so she could get through the ceremony. Bernice knew that this event signaled that they could not go back to their childhood. Pearl had begun courting. Relationships at home could never be the same again.

When Bernice graduated from Mt. Moriah Academy, she was thinking she might want to be a teacher like Nina Brown, her favorite there. Bernice's parents supported her choice. They must have reasoned, like many other parents, that teaching offered a woman a respectable way to make a living. Teaching jobs were opening up for women in North Carolina early in the century. Graded schools replaced the one-room school, and counties began to vote funds for the erection of schools for this new way of educating. Administrators saw the advantage of hiring women: they could be offered cheaper wages than men. And although men had dominated teaching earlier, outnumbering women three to one, by the turn of the century, women had about half of the teaching jobs in the state's classrooms.[48]

To become a teacher, Bernice would need further education, and her mother and father were willing to do whatever was necessary to provide the money. They decided to send her to high school to prepare for college entrance.

Bernice had to go to high school in Cary (on the other side of Raleigh) one year to prepare for college. This was the first public high school in the area, and it was a boarding school. Although it was only about twenty miles away, she could not often repeat the expensive forty-five-minute train ride home. But she soon adjusted to living in a dormitory and liked it. She had grown tall. While at home, she had tried to slump so she would not attract attention; now she was with older girls and her height was no longer embarrassing. She was dark-haired, slim, and lovely. She had three beaux, one after another.[49] Bernice Kelly had a grand graduation at Cary High School; her mother and sister Rachel Floyd made a silk dress for her to wear.

Next year, she went to Meredith College, a Baptist college for women, founded in 1891 and situated in the heart of Raleigh. This was the era when religious groups, especially Baptists, objected to the direction education was taking. They could see that such colleges as the state's Normal School in Greensboro, which trained teachers, would grow with the use of taxpayers' money. More and more, local officials would lose control of education as teachers would insist on different ways to teach and on different subjects. Baptists, history-of-education scholar James Leloudis asserted, had a tradition of local control of their churches and of education and did not want to give that up.[50] It is not surprising that the Kellys, loyal Baptists, chose Meredith.

For the first time, academic work was hard for Bernice. She was so homesick she wrote her parents that she should come home because she was going to have typhoid fever. They wrote back that they were sure the doctor at Meredith could handle the situation.[51]

In the college dormitory she sat up after lights-out to write poems in the dark. One night she attempted to build a tent with her silk graduation dress around a light bulb so she could see to write. Suddenly there was a flash of light and the smell of singed cloth. The dress was no more. At first she thought the power surge was the effect of Halley's comet coming too close to the Earth. She had heard predictions of dire consequences of this comet's nearness. But in the morning the college president announced that a blown fuse had been replaced and the damage repaired. Bernice remained silent about her deed, but a few years later, when she was an officer in the Student Government Association, she was lenient with freshmen who blew fuses.[52]

She continued to write, but now she wrote short stories for the college publications and was soon appointed to the staff of the college literary magazine. Mostly she studied Latin, English, and science courses. Tall and strong, she played on the basketball team. She began to enjoy college. Her teachers took advantage of being in the state's capital and made sure their students attended the cultural events there, such as meetings of the North Carolina Literary and Historical Association. They went on excursions—trips to the state fair were favorite annual events. Friendships she made at Meredith lasted a lifetime. Even forty years after graduation, she would get letters from former classmates telling her the details of their lives.

But the childhood determination to be a writer waned as Bernice neared twenty and her college graduation. She had enjoyed a conventional life up to that point; she had known happiness in it. She had observed the happy Nina Brown—now Mrs. Thomas William Elliot, the married schoolteacher at Mt. Moriah Academy—who had become a role model for her. And formal education sometimes has the result of pulling down dreams from the sky and fastening them onto solid earth; in the transfiguration into practical plans, much is obscured.

The dreamer plods on. At Meredith, Bernice decided definitely she would be a teacher and nurture writers rather than be one.

Later in life, when she needed to sum up herself, she said simply, "I am a Baptist and a Democrat." Harris's upbringing was probably characteristic in a general way of the place and time and social class. Ben Robertson, a writer who grew up in a landed family in South Carolina in the generation just after Bernice Kelly's, recalled that the objective of his parents and relatives "was to set me in the mold—to make me a Carolinian, a Democrat and a Baptist. Once they had accomplished that—well, hell and high water could try as they liked."[53] Bernice would use this heritage in some surprising ways.

2

No Flowery Bed of Ease: Miss Kelly, Teacher

Bernice Kelly's first teaching job after graduating from Meredith was in Beulaville in Duplin County, North Carolina (about twenty-six miles northwest from Jacksonville and the North Carolina coast). The school's funds gave out before the year ended and it closed early, and so her stint there was brief. She was greatly disappointed because she was enthusiastic about teaching and ready for a demanding job. She got just that when, in 1914, she began her second teaching job, this time at South Fork Institute (near Maiden, North Carolina, in the foothills of the Appalachian Mountains). It was a religious institution for training future ministers, but some students already had families, and so their wives and children came to class with them. Because Bernice had a religious background, it was not difficult for her to fit in: she knew how to get their attention. She said that she "used the Bible as a basis for grammatical studies so greatly needed by these mountain pastors."[1]

She had to attend services every Sunday where she would wince as she listened to one of her preachers "slaughter cases and number and gender and pronunciation all over the pulpit platform." She admitted, "Iniquity was being broadened in my mind to include murder of the King's English." Next week in class, she would introduce examples—in disguise—of some of Sunday's worst grammatical errors.[2] She got into arguments about English usage, but she remarked, "Only two preachers were openly antagonistic to my efforts to introduce better English into the pulpits of the South Fork Association, and they stopped after a while."[3]

"It was challenging—this job—oh, very challenging," she said.[4] Her students knew very little, and she was aware that she did not have much experience teaching. Nevertheless, she described it as a place where she made "fine friendships" and where "choice students" came to her classes: "Some of these pastors, like B. E. Morris, went on to college and became influential in broader ministries. Others served where they were. I have hoped through the years that case and gender suffered a little less in the pulpit because of my stay at South Fork Institute." She remembered with pride such students as Hubert Heffner, who later became a university professor of English literature and attributed his love of Shakespeare to "Miss Kelly."[5]

While she was teaching at South Fork, the First World War began. Bernice's three brothers were serving in the United States forces: William Olive was in France, Darwin on the eastern coast of the United States, and Elwood with the Atlantic fleet. The war was also claiming her students. Letters came to her from "Somewhere in France." She felt bewildered—she did not know what to do to help them. (Most of the students were only a few years younger than she was.) She agonized over them: "What was there to do for my boys who were caught up from their parsing, their themes, their blue-eyed loves into the maelstrom of European mess but to send them poems, candy, gray scarfs knit with my own fingers, letters—and to pray?" She remembered with deep sadness a "brilliant Methodist youth," Lawrence Peeler. Something of her bitterness over the loss of life in the war she indicated in this sentence about him: "At eighteen he enlisted in the Army and did what he could to make the world safe for democracy: at least, he was blown to bits by a machine gun in France."[6] Later in her life she reflected, "A teacher's life is her pupils; who doesn't count them over, every one apart?"[7]

In the immediate situation, she had worries also. The school became a nest of political intrigue, denomination politics, and mismanagement—all the things that, in her view, finally wrecked it. Because the school became defunct, she was never paid some of the salary owed to her.

In 1916, when she was twenty-five, she signed a contract to teach English at the high school in Seaboard, North Carolina. However, the

farewells at South Fork were not easy for her. All of her life she remembered the last day at the Institute, when one of her students, a tall
mountain youth, stood by the wagon in tears:

> The music teacher, the primary teacher, and I went out to the road to
> tell two of our students whose going left us alone in the dormitory,
> goodbye. These two had been very close to us, and parting was difficult.
> The father had driven in his wagon from the foot of the little mountain
> eight miles away to fetch home his boy and girl. All of us stood at the
> road-side crying quietly, realizing that we were saying goodbye not only
> to two we cherished, but to an institution, to an idea. The music teacher
> who had recently lost her mother and father, who no longer was young,
> philosophized brokenly: "Partings like these make us realize how to ap-
> preciate our heavenly home where there'll be no more partings, no more
> tears." I wanted to kill her.[8]

Bernice went on to summer school to complete the requirements for
obtaining a teaching certificate. North Carolina's public school system
was expanding; the state was pouring money into schools. It was clear
that the teaching jobs would be in the public schools from then on.
The state required a teaching certificate, so it was important to get
one, but she depleted her funds.

She had to borrow money to go to the teaching job in Seaboard. As
it turned out, the town was not by the sea—it was about sixty-three
miles from the ocean. The name came from its being a stop on the Seaboard Railway line. It was located in Northampton County whose
northwestern border was the Virginia line. Seaboard itself was so close
to the border between North Carolina and Virginia that bootleggers
running from state police could, in a ten-minute chase, reach the next
state and safety.

Looking back on the decision to go to Seaboard, she declared, "It
was not until I accepted work in Seaboard, that I really came home."[9]
She taught various subject combinations: four classes of English and
four classes of Latin some semesters. Sometimes, four English classes
and four history classes or five English courses and one science course.
The best, to her, was four English courses and several in dramatics.[10]
For the next eleven years, Bernice taught English every semester and in
a way people there had never seen before. Bernice's student Elizabeth
Bullock said that when she went to college, her professor was astonished with the understanding of English sentence structure she had
gained in high school.[11]

In addition to teaching, Bernice did the usual things schoolteachers did: coached the debaters, raised money for the school, attended meetings of the Betterment Society (forerunner to the Parent-Teacher Association), kept study hall at night for dormitory students, tutored students privately (for free, of course), attended choir practice at church, taught Sunday school, gathered stories for the local newspaper reporter, and cleaned the school when necessary. "I gave everything to this school, including my health," she said.[12]

Bernice's childhood determination to be a writer had changed in college to a desire to teach others to write, and now she got her chance to teach writing. She admitted she wanted to discover good writers. But now, there was a more encompassing motive: "The will extended beyond any discovery motive; it included the wish for a good life for my girls and boys. A good life was writing."[13]

At the beginning of her teaching in Seaboard, she discovered a powerful genre for her students' writing. In the summers she alternated between teaching summer school at Washington Collegiate Institute in Beaufort County, North Carolina (a program to train public school teachers, located on the coast at Washington, North Carolina), and attending classes in Chapel Hill at the University of North Carolina. There she decided on a whim to take a course in drama. She described the first time she encountered the founder and head of the drama program at the university, Frederick Koch: "On our first day in his class he sat on the table and dangled his feet and talked with zest about the unwritten folk drama and won me forever to his idea. He won the others. Staid and sedate teachers and principals and newcomers alike fell under the spell of Proff Koch. His class became an oasis in the Sahara of pedagogy and credits. We turned toward the long table in an upstairs room of the library as toward a feast."[14]

Frederick Koch, as a graduate student himself at Harvard, had listened to his professor George Pierce Baker urge his students to nurture the creation of a native drama that would express the common people's experience. A nationwide development in drama resulted when these students went to universities throughout the country with this sense of mission.

In North Dakota, Koch did such outstanding work in fostering regional drama that the president of the University of North Carolina, learning about Koch's work and noting a similar need in the Old North State, offered him a job. Koch came to North Carolina in 1918.

His goal was to get his students to listen to the stories around them and to write plays that gave voice to the concerns and aspirations of their own people. Legends, superstitions, customs, narratives of personal lives—all were oral literature that could be dramatized in folk plays. The vernacular of the region would be used. The plays could be whatever the students felt they wanted to write—realistic or purely imaginative.[15]

Koch had "boundless enthusiasm" and imparted to his students, including Bernice Kelly, his conviction that *they* had a mission. She said, "How that little man in the Norfolk jacket did inspire!"[16] Paul Green and Elizabeth Lay Green, Betty Smith, Frances Gray Patton, and Thomas Wolfe were also his students. They would each write plays that together formed a body of original work which articulated both the dilemmas and feelings of their fellow North Carolinians and also universal human emotions.

To produce original plays, Koch organized the Carolina Playmakers in 1918. He wanted to involve people all over the state in writing and producing plays, and so he established the Bureau of Community Drama and appointed a field secretary to set up drama centers throughout the state. He originated an annual spring festival of plays at Chapel Hill in 1925—a competition to which people at the drama centers throughout the state brought their best work. Bernice Kelly's students in playwriting took their plays to the festival in Chapel Hill; in her first playwriting class, her student William Ivey Long (who later became a professor of theater) wrote the play that won first prize that year.[17]

After that, every student wanted to write, and Miss Kelly organized the Seaboard Players to produce their plays. She began to spend all her evenings working with students on revisions of plays and rehearsing the ones ready for production.[18] Often when they took plays to the festival, they won the prize.

She also arranged to take her students to see performances of Shakespeare. And then for the next five years they put on a Shakespearean play at the high school in celebration of the commencement. During one evening's performance of *Julius Caesar*, she caught a glimpse of a young boy in the audience: "There still lingers hauntingly a certain intensity of interest, of inscrutable aloneness caught on the face of one boy as he leaned over the balcony rail watching Brutus fall on his own sword." Later, when he was a young dentist with what everyone thought was a brilliant future, he killed himself. She remembered that look on his face.[19]

One year Macbeth played his role so convincingly that the commencement audience knew that "the wages of sin is death." The student who played Macduff—who later became a university professor—said his "horror, horror, horror" in such a striking way she heard it for years afterwards. In the middle of the "in thunder-lightning-and-in-rain" speech, the Seaboard train whistle blew like a scream. One of the witches (later a North Carolina State College official) was so terrified that he had to make sure he was still himself and pulled up his witch's robe to see if he had his tweed trousers on.[20]

She delighted in following her students in their later life, noting that the one who played Shylock and clamored for his pound of flesh became a doctor who ended up practicing in Hong Kong and "had to do with many a pound of flesh." She observed that wise and assertive Portia, who married and had a family, still managed to keep a little of Portia about herself. And Bassanio became a Greensboro lawyer—having heard his first case on the Seaboard high school stage. King Claudius extracted teeth in the Carolina mountains, and Queen Gertrude taught in a country school. Horatio kept books in Raleigh. She added, "Perhaps with a difference."[21]

But Lady Macbeth, in the years to come, changed the conversation when the production of *Macbeth* was mentioned. Only in the privacy of her kitchen, alone in the house, with whatever was cooking on the stove burning, did she pace and say, "All the perfumes of Arabia will not sweeten this little hand." Bernice Kelly Harris confessed, "Yes, I played Lady Macbeth." At the last minute, when the actor who had rehearsed the part could not go on stage, Bernice had to take the role because she was the only one who knew the lines by heart.[22]

Directing, producing, designing stage sets and costumes—all gave her a direct knowledge of the theater. She said that if she had to name a single piece of work that gave her more pleasure than any other those eleven years, it was their "adventures with Shakespeare."[23]

Meanwhile, her social life became more interesting than even she expected. When she began teaching in Seaboard, she lived with a family in town, and later, when the teacherage was built, that was her home. She enjoyed the late-night conversations about men and life with the other young unmarried teachers. The widowed teachers entered those conversations with a dose of realism. One of the matrons told the young ones that they were too "sloppily idealistic." She promised them if they did not make a mess out of living or dying, she would give them an A.[24]

Bernice was trying not to make a mess out of living. She was working hard; she was saving her money, as became a responsible person, in her view. At South Fork her salary had been so low she even tried selling encyclopedias to make extra money. But she hated the sales talk and in the end lasted only a few days at it, making just about enough money for a train ticket home. Now, at Seaboard, her salary was more than she was used to getting, and when monthly salary checks (although still small) came in, the young teachers "lit out for Norfolk" to shop. She loved these trips: "There was something about the ferry crossing that to us inlanders who had crossed Walnut Creek bridge with trepidation in our childhood was positively glamorous, daring, adventurous."[25]

One day when she went to Norfolk with other teachers to shop, she stepped out of character. It was a heady experience—the first time she had had money to spend on something as frivolous as an outfit she did not absolutely need. She splurged and bought three dresses, one a blazing red, and agonized over it:

> All my life I had wanted a red dress with black touches and had been restrained. Even since choices had been mine, I had been held back by an ingrained sense of fitness. Red had not been among the choices of color women wore when I was a child. . . .
>
> Secretly I had gleaned red rose petals off the ground and colored girls' dresses pictured in the Readers. I had watched spring birds fly from quince to frangipani and identified myself with cardinals. I had gazed into winter fires that leaped against the soot of chimney backs like playmates at hopscotch and dreamed of myself in flame dresses with piquant touches of black.
>
> I had caught red and black butterflies to bite off their heads and make the ritual wish for pretty clothes. Only, I had always let them go free and so had kept wearing pastels and browns and white.[26]

Back in the teacherage, she put on the red dress she had bought in Norfolk and looked in the mirror. Suddenly she became homesick for Poole's Siding, for her mother and father, brothers and sisters, for the cousins and aunts and uncles.[27] But there was also a realization that it was 1918, that in another decade she would be nearing forty. She reflected that it was "time to preen some plumage."[28]

She looked in the mirror again and decided the red dress did something for her.[29] There was a moment of delight and defiance, too: she had bought not one but three dresses. She had spent a total of forty-nine dollars and ninety-five cents on spring—and hope, too, no doubt. For this extravagance was part of a design: she was about to go on a Sunday afternoon drive with a Seaboard businessman, Herbert Harris.

Strict rules forbade the teachers from dating except on weekends, and even then there was a curfew. Chaperons—often the widowed schoolteachers—accompanied any couple who wanted to venture from the teacherage parlor. One of Bernice's fellow schoolteachers wanted to go out for a Sunday drive with a local man. Herbert Harris had a car, and so it seemed convenient to ask Herbert to take them and to arrange for Bernice to go, too, as chaperon.

It was not quite that innocent, however. Bernice had been very much aware of his presence in Seaboard on several occasions. One afternoon, a cotton gin employee had rushed over to the dormitory, asking if there were any white cloths to bind Mr. Harris's hand, which had been hurt in an accident with the machinery. The matron and Bernice went quickly to the gin and bandaged the crushed finger. Bernice thought that their eyes met, that an awareness was sparked.[30]

She was excited that Sunday she was to go with him on the outing. Herbert's car was a brand-new Grant. The other teacher and her beau got in the back seat and pretended they had complete privacy. Accordingly Bernice and Herbert pretended not to notice the lovers in the back. At a favorite courting place, a spring deep in the woods, Herbert and Bernice sat on a huge rock and chatted. After a little while, she felt so awkward that she excused herself, saying that she needed to pick wildflowers for her classroom. When she came back to the rock, she saw him climbing the bank, carrying a handful of violets. She was touched that this businessman had concerned himself with wildflowers—for her.[31]

Back at the teacherage, she thought again about how the matron had described for the unmarried teachers the town's eligible bachelors. Regarding Herbert, the matron had said that he did not come from a marrying family. She cautioned Bernice: a moth flying too near the flame gets singed.[32]

Bernice had found out some things about him for herself. Herbert Kavanaugh Harris was part owner of a cotton gin business called Bradley and Harris. He, with his brothers, owned timberland and farmland, houses and livestock. He was an eligible bachelor, to be sure, but he was closer to forty than to thirty. He had not yet shown any interest in marrying. Bernice was wary—the matron's other predictions about men had come true.

Even though wary, Bernice accepted the invitation when Herbert made it clear that she was to go out with him again. Although the custom of the times was that a couple going for a drive took with them a chaperon, Herbert simply declared that they would not have one. Their first Sunday drive alone was tense: "Without the widows along, there was too much awareness of the extraordinary in the afternoon outing. There was constraint between us. Each was conscious of the awareness of the other. We tried too hard to make the ride unimportant."[33]

And there were tense moments on the next drives as well. The more she saw him, the greater the tension she felt. She was both attracted and afraid of the attraction.[34] She kept telling herself not to get involved.[35] But she watched Herbert's Grant turn into the teacherage's driveway weekend after weekend—she never tried to stop him. She remembered, "Following that ride to the Springs, the days had a touch of fantasy beyond any dramas my Seaboard Players ad-libbed through."[36]

Only once did they have an outright quarrel. Herbert was late in meeting her to go to a social event. She went with a man who was with her friends at the teacherage, hoping Herbert would see them, no doubt. Herbert did see them and he was livid.[37] As she suspected, if there was one thing Herbert hated, it was to be beaten in a competition.

In the midst of this growing intensity in the relationship with Herbert and of such success for her students and herself in drama, Bernice was caught up in an unanticipated anguish. In the summer of 1920 when she went home for the summer break, Bernice realized that her mother was not well. One day, her mother took her to a trunk and opened the lid for her to look inside. There she saw new stockings, freshly pressed underclothes, a black dress with a ruffled white collar, clean sheets and bath towel, some scented soap. "Everything's here that will be needed," her mother said. She had already had several heart attacks, and she had packed the clothes she wanted to wear in her coffin. Bernice was startled by the "sureness of her statements." She did not want to believe what she heard and tried not to believe it.[38]

That summer while Bernice was with her mother on the homeplace in Wake County, her students were scheduled to put on a play in a town near her parents' farm. Not wishing to leave her mother for any length of time, she called and appealed to another director, who organized the troupe and got them there. But she felt she should at least attend the play to give them moral support. Her father and brother were with her mother; her mother said that she felt all right and that Bernice should go to the play. Bernice decided to go, but she continued to be uneasy.

Returning home that night, Bernice saw her mother in her long white gown with her beautiful white hair in braids, waiting at the front door to let her in. Her mother had often done this because she could not sleep when one of the children was out late. Bernice came in, glad to see her. But suddenly her mother vanished, and when Bernice went to her parents' room, she heard the measured breathing of two parents asleep. Next morning her mother said that she had not gotten up during the night; indeed, she was not strong enough to walk at that point. Within a matter of weeks, she was dead.[39] Apparently, Bernice wanted so much to have her mother back as she used to be that she created an illusion more real than the reality she was living through. At the same time, by imagining her mother suddenly out of sight, she was preparing herself for her mother's going as surely as her mother had prepared herself by getting together "going away" clothes.

In later years, Bernice recounted her sorrow over her mother's death again and again. In her own last year, reviewing the most significant events of her life, this was the first that came to her mind: "In my twenties, I lost my mother."[40]

Within two years, her father remarried—he was sixty-four; the bride was thirty-eight. Bernice and her brothers and sisters were dismayed at what they considered a lack of respect for their mother's memory. Bernice described her reaction in unpublished pages: "It was not a happy occasion for us. It fell too close upon the anniversary of Mama's death. Besides, we shrank from the idea of Papa's remarriage, for it seemed to alter his identity and change our family pattern."[41]

Bernice and her brothers and sisters did not want an open confrontation with their father, however. They were determined to treat his new wife cordially, and so she became known in the family as "Miss Myrtle." In southern culture, "Miss" is added to an elderly woman's first name to indicate respect; however, a relative would be addressed as aunt, cousin, or the like. The choice of "Miss Myrtle" indicates a distance from the speaker.

Her father's remarriage made it clear to Bernice as she approached her thirties that she would have to acknowledge that her mother was gone and that home would never be the same again. She remarked in a sentence omitted from the autobiography published years later, "Always she [her stepmother] had been kind and welcoming, but common sense told me I was no longer a fitting design in the new pattern."[42] She would have to create her own family.

The summer after her mother's death, when the school semester ended, she went back to the family home in Wake County. She always packed her trunk, keeping in mind her little niece Rosalie, Rachel Floyd's daughter, because the child liked to help her unpack. "For this little blonde niece I made the plain metal trunk as much treasure as I could," she said.[43] Bernice always had a surprise for each niece and nephew.

She was planning to go on to Chapel Hill to attend summer school at the University of North Carolina, where she could continue to study playwriting with Professor Koch. And she had been considering accepting a contract to teach in another town in the fall, in a larger school. It would give her the chance to put some distance between her and Herbert, to give her respite from a relationship she expected could only end in disappointment for her. But she had also been offered a contract to teach in Seaboard again. In the midst of her packing for the trip to Chapel Hill, a letter came from Herbert—a love letter. It was based on a form letter. Years later, she sent an account of receiving this letter to her biographer Richard Walser. She said she had burned Herbert's love letters, but she was willing for Walser to see this odd sheet describing her reaction:

> With sudden clarity I envisioned some kind of Manual that had served the strictly-business man. Otherwise, he would have been lost among sentiments so alien to cotton gins and standing timber and columns of figures and land. I was moved by every stilted phrase, every quote from LOVE'S YOUNG DREAM, every strained paraphrase of poetry.
>
> For all my facility with words and my emphasis as a teacher upon originality of expression, I found myself countersigning, "Oh, there's nothing half so sweet in life as love's young dream."
>
> I signed the contract to return to Seaboard.[44]

Bernice was as surprised at the mutual attraction as any observer. No matchmaker would have paired them. She admitted,

> He was quick and fiery and explosive, I was inclined to contain. He did not have formal education, but he had all the business and money sense, the common sense that I lacked. His ideas about life and people were at variance with mine. His intense family sense bordered on Shintoism, sometimes it seemed. He was shrewd and wary, I was over-trustful. He was not socially inclined, I was. He had a sense of humor that often left me plodding behind. He was low in stature [page fragment ends][45]

She was dark-haired, tall, slender, and dignified in bearing.

Somehow, an emotional bond had been formed. "I knew by now," she said, "that it was, mysteriously and extraordinarily, the two of us."[46] She wanted to teach another year and to get to know Herbert better. She agreed to an engagement but was relieved when he said they would wait a while to get married "because of family commitments." The engagement stretched out for six more years, but it was a time in her life she remembered fondly: "So much about him, I discovered, was endearing. There would be no further use of Manuals to evoke intense tenderness for the belabored business man handing in papers. Herbert had become relaxed and natural once our understanding was complete, and he expressed his love sanely rather than articulated it in poetry. Even his relegation of love to the exigencies and half exigencies of business was endearing, once I adjusted to it."[47]

She would find out later that there was a great deal she would have to adjust to. But for a time she was happy being courted by Herbert and teaching—even though the teaching job was, as she said, "no flowery bed of ease." Indeed, every minute of her waking hours was taken, and years of her youth which she might have spent writing slipped by.

3

Shamelessly Just Married Before the World

At the end of the school semester in 1926, Bernice went home to Wake County, planning to stay a short time and then to go on to summer school. Three weeks later, as she was packing summer clothes, Herbert suddenly arrived at her father's house. He told her he had decided to marry right away.

Immediately she began making arrangements for the wedding, which was to take place the next day. The minister's wife put flowers in the church. Bernice's sisters helped her find "something old, something new, something borrowed, something blue." Her stepmother was not feeling good and could not do much to help, but she tried. She confided to Bernice that she was pregnant—a development none had expected, certainly not the grown-up children of the sixty-seven-year-old father.

Bernice and Herbert were married in the Mt. Moriah Baptist Church. After the vows, she glanced at Herbert, standing beside her. He seemed remote. She said, "For all his handsomely tailored wedding suit he did not look like a bridegroom." He looked, she thought, "BRADLEY AND HARRIS." He looked like cotton gins, land, and timber. "And he looked lost." She moved closer to him and slipped her arm into his, "shamelessly just married before the world."[1]

They boarded the train for a honeymoon in Washington and New York. Her nieces and nephews knew from schoolbooks what should be seen in both cities, but Bernice and Herbert saw little of Washington, and they never got to New York. Mostly they shuttled between hotel room and restaurants. "What were thoroughfares or galleries or playhouses, with a new world of our own to explore?" she said.[2] "We stayed in our room. The mystery of oneness deepened. There were times when out of vast happiness I thought to myself, 'How can such things be?' " She added, "For an interval he was not a business man."[3]

But soon Herbert became the businessman again, and he grew impatient to return to his businesses in Seaboard. It dawned on her that Washington was as far north as they were going. Any train they might board would be headed south toward Seaboard. She acquiesced. Sheepishly, he tried to coach her on what to say if anybody asked what they saw in New York.

And so they took the train to Seaboard. When they arrived, there was no one there to meet them. She had hoped his family would be there.

It was the end of May 1926. Bernice was thirty-five; Herbert was forty-three. She "wondered what the composition of life would be for us in this little town, what its savor was going to be."[4] Seaboard Township had only about 2,500 people[5]—she already knew many of them. Although she began her life now as Mrs. Harris, the townspeople always affectionately referred to her as "Miss Kelly." She had been involved in two centers of town life, church and high school. Now she would begin to explore the other aspects.

Bernice's world was a farming world even though she was a town dweller. Two main streets with small intersecting streets constituted the town. But from nearly every window, townspeople looked out on the flat fields: a bright green sea in spring, a white sea of cotton in late summer.

Seaboard was dominated by the railroad; trains made stops there day and night. Near its tracks, cotton was ginned and bound for transport. In 1920, the total value of all crops in Northampton County was $4,664,394; of this, cotton's share was $3,664,321. No other crop came near it in importance,[6] but in season, other crops, such as peanuts, would be bagged and loaded on the trains as well. Passengers boarded and strangers alighted. Everyone listened for the train whistle and marked the time of day.

Northampton was a large county, and 69 percent of it was farmland.[7] Nearly everybody farmed or served farmers—whether it was the town doctor or the railway station master. Most of the farms were small by today's standards, 20 to 49 acres. But there were huge farms as well, with farm managers and tenant farmers and a non-laboring class of owners or gentry. In all, farms in Northampton County numbered about 3,500; but only about a third were owned by the people who worked them. Landless farmers were more typical of the county than the landed.[8]

The population profile for Northampton County showed that blacks greatly outnumbered whites—13,062 to 9,261.[9] But whites owned twice as many farms as blacks. Among the landless—tenant farmers and sharecroppers—there were 556 whites and 1,535 blacks.[10]

Clearly, black farming families were disproportionately represented in the landless group. Slavery had ended only about sixty years before, and it was still hard for black farmers to get credit to buy land. And in other ways black landless farmers were even more vulnerable than white. Laws favored owners who wanted to keep both white and black laborers from challenging authority or even just leaving to seek a better contract; but white owners' control over black workers was also reinforced by extra-legal controls, such as the punishments carried out by the Ku Klux Klan.[11]

Among the white gentry in Seaboard Township, the Harrises and the Edwards were the most prominent families.[12] The gentry owned much of the land; they owned the banks. Their sons were the judges and lawyers. They were the employers of farm managers and families of sharecroppers and tenants.

In this social pyramid, between the elite at the top and the landless at the bottom, there was a small middle class of farmers of moderate-sized farms, storekeepers, and managers. They were afraid always of sinking to the bottom of the pyramid. Even those farmers who owned substantial acreage and employed a tenant with his family had a hard time surviving a series of bad years with crops. And although some poor black families and white families were able to buy and keep small holdings of land, for them one or two bad crop years often meant debt and foreclosure—and sinking into the tenant and sharecropping labor force.

Everyone knew the family history of everyone else. Sharecroppers and tenants might move from place to place, but usually they stayed within Northampton County, continuing in a society in which, if people didn't know you personally, they knew your reputation and knew who your forebears were. White and black, although often blood kin, kept up the illusion of separateness. Black women tended the white babies and cooked white families' food and nursed the ailing whites. Black men were craftsmen, small farmers, day laborers, or sharecroppers. Because black women worked in whites' homes, they participated in two cultures and knew more about whites than the whites knew about blacks.

For white people of means and leisure time, life was pleasant. Men groomed horses for show. They hunted deer. Young and old played baseball. The county even had a league with paid players. The Seaboard field had the train tracks as a left field boundary. When one player hit a ball into a passing boxcar, it went all the way to Richmond, Virginia. The local joke was that this was the longest home run in the history of the county.[13]

Two churches—Baptist and Methodist—were large and well supported. A smaller church, Presbyterian, struggled along. Although church doctrine forbade card playing, that did not stop anybody. And if alcoholic beverage was desired—the Devil's work—a discreet knock at one's back door brought that, as well. Or when an anonymous individual went to Roanoke Rapids or Weldon, he could pick up a supply for himself and his friends. Certain individuals, like the town doctor, could even sit out on the porch in the late afternoon and have a cocktail. This was not mentioned at church.

Eating was a chief pleasure for the well-to-do. In this farming community, fresh food (or canned or dried) from one's land was available in abundance. Preparing it was a major concern. The busy town doctor, John Wesley Parker, for example, could spend forty-five minutes with his friends talking about what they were going to cook and how they were going to cook it.[14]

This was the world into which Bernice came as the wife of one of the richest men among the gentry. What she would do in the long run in this setting, she did not yet know. Now, as a town matron, she became involved in various women's activities connected with the church, such as the women's circle and the Woman's Missionary Society. She sang in the choir, and all her years in Seaboard she taught Sunday school at the Baptist church.

But she was also a card player. Women had rook parties at which five or six tables of rook players were served a three-course meal.

(Rook was the popular card game at the time; bridge did not come into favor in Seaboard until later.) Bernice spent time going to these rook parties and figuring out what she would serve when she was hostess.[15] An observer of town life said that she was a part of all of it and she "enjoyed the hell out of it," but that somehow she was "above it, too."[16]

At first Bernice and Herbert lived in the teachers' residence. Herbert had lived with his widowed father and his father's other grown-up children, all of whom were unmarried at the time except for one son. There was no question of Bernice and Herbert living there. However, there were rooms available to them in the teacherage because she had not expected to marry that summer and had signed a contract to teach in the fall. But their rooms had neither water nor cooking facilities. Herbert decided they would build a house. She dreamed of a white house with a lawn stretching before it where children played. He picked out the site, bought the land, and built a red brick house.[17]

When they went to Norfolk to buy furniture for the new house, Herbert remarked, "We're not going to pay the world for furniture, but we'll keep looking till we find something that suits us." She was worried about money. He told her they'd find out what suited them and then see to the price. She liked that: "It was a refreshing experience to be suited first and ask for the price second. I was not yet adjusted to the solid security Herbert represented."[18]

When they went to a restaurant for lunch, it felt strange not to have to look in her purse to see if there was enough money to pay for what she wanted to eat. It was something she, and all her friends who were schoolteachers, had done automatically for years.

Herbert approved of her choice of furniture but insisted on looking around and comparing before closing any deals. When he did get to the bargaining point, she watched, fascinated. Later she would get used to his strategy: even if he bought a pair of shoes, he would point out all the flaws that justified his demand that the merchant cut the price. "I came to believe that the rock-bottom prices Herbert held out for were not motivated by the saving involved so much as by victory over the other businessman." In time she became accustomed to "the little comedies" he staged. And in Seaboard, she thought the merchants had figured him out and jacked up the prices when they saw him entering the store because they knew he would not buy until they brought the prices down.[19]

When the house was finished and the furniture put in place, each piece seemed "animate and dear." Bernice turned on all the lights and went outside in the darkness to look at their home. Hearing Herbert's car, she quickly ran in and turned the unnecessary lights out. But later, he insisted they turn on all the lights and go outside to look. Excited, she said, "There'll be spring and summer and fall and winter. And Christmas. And weekdays and Sundays. . . ." The drama of the moment did not impress him, but damage to property did. He replied, "I took out wind insurance with Rip Foster today."[20]

For their first Christmas in the house, they gathered greenery in some woods he owned. Doing this reminded her of Christmases when she was a child. She talked to him of those past Christmases, when she had felt her family's richness even though there was no ready cash or standing timber. At the end of their hunt for greenery, she saw that "the holly he finally chose was loaded with luxuriant berries, the running cedar was richly green, the mistletoe was rarely delicate with its white waxy balls." Then she understood: "He was summing up richness too." It was a December morning she remembered all her life. She wrote, "I wanted to encompass the land with our happiness, to leave little fragments of it as reminders, to relate ourselves richly to the world around us. Forever afterwards now this standing timber would have something of our oneness. We had gathered Christmas greenery here to deck our home."[21]

She splurged and bought white lights for all the windows, twenty-three electric candles in all, but then she started worrying because he might not like them—other houses had red, blue, and green lights. And she feared he would hate the expense. At first she was too nervous to turn them on, but she took heart. She watched for his car that night. When he came home, he drove slowly past the house and then drove past again. To her relief and delight, he came in and said they had the prettiest lights in town.[22]

Bernice had come from a very sociable family and missed the Sunday afternoon visits of aunts, uncles, and cousins. She had been impressed with what she could imagine about Herbert's family: "I was pleased at the apparent intense family loyalty and closeness, for it promised a precious fellowship for me, too."[23] Some months after her marriage, she received an invitation for her and Herbert to come to dinner at the homestead, his father's house. The meal was "bountiful," the atmosphere was "frosty": "There was an odd lack of table talk. Not knowing why and wanting to do well, I chattered away. I shouldered the responsibility of conversation. His father, Herbert informed me afterwards, believed in eating at the table and talking later. Unaware at the time, I kept trying. My efforts floundered. In silence we finished the meal."[24]

She thought Herbert's father a handsome and remarkable old man. He had original ideas. But he was a formidable patriarch, a "rod to check the erring and reprove." Bernice saw that for him "sons and daughters did not get too old to be checked or reproved." He demanded that they give him respect, obedience, and devotion, and they complied. She described her relationship with him: "Mr. Harris and I made it all right. We were friends, though always with a certain guarded tentativeness between us. He could not be sure about daughters-in-law. I was unsure too and eager to please."[25]

Herbert finally told her that his father had not wanted him to marry. Especially he did not want him to marry a schoolteacher because such women were used to having their own money to spend and were apt to be "hard on husbands' pocketbooks."[26]

The first Christmas in their house, Bernice invited Herbert's father and brothers and sisters to their home for dinner. She cooked. They waited. No one came. No excuse was ever offered.[27]

Herbert had two sisters, Anna and Zenobia—neither married. Rumor in the town has it that when his sister Zenobia was away teaching, she could be the life of the party. In summer, when she returned to Seaboard and the homeplace, she saw no one. Once a suitor came to the house, and her father made it clear he must never come again. After teaching for a few years, she came home to stay at the homestead, which was on a large farm three miles out of town. Sometimes townspeople would not see her for a year. Anna, the other sister, stayed at home also. Jethro, one of the two unmarried brothers, lived there as well, but it was his prerogative as a male to be involved in the family's town businesses.[28]

When Bernice and Herbert had not been married very long, Beatrice Harris, the wife of Herbert's married brother, Whit, came to visit. Bernice was delighted, sure that they would be friends. They had both been teachers, and so they would have much in common, she thought. However, the sister-in-law got to the point of her visit very soon:

She startled me with her precipitate advice. "Go ahead and have a family!" she said with odd urgency soon after her arrival. "Don't wait!"

In impassioned tone she told me then how she had wanted a family, had meant to have children. But other influences had proved stronger and she had remained childless.

"But why—?" I was bewildered at the revelations.

"Property!"[29]

Bernice was left dazed.

Her hopes for a friendship evaporated. "There should have been a close bond," she wrote in her autobiography (pages she chose not to publish). "But I learned early there could be no real closeness with opposing sides among family and friends, whatever personal liking there might be."[30] And now the picture became clearer: Bernice was on the opposing side. She was the threat the family members perceived. She might have children, who would take Herbert's wealth from them—at best, they would have to split inheritances eight or nine ways instead of six. The sister-in-law may have felt some empathy with Bernice, but she stayed on the family's side (undoubtedly in an attempt to consolidate her own position). Ironically, it was not Whit but a younger brother, Otis, who defied the family: he moved to Norfolk, Virginia, married, and produced a son.

The family let Bernice know she was not one of them. Herbert's father died suddenly of pneumonia while she was visiting her own father for Christmas in Wake County. Some friends in Seaboard decided she should know and called her brother William Olive in Raleigh, who drove out to the family farm to get her. Immediately, Bernice and her brother began the five-hour drive to Seaboard and arrived just in time for the funeral. She remarked, "Herbert seemed pathetically surprised and glad to see us."[31] She was not invited to ride in the family car but walked behind it with other townspeople.[32] A similar situation occurred later, when Herbert's oldest brother Whit died: they did not tell her, insinuating that she was not one of the family.[33]

She longed for a family of her own. When a bride came to the Harrises' house to dress for her wedding, Bernice imagined it was her daughter. The young woman's face shaded into a boy's face as Bernice imagined her son.[34] One Christmas soon after their marriage, Bernice tentatively approached Herbert with her longing for a child:

> On Christmas Eve that year Herbert and I sat in the candlelight of our bedroom and listened to the radio music and ate white fruitcake

and candied ginger and toasted peanuts and had no sense of being second-rate. The muted notes of "Oh, Little Town of Bethlehem" and of "Silent Night" seemed no less sacred because we relished our bounty.

Later after we had gone to bed, I turned to Herbert . . .

"Who knows but there'll be three of us another Christmas?"

"I do!" he spoke out impetuously.

"I mean, we might have a baby."

"I know what you mean."

"A little fellow with brown eyes," I thought.

He yawned.

"With brown eyes like yours . . ."

"You don't have a thing to worry about. You ought to know that."

"Worry, when—?"

"Let's go to sleep! I have a headache." He turned away quickly. Soon he was snoring gently.

My silence was not acquiescence to his attitude that increasingly dismayed me. There would have to be a showdown before another year ended.[35]

The next Christmas the showdown came. She made her plea again as they sat watching the snow whirl around the window. She was moved by the beauty of the scene. She remembered, "I was aware that the summation of it all was to pass beauty on from heir to heir, to pass life on—I tried to explain how I felt."[36] There was a stillness in the room.

Then he gave his answer. The answer was still no, and now it was clearer and more emphatic. When she asked why, he "blurted out angrily, 'Haven't I got all I can finance?' " He left abruptly and went upstairs to bed. She sat alone by the radiator and then went upstairs, too.

There was a waiting silence. I felt his anger subsiding. He coughed, he cleared his throat, adjusted the pillow, reached out for the extra blanket. I knew he was in need of reassurance of some kind. It was palpable there in the room, his reaching out, the maze he was alone in.

He had to be alone in this, alone and comfortless.

Then he blurted out, "Do you think I'd let you go through that, at your age?"

"I want to." I moved over to the bed and sat by him. I made my plea, concluded my brief. I knew this would be the final adjudication.

"No!" He was final. "No babies!"

The rejection was absolute. It was incredible that it should be babies against trees, the little fellow with brown eyes against standing timber.

I went back to the window and watched the cold animated whiteness awhile longer. It did not turn back into the beauty of the earth that night.[37]

She carried the loss inside of her from then on. When her little nephew Gordon Kelley came to stay with her while William Olive and Mary went on a vacation, it was such a treasured time that Bernice remembered it always. Years later in a letter, she reminded him how he had taken the crib guard that kept a small child from falling out of bed and put it under Herbert as he napped on the sofa. "You were once my little boy," she said.[38]

Even in her seventies, when Herbert had been dead twenty years, she still grieved over her childlessness. Once when a friend, Ed Hodges, a journalist, was visiting her with his young children, she shocked him by suddenly blurting out her anger against Herbert because he had not let her have a child.[39]

She sought, as best she could, to maintain a sense of family and ongoing generations by being in contact with her brothers and sisters and their children. Occasionally, Bernice's brother William Olive and his wife, Mary, and little Gordon came to spend a weekend. And in the late 1930s, they had, besides the toddler Gordon, a new baby, Alice Jo. Bernice delighted in them. She loved Olive dearly, and Mary was as close to her as a sister. She always addressed her letters to them as "Dear Folks." Mary had been a teacher also, and like Bernice, she wrote plays. William Olive was a teacher and later, a superintendent of schools. Their stays in Seaboard were highlights of the year for her. She visited them in Raleigh whenever she could, and she tried to get back to Wake County regularly to see her father and other family members. Especially she loved being there at Christmas, which was a major event among her mother and father's children and grandchildren. All her visits were special occasions for her extended family. Her nieces and nephews saw her as a hero from the outside world.

In the spring, Herbert would buy a huge rockfish (a channel bass) and he and Bernice would pack it in ice and drive with it to her father's house. They would cook a huge pot of fish stew, a Northampton County dish called rockfish muddle, made with potatoes and onions. Family members would gather, bringing the "side dishes" and desserts.[40] These times brought back to her the happy feelings of being with the family she had known in childhood.

Meanwhile, her dependence on Herbert grew. She tried to learn to drive the car, but on one occasion she scraped the fender against the column of their porte cochere. (At that time houses were still being built with a porch roof projecting over the driveway so passengers could alight without getting wet in the rain.) Herbert delivered such a tirade about her marring the car's surface that the neighbors heard, and so then did all the town. She quit driving.[41]

Bernice tried hard to please. She worried about household costs because expenses distressed Herbert, and so she tried to be thrifty. A challenge was to keep the cost of groceries for each week under four dollars, but she dreaded the day in the month when the bank statement came because the canceled checks upset him. It was customary that a married woman did not teach, so after her contract with the Seaboard high school ran out, her ability to make money had ended, and all of her own savings had gone into building the house.[42]

She discovered that he had such "terrific headaches" when worries preoccupied him that she shied away from provocative topics in conversation. She tried hard to care for him in other ways as well. He worked so constantly at the cotton gin that she would take him meals and then stand over him to make sure he ate. She described the scene: "He was skilled in mechanics, so that often when I arrived with trays he was repairing machinery dangerously high in the gin building. He and Mr. Bradley, senior partner, shared the office work and an incredible capacity for activity. They were devoted. Many times after being together from early hours of morning till bedtime, they stopped on the way from work at the street corner in front of their houses to talk awhile."[43]

Herbert's brother Jethro was a silent partner in the cotton gin business. Another brother and Herbert had a fertilizer business. And he had shares in still other businesses. In spite of profits from these enterprises, he figured incessantly—furtively, she thought—but she said he "was never quite satisfied with the dividends and profits he made from his investments."[44] But he did have real losses to deal with: in their first year of marriage fire destroyed part of his timber, and later a cotton gin burned.

Bernice was a little jealous that he had these partnerships in which she was not involved. She wanted to be in on "Harris and Harris" also.[45] Each year they would have a gigantic backyard garden. A neighbor asked her why, with all their money, they worked themselves like horses. The reason was simple: Bernice had been, above all else, a farm girl; she could not bear to let spring pass without planting. And she enjoyed harvesting the vegetables, but processing so much food was another matter. In the pre–freezer era, things had to be canned, and so the wood-burning cookstove was fired up even on the hottest summer days so the pressure canner could reach boiling point. Sometimes, she said, the pressure canner was kept going all morning and all afternoon. Jars of beans, squash, tomatoes, and corn lined the pantry shelves. She said that at first it was wonderful.

> It grew less wonderful as Herbert increased the pressure on me. He was a slave driver, I told him sometimes when he came in with still another bushel of beans to be processed. At first I was puzzled by his insistencies. When the pantry shelves were loaded with quart jars of vegetables, there was no let-up. The cellar had to be filled. New jars were bought, more garden produce garnered and pressure-canned.
>
> Then it became clear. Herbert was racing. He was out to beat neighbors, family. He wanted to brag on our supplies. I was touched. It seemed to make me still more Harris and Harris.[46]

At last, late fall would come and she could turn her attention to other things. She had been an enthusiastic teacher of writing. Now she renewed her childhood dream of being a writer. And, in truth, the "solid security" Herbert gave her meant she had, for the first time since childhood, the leisure to write. She began by describing her observations and feelings in a personal journal she called "My Day." (She was influenced by Eleanor Roosevelt, whom she admired and who at that time was writing a newspaper column with this title.) Bernice also started writing human interest stories for the local papers. She already knew the town well enough, but she also wanted to know what was happening outside it. She began to accompany the county caseworker on visits to tenants' and sharecroppers' homes. Everything she saw was important to her: Seaboard Township was a whole world of fascinating people. Journalist Roy Parker Jr., whose mother and aunt made their home in Seaboard, mused, "I lived in the midst of all that stuff that so fascinated her and I thought, 'Hell, this is the dullest place.' " But for her, he remarked, everything and every person held a mystery and a story.[47]

Soon she was publishing articles in the local papers—for the Norfolk *Virginian-Pilot*, the *Jackson News*, the *Bertie Ledger*, the *Hert-*

ford County Herald, and the Raleigh *News and Observer*. She wrote personal-interest stories and accounts of social events. There were such deadly boring topics as the card parties, and these write-ups had to follow a rigid formula, but she did her best to make them interesting. She wrote accounts of weddings, especially what the bride wore, to the smallest detail. And she even reported the frog-fries.[48]

In the personal-interest stories, she described such individuals as Sallie Jordan, an African American woman with ten children. For years Mrs. Jordan had sent her children forth to participate in seventh-grade graduation exercises but had not seen one graduate because she did not have proper clothes to wear to the school. At last, she did have the right clothes and attended the event, seeing for the first time one of her children receive a diploma. In high spirits, Sallie Jordan advised the country to keep "rosy with Roosevelt!"[49]

Although many of these human interest stories had a black citizen as hero, there were also humorous ones that perpetuated commonly held notions about African Americans. In one, mourners slink away from a funeral to steal the deceased woman's chickens. Later, after Bernice had done in-depth interviewing for the Federal Writers' Project in the African American community, she did not use stereotypes.

Bernice received awards for her newspaper reporting.[50] And meanwhile she started writing short stories. Herbert could not understand why she would spend time "scribbling." "It was not necessary," he said. "If it was to keep me company that I wrote, well—wasn't he there?" If it was to make money, did he not make enough money?[51]

She thought that it was *because* he was there that she had "bounty to share." She felt snug and secure in the marriage relationship. Once, when they attended a wedding, she observed the widows present; she had some empathy, but she knew the married women could not really understand what widows might be feeling. She thought, "We were homed, secure in husband's affection, paired. We would be dear to somebody in our old age."[52] She remembered the tablets she had filled with her writings in childhood, expressions of her longing and groping. "Out of fulfillment I wrote now," she said.[53]

Not long after their marriage, Herbert was diagnosed with high blood pressure. Not wanting to upset him, Bernice refrained from writing in his presence. She would accompany Herbert when he went out to check on his property and would wait in the car for him. In his absence, she would write. When daylight waned, she would hold a flashlight so she could see the paper. Possibly all her accommodations had some effect on her own health. Soon after the marriage, she began to have problems with "nervous indigestion." This could have been a physical manifestation of psychological stress. She also suffered from anemia and low blood pressure.[54]

She kept writing, and in 1934 she sold her first short story to the *Saturday Evening Post*. It was called "Bantie Woman" and it was different from the usual love stories published in magazines. In the story, a widower spies a very small woman who works with great strength and perseverance. When he can at last claim a small farm, he travels to get his dead wife's coffin, thinking she will rest better in land he owns. With the coffin in the back of his wagon, he drives to find the little woman to ask her to be his next wife. And with dead wife and living wife in the wagon with him, he sallies forth to his land. His little living wife is pleased to be with a man who has shown such tenderness for a wife, even caring for her after death.[55] It was the feeling of being dear to somebody that Bernice herself prized.

When the check for the story came in the mail, Herbert happily deposited it in his account at the bank. He said he could not understand why anyone would pay so much for so little. But he was pleased and said that now he would hold the flashlight for her.[56]

Nevertheless she still did her writing when it would cause the least annoyance to Herbert. In the daytime she wrote when he was not at home and when she was not required to attend a social event. In the evenings she would sit beside him and listen to the radio or go out in the car with him.

According to neighbors and friends in Seaboard, Herbert had a reputation of being hard to live with. Bernice reinterpreted his tirades against her as being expressions of their closeness. She said that she felt cherished when he ranted most.[57] But she could not reinterpret his refusal to have a child. All her life after the confrontation, she held it against Herbert. This is the one subject in her autobiographical writings in which Herbert appears as a mean person.

However angry about his denial of her dream of having children, Bernice Harris could not have just walked out of Seaboard and left this marriage. Other southern women writers of her generation claimed for themselves freedom to divorce, but not without wrenching hesitation. Katherine Anne Porter, just a year older than Bernice, divorced the first time after nine years of a very unhappy marriage, and even so her father was angry at her for doing that.[58] But for Bernice Kelly Harris, there was no divorce. Unlike Porter, she was too much a member of a church and a believer in Christian doctrine and too tied into a conservative community to divorce a husband. And, in truth, she loved Herbert and she wanted the conventional life she had in Seaboard.

She acted according to the expectations for a southern lady. Anne Goodwyn Jones, discussing women writers in the late nineteenth and early twentieth centuries, declared that the "finest act of the southern lady, [was] devotion to a superior man."[59] And if he was not superior, the southern lady pretended that he was. Bernice hid her intellectual gifts and magnified Herbert's abilities. She was loyal and devoted to her husband, as her mother had been to her father. And like her mother, she was obedient. She fulfilled the expectations for a southern lady by taking care of her husband's physical needs and tiptoeing around him so as not to displease him. She took care of his psychological needs as best she could; she always deferred to him. (She called him "Mr. Harris," as ladies at the time would do.) She was certainly self-sacrificing. She was a master at being the gracious hostess; her natural reaction to another person was one of being interested. But she had also perfected the skill of being controlled and polite.

However, she also defied the tradition. She described her honeymoon, alluding to sexual experience with Herbert in glowing terms, although southern women were supposed to be innocents. She did not just read books, as might be expected of her in order for her to converse in polite society. Instead she started writing her own.

She defied traditional expectations in still another way. Southern women were supposed to accept dependency: a woman who made money by working provoked questions about her husband's competence as a provider. But Bernice hated not being able to contribute money to sustaining their household. Her dream was that they would be equal partners, "Harris and Harris," and she doggedly pursued this while Herbert just as stubbornly denied the importance of her monetary contributions, all the while pocketing the money.

She endured, and her solution was not unusual for a southern woman writer—she lived by exploring in fiction the questions she could not talk about out loud.[60] And writing fiction was the one endeavor in which she could do as she pleased. In the "real world"—whether it was the public world of the town or the private world with

Herbert—she was contained and conforming. In her fictional worlds, her rich inner life, the "life behind the mask,"[61] could be articulated. And by writing, whenever she could, Bernice Kelly Harris made some part of each day exciting and limitless—as she had done in her childhood when her imagination created such dazzling vistas.

4

Northampton County Produces Cotton, Peanuts, and Plays

Being so much a part of town life and having the liking and respect of other women, Bernice Kelly Harris was ready to use all her influence to carry out Koch's challenge to his students. She had had on her mind for nearly ten years—since she took Koch's classes—that she would move beyond high school dramatic production to develop community playwriting and play producing. And she missed teaching. Within a few years of her marriage and the consolidation of her position in the town, and while she was writing short stories for magazines and articles for newspapers, she also began pressuring women and men to come to her house to learn to write plays. By all accounts of people who knew her, she was so likable and encouraging that it was hard to refuse her.

Bernice said that she stayed awake nights devising ways to inspire her students to think about characterization and plot—and pondering what she could serve as refreshments. Her method was to get them to talk about stories from their lives or from the lives of people they had known or heard about. But sometimes they really wanted to talk about gardens, recipes, and gossip. She kept them on target. It was difficult in a beginning playwriting class to get students to see that ordinary language had to be used in an extraordinary way, and she worked on that. Also, she said that she focused on "the difference between situation and dramatic situation, explaining the importance of relation-ships therein."[1]

Sometimes the debates over themes in the Harris living room were loud and hot. Especially they debated one theme in a play that man's greatest passion in life was love of money. The wives in the group ar-gued that it was romantic love. Bernice commented that they had no trouble with another theme—the wages of sin is death—until one member made a local application a little too pointed. Bernice hurried them into discussion of a safer theme, the eternal vanity of males. They liked talking about character. She insisted that an interesting charac-ter, whether adulterer or saint, did not make a play. "The character," she emphasized, "has to react to a situation, has to be shown in action, has to set out to do something or fail to do it."[2]

Her students began to see that there was "authentic drama all around."[3] Each would write a scene and Bernice would work with the writer on it. The writer revised and began work on the next scene. Over a few years, with a somewhat changing membership, twelve women and two men wrote plays that were produced. A minister wrote a play about the rich young man who cannot turn from material gain to spiritual gain. A townsperson wrote a play about a county of-ficial who sought the moonshine maker to arrest him but unwittingly drank up the evidence. Annie Bradley, the wife of Herbert's partner, wrote a play about a widow's last fling at romance in *Seliney's Last Dance*. A teacher, Mattie Griffin, collaborated with Bernice on *The Elopement*. It won a prize at Chapel Hill. (For a while, Bernice re-mained the silent author on that one.)[4] And often her students' plays won prizes. She described all of her students' work with great pride.

Harris believed that local situations and human relationships were as interesting as anything about sophisticated urban people that was often presented in fiction. She argued that the struggles of the people next door and across town are not necessarily only regional but that they have universal significance. "Villains and saints, domestic tangles and wedded bliss, divorce, suicide were no less dramatically motivated because they occurred in a precinct than in New York," she declared.[5]

Soon she managed to get people together who were interested in producing the plays. Then she appealed for help to the groups she was involved in and had worked hard for or to people she had done favors for. The community became involved. Men, after working on the farm or in the store or at the gin, built sets and wallpapered and painted them. The props group scoured the countryside for a spinning wheel of the right vintage and other props that would be representative of the era. Wardrobe mistresses studied the *World Book of Styles* and designed patterns so that the costumes would be authentic.[6] Furniture went out of people's living rooms and onto the high school stage. Some furniture became worn out from so much traveling.

Actors came from all social strata in Seaboard and the surrounding area—lawyers and farmers, housewives and teachers, county home-demonstration agents and ministers, sharecroppers and bankers. The town policeman took the part of a Confederate lieutenant. One farmer—a character himself, a "cross between Ichabod Crane and Abraham Lincoln"—said, " 'Twan't hard for me to learn my part; all I had to say was, 'Sure, sure.' And didn't I say it good!"[7]

Opening night always had the whole town in excited frenzy. Nobody could miss the show because nearly everybody had had some part in it or had contributed something.[8] Bernice loved the feeling of community that these dramatic productions aroused.

She started organizing towns throughout the county as units of the Northampton Players. County-wide and local slates of officers were selected. She met her good friend Vaughn Holoman in this way and made other friends throughout the county. People drove ten to twenty miles to attend playwriting sessions or rehearsals or to work on sets. Harris repeated with much pleasure the saying going around then: "In Northampton County we produce cotton, peanuts, and plays."[9]

Playmaking was not always as easy as Bernice Harris made it sound, however. Ruth Vick Everett, as one of Harris's narrators for the Federal Writers' Project, spoke frankly of the troubles she encountered in putting on plays there. Everett was a teacher in the Seaboard high school in 1927 and headed the school's dramatics club. She also became head of the Northampton Players. During one play, the leading lady said, "Damn" and lit a cigarette. The Baptist preacher and his wife made a show of walking out. (Everett added, "The same preacher had more than one congregation to walk out on him because of rumors about his personal life.") She described another occasion, after first night of a biblical play:

> One Sunday night as I started home from the beautiful production of "The Terraphim," the immortal love story of Jacob and Rachel, I was

waylaid by the irate husband of the leading lady. "Now, look here, Mrs. Everett," he said, white-lipped in the moonlight, "don't you ever put my wife in an immoral play like that again." Rachel, who was a teacher in our school and one of my best friends, was terribly embarrassed by her husband's anger; since that night there has been a rift in our friendship, though I saw to it that she was in another religious play two years later. I went straight to the Methodist preacher who also had a part in the play, and he consoled me by reminding me of the limited horizons of some of the audience.[10]

One could conclude that drama was taken seriously in Seaboard—and also that Bernice preferred not to notice local limitations in the understanding of the art. But inevitably the interest in playwriting, not play production, waned. Bernice began writing the plays herself. She appealed to J. O. (James Ostler) Bailey, a professor in the English department at the University of North Carolina, to direct her in a correspondence course on writing plays. He was young and aware of his lack of practical knowledge of theater and playwriting, but he was interested in her ideas. Sometimes his criticisms were on the mark, sometimes his advice was sage, but always he was honest with her and supportive. He became and remained a mentor and friend to the end of her life.

She began to turn out plays for the Northampton Players. From 1932 to 1938, she had a play ready for production every year. The first was *Ca'Line*, which was based on the homeless woman she had known in childhood (described in chapter 1.) Ca'Line, spinster of uncertain age, distant kin to many families in Poole's Siding, worked at each house until her services were no longer needed. She did not fear work, she feared only ending up in the "poor house"—the county institution for elderly paupers. And her worst fears came true: when she became old, her relatives packed her up and took her to the poorhouse, despite her wailing. Later, when they brought her back for a visit to the country, she told them she wanted to return to the poorhouse. There she had electric lights and indoor plumbing and was called "Miss Caroline." At the end of the play, the relatives concluded that Ca'Line had gone to the poorhouse and gotten "the big head."[11]

The next play, *Special Rates*, was produced in 1933 by the Jackson Players (a unit of the Northampton Players) in Seaboard and in 1934 by the Carolina Playmakers in Chapel Hill. The main characters are two old widowers, Alf and Nath, who live together and spend their days bickering and arguing. Alf has been courting (with less than en-thusiasm) a local woman. When his daughter Mittie, from whom he is estranged, hears a rumor about the possibility of his marrying, she ap-pears in Alf's farmhouse. She wants to make sure she stays in his will. Meanwhile, the courted woman, Gussie, arrives with plans for instant marriage. She tells Alf how she will change the house and insists he sign a new will making her—as his wife—the sole beneficiary. They will take advantage of special rates offered by the railroad to go on a honeymoon. While her back is turned, Alf and Nath review the situa-tion:

> ALF. We was a-makin' out right good here . . . I and you. (He sits by the bed Nath has crawled into.) Had it quiet and all to ourselves.
> NATH. Yeh.
> ALF. Stripped and washed often enough, without women-folks a-tellin' us when to wash.
> NATH. (*Innocently*) Or shave.
> ALF. We cooked our vittles to suit ourselves and heard good speakin' and read and chewed and spit where we pleased and— (There is a lumbering above as Gussie moves furniture to put it where she wants it.) Nath![12]

Nath jumps out of bed, sticks his feet in his shoes, and heads for the railroad tracks with Alf. *They* will take advantage of the special rates and go to Washington—a place Alf has always wanted to see. Alf says he will send Gussie a postcard saying no to marriage.

The Seaboard Players (another division of the Northampton Play-ers) took *Judgment Comes to Dan'l* to the Community Drama Contest in Chapel Hill in 1933. One of the actors, Irene Harris (wife of Her-bert's second cousin), was pregnant, and delivery was imminent; but since she was in bed during most of the play, she could be a convincing seventy-year-old. She was one of the two elderly women, Cynthy and Liza, who sit propped up in bed as the play opens. On the way to Chapel Hill, the featherbed, their main prop, popped a seam, and the cavalcade of players' cars and trucks strewed the highway with feath-ers like a trail of glory.

Cynthy and Liza have figured out how to be weak and sick so that a niece, Etta, will take care of them. A local farmer, Dan'l, loves Etta and wants her to marry him. The old ladies will not consent; they know they would have to share Etta's attention with him. Suddenly, the house shakes. It is an earthquake, but they take it as a sign of God's Judgment Day. Liza and Cynthy get out of bed so they can kneel down to pray. They decide they had better do the right thing by Etta and let her marry Dan'l. They grab quilts, wrap themselves up, and go outside—revealing to themselves and their world that they can move around and take care of themselves.[13]

In *Three Foolish Virgins*, the winning play in the drama contest of original plays at the University of North Carolina Playmakers Theatre in 1936, the curtain rises on Miss Sue Wren, "a diminutive creature of seventy." She is at her spinning wheel, spinning rolls of carded cotton into thread. Near the fireplace sits her sister, Miss Sarah Wren, "smaller and a half-hour younger." She is sewing a dress for a doll. Sue accuses Sarah of worrying about Cling Austen, who lives in the tenant's house nearby. They decide that their fifty-year-old niece Tommie will marry Cling and move him over to their house where they can keep an eye on him. When Gracie Bell, a neighbor, comes in to tell them *she* is going to marry Cling, they show her the door. Sarah, fearing there is no time to waste because Gracie Bell intends to marry Cling, orders Sue to go over to Cling's house and tell him he's marrying Tommie. Sue is also to ask their nephew, Jim, to drive Cling and Tommie to town for the license.

Sarah then tells Tommie her fate. Tommie says she would rather die than marry Cling and that Sarah can marry him if she wants him in the house. When Sarah confesses that once she and Cling were sweethearts, Tommie uses this information to convince Sarah that *she* should marry Cling. Sarah goes to get ready. Seventy-five-year-old Cling arrives with all his pills packed for moving. He thinks he wants to marry Tommie, but Tommie tries to convince him otherwise. He says, "I ain't satisfied with the change—a-switchin' women on me." Tommie gets mad and throws his pills out of the door.

At that moment, Sarah appears in her best clothes. Cling complains that Tommie has ordered him out. Tommie says she has changed her mind:

> TOMMIE. I'm goin' on over to Emporia and get hooked up, and tomorrow you'll see him on the woodpile, and by spring a-breakin' up new grounds. I just throwed away all that mess o'medicine, and next—[14]

She dashes out to put on a clean pair of overalls to get married in, saying, "I'm goin' to wear the breeches at my house. I'll get married in 'em!"

Cling decides against real work and against marriage to a woman he cannot manipulate. He declares that he wants to marry Sarah. When Jim's horn honks, he grabs Sarah and they leave for town and the preacher. Tommie starts making a wedding cake. Sue puts her doll away in a trunk, saying, "Come on, sonny; we got a big baby to nu'se." But Tommie tells her aunt to put the doll back in its place—a portent of the way Tommie will prevent the old man from being too much the center of attention.[15]

A Pair of Quilts, produced in 1938, concerns the rivalry of women who want to make the quilt that will win the prize at the local fair. One is so determined to see a quilt she thinks the peddler has in his possession before her rival sees it that she becomes the dupe of the peddler: he sells her back her own quilt. Much of the humor is in the juxtaposition of two accents—the peddler is originally from the Middle East (both Syrian and Jewish immigrants made a living as peddlers early in the century) and the housewife Cornie is an East Carolina native. It is the difference in speech that had so fascinated Bernice as a child when the peddlers came to her father's house. The peddler here has much insight into the desires of rural North Carolina women. Here he persuades Cornie to buy still more of the treasures in his pack:

PEDDLER.   All preddy womens need preddy jew'lry and fancy combs do decorade dhe hair. You god a fine head of hair, but you bound do have somedhin' do set id off. (*He places the fancy comb in her hair.*) See dhere? Pud id jusd behind de ball—make you look like de town womens! (*The Peddler goes around the chair.*) Ged de blue ribbon, have you picdure dook wid dhis. Jusd fifdy-five cend. Sdunnin'! Make you look like Queen Vicdory! (*He holds the mirror before her.*)

CORNIE.   (*Wondering at the difference in her appearance*). Well, don't a little thing make a change in a body's looks?[16]

This play and the others were what Harris referred to as "country comedies." They are gentle comedies; their characters are not the gentry but simple farming folk, and the fun comes from the exposé of human foibles common to us all. Yet they seem quaint to the contemporary reader. Since they were written, urbanization and mass communication have drastically changed lifestyles. The plays are still funny, however, and the dialogue is still lively. One theme is the lack of understanding between men and women. Miss Sarah in *Three Foolish Virgins* explains that men are different and inclined to be bad, but there is a remedy, "I ain't goin' to deceive you, men *has* got natures, but—but they got Bible for it."[17]

Harris wrote two social protest plays. The first, *His Jewels*, was originally produced by the Seaboard and Woodland Players and taken to Chapel Hill to the drama contest in 1935. The play opens in a church, where three girls, Ruby, Garnet, and Pearl, are trying to make a home. Ruby stands at the woodstove used to warm the church; she is trying to cook bacon. Little Pearl is lying on a back bench. Garnet is trying to warm her with an old quilt. They try to get Pearl to eat a bite of the bacon, but she is too sick. Their father, the widower Ed Harper, comes in, having tramped through the countryside all day looking for another place to sharecrop. The previous landlord has turned them out, fearing he will have to pay for a doctor for Pearl. Ed is greatly distressed to see how sick Pearl is, but Garnet and Ruby assure him she has eaten. He feels her forehead and knows she has a fever, and he hears her cough. When they see church members coming in to the church to practice a play, they hide.

The church members' play is about the Gentile who says he seeks Jesus and the Messenger who says that Jesus' jewels are the ragged child and the beggar. Whoever recognizes the jewels and takes care of them as a good steward of Jesus' possessions will meet Jesus, the Messenger declares. One actor throws open a door unintentionally and reveals the hidden, ragged family. The church people immediately turn the family out into the cold.[18]

Like *His Jewels*, the other social protest play, *Open House*, exposed the injustices of the sharecropping system and the hypocrisy of churchgoers. *Open House* was the winning play in the festival at Chapel Hill in 1937. It is based on a sketch called "The Butterbean Woman," which Harris had published in a local newspaper about a family evicted by a landlord. The Butterbean Woman, as she was known locally, raised and sold vegetables and worked her landlord's cotton crop. Harris had interviewed this woman and was haunted by her family's desperate plight. Harris wrote:

Three weeks ago the landlord told the Butterbean Woman and her family to vacate for the occupancy of another tenant. She had nowhere to go. She tramped seven days over a wide territory hunting a house to move in. She could find no place. On Friday in March at three o'clock in the afternoon two officers, dreading their job, evicted her. They placed her three beds, three mattresses, safe, bureau, washstand, stove, chairs, two dogs, five chickens, quilts and clothes by the side of the Sea-board-Gumberry highway. She and her family parked alongside ("I didn't kick up," she declared) where the walls were the evergreen horizon, her roof the blue sky, her pictures still life and landscapes, and her neighbors highway traffic.[19]

When the play opens, the officer and constable stand on the highway, staring at the ragged children. The mother, Mrs. Jernigan, makes a fire—the smoke curls upwards without benefit of a chimney. She tells the children to fix the beds ready to lie in, and her invalid husband puts himself to the task of making a broom. An ex-officer comes by to have a look. He advises Mrs. Jernigan to go on relief. She refuses: "We ain't that kind of folks." He tells her to vote against the landlord and to vote for him, the ex-officer. He leaves. The baby in the cradle whimpers. Another child scrapes the sugar barrel and dips a wet rag in it to make the baby a "sugar-tit." There is no milk.

The church's pastor comes to visit the family. When he finds that the landlord is one of his best-contributing parishioners, he bows out. He says he'll come back when the weather is not so cold, and meanwhile he'll report the case to his missionary circles. A one-legged man on relief arrives to warm himself by their fire. He tells them to write the president about the landlord's dirty dealing. Women from the church circle bring a little food, some blankets, and some clothes. When one looks into the cradle, she realizes the baby has died. The churchwomen leave.

A black woman and her two children pass by and stop, and Mrs. Jernigan shares with her the food the churchwomen brought. The landlord returns—he is beginning to worry about his reputation. He meant for the officers to move her out of the house but not all the way to the road so people can see. He is angry with Mrs. Jernigan because she insisted on the highway. He tries to convince Mrs. Jernigan to take the dollar he offers and move somewhere else and go on relief. Her reply is, "I come from working folks." The circle leaders return to get the dead baby for burial. Mrs. Jernigan has the last words in the play: "I'll bury him. And we won't be needin' no relief."[20]

The two social protest plays have impact. Harris knew what she was writing about: on her rounds with the county agent, she had seen how people were living. Her ideal was the independent yeoman farmer such as her father had been; in her view, the worst thing that could happen to any human was to be landless and homeless. The independence of the Butterbean Woman touched her deeply, and the words she gave her character Mrs. Jernigan are words of defiance.

All of the aforementioned plays are folk plays in several senses. Certainly the speech characteristics of eastern North Carolina are reproduced. In *Three Foolish Virgins*, when Tommie tries to convince Sarah to marry Cling, she says, "You're the one that's traipsed through rain and sleet to take him hot biscuits and herb teas, washed and ironed for him, and fixed his clothes and medicine and poulticed his risin's."[21] People in other places might talk of trying to get a swelling to go down by applying a wet application of herbs, but these are the terms used in Eastern Carolina. A character in some other place, some other time, might say "slogged through rain and sleet." But "traipsed" has, beyond the surface meaning of walk, a connotation not only of determination but of a ceremonial gait.

The old sayings that shaped lives for generations are integral to plot. In *Special Rates* when Alf and Nath argue, for example, Nath resorts to a saying he knows will evoke a spark of recognition in Alf. He says the woman is "fixin' to make her nest here."

ALF.   I'm boss here.
NATH.   Crow then, while you can, for feathers is goin' to fly when she gets you tied up and makes a Methodist out'n you.[22]

Common misconceptions are used. Typical of the way the two old men bicker, Alf evades the subject of Gussie by introducing the old rivalry between Methodists and Baptists, drawing on the common man's misbeliefs in that culture:

ALF.   Never! I wouldn't send my soul to torment. . . . How you 'spect to keep out'n torment and you never been baptized?
NATH.   Methodists don't need wettin' all over; they ain't that mean.[23]

The metaphors are taken from the farming way of life. Mittie in *Special Rates* tells Nath about Gussie's persuading her father to marry,

"I ain't goin' to take it settin' down." Nath comments, "There ain't nothin' you can do, and nothin' I can do to keep him from mirin' up to his head."[24] It is the word choice of rural workers who must deal with spring and fall rains and all the mud and animal waste that one sinks into.

Harris uses beliefs that kept in check the would-be challengers to this society's norms, such as the belief that an earthquake is an announcement that God's Judgment Day is soon to come. In *Judgment Comes to Dan'l*, Minda, the cook, tells Etta, who wants to know where her aunts have gone, that they have vanished in the "battin' o' yo' eye." She adds, "Don't de Good Book say 'twould be lak dat at de End o' Time?"[25]

Harris based her characters on individuals she had known, on the life situations of ordinary people. She candidly admitted:

> To write as authors do these days, "the characters in this book are fictitious and any resemblance to living people is purely accidental," would be untruthful. It will be strange if resemblance to living persons is not traced, for the plays were written for the most part with an eye on certain people in my experience. Their physical characteristics, their ages and names, their stations in life have been changed to suit the exigencies of the occasion, but they have all breathed the breath of life—in eastern North Carolina.
>
> Only four are actual prototypes: two of these dear ones are dead, and the other two say they don't mind being in a book. The situations in which they are placed are basically authentic, though the plots are invented. There *are* three "Virgins" of fifty, seventy-two, and eighty years (dear "Miss Sarah" has passed on) who live together in a little cabin in Northampton and spend their days spinning, quilting and "waiting for a sweetheart." There *was* dear Ca'line who finally had to go to the poorhouse after a lifetime of aversion to the idea and who came back to visit among her folks a little "stuck up" because she was living so much better at the Wake County Home than they were. There *was* an eviction of tenants along the highway near Seaboard in 1936. Apparently the landlord had plenty of reason on his side, but the evictees were appealing drama none the less as they set up housekeeping along the highway that cold day. The other eviction, in *His Jewels*, was in the news under another date line, but the Harpers were drawn from a family of white sharecroppers on a Northampton farm. The earthquake of course was not peculiar to eastern North Carolina, but the memory of the terror it brought here still makes dramatic stories out of which other plays might

well be written. And I doubt if I left myself out. Maybe I am in the Church Group in *His Jewels*; perhaps I might have been, under a different set of circumstances, a "Miss Ina" or a Circle Leader in the play.[26]

Speech characteristics, sayings, and metaphors from the culture, beliefs, and authentic characters and situations—all are significant features of Harris's folk plays. Beyond these is Harris's understanding and compassion for those our society passes by. The elderly figure prominently in her plays, but as Koch said in his introduction to a published collection of her plays, *Folk Plays of Eastern Carolina*, "They more nearly please themselves then than at any time in life, and while the turn their pleasure takes sometimes has its pathetic overtones there is natural and delightful comedy among them."[27] There is, as well, a stubborn independence in her elderly characters that wins our admiration. Koch compared Harris's plays to other plays of rural life: "In the seemingly commonplace lives of her neighbors Mrs. Harris had found moments of great excitement and recorded them in their natural rhythms and colorful vernacular—as Edgar Lee Masters did for Spoon River in Illinois and Thornton Wilder did for village life in Vermont." There is, he said, a "haunting beauty" pervading her plays.[28]

Without knowing intimately the culture she portrayed, Bernice Kelly Harris could not have written these plays. Without being so much involved in the life of the community, she could not have inspired the community effort that made production of the plays possible. If it is difficult for the contemporary reader to understand why this gifted writer spent time teaching Sunday school, going to women's circle meetings, accompanying the county agent on her rounds, playing cards with townswomen, cooking for the visiting preacher, chatting at the post office, the answer is that she loved it all. But her awareness of others' feelings, her sensitivity to the nuances of a word, and her observation of everything around her made these experiences a never-ending source for her writing.

5

Farm Girl Compelled to Write: *Purslane*

Near the end of the thirties, just as Harris finished writing the last play—*A Pair of Quilts*—the circumstances of her own life were vexing. Nervous indigestion and anemia continued to trouble her. Her overworked doctor, John Wesley Parker, prescribed a small dose of whiskey once a day—not an unusual remedy at the time. Now she came to recognize the bootlegger's tap on the back door at night. Herbert would meet him and discreetly hand him money in return for the paper bag with its heavy contents. He would prepare the toddy for her.[1]

In addition to her health problems, she worried about Herbert, whose blood pressure was constantly elevated. He continued to have anxieties about his property. Especially traumatic was a lawsuit involving inheritance when Whit Harris, his older, married brother, died without a will. His wife, Beatrice, survived; and his brothers and sisters, who were by law "collateral heirs," sued the widow to get the property. Herbert and his brothers and sisters claimed that there had been a marriage contract between the deceased brother and his wife stating that at his death, all his property reverted to his brothers and sisters. No such marriage contract was found; nevertheless, the lawyer got a settlement favorable to the collateral heirs.

However, Bernice sensed that there was some deeper meaning underlying Herbert's and his siblings' obsession with property: "I had an odd feeling through it all that it was more a matter of first loyalties than of property," she remarked. Each family member felt compelled to put the Harris family first; one way to demonstrate family unity against the world was to guard the family's wealth. Herbert and his brothers and sisters seemed to have distrusted all others, and consequently they clung to each other: together, *they* were a mighty fortress; *they* would withstand the onslaughts of the terrible outsiders. And Bernice realized that wives were definitely outsiders. She wrote privately, "It was sad, I thought, about wives."[2]

However sad she might feel, however much she might identify with Whit Harris's widow, and despite the fact that Herbert also steadfastly refused to make a will, Bernice remained on her husband's side out of a sense of loyalty. But she was by this time heartily sick of thinking and talking about property. She tried to get away from this kind of preoccupation by writing a novel: "I felt impelled to make some kind of affirmation about people who without property holdings knew vast bounty. I made that affirmation in a novel. I called it *Purslane*."[3]

It seemed like a natural progression to write a novel. She had been encouraged by the editors of the papers who published her articles to write longer works. And she was still writing her observations about life around her in her personal journal, "My Day," with a vague idea of using the writing in some way. She was also reflecting on her family life when she was a child, longing for the feeling of being enfolded in a family with love and acceptance. "I had known the warmth and fullness of family and community life, had savored values that had nothing to do with money," she said, explaining why she wrote the first novel.[4] She could not have in the present that feeling of being enveloped in a family, but she could recreate it—could live it again—in fiction.

Her doctor told her to rest, and Herbert did not want her to write, but write she would. She knew that rest would not make her happy: "Writing was better medicine for me."[5] She once described herself as "a farm girl compelled to write."

Indeed, her first novel, *Purslane*, is the life she knew as a farm girl; it is about independent yeoman farmers, men and women, in Piedmont North Carolina at the beginning of the twentieth century. She gave it the title *Purslane*, the name of a plant commonly found growing on its own there. For her, purslane was symbolic of the people she had known—who were her characters in the novel—growing on their own and as much a part of the place as a native plant, rooted in a particular place like a plant.

She began the novel by evoking a feeling. The first lines were from a song:

> Oh my darlin', oh my darlin'
> Oh my dar-r-lin' Clementine,
> You are lost and gone forever—

> The sad finality of the song, the gloomy blue haze yonder above the Neuse River, the wood dove's lonesome call from the huckleberry swamp, the weariness of a long Monday were suddenly too much. The boy Calvin, drooped listlessly astride old yellow Nellie mule, gazed forlornly into the blue river vapor with the eyes of a wanderer who yearns for a haven beyond his reach.[6]

The family was returning from a day of chopping cotton in the fields. Dele Fuller, the mother, studied the set of her son's head as he rode the mule ahead. John Fuller, the father, drove the wagon, his mind on the cotton crop. His daughters, Letha, Kate, and Nannie Lou, were seated in the flat wagon body.

Dele knew what was causing Calvin's despondent mood. He was in love with Milly, the daughter of a rich man, Nick Pate, Dele's distant cousin. Dele, during the "silent morning in the cotton rows," had been trying to think of the words to say to him:

> You're worth two of her, Calvin—Dele went over the words row after row, knowing she could never speak them, for all her practice—No boy's got your looks. You always had looks from a baby up. She's not pretty and no bigger'n a washing of soap. The world's full of girls, pretty ones. Let her go, Calvin. (5)

Dele explained one day when Calvin asked her point-blank why Milly's parents rejected him:

> "Why should they cut up, if I'm the one she likes?"
> "It isn't just you, Calvin. It's us—not so much us as what we don't have. They feel above us, I reckon. They think we're just—pusley."[7]
> (154)

Calvin resolved to make money so he could own a farm. Somehow, he would win her parents' respect and permission to marry Milly.

Calvin and Milly attempted to spend time together; many of the novel's events gave them a chance to do so, and they tried their hardest to be together. But Milly's parents, Joyce and Nick Pate, were able to keep them separated most of the time. Finally they sent Milly away to a relative in Philadelphia. Calvin, in an attempt to make money, agreed to play baseball for a club in Alabama. He was a successful ballplayer and began to save money from his modest salary for the farm he dreamed of owning in order to win Milly.

In the meantime, Milly's parents put an announcement in the newspaper that she was to be married to a man in Philadelphia. Dele hesitated to tell Calvin, then decided she must. And so she wrote the letter to him. Consequently Calvin quit the ball club and returned home with a wife. Too late he received a letter from Milly saying that she had run away, gotten a job, and planned to return to Calvin. He took a fatal dose of laudanum. The men in the family and neighbors tried to keep him on his feet and make him walk. They switched him with sticks in an effort to keep him aware and conscious. But after some time Dele stopped them, telling them to lay him on the bed: "I want him to have peace." She explained, "He wanted us to cover him up and blow out the light and leave him to himself." She blew out the light (316).

The Eden Harris had created was shown to be a garden with a basic evil, a serpent, which was social class. Class differences—based on landownership and money—formed the basis of the plot. The large landowning class, represented by Nick Pate, was presented as pretentious and without a real sense of community. The need of this class for status and wealth overrode all other considerations.

Class difference also fueled a minor plot which began when an itinerant family, the Hewitts, moved in as the Fuller's sharecroppers. Everybody felt that the Hewitt family was lower on the social ladder because they owned no land, so the small-farming class was not without their own snobbery.

John and Dele Fuller did not spread gossip about their tenants' situation because they felt it was their responsibility to take care of the Hewitts, but their neighbors found out about the Hewitts' desperate poverty. People in the community brought them so many of their own clothes that one man declared, "Law, Puss gave away so much I started to collect the wrong children after church" (167).

The pretty daughter in the sharecropping family, Sally Hewitt, felt strongly attracted to Uncle Job's son, Ellis Pate, who came with his father to the Hewitt shack to read the Bible to the family. Hoping to impress Ellis, Sally joined the church. Later, she found Ellis alone in the church building. He put his arms around her at first to comfort her from the thunder and lightning outside, but the feeling of the woman in his arms aroused desire. They became sexually involved.

When Sally Hewitt became pregnant, she was turned out of the church by the "vigilant committee." And John Fuller, at his wife's insistence, threw the entire family out of their home. Real hypocrisy existed among them. Ellis Pate, the young man who made Sally pregnant and who was respected by all as the future preacher, pretended to be innocent. Ironically, he preached a sermon on motherhood during the Christmas season. "Motherhood," he assured his listeners, "is a beautiful thing" (255).

The church members did not look very hard to find the father of Sally Hewitt's child because it was certainly one of their fathers or sons or brothers. Uncle Millard remarked laughing: "Every woman in this neighborhood's mad with her husband. Just watch till the favor pops out" (250). Ellis Pate, who made her pregnant, prayed God not to reveal this information. When the Hewitts rolled away from town in their wagon, he said to himself, "God is good" (252).

And yet, Harris shows that the community was not monolithic in refusing to question their own behavior. Individuals reacted differently to Sally's giving birth to a child out of wedlock. John did not want to evict the family as long as its members were working. He could not "see that the Hewitts' girl having a baby had much to do with raising cotton and tobacco." The preacher remarked, "Well, this is what sin brings in its wake." Aunt Sugar thought John would learn a lesson and stick to "niggers" like other folks and not take in "white sharecropper trash." Ca'line, herself a near outcast, said simply that if a woman wants to wash diapers, it's nobody's business but hers (246–252). Milly's mother, Joyce Pate, the would-be aristocrat, gave Sally Hewitt information on feeding and caring for infants without noticing that Sally had no food and no access to water for bathing the baby (252). Uncle Wes reflected with his wife, Mary:

> "I reckon we all had a hand in it."
> "In what, Wes?"
> "Ruinin' that girl."
> "I reckon so, Wes." Aunt Mary had no idea what he was talking about, but Wes was usually right.

"If she *is* ruined."

"She *did* have a baby, Wes."

"We all had that baby I reckon."

"We all had a hand in it, is the way I see it." But Uncle Wes did not
have the words to explain what was in his mind. He was so still that
Aunt Mary tipped out of the room. (253)

In the same way that they reacted differently to Sally's having an illegitimate child, individuals in the community experienced religion
differently. Harris gave no simple endorsement for this force in their
lives, but examined the meaning of religion from different perspectives.

For the little girl Nannie Lou, who did not like to take chances,
"God" is the word in the reader she declined to say. There was some
power there—not always kind—that she would rather not tangle with.
After she was baptized, she thought, "Jesus was her Saviour; there was
fried chicken, ham, cabbage, pound cake, cucumber pickle in the cup-
board at home—she didn't mean to think of eating, dear Jesus, but she
had been baptized on an empty stomach, and anyhow when she was
happy she always thought of eating" (83).

Dele also did not take chances where God was concerned. She answered the statement made by neighbors that as soon as the Hewitts
came, she and John had to pay for a coffin for Mrs. Hewitt's baby and
a doctor for her broken leg. Her answer was, "I rather pay for coffins
and doctors' bills for the Hewitts than for my own folks." She added,
"I'm just thankful we're all well." But she was thinking that "whatever they sacrificed for the ills of others was somehow a pawn paid to
Somebody. . . . It was pneumonia weather" (171–172).

Revival meetings were designed to arouse religious fervor in the regular church members and to inspire others to dedicate their lives to
this particular brand of Christian belief. The preacher urged back-
sliders to leave their fleshpots and come up to the altar. They sang
"Come then and join this holy band/And on to glory go." When the
meeting was over, "the brothers and sisters returned home and took
up their fleshpots where they left them—milk pails and swill buckets
mostly" (229).

The emphasis in the church sermons was on the evil consequences
of alcohol (although few did get drunk) and sins of the flesh (which
implied extramarital affairs, something they feared already). The ser-

mons were not on hypocrisy and lack of compassion, their faults in reality.

And yet religion was certainly relevant. Harris showed that religious ritual provided order in their lives: it was the social life around which they marked the major events of their lives and the smaller events within each year's season. There was a sense of oneness in this common undertaking of preserving religion—the cause that transcended their individual causes. Not only was it their experience of communion with each other but it was their chance to be in communion with whatever force in the universe there is that is just and all-knowing. It was the reinforcement of their belief that there is such a Being. Otherwise, their spirituality was felt in the contact they had with the natural world. But even here, the supernatural was felt to be close.

The power of the church was consonant with the power of the father in the family. Neither was necessarily benevolent. John would not give his consent for his daughter Letha to marry a local man, Victor. Letha ran away, but at the last minute she could not marry Victor and risk being turned out of her family forever. She walked the miles home. In spite of her returning home without marrying, John did not speak to her for a long time. Punished by her father's silence, Letha realized she had nevertheless lost Victor. Dele felt sad, knowing that Letha would always be in love with Victor and that Letha's role in the family would inevitably be that of the unmarried sister who cares for her married sisters' babies (106). Milly's defiance of her parents at the end of the novel is thus put in a context that makes her courage even more unexpected.

John's stubbornness in refusing consent to Letha's marrying the man of her choice prevents the reader from seeing him as a compassionate person. On the other hand, Harris gave the details that reveal how caring these individuals could be. When Aunt Charity was dying, she longed to have a bed to herself so that if she moaned and moved about to distract herself from pain, she would not awaken her husband, Mr. Bill. He agreed to sleep in the other bed in the room, but he was lost without her—he was unused to sleeping alone after many years of marriage. Miss Charity felt relief when night came and he lay down on the other bed, but soon she was aware of his distress:

> Suddenly a peculiar quality in the breathing on the other bed arrested her. A quick fluttering intake of breath, and then Mr. Bill blew his nose, like a head cold. She listened tensely.

Mr. Bill was crying, crying like a little boy after a bad dream. The minutes passed. The clock struck one . . .

"Bill—"

"Hunh?"

"I wish you'd come over here and lie with me. I been havin' bad dreams again, and—and I'm scared."

"That's foolishness. Ain't nothin' goin' to hurt you, with me right here."

But he came [to her bed] with alacrity. Soon he was snoring contentedly by her side. She braced herself against the next wave of pain. (274)

As the women bathed and dressed her body after her death, their tender care with her was shown as well: "Aunt Mary eased the sheet back over the wasted body and washed the feet and legs carefully, as though not to hurt Miss Charity. Dele gently soaped the flat yellow breasts which had once given sustenance to lusty life" (286).

Tender moments like these were interspersed with the understated humor often found in Harris's plays. Cousin Sim had a spell (probably an epileptic seizure). "Even Fatty stopped eating pie to stare openmouthed with his companions, who had never seen Cousin Sim have a spell before and had wanted to" (206).

There is humor also in characters' actions, such as the machinations of housewives to get rid of Cousin Sell, who would come and stay forever if they did not arrange some event that would speed him on his way. Several would stoop to indulge his suspicion of ghosts in the house because this always caused his quick exit, or would announce a flare-up in the house of a contagious disease that would have him packing his shirt.

Each character—no matter how small—comes alive. It is by the accumulation of precise detail, the vivid description of the telling gesture, that Harris accomplished this. Typical of her writing style is this description of Nero, Nannie Lou's dog, which makes the dog—however small his part in the story—unforgettable.

Nero was a small, curly black dog with no pedigree to speak of, but with what the teacher called personality. Lacking dramatic and swashbuckling instinct, he never jumped into water to retrieve a stick for Fatty or the other boys, nor stood on his hind legs to amuse his public. He might have tried to rescue a drowning child or kept a vigil at a master's grave, but drama passed him by; so he kept the even tenor of his way. Never puppyish and increasingly unplayful, he took his doghood seriously. His energy was always purposeful; he was not above killing a rat in the corn crib or catching a young rabbit for a meal, but he did it definitely, neatly and without a flourish. (222)

The new widower, answering roll call in church, was described with a few deft touches: "Mr. Tom Smith delivered an impressive "Here" through the new false teeth he had bought since his wife died, and then looked over toward the women's side, twisted his mustache, and fingered the fifty-cent piece in his pocket" (242).

The homely, vivid metaphors drawn uniquely from that culture abound in the novel and are often humorous as well. As the men tried to improve John's tenants' cabin, Uncle Millard remarked that the outside of the house still looked like an old lady pulling up her skirts to squat down (162). The precise word choice characteristic of Harris's earlier writing also permeates the novel. After Mrs. Hewitt's baby died, Calvin and John bought a white pine coffin with brass handles and a white silk lining. The women fashioned a shroud of white muslin. Aunt Lina slipped "a cluster of pink geranium in the waxen hand." Without meaning to, "they had made a stranger of the baby forever"(166). The placement of "pink geranium" and "waxen hand" beside "stranger" conveys a striking picture to the reader—and also a sharing of the eerie feeling that swept over her characters.

Just as she used the folk sayings in this culture, Harris made the folkways of this region and time an integral part of the novel. Her work is similar to Thomas Hardy's in this respect. Especially interesting is the account of the rural wedding of Dele and John's daughter Kate to Garland, a neighbor. After the marriage ceremony, there was a traditional supper at the bride's parents' home. Then the bride's girlfriends accompanied the bride to the new place she would make her own home. They dressed her for bed and went outside. As expected of her, Kate knelt by the bed to pray. Usually the couple's friends played a practical joke. On this wedding night, Garland guessed the joke and deprived the listeners of their fun by untying the cowbell from the bed springs (220).

The adolescent girls got together for a party and spent the night together. They played the usual games: they set the "dumb table" to find out what their future mate would be like. Each girl put her own and one other's knife, fork, plate, and cup on the table. She put two chairs, side by side, at the place settings. But the game changed abruptly when the wind began to blow and the door flew open. In the open door, an apparition appeared to Margery, who secretly longed to see a sign that she would end up with Calvin, whom she wanted. But what she saw left her shaking. The girls were so frightened, they became silent and subdued (114–115).

During the Christmas holidays, the adolescent boys dressed up as women and went visiting—by custom each family had to entertain the strangers. But one hostess, the very old Aunt Becky, thought that among these masqueraders was the ghost of a long-dead resident. The boys left hastily (155–156). The games they played, Harris showed, were never far from an awareness of the impingement of the supernatural on their natural world.

Also characteristic of these folkways was the interaction based on racism. Harris showed their racism in subtle ways—for example, by revealing John's thinking: "Although Mr. Hewitt had made no complaint when he saw the poor shack that would house him, John felt that because his tenant was white the window lights must be mended, the steps patched, and some of the loose boards nailed up." He and Calvin scraped the newspapers from the inside walls and applied a coat of whitewash, added a new mantel, patched the roof, put a ceiling in a room, and laid a new kitchen floor (162–163). The condition of the house when a black family lived there is made clear in this indirect, but very effective, way.

She reproduced the dialect the African American tenant farmer Jessie used, showing how he communicated to get what he wanted: he knew how to deal with whites. She also showed that Jessie had some power in the relationship with his boss, John Fuller. When he decided to return to John's farm, despite John's lagging in his decision to let him, Jessie simply told him what time to send the wagon—the time that he, Jessie, would be ready (248).

There is, throughout the book, a celebration of bounty, as Harris had known in her childhood. The rivers abound with fish, the fields with cotton, collards, and corn, the pasture with livestock, and the tables with food. They have their fill of what the earth offers. It is touching to read about the friendship of two elderly women, Aunt Sad and Miss Jennie, who met and cooked together. Although there were only two of them dining, they had to have the satisfaction of a full table:

> Between stirrings she spread the white damask over the dining table, although Miss Jennie begged her, as was custom, not to put on the Sun-

day cloth just for her. Not much of the white showed by the time the platter of chicken fricassee, browned squash, buttered potatoes, green snap beans with slices of ham on top, red beets submerged in vinegar and sugar, stewed tomatoes, pickles, preserves, hot biscuits and corn bread, peach pie and gooseberry rolls, a dish of cup cake, the caster in the center with its vinegar cruet, salt and pepper, were placed on the table.

Neither of the women ever ate very much, but something in each was satisfied by the hot and tiring preparation and the appraising pause when each woman looked over the food and saw that it was good. (65–66)

Against the bounty of the earth is juxtaposed a psychological hunger that defied words, but it was transformed by each character into something that could be expressed. Ca'line felt a compelling need to belong to a place even to the grave. Dele focused on her son's well-being, his happiness would be her heaven on earth; and Nannie Lou longed for the beautiful words that would transport her. Sally Hewitt dreamed of having the love of Ellis Pate and the life he could offer. Calvin hungered for the presence of Milly at his side, and Milly, for emotional intimacy with her mate, Calvin. When Milly realized that Calvin had been outside her house and she had missed him, she felt a terrible longing: "Milly, standing at her window upstairs, almost cried out across the darkness as she saw the hunters turn into the field. At the gate there had been one to whom she had called wordlessly, who was touching her across the moonlight, to whom she was pouring her heart" (126).

At the end, when Calvin had drunk the drug that would kill him and he begged those around him to give him the thousand years' sleep he craved, his mother made them grant his wish. "He got so little he wanted," she said (316).

The novel ended as it began: farming people go about their tasks and take whatever comfort they can in the work of their hands:

John walked off to the lot alone in the darkness. He gave old Nellie an extra bundle of fodder.

Dele, going over Calvin's clothes, came across the little sailor suit he had worn in the school picture years ago. There was a hole in the pocket. She mended it. Then she handed Uncle Wes the clothes she wanted Calvin buried in. (316)

Like many writers, Harris stated at the beginning of the book that the characters are fictional, that no resemblance to living persons was intended. But in her autobiography, Harris admitted, "Persons living and dead are distilled into fiction." She added frankly, "They are sometimes illumined by an identification less 'purely coincidental' than is indicated in prefaces to novels."[8] In fact, she used everything, whether actually experienced or secondhand, creating characters from one individual or making a composite of several. Nannie Lou, always writing and dreaming of being a writer, was very much like Bernice Kelly Harris as a child. Ca'line was the same woman who had come to her mother's house to work. She had, of course, already been the subject of a one-act play, and in this novel she returned. A few of Harris's own family members were also pictured in scarcely disguised form: her father, for example, was the model for John Fuller, and Dele was modeled on her mother. Other individuals from her childhood—uncles, aunts, grandfathers, cousins, neighbors—stayed in Harris's mind and figured in her writings.

Stories she had heard growing up also reappeared in her writing. Some are funny; some are stark and tragic. Jonathan Daniels wrote in his review of *Purslane* for the *Saturday Review of Literature*, "Mrs. Harris only injures her portraiture when she tries to pull drama and tragedy into her book."[9] But Harris felt drama and tragedy *were* an integral part of life among these people she knew so well. Irate about Daniels's pronouncement, she wrote her mentor and friend, J. O. Bailey: "I try, eh? I'll swear it was no effort, any more than turning over a hoe-cake when one side is brown. I've heard my father tell that laudanum story so many times. He was one of the neighbors who helped with the walking and the little switches."[10]

The homely tasks, soap making, rolling out pies, plowing the fields, churning butter, are recreated in detail. The old sayings are expressed and applied. The images, humorous and vivid and never self-conscious, are those she grew up savoring as well as those that came from her unique way of looking at things. The social activities are those she participated in and observed. North Carolina's poet laureate, Sam Ragan, said he never found a false note in any of Harris's writings.[11]

Typical of testimony people wrote to her after reading the novel is this passage from a stranger's letter: "I read *Purslane* last summer, and to me it was living. Not many experiences I've had as a child of the soil were omitted from your story. Many of the little ups and downs that had sunken into subconsciousness came to life when I realized that those simple ordinary happenings were appreciated by one inspired to write."[12]

Harris did what she intended to do in this novel: she offered the story of a community of southern yeoman farmers at a particular time—a time before industrialization. It is a picture of an entire community, all classes, white and black: from the way they made soap to wash themselves to the way they arranged themselves for sleep.

Purslane is, however, much more than excellent reportage. It is an exploration of how people in this farming community in the South early in the twentieth century gave meaning to their lives. This is a study of a culture in which the things people are most sure of are tested and often found lacking. And often they cannot afford to see that. Harris makes no condemnatory judgment about this way of life; rather, she tells the story. And she tells it in such a way that she is honest about the shortcomings as well as about the goodness and courage of many of these individuals.

She emphasized that the values of honesty and hard work were an integral part of this small farmers' culture. Loyalty in the extended family, another value, was consistent. And so, eccentricities among individuals were tolerated—if an aunt was a little strange, people worked around that; if another was stingy, relatives somehow compensated for the aberrant behavior; if an uncle advised the bridegroom to read the Bible every night before he went to bed with his bride, the elder was listened to respectfully. In the worst of struggles, people took courage and plodded on. And in tragedy, they stayed together. There was a value in sharing. Unless someone violated the sexual code openly or drank to excess—such behaviors would be an open challenge to their value system—the community would help when help was needed.

When she finished writing the novel early in 1938, Harris did not know what to do next. She sent it to her mentor, J. O. Bailey, in the English department at the University of North Carolina, with the expectation that he would tell her whether it was good enough for her to try to get it published. He sat up all one night reading it, and in the morning he walked it over to William Terry Couch, the editor of the university press. As soon as Couch read it, he wrote her his decision to publish it, although the press had never published a novel before. It came out in 1939. McClelland and Stewart, a Canadian publishing house, issued the novel in Toronto, and Putnam's of London published the novel abroad under the title *Pate's Siding*, thus providing an international market.

Harris was stunned at the novel's reception among the public. Reviews appeared in a range of periodicals. In the *New Yorker*, Clifton Fadiman wrote, "*Purslane* stands apart from most regional books I've read in its quality of intimacy and tenderness."[13] The *New York Herald Tribune* critic declared, "It is not afraid to touch the dirt in which the Fullers delve for a living; but neither is it afraid to follow their aspirations when they soar; it laughs at the Fullers, uproariously, as they laughed at themselves; but it knows their pain, too, and their sorrow it skillfully and justly links with the tragedy of the world."[14]

In the *New Republic*, the reviewer Caroline Gordon described *Purslane*: "Every kind of man and woman it takes to make a world is found in this community of small landholders living at the turn of the century on the banks of the Neuse River in middle Carolina." She pointed to the authentic detail that characterizes the book: "It is a special quality of imagination—the same freshness and immediacy of perception that is found in the poets whose songs are preserved in the Greek Anthology." Gordon said that few modern writers have this, that she could think of only three others—Stark Young, Elizabeth Madox Roberts, and Katherine Anne Porter.[15]

In "What I Liked Last Week" in the *Los Angeles Times*, the reviewer said, "People who know the rural folk of the South as they lived and spoke around 1900 will recognize at once the wholly authentic atmosphere that surrounds the simple folk who come alive in its pages and probably will agree that here at last is the real voice of that region."[16] One reviewer compared her to Thomas Hardy, saying that she had charted a Wessex here in America.[17]

Nevertheless, there were criticisms, and they were centered on the meandering plot, some critics wondering if there was a plot at all. The novel does have a plot—it is essentially a Romeo and Juliet story—but it is the life of a rural southern farming people early in the twentieth century that the novel is focused on. It is not the story of a tragic flaw in an individual but in a community. This is not the tightly controlled style of Ernest Hemingway: the plot is not inexorably advanced. There are sidetracks, such as the gathering of herbs in the woods or soapmaking. But there is a richness in the texture, too. Romeo and Juliet's story must be seen within the particular context and historical moment in which they had their being; so, too, Calvin and Milly's tragedy is placed within a culture whose limitations make their tragedy almost inevitable.

In the 1920s and 1930s, sociologists like Howard Odum and Rupert Vance and journalists like W. J. Cash were examining social change in the South caused by industrialization. A group of intellectuals, called the Agrarians and including Robert Penn Warren, Allen Tate, and John Crowe Ransom, were concerned with the same development and expressed their anguish over the loss of the traditional southern way of life in a collection of essays, *I'll Take My Stand: The South and the Agrarian Tradition*, published in 1930.[18] They feared that as industrialization proceeded, old values would be lost; they would be replaced by a materialistic outlook, and man's spiritual and aesthetic needs would be neglected. In rebuke, they pointed to values and human relationships in an agrarian way of life that they thought had been characteristic of the South earlier.[19] The Agrarians believed there had been a time when large landowners and yeoman farmers had lived in harmony. Harris examined this agrarian society and refused to idealize it—even though it had been a way of life she had known well and loved. She presented it as a class-ridden society capable of injustice towards the vulnerable, white and black.

The thirties and forties, which were characterized by an outburst of creativity especially in literature and historical research, were recognized as a southern renaissance. Like the Agrarians speaking in *I'll Take My Stand*, many novelists insisted on love of the land as being the constant in southern culture, choosing as their main characters the landed aristocracy. In Caroline Gordon's *Penhally*, for example, the contemporary generation in a southern aristocratic family is represented by two sons, a farmer and a banker.[20] When the eldest son, the banker, sells the family land simply because he can get a good price, his brother shoots him. In *Penhally*, loyalty to family members who have gone before and to the land they lived on for generations are values worth killing and dying for.

But Harris takes as her main subject the small farmer, not the aristocrat. And she also presents white and black landless families, showing that they are as much a part of southern life as the landed. The supposed universal value placed on family land by southerners is shown in Harris's novels to be a class-bound value. It is true that the gentry and the small landowners alike judge people on the basis of whether they have land or not, but Harris seems to say this is an artificial boundary between individuals and is destructive of other values. In this, regard, *Purslane* is close in theme to Elizabeth Madox Roberts's novel *The Time of Man* (1926), which presents the life of a woman from a landless family, and to Ellen Glasgow's *Barren Ground* (1925), which narrates the struggle of a woman to make her small farm successful. Like Harris, Roberts and Glasgow were acutely aware of social class and sharply delineate this background against which their characters move. In *Purslane*, as in *The Time of Man* and *Barren Ground*, the really interesting people are the plain, small farmers.[21]

Both Roberts and Glasgow realistically describe the backbreaking work that farming requires. The land is a means to an end for their characters, a way to make a living. However, Harris delights in describing her characters' closeness to the land and in showing the indissoluble link between the human and the natural world. It is not so much preoccupation with owning land as with living intimately with it that brings her characters a sense of well-being.

Harris had spent childhood in the outdoors; she knew the name and use of every plant, the call of every bird, the habits of every animal. She had felt the rough touch of oak tree bark and the jagged leaf, watched the wind shift pine branches to send a shaft of sunlight falling on the smooth pink petals of a lady's slipper. She had also seen the wind twist leafless branches mercilessly and felt the "shower of icy drops" (173). And like Dele, she had gathered sweet potatoes, "loving the feel of the soil on her hands, the acrid odor of frost-bitten vines, the mellow ripeness of the harvest" (233). She conveys the immediate, sensuous pleasure of living close to nature in the farming way of life. She revels in its beauty:

> Down the hill bordered by the apple orchard—Grandma and Aunt Lina had to have a lapful of those winesaps. Slipping across the pea patch covered now with dew-laden grass sparkling in the morning sun, she [Nannie Lou] pulled the red lusciousness from the lowest limbs and filled her little plaid gingham skirt. Along the road the sumacs hung with reddish berries, which Aunt Puss made her children eat to keep them from wetting the bed. Nannie Lou tasted the rough sourness, carefully avoiding the cow itch vine. (89)

Harris's lyrical writing about farming life sets her apart. But as this paragraph shows, there is characteristically a homely touch that interjects a gentle humor even in this celebration of nature's beauty.

Nevertheless, *Purslane* is not a plea for return to an agrarian system; the feeling that this Eden is in the past pervades the novel. Perhaps she asked herself, What have we brought from this farming way of life? How are we the same, how are we different?[22]

Bernice Harris was not a part of the intellectual movement which produced *I'll Take My Stand*, nor was she connected by friendship ties to her contemporaries who were novelists. But with the publication of *Purslane*, the outer world came to her. She had what she described as a "wonderfully exciting time hearing from New York and Boston and London editors, as well as writing to them." They were all interested in publishing her future work. They invited her to New York and London; they even offered to come to Seaboard. They sent her so many books that she had to buy more bookcases. She sent them swatches of purslane from her garden. Of course, the weeds arrived dried up and scarcely recognizable. John Woodburn, the editor at Doubleday, called them "cadavers" because they were "dead on arrival."[23]

And she felt happy because she had offered the story "of the good people living along little roads of sand and ruts, enduring and worthy to endure."[24] But the best thing about the novel's success was her conviction that it had a positive effect on her relationship with Herbert. It brought in money and thereby she gained his respect, she thought. She looked for signs:

> It was becoming symbol of Harris and Harris. Herbert told Walmus, the handy man, not to dig up the purslane in our garden. Walmus looked at his employer as though certain Mr. Hub-but had lost his senses. "What, leave pusley in the middle of the butterbean rows?" he demanded. Herbert ordered it left.
>
> He saw the sense in the swatches to New York. He saw the sense in royalties. I was writing openly now. Hitherto I had more or less worked secretly or only when he was absent.[25]

He even tried to read *Purslane*. He did plow through, although she assured him he did not have to finish. When he finally read the last page, he told her how the story ended. "She mended the hole in his pocket, did she?" Bernice remarked that like a schoolboy "who aims to prove he deserves an A on his book report, he added: 'What did you let him die for?' "[26]

She was the first woman to receive the Mayflower Cup, an award given for outstanding writing about North Carolina by the North Carolina Literary and Historical Association. This was the first time a novel had received the award. When she arrived in the Hugh Morson High School auditorium in Raleigh on the evening of December 8, 1939, to receive the award, Herbert was with her, smiling. The times she had gone to the meetings of the association with her history teacher when she was a student at Meredith came back to her.[27]

Her fellow citizens in Seaboard received the publication of a novel by one among them in different ways: One said, "She's bound to be smart—anybody that can use commas and periods in a book that long is bound to be smart." Another said, "I don't see what she would write a book for; she's got a husband."[28] But many neighbors were proud of "Miss Kelly." One neighbor borrowed a copy and took three weeks to read it. He told her, "It made me sleepy to read it, how come I to keep it this long." He added, "But it's the best book I ever read, except mission study books Cousin Bettie brings back from circle meetings." What really delighted Bernice was his final comment: "They're always after me about my big words, but I just tell you, your book's obnoxious!"[29]

The Seaboard Woman's Club gave her a banquet, complete with flowers and an original poem paying tribute. She was pleased and remarked, "Seaboard came through for the home-town author."[30]

Extended family in Wake County were proud of their kinswoman for writing a book, but they didn't think she got "the story just right here and there."[31] Harris took this with a sense of humor, realizing that there was so much family history in the book they could easily forget she was writing fiction. And when neighborhood children and her nieces and nephews came to visit, they played with the huge shining cup that sat on the table in the living room. It was always nicely polished.

Bernice Kelly in her late teens, probably while she was still a student at Meredith.

Courtesy Sandra Poindexter

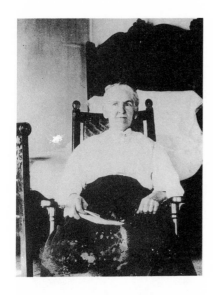

Bernice's mother, Rosa Poole Kelly.
The photograph was made in 1918.
Courtesy Alice Jo Kelley Burrows

Bernice's father, William (Bill) Kelly
Courtesy Alice Jo Kelley Burrows

The Kelly homeplace in what is now Clayton, North
Carolina, in Wake County.
Courtesy Alice Jo Kelley Burrows

Bernice Kelly and her brother William Olive. Photograph probably made in the early 1920s.
Courtesy Alice Jo Kelley Burrows

Bernice's sister-in-law, Mary Sullivan Kelley. The photograph was made for a Wake Forest College publication probably about the time she became engaged to William Olive Kelley, 1923.
Courtesy Alice Jo Kelley Burrows

Bernice's brother, William Olive Kelley. Photograph was made probably about the time he was a senior at Wake Forest College, 1923.
Courtesy Alice Jo Kelley Burrows

Photograph Bernice had made for the *Virginia Pilot*
(Norfolk, Va.). She is probably in her early thirties here.
Courtesy Alice Jo Kelley Burrows

For the publication of *Folk Plays of Eastern Carolina* in 1939, photographer
Charles Farrell went to Seaboard and set up shots to illustrate the plays. He
photographed Bernice Harris interviewing Mrs. Jordan (the Butterbean
Woman), who was the model for Mrs. Jernigan in the play *Open House*.
(Bernice had interviewed her for a story that she published in a local paper
earlier in the thirties.) The following dialogue appears with the picture:

AUTHOR: "Whom did you vote for, Mrs. Jordan?"

MRS. JORDAN: "I don't vote. When I get ready to put on breeches I'll vote.
Last June they swarmed over here worse'n flies 'round a
'lasses pot. But they never got me to go to no poles."

*Courtesy North Carolina Collection, University of North Carolina Library
at Chapel Hill*

"I feel like I want to sing." A line spoken by Dan'l in Bernice Kelly Harris's play *Judgement Comes to Dan'l.* This is a recreation of a scene from the play; it was published by Charles Farrell as an illustration for *Folk Plays of Eastern Carolina,* published by the University of North Carolina Press in 1939. The dialogue appears with the photographs.

Courtesy North Carolina Collection, University of North Carolina Library at Chapel Hill

"You look like Queen Vicdory!"—the peddler says to Cornie in Bernice Kelly Harris's play *A Pair of Quilts*. This is a photograph of the Carolina Playmakers production in 1938; it is reproduced in *Folk Plays of Eastern Carolina*.

Courtesy North Carolina Collection, University of North Carolina Library at Chapel Hill

6

Haunting Work: The Federal Writers' Project

With the publication of *Purslane*, Bernice Kelly Harris's writing began to be compared with Erskine Caldwell's novels *Tobacco Road* (1932) and *God's Little Acre* (1933).[1] They were both writing about the plight of southern farmers in poverty in the thirties. But the two writers differed in approach and in their own needs. Caldwell roamed the backroads, streets, and bars to observe ways of living a life. Harris took a very close look at lives immediately around her, observing the lifting of a chicken breast at table, the moment's hesitation before inviting a lover into the house, the glance of a widower as he jingles a new coin in his pocket. She attended to the details of daily living in an apparently innocent environment and discerned the drama and heartbreak going on. She could describe the violent physical act, but often it was the subtle, devastating psychological blow that commanded her attention. Caldwell observed the physical violence and overt degradation of the social environment he moved in and portrayed it with brutal honesty.

Both Harris and Caldwell knew what rural poverty was from direct observation. The decline in prices for agricultural products began with a sharp drop in 1920. By 1926, prices were below the cost of production for cotton and tobacco, the principal crops throughout the Southeast. Small farmers, after working all year and making nothing, sank further into debt and had to sell whatever land they had. The class of landless farming families multiplied fast in the thirties. Sometimes in official documents, distinction is not made between the landless—sharecroppers and tenant farmers—but rural people knew the difference. Tenant farmers held a contract (usually verbal) with the landlord, who provided a house and acreage. The entire family farmed twenty to forty acres of the landlord's land and divided income from the sale of the crop with him equally. Or, the tenant might supply the mule and some equipment and get a larger share of the harvest. When, after losing money on crops year after year, the formerly landed farmer had to sell his mules and equipment, he became a sharecropper. Sharecroppers were simply laborers who had nothing but their backs. Sharecroppers always gave the landlord at least half the crop, and they were usually in debt to the landlord for money he furnished them through the year. After a few years the debt was so great that it was impossible to move—sharecroppers were nearly as bound to landowners as slaves had been earlier.[2]

Both writers were aware of the terrible psychological costs of economic failure that had gone on for a decade. But Caldwell's treatment of hunger in *Tobacco Road* is unrivaled in its power—there is a basic rawness to his writing and images so vivid they last a reader a lifetime. Harris has an unrivaled ability to convey to the reader the way people made sense of these experiences and tried to go on living.

Some critics preferred Harris's writing because it presented a different view of the story of rural poverty in the South from Caldwell's. Especially, they were repelled by the explicit way Caldwell described sexual encounters in *Tobacco Road* and *God's Little Acre*. These two writers, Harris born in North Carolina in 1891, Caldwell born in Georgia in 1903, were both brought up in religious households; but Ira Caldwell, a minister, encouraged his son to question received truths, while Harris's parents demanded conformity. Thus, Harris, contained and conforming, needed to visualize order in human society. Caldwell, often unable to control his violent urges or restrain sexual desires and questioning whether anyone should, presented a world of people who are without restraint. In his novels, copulation occurs without much thought of consequences. Harris saw humans as existing within a moral framework even when they try to deny it. Sally Hewitt lies down with the future preacher because she hopes for a life with him; and he is attracted by the comfort of being loved and of loving as much as by her beauty. However, Caldwell's images of animalistic behavior are also derived from his own emotional pain at witnessing such suffering of hungry, hopeless people. His attitude could be described as a taunt: Treat people like animals—see what you get?

Caldwell's *Tobacco Road*, his recent biographer Dan B. Miller asserts, "is a novel of violent incongruities—between sympathetic admiration for gritty farmers and vicious ridicule of their faults; between images of dignified endurance and heartless sketches of outrageous buffoonery; between calls for social reform and testimony to hopeless depravity."[3] Indeed, Caldwell makes some bitter jokes at the expense of sharecroppers and tenant farmers. Harris writes about the share-cropper family with much compassion in *Purslane*—there is no joke at their expense. She can laugh with and at the middle-class farmers; she can portray the gentry with disdain, but never did she lampoon the really down-and-out. Nor are the sharecroppers hopelessly depraved in her writings: in *Purslane* there is an innocence and tenderness about Sally Hewitt even when she is being conniving. And the black share-cropper knows how and when to assert power; he is not just a downtrodden victim. Harris's sharecropper Ed Harper in *His Jewels* has dignity; in *Open House*, the sharecropper Mrs. Jernigan has the last word.

Perhaps one important difference lies in the authors' distance from the human subjects. Caldwell, in rage against a society so blind to the sufferings of a whole class of people, focuses on the desperately poor rather than on a range in the social strata. He looks at them as an observer. Harris, also writing from a stance of exposing social injustice, nevertheless presents several classes and examines their interaction. Hers is not just an observer's view: she feels like a participant. In *His Jewels*, she said, she was probably one of the hypocrites, a church member who comes to practice a play about social responsibility and throws the homeless family out of the church. In *Purslane*, her mother and father and she herself are central characters revealing both good and harmful behaviors in their interaction with the sharecropping family.

Harris liked Caldwell's *Tobacco Road*. In the novel she was writing in late 1938, *Portulaca*, she has the main character, Nancy, defend *Tobacco Road* when women in a book club say it is just smut. Nancy says, "We can't isolate either ugliness or beauty. It's all in the pattern of life." When the women say the South is not like Caldwell's picture, Nancy asks if they have gone out to look.

And Harris has Nancy write a story about incest. The sexual exploitation of a child by her father and also by the landowner is described with the same fearless honesty Caldwell's work showed. In *Portulaca*, the editor rejects the story because people do not want to read that sort of thing, he says. It is a good bet that Harris herself had received such a rejection letter on this story.

But critics were afraid Caldwell's representation of "hopeless depravity" would support the position of those who said nothing could be done. A sociologist doing field research among southern tenant farmers in the mid-thirties wrote, "Failure has often been accounted for on biological or moral grounds, that is, sharecroppers remain sharecroppers because they are of bad hereditary stock, poor whites, or because they do not have the middle-class virtues of industry and thrift, or because they do not care enough to improve their status."[4]

One of those concerned about this image was William Couch, the editor at the University of North Carolina Press, who was sure that no one reading *Tobacco Road* would want to help the southern poor. He had in mind a strategy for informing the public differently. The manuscript for *Purslane* was on his desk, and he was determined to publish it. But now he decided to contact Bernice Harris about another matter—a project for which he thought she would be perfect. He had taken on the job of regional director for the Federal Writers' Project and was looking for interviewers who could also be good writers. She was instantly intrigued.

The Federal Writers' Project was part of a brave new experiment that the federal government undertook in 1935, as part of the Works Progress Administration. It turned out to be the most extensive support to the arts that any nation had ever given. President Roosevelt had appointed Harry Hopkins to oversee the Works Progress Administration, and Hopkins was eager to try out his ideas: he wanted artists, musicians, and writers involved. He explained, "Hell, they've got to eat just like other people."[5] So, with the support of others close to the president, Hopkins created four main divisions for the arts under the WPA: organizations for theater, fine arts, music, and the Federal Writers' Project.

For the latter, the aim was to hire unemployed writers; their task was to produce a guide to each state's economic and cultural activities as well as its natural resources. Journalist Henry Alsberg was appointed the nationwide head of the Federal Writers' Project. The director for North Carolina was writer Edwin Bjorkman, who kept his office in Asheville but also set up regional directorships. Couch, who continued to be the editor of the University of North Carolina Press, was made an associate state director and in 1936 regional director for the southeastern states. He conceived the idea that in addition to the guides, southern writers would document the lives of common people.

Couch believed that up to that time, the common people had not been accurately represented. After reading *Tobacco Road*, he had studied Caldwell's and Margaret Bourke-White's photographic essay, *You Have Seen Their Faces* (1937).[6] He questioned the extent to which writings like these were outsiders' interpretations. Were publications like these at all like the people's views of themselves? He doubted that. Couch hoped to publish volumes in which people could speak for themselves. He thought that if he could get firsthand accounts informing the public about the struggles small landowners and landless farmers carried on, he could influence policy makers on the state and local level to do something to help them. [7]

Couch soon realized that the chief problem would be in locating unemployed writers who could convey the people's experiences. The guidelines stated that only 10 percent of the writers could be individuals not on the dole; later, the percentage was raised to 15 and then reduced to 5.[8] Bjorkland had looked over the list of people receiving unemployment compensation in North Carolina and could find no writers at all.[9] Undoubtedly, writers had long ago given up hope of making a living writing and now described themselves as seamstresses, secretaries, house painters, carpenters, and so forth. All over the country, administrators had to confront the riddle, Who is a writer? The WPA guidelines could be interpreted to mean anybody who could write English.[10] Couch hired unemployed people who had some education; he stayed within the guidelines by appointing only four published writers who were not receiving unemployment compensation. These four were Ida Moore, a teacher and administrator in adult literacy programs; Muriel Woolf, an administrator; Leonard Rapport, a young writer who aspired to the forestry profession; and Bernice Kelly Harris.

Couch asked Harris to interview for the Federal Writers' Project because he knew from reading the manuscript for *Purslane* that she was knowledgeable about the culture of farming communities and that she had empathy with rural people. But he probably also expected her to present a picture of poor farmers that would inspire respect and desire to help. In his letter inviting her to participate in the project, Couch told her that she would have to travel around a lot—at her expense, of course. He said he'd pay $100 a month for two, three, or four months. He concluded with an argument he knew would be irresistible to her:

> There are several reasons for my thinking of you in connection with this work. First, I believe you can do it better than anyone else I can find and that the stories you write will be authentic and interesting. Second, I am extremely anxious for you to do more writing of the kind you have done in your volume of plays and in *Pursland* [*sic*], and I believe this writing would provide more stimulus than anything else you could do. Third, I believe the books we shall get out of this work will be about as good as, perhaps better than, anything ever printed on the South.[11]

Bernice had to ask Herbert if she could do this, but she might have suspected he would not turn down $100 a month.[12]

Couch presented Harris and all the writers with a topic outline prepared by Ida Moore in which the interviewers were to get information in such categories as family size, education, income, religion, diet, medical needs, and use of time in each season.[13] He charged the writers: "In so far as possible, the stories should be told in the words of the persons who are consulted."[14]

Couch's instruction to writers to take down and represent in published form only the words of the narrators or summarize only their words was a worthwhile goal to aim for. Before the days of tape recorders, however, accurate recording of dialogue was not an easy task. Leonard Rapport charged that some of the stories are not authentic. He believed that Couch should have hired sociologists to do the interviewing and not writers: writers turn things into fiction, he said.[15]

Apparently, Bernice Harris and Ida Moore, and other field-workers as well, took down notes as the narrator spoke in the same way a secretary took dictation. Others may have taken only rough notes and later added words to the testimony as they remembered them. Occasionally Harris might have done that, too—parts of some interviews were reported in paraphrase. In the general collection of the Federal Writers' Project, whole life histories were sometimes paraphrased. Assistant editors sometimes wrote stories, basing them on rough notes taken by the field-worker. And editors might have omitted things; in fact, in one known case, an editor changed the narrator's words.[16]

Scholars and general readers have subjected the stories to a critical review. To evaluate authenticity, if readers had tapes of these stories, the transcript could be checked against the recording and inaccuracies spotted. But without such technology, the account can be looked at for consistency in point of view and speech characteristics.[17] The narrative can be scrutinized to see if it is contrived so that it follows a conventional plot line—the reader can determine if the story is too "pat."[18] To evaluate the usefulness of the evidence for a history of American life at the time, other questions can be asked, such as, "Is this a full life history, or is the narrator on guard and therefore reticent?"

As a playwright, Harris was used to focusing on each word in a speech. She had become sensitive to characteristics in the speaker's discourse and alert to the particular way each person structured the life story. In the accounts Harris wrote for the project, she allowed herself expression only when she was describing setting or character (and on rare occasions, her reaction). The testimony itself in Harris's stories is unique to each narrator, and speech characteristics are consistent within the text. Harris did turn the testimony into fiction—but not as Rapport expected fiction writers to do. She did this long after the eighty-two life histories she wrote for the Federal Writers' Project were deposited in Couch's office.

Rapport pointed to the work of his fellow interviewers Ida Moore and Bernice Kelly Harris as examples of texts that *do* stay close to the original testimony of the narrators. Scholars and critics of the project have agreed with Rapport in his judgment of Moore's and Harris's work.[19]

In his letter of 13 October 1938 inviting her to join the project, Couch told Harris to get stories of tenant farmers and small farm owners; but later he gave her free rein to record any story that contributed to documenting the life of the community.[20] And so, Harris interviewed a range of people—women as well as men, blacks and whites, rich and poor—often choosing as narrators people she had known since the 1920s. She recorded the life stories of day laborers, tenant farmers, and sharecroppers; often their words reveal that they had met her in some way previously. She also interviewed landowners, cotton gin workers, schoolteachers, merchants, a minister, a justice of the peace, a country doctor, and an undertaker. And she chose a variety of activities in the community to document—from the adult literacy classes to the country store crowd's conversations. Now the character of her visits to people changed from just accompanying the county agent as an observer to carrying out her own systematic, in-depth interviews.

Like Studs Terkel's published work, Harris's life histories (and those of her colleagues) do not often contain the questions asked—the reader must infer them from the answers. The answers also tip us off to the kind of interaction between narrator and interviewer that was taking place.

It is clear that Bernice Harris was at ease with whomever she was talking to and usually had no trouble getting narrators to talk. Herbert was along, too: he had offered to drive her around when he gave his consent to her doing the project. A landowner and cotton gin owner, he was viewed in the community as a hard man to deal with, but he was also seen as an honest man. Sometimes he stayed outside of the house when she was interviewing; sometimes he was a silent companion in the interviews. Sometimes, he was not so silent, as this excerpt from a life history reveals: the family had a three-string banjo (with only two strings) and a little mouth organ which they used to play "Nellie Gray." Bernice admitted, "Mrs. Lee, a soloist, is soon joined by the visitor's thin soprano, by the visitor's husband's foot-patting."[21]

Bernice and Herbert both experienced the hospitality of the narrators. On one occasion when they picked up a narrator at the country store to give him a lift home for the interview, the old bachelor invited them to stay for supper, saying, "I tell you what you all do. Take me home and stay and eat supper with me. It won't be no trouble to me. My supper's done cooked, hangin' in the well. . . . I won't give you nothin' but chicken muddle. It ain't as good as the last one I made, how come I want somebody to help me eat it up" (F439, FWP).

And Bernice said when she mentioned that the government was the instigator of the visits, the welcoming reception was "open sesame." She observed, "The government at that time was the Great White Father for so many."[22]

But Bernice could draw on her own reputation in Northampton County as a schoolteacher, Sunday school teacher, and play producer and director. She had taught some of her interviewees in the high school in Seaboard in the years before her marriage, and she continued to teach several in Sunday school. One narrator declared, "I rather hear you teach the [Sunday school] lesson than to eat when I'm hongry"(F458, FWP). Occasionally a narrator made some reference to a play he had acted in that she directed.

Her reputation as a kind and compassionate person undoubtedly influenced the narrators to regard her as a potential friend. This is evident in many of the life stories. When Harris asked the routine questions about diet of a ninety-five-year-old narrator, the woman declared that she hated to eat much because she was depriving the family's little children of food. The woman asked at the end of the visit: "Bernice, can you sing 'Will There Be Any Stars in My Crown' before you go?"(F428, FWP).

In another household, after the husband had bragged about the clothes he had bought his wife, the wife whispered a request to Bernice for any old clothes or old shoes she could give her. Bernice must have said yes, because the next morning the wife walked the miles into town to the Harris house to collect clothing (F465, FWP). Bernice understood that the husband had indeed bought his wife some clothes, but that that had been years earlier—a detail he had forgotten. Another narrator, at the end of the interview, told her, "You bring me some scraps [for quilting]. Don't you forgit now!"(F454, FWP). And a male narrator urged her: "Don't you want a little 'possom grease to take home with you? If it don't cure the deafness you say you got in your family, it sure won't hurt it. Let me get you some"(F466, FWP).

Most often when Bernice was talking to a black person, the relationship was cordial. In the interview with an African American farmwoman, the narrator addressed her affectionately, as in this example in which she described her poverty: "It is tight, child, tight as Dick's hatband"(F442, FWP).

In another situation, in which she did not already know the African American family, Bernice described her reception by a mother and daughter: "At first there is an almost defensive air about the women; their speech is a little guarded, the looks they exchange a trifle significant. This is soon explained by Sally [daughter] in her crisp, consonant-stressed sentences: 'When you first come, we thought maybe you was another one of them Northern women with some more Holy Dust or something' " (F449, FWP). She referred to an earlier incident when a white woman came to the door, trying to sell them "Holy Dust" to ward off evil.

A giant of a man, with a yellowish tinge to black skin, wearing faded overalls, a denim coat, a black felt hat with brass stars on a white hat band, two yellow tusks protruding from his gums, politely answered her questions. But when she asked the required question about religion, he warned, "Don't you git after me to join de church now 'cause I ain't a-goin' to do it!" When he got tired, he simply said, "No, Madam, I ain't goin' to tell you no more stories today. No More!" And he walked out of the house (F437, FWP).

In still another visit to a self-contained community in which whites and blacks had intermarried and then kept to themselves, the woman who came to the screen door never opened it: "Yes, I live here. Yes, I been sewin'. No, my husband ain't home. No, I can't tell you when he'll be back. I don't know where [sic] I got time to talk to you or no. What you want to talk about?" (F444, FWP).

The life stories in that community were truncated, with many important events omitted, as Bernice stated.[23] But in most life stories, the easy, warm, trusting relationship of narrator and interviewer can be felt; the ambience is one of a conversation between old friends. When that is not the case and something is awry, Harris tells the reader.

The effect of firsthand knowledge of how people lived reinforced her feelings about social injustices and charged her writing. Bernice said that when she juxtaposed the landlords' stories against those of tenant farmers and sharecroppers, it was "illuminating."[24] For example, one of the largest landowners in the state told her, smiling, about the best advice he ever got in his youth: "Son, the best system is to see that the sharecropper has just as little as possible and that the landlord gets it all"(F423, FWP). Harris could place this life story beside that of a farming woman who declared to her, "I will tell you the God's truth, we ain't got nothing. Not nothing! Even the turnip patch failed us this year. We had one hoe-cake of cornbread for our Christmas dinner."[25]

She recorded both perspectives—white and black—on race issues, as well. Beside the story of the justice of the peace who declared he always found some way to refuse to register black people to vote,[26] she placed the account of the educated black cotton gin worker. He had lost a leg in an accident at the gin and could get only occasional unskilled jobs from the welfare office—work such as digging ditches.[27] This was obviously not an appropriate job for a one-legged man, nor for a man qualified to do white-collar work. In another narrative, she presented the life story of the black farmer who described the fraudulent way his land was taken away (F421, FWP). In this account, she refused to change any names to protect anonymity (it was the usual practice, unless the narrator wanted the real name used). She wanted people to know who was responsible for this injustice.

When Bernice wrote the account of a women's group at church, she used juxtaposition of testimony from two stories within one report. The group employed needy women in their sewing room. The piece begins with the women talking about who "deserved" their help: they pointed to sons in one family who were too lazy to help themselves. Bernice then placed in the text the testimony of members of that family. The father (who had tuberculosis) had walked off and not returned. He had left the mother with a houseful of children. The two sons in late adolescence, who appear to have had some mental deficiency, had tried to make tools to do work. Much of the testimony concerns the way they had tried to get jobs. At the end of the piece, Bernice placed the last line of the minutes of the churchwomen's meeting, "If those Hargraves boys won't work, let them go hungry" (F455, FWP).

Bernice thought she knew what people's lives were like; but these firsthand accounts she wrote down for the Federal Writers' Project as she sat with people in their homes jolted and troubled her. The interview with the woman mentioned above who had nothing especially worried her. Even after twenty-five years, the memory was still vivid in Bernice's mind. Bernice remembered that at first glance inside the shack, she knew this was a life of desperate poverty. The woman talked to her about injustices of landlords, farming losses, the birth of an illegitimate child, her sins, the cost of operations. At the end of the interview, she followed Bernice to the door and whispered "with a kind of desperate brightness in her voice": "Last fall the doctors over at the Rapids took out all my female organs." Bernice surmised that the woman wanted to tell something that would distinguish her from all other paupers.[28]

In that same interview, the woman recounted how her little girl had come home and said her teacher told her Santa Claus was coming. The girl, Clayra Virginia, instructed her mother to take down from the mantel the small Santa Claus that stayed there year-round because if Santa Claus saw a picture of himself, he would not come. The Santa Claus was removed. The mother had nothing to put in a stocking. During the night, she put the Santa Claus back on the mantel because she would rather the child would blame her than lose all hope that a

Santa Claus existed and would someday bring her some good (F441, FWP).

Bernice admitted that she was shocked by the wretchedness of many of the people she talked to. She had grown up in a farming family where there was not much cash on hand, just her mother's butter and egg money and change from the sale of Native Herb Pills, but she always had shoes to wear and plenty to eat and her own pennies to buy books. Now she listened to the details of lives she had not imagined. One starving narrator told her that the government ought to hire a man "to go round and kill up all the pore folks." The narrator laughed and said her son wanted the job because "all pore folks does is take up room" (F462, FWP).

"Hopelessness," Bernice said, "waited for the release of death." But she also saw "human dignity struggle for expression."[29] Certainly, the respect she had for each narrator comes through in the life histories; even with the bigots, she tried to see the world through their eyes, to understand how they had become the way they were.

Indeed, each narrator was for Bernice an individual, and many were so unforgettable they appear later in her novels. One of the narrators was Miss Sis, a seventy-five-year-old woman who was determined to learn to read. She often had to walk the four miles to the adult literacy class, and when she got too hot or her blood pressure went up, she stuffed her bonnet with cool green leaves. Harris described a moment with her: "And with what militancy she read the gentle Shepherd Psalm the afternoon I was there! With what creative militancy she lived. And when time was out for her here, she did not make a mess of dying. She sat in her chair and waited for death, as for company."[30] Miss Sis became the character Miss Partheny in Harris's novel *Sweet Beulah Land* (1943).

In addition to Miss Sis, Harris drew upon several narrators' accounts to present in fiction later the physical and psychological world of the elderly widow who has no resources—except her sense of herself. One of these outstanding women was the ancient African American woman Lettice Boyer, who told Harris, one October afternoon in 1939: "I was here when Nat riz, and when de stars fell, when de war come, when de surrender was, when it was de earthquake—and I's still here."[31] Harris would later use these words in her novel *Sweet Beulah Land*.[32] Lettice Boyer was one of the individuals who influenced the composite portrait of Aunt Cherry in the novel *Sage Quarter* (1945)—

the person who remained loyal to the narrator, Tiny, when her own white aunts went against her.[33]

One narrator, Lucy Ivory, became the inspiration for Harris's novel *Janey Jeems*.[34] From this interview and others with black farming women, Bernice gained specific knowledge of the intimate details of this kind of life as well as their particular way of seeing and expressing their experiences.

There was sometimes an engagement with the narrator on such a deep emotional level that even Bernice was astonished. She went to interview a seventy-four-year-old black woman she seems to have known already, Tank Valentine Daughtry. The woman's physical appearance fascinated Bernice: "Two braids of thin gray hair were wound tight with strings across the top of her head. From her ears dangled gold earrings. A silver signet ring flashed on her finger. Large safety pins were strung along the front of her dress like medals. Her tiny feet were encased in narrow brown high-top shoes, pointed at the toes as an elf's should be" (F469, FWP).

At first, Bernice watched the setting sun and wished that Mrs. Daughtry would wait until after she left to carry on her conversations with the Lord. But Tank Daughtry soon began her story of how she had married a man who worked for the railroads, how he had died and left her with six children, how she had sold his horse and buggy and bought seven acres of land, and how she had planted at night after working all day. She recounted all the jobs she and her children had done for white people to get money to keep the land.

Tank Valentine Daughtry dramatized the stories, "acting the parts so vividly that the dramatis personae were projected in person there in the quaint cluttered setting of her cabin." But it was the songs and dances she did with such verve and imagination that worked magic on Bernice. One of the songs Bernice put in the mouth of the wild, independent woman Valentine in her novel *Janey Jeems*:

> I'll build me a eyrie
> In the mountains so high,
> Where the wild birds will see me
> As they pass by. [35]

Telling the story of her husband's courtship, Tank Valentine Daughtry described how she pretended to be spinning to fool her father into thinking she wasn't just waiting for the chance to run away to get married. While she spun, she sang a love song:

> "The peach trees is all in bloom."
> Zoom, zoom—
> "The peach trees is all in bloom."
> Zoom, zoom—
> "The peach trees is all in bloom.
> Come, my love, and go with me.
> Go with me to the wedding, oh."[36]

When her Doubleday editor, John Woodburn, came to visit her, Bernice took him to hear Mrs. Daughtry's ballad. He wrote to her later to tell Aunt Tank that he wished they had been contemporaries, he would have loved to take her to a dance.[37] When Bernice was writing *Sage Quarter*, it was this song that established the mood for the novel. She remembered in such a way that we can glean the feeling the ballad evoked in her: "It was thistlebird's per-chic-oree, lambs bleating in the meadow, pink fog of blossoms upon upturned furrows, June apples reddening above a white hammock that was never realized except in dreams."[38]

Couch's prediction that Harris would find stimulus in these face-to-face encounters came true to a greater extent than even he could imagine. Harris's intimate knowledge of life in the South was now greatly enriched by her work on the Federal Writers' Project.

The general picture, however, is not so fortunate. The Federal Writers' Project was under attack by 1939, and its end seemed imminent, though the death was slow in coming. From the beginning, the arts projects were constantly the target of politicians who charged that they were Communist-inspired. By 1941, the nation's energies were directed to the war effort, and so in that year the projects were denied federal support. For a time they had to depend on the states. The next year a new arrangement was made whereby the remnants of the writers' project became a unit of the War Services Subdivision of the WPA. This unit was abolished altogether in 1943.

But even in the short time that the Federal Writers' Project existed, much was accomplished. Fifty-one guides and hundreds of other publications were produced. More than a thousand life histories were collected; and although a small number may be faulty, the great majority give us an authentic picture of life in the South in the thirties.

For Bernice Kelly Harris, the characters, situations, individuals' philosophies, and actual words in the life histories she recorded with her pencil were haunting. In the novels that followed her interviewing for the Federal Writers' Project, she felt compelled to give these narrators voices again.

7

Taking Risks: *Portulaca*

While Bernice Kelly Harris was conducting interviews for the Federal Writers' Project, she was working on her second novel. In this novel, the girl Nannie Lou in *Purslane*, who aspired to be a writer, has grown up. Now she is the principal character of the book and her name is Nancy. Nancy is married to a businessman, Kirke; they live in a small southern town Harris calls Bonwell. Harris named the novel *Portulaca*, a reference to the cultivated version of the wild plant purslane, and symbolic of the farm girl who has become the sophisticated townswoman. It is a frankly autobiographical novel.

Nancy writes stories for magazines and the social news for the local newspaper. Kirke does not understand why she is always typing. He complains that it costs money to mail her stories off. One night, she begs him to listen to a story she has just finished. He changes the subject to the amount of money she is spending. When she insists on reading the story, he develops a headache, takes a BC (a headache medication), and nods off to sleep.[1]

Neither does Kirke seem interested when Nancy investigates charity cases in her position as head of the welfare committee of her church's district organization of ladies' groups. As she visits families, the character Nancy becomes aware of how desperately sharecroppers need adequate nutrition, health care, and shelter. She becomes cognizant especially of the hard lives of rural women, black and white.

Nancy writes a short story about a very young girl who is sexually abused by her father and seduced by the landowner (the story mentioned earlier in the comparison of Caldwell's and Harris's work). She sends it to the New York editor, who has promised to publish a collection of her short stories. He replies that his publishing company does not want this story of incest, saying that "this was not part of the Southern scene." "There might be isolated instances," he writes to her, but this has "little to do with the true South" (43). Nancy is effectively silenced.

Next, Nancy appeals to the church committee to do something about the plight of the sharecroppers, but the members want to send their money to convert pagans in Africa. Finally, one day Nancy's husband, Kirke, who is the owner of the town's general store, asks where she's been, and she tells him she has been visiting sharecroppers. The following dialogue appears in the novel:

> "What business did you have there?"
>
> "Nothing more definite than—Kirke, I told you I had been appointed welfare chairman of the district clubs."
>
> "I don't get the connection."
>
> "It's too vague in my own mind to explain clearly, but I have a feeling that a great many of our club and church objectives are impractical, intangible, and that we need to touch realities and formulate programs that will be applicable to conditions that actually obtain among us."
> (256)

The conversation continues with Kirke telling Nancy she has no common sense. He tells her she has made people in town angry. He concludes by saying that she is ignorant and that he will hear no more from her, that she will "cut out this foolishness." His last words to her are these:

> "You'll behave yourself if you expect to remain a wife of mine. Now get to bed! And never let me hear any more about this as long as you live, or there'll be serious trouble between us! Never, as long as you're a wife of mine!" (256–261)

Nancy thinks about this. She then goes meekly to bed, never visits a sharecropper's cabin again, and never even speaks about their plight again. Every occasion in *Portulaca* when the time to oppose her husband and the community comes up, Nancy remains silent.

Nancy has a growing sense that she is less important to her husband than his family and his business. Even at the beginning, he makes it clear that his real home is where his sister and brother live—with Nancy he has only a house. He insists he will be buried in the family plot. He adds that she can be buried there also if she wants to be.

Nancy's best friend, Ellen (who is married to Kirke's brother), states emphatically that she does not intend to let her wealth go to Kirke's family. Ellen tells Nancy that she has a will that stipulates that at her death the wealth she had brought into the marriage will revert to her own family.

Ellen dies in circumstances that are questionable—it is either a murder or a suicide. Nancy is staggered. She observes the behavior of those around her like a woman in a dream:

> Clint nervously passed the empty box of capsules around among the friends who pressed upstairs, as evidence of the way "poor Ellen" went, until Fred took the empty box and hid it from "poor Uncle Clint." Nancy was burdened all the more because she had to hide her troubled doubts deep within herself. All of Ellen's associates were too defensive, too sorry for "poor Clint," too careful to avoid one another's eyes and to conform to the conventional pattern of community order and decency at "such times." Clutching desperately at some fellowship in the despairing helplessness of her perplexity, she asked Kirke if he did not think Ellen's death seemed very very strange and oughtn't somebody—
>
> Kirke did not let her finish the question. Very solemnly and sternly he warned her never, as long as she was a wife of his, to even think, much less voice, such an idea. "Strange" was a word she must never use again in this connection, or she would start trouble that could not be stopped this side of a court of law. An utterly ridiculous word, strange. (302)

When Nancy writes the obituary for the newspaper, she takes the line adopted by the male elite in the town (that is, her husband's and Ellen's husband's business associates, including the town doctor): she explains cause of death as heart failure. Ellen's will is never found. When her family objects to Ellen's husband's taking all her property and brings the case to court, begging for witnesses to testify about the existence of Ellen's will, Nancy remains silent. But she asks *herself,* "Should I run away? From Bonwell? From myself?" (310).

A little later, during the night, Kirke and Nancy have a fire in their house. It's the townspeople who rescue her, and it's the townswomen who give her their best dresses so she will have clothes. Nancy is touched. She has kept quiet about any criticisms so that she can play the role of southern lady, challenging no behavioral norms, and now she reaps her reward—the community's support.

But Nancy is still troubled about the way she lives her life. She fantasizes about escaping to New York, even having an affair with her editor. Certainly just leaving is one way to end the double life she lives in Bonwell—outwardly a respectable married woman and church leader, inwardly an artist and social critic.

Near the end of the novel, she does go to New York. And while she is waiting in the hotel room for the editor's return for a romantic tryst, she feels a "tug of loneliness, of fright, and returning nausea" (332). She remembers her childhood when she went to spend the night with her Grandma and Grandpa and cried for wings to take her home. She bolts and takes a taxi to the airport. In the end she cannot bring herself to have an affair because that would cut her off from Kirke. She cannot leave home. She returns to the safety of the little town, the emotional security in her marriage to Kirke, and the comfort of having a place in the community.

This is a strange novel in that the woman who is the main character is an anti-hero. She is also the author's alter ego. The similarities between Bernice Harris and Nancy are unmistakable.

Both Bernice and her character Nancy had a "dual consciousness": the self that conforms to society's definition and the self that is different from that definition.[2] Bernice Harris was conscious of the fact that she wrote, like Nancy, to keep her sense of who she really was.

In the legal battle over inheritance, Nancy plays a coward's role, as Bernice did in life when she supported Herbert in taking the property away from Whit Harris's widow. The real situation is similar to the fictional one—a legal paper that is never found. This loss of a document is so convenient for "collateral heirs" (Ellen's husband's family in the novel, Herbert and his brothers and sisters in life) that it is suspicious. Bernice stayed silent and so does Nancy.

Certainly Nancy, her alter ego, is a character who arouses ambivalent feelings in the reader—sometimes sympathy and sometimes anger. Bernice Harris expresses in this novel the ambivalent feelings she had about herself in her role as unprotesting, always loyal, wife.

In the novel, Nancy keeps begging Kirke to make a will. He refuses. Similarly, Bernice begged Herbert to make a will. He refused. Bernice feared, from observing what happened to his brother Whit's widow, that if Herbert died before she did, his family would take most of his property and investments. (Her fears would come true in 1950, when Herbert died.)

Other similarities between Bernice and her fictional character Nancy abound. Like Bernice, Nancy longs for a child. Like Herbert, Kirke says no to Nancy's urgent request. Bernice had been a fired-up teacher, and suddenly she had nothing except the ladies' social events in the town to occupy her thinking—like Nancy in the novel. Bernice became involved in teaching playwriting and producing plays; Nancy leads the Pen Club of Bonwell. Harris's account of the fictional group sounds like the writing groups she led in her own living room: "The talk swerved from story motivation to pickles and nail polish and caskets. Seven of the members brought stories to the next meeting. Nancy found Grace's story improbable and melodramatic. Steenie had buried hers in a muck of profanity. Lila had rattled too many family skeletons. All the stories were vaguely resented, because each member of the Pen Club identified herself or some of her family with the various situations outlined."[3]

Nancy investigated social conditions for her churchwomen's group just as Bernice interviewed for the Federal Writers' Project. The experience profoundly affected Bernice and she makes it troubling for Nancy, but she also writes a plot that stills Nancy's critical voice.

On the surface the novel is a critique of small-town society—its pettiness and generosity, its illusions and practicality, its hypocrisy and genuine concern. Harris's awareness of social injustice infuses the writing. No one can read *Portulaca* without becoming aware of the pain and want in the lives of the rural poor, then and now. And she makes clear the hypocrisy of the church people and businessmen as they spout the approved Christian sayings and at the same time exploit their workers. The situation is comfortable for the white elite. They fear change; thus, the women sense danger if they rock the boat, and so they indulge only in activities that challenge nothing.

Harris's writing deals with the interplay of race, gender, and social class in this small town. She strips the courtly manners of white men from the situation and reveals their bullying of women. She shows the way some white women worked black women with hardly a thought about how these women might manage when, dead tired, they came home to their own children.

She was treading on a lot of toes. To be a critic of the society in which you value acceptance as highly as Bernice Kelly Harris did is a risky business. You have a lot to lose—that feeling of belonging to a place, of the shared identity with others in your community, of the comfort of friendships, of the intimacy and support in the relationship with your mate. This was what Harris wanted above all else. She kept quiet much of the time, but she was not quiet in this book. She was no politician, making public speeches: she was too much a private person for that. Characteristically, she wrote out her distress in her novels. Possibly, she thought fiction could be as powerful as any official document or purely political speech. By evoking emotion through the telling of a story, she would give the ideas she was communicating an impact.

Under the surface layer of social criticism in *Portulaca*, there is a deeper layer of meaning, a theme that appears in Harris's later novels and in the writings of other women. The theme deals with the psychological dilemma, To what extent can I remain myself and still be connected to another? In his essay on the fiction of another southern woman writer, Eudora Welty, Robert Penn Warren treats this theme briefly: the dilemma as he phrased it is between the need for love and the need for separateness.[4] In Welty's *Delta Wedding* (1945), for example, the child protagonist tries to keep a few secrets about her life to herself so that she can still feel like herself, all the while trying to conform to the extended family's behavioral norms so that she can be part of them.

Harris explores the theme, asking what connection means for both Nancy and Kirke. For Nancy, connection is the emotional security of the kind we feel when we are truly home among our own; it is the tie that keeps us from being adrift alone in the world. For Kirke, connection means the preeminent social and financial position that empowers himself, his sister, and his brother. It is power and advantage that he seeks in relationships in the community. Neither Nancy nor Kirke can risk losing connection, as each defines its meaning.

Kirke is obsessed with his money-making enterprises and cannot tolerate his wife's behavior when it might result in his losing business. Nancy chafes against the rope he tightens around her. She passionately desires autonomy, the freedom to act according to her own conscience, to be herself with whatever quirks of personality, goodness or flaws there are, to direct her life so as to develop her creativity. She thinks about running away to New York and just sacrificing connection. In the end, she cannot give up her need to belong; instead, she denies her need to be herself.

Just as *Purslane*, in contrasting material bounty with emotional hunger, expresses more than just a way of life in a farming community at the beginning of the century, so *Portulaca* is more than just a novel about small-town life. *Portulaca* addresses the need for individual freedom within the context of belonging. It is a timeless and universal theme.

After writing the ending to the novel in the fall of 1939, Harris had a difficult decision to make about publication. She sent the novel to William Couch at the University of North Carolina Press. He wrote her that he finished reading it at two o'clock in the morning. He added, "I have read few manuscripts that I would rather publish."[5] Soon she was hounded by editors of large commercial presses who wanted the novel, but Couch reminded her that the university press had done a good job of publicizing *Purslane*.[6] New York publishing companies continued to apply pressure, and especially John Woodburn, an editor at Doubleday, was assiduous in pursuing rights to publish it. He even appeared with Mrs. Woodburn outside her door one night in Seaboard.[7]

Woodburn and Couch met in New York to discuss publication. Later Couch wrote to her that she should probably go ahead and let Doubleday have it, but the tone of his letter was angry. Still, he told her he'd publish her autobiography if she decided to write one twenty years hence and anything else she wanted to send him.[8] She really wanted to publish with Doubleday, and she went with that company, though she may have felt some lingering guilt. Doubleday published *Portulaca* in 1941.

Contemporary reviewers saw this novel simply as a portrayal of various aspects of small-town life: they were not attuned to Nancy's psychological dilemma. In fact, almost all the reviewers concluded that Nancy made the right choice at the end when she returned to her husband and her town. The reviewer for the *New York Times* wrote condescendingly that women might like it: "It scores heavily, first of all, as a detailed picture of small-town life, which, written with a kind of breathless intensity, ought to prove especially interesting to women readers; its accounts of church suppers, marital mix-ups, and of all the simple, homely things that go into a familiar mosaic, have the fidelity, the warmth and the glowing colors of Dutch genre paintings." But he concluded that it was just another critical look at the *petite bourgeoisie* in a small town.[9]

The most that reviewers could say is that this is the story of "a southern woman's struggle against pettiness in a small town."[10] One reviewer, in Raleigh's *News and Observer*, did conclude, "In the end you get the impression that Nancy, for all her yearning for escape, yields to the Town both weakly and happily. Possibly that, too, is one of the implications of intimate living that Mrs. Harris sought to convey."[11]

But that the novel dealt with a woman's having to choose between her need to act on her conscience and her deep emotional need for connection is discussed nowhere in the critiques of *Portulaca*. That the novel is a strong indictment against a society that forces a woman to make such a choice was not glimpsed. In the forties and fifties, the intellectual and social milieu did not yet permit this kind of analysis.

One point all the contemporary reviewers agreed on is that there is no bitterness toward people. The *News and Observer* reviewer wrote, "There is both truth and beauty in her *Portulaca* along with the wisdom that comes from a keenly observing and tolerant mind, for there is no warping bitterness in Mrs. Harris' account of small-town life. And that requires the touch of an artist to complement the ability of a reporter."[12]

Poet Sam Ragan compared *Portulaca* to another novel of small-town life published twenty years earlier, Sinclair Lewis's *Main Street*.[13] He said an important difference is the compassion Harris showed toward people in small towns.[14]

There are similarities in the two novels. The hero of *Main Street*, Carol Kennicott, tries to get townspeople to make their town more beautiful and to make their forays into literature deeper. Nancy wants Bonwell's citizens to become involved in social justice issues, such as the plight of sharecroppers. Both women accept defeat.

Harris's Nancy is entangled in a web of family relationships; Sinclair Lewis does not make much of family in his novel—the deep need for connection is not emphasized. But there is an even more important difference. Nancy is so much involved in community life that she participates in the cover-up, but at the same time she reflects on her own behavior. Carol Kennicott does not castigate herself, but Nancy is wracked by the realization of her own cowardness and blindness. Harris offers a closer look at a woman's inner self than does Sinclair

Lewis: *Portulaca* is not just a sociological portrayal of narrow-minded attitudes in a small town but a delving into the psychological effects on a woman of conforming to this kind of community.

When Couch first read the manuscript, he told her it would finish her off in Seaboard.[15] Bernice was afraid of that. She was also afraid it would finish her off with Herbert. Ironically, she dedicated *Portulaca* to Herbert even though she knew he would not read it. But she was still apprehensive because he might hear talk about it and she agonized: "Though Herbert was not to read *Portulaca* himself, reactions would sift through to him. Had I made a fool of myself again?"[16]

Bernice also worried about Herbert's family's reactions: "Nancy, the heroine, related the religion of blood to lawsuits over property. Property, held in relentless trust for a family that did not believe in heirs, had stood in the way of Nancy's having a son. Would the novel seem impersonal enough?"[17]

And the thought crossed her mind that people would think she herself had had an affair with her editor: "What would be made of the Constant-Nancy romance? There had been an editor in my life as well as Nancy's, of course, only in mine he was legion and the romance had been impersonal as publisher's bond. Would composite be acceptable, or would literal be ascribed?"[18]

Actually, her London editor at Putnam's was named Constant Huntington—Harris had given Nancy his last name and her fictional editor, his first name, Constant. The Putnam editor wrote to her, "Just at the moment I am a little bit confused by finding my name scattered about among the characters, but you are certainly welcome, and no doubt I shall get used to it as I read on."[19]

Harris named the town Bonwell, but no one was fooled—it may have been a composite of small towns, as she maintained, but one in which Seaboard figured prominently. She was greatly worried about what would happen when townspeople read the novel. Would Seaboard women in her playwriting classes see themselves in the account of Nancy's writing group? She has Nancy explain to the Pen Club (and to Seaboard readers): "Nancy, sensing the disturbed cadences, suggested that all the materials used in the afternoon's assignment were representative, not actual; that there were hundreds of situations so similar that it was easy for people to read themselves into stories, to identify themselves with people in books where no similarity was intended."[20] But she said frankly, "I doubted that Nancy's apologia would keep me from being 'finished off.' "[21]

And how did the little town of Seaboard in general take this? Harris braced herself for the reaction: "After the publication date," she admitted, "I laid low." A neighbor, spying her in the back yard, called across the fence, "I've ordered your book. I hear I'm Ellen."[22]

But for the most part, Harris was surprised by the reaction—or lack of it. People thought they saw their enemies in the book, not themselves. They laughed at the ones she had "hit hard."[23]

Her friend Elizabeth Harris (Herbert's second cousin) said that what the town's women objected to was that Bernice had told about the social cliques. Elizabeth and Bernice had started having contract bridge parties. Some individuals felt left out; their feelings were hurt. When they saw this reported in the book, they treated Bernice coolly from then on.[24] (Bernice denied this in the published pages of her autobiography.)[25] On the other hand, Betsey Bradley Merritt, who grew up on Bernice Harris's street, said her mother made her read *Portulaca* because Miss Kelly "said what it was really like." Merritt surmised that the townspeople were, like her mother, proud that one of their own had written a novel.[26] It is unlikely that Herbert's brothers and sisters read *Portulaca* or any of her work. Herbert did not read it. Eventually Harris concluded that most people in the town never read the novel in its entirety: some were not readers, some read other things.

And she was feeling appreciated outside of Seaboard. As the author of *Purslane* and now a second novel, she continued to receive invitations to speak. She turned down requests to speak in New York and Atlanta. She had to stay close to Seaboard because she was concerned about Herbert, whose hypertension was growing worse. Her worrying about him created problems for the management of her own health. Or, as she said, "His condition sharpened my nervous tension." She was taking too much medicine, she thought.[27]

Still, she felt she had a duty to readers to talk about the writing, and so she accepted invitations to speak if she could go and come back in a day. Most often she continued to be guest speaker for women's clubs. Women in these clubs wanted to improve their own education in the arts and also to initiate arts projects in their towns.[28] For Bernice, literature made all the difference in the quality of life a person had. She was pleased to be with a group of women who interested themselves in literature. And once she began speaking, she enjoyed it—and the butterflies in her stomach stopped flying. Surprising to Bernice, the accounts of her speaking were positive. A friend in Chapel Hill, Walter Spearman (professor in the school of journalism at the University of North Carolina), wrote her, "I hear that you made a fine talk to the alumnae at Meredith—and that you were quite the belle in Charlotte."[29] Friends, especially Josephine Parker, the adventuresome wife of Seaboard's doctor, John Wesley Parker, drove her to speaking engagements.[30]

One invitation came from a group of women writers in Raleigh who called themselves "The Strugglers." "We need some inspiration and a fresh start," they said.[31] Bernice went, probably because her sister-in-law Mary was in the group. Bernice became a member and attended their meetings for the rest of her life, cherishing the friendships she made among them.

Now in her late forties, Bernice Kelly Harris was feeling her power as a writer. Her fears about the novel's reception in Seaboard did not take center stage for her: she was elated over the novel. Thinking about it decades later, she remarked that *Portulaca* still seemed to have "certain explosive potential."[32]

8

Friendships and *Sweet Beulah Land*

On the farm in Wake County a yeoman farmer's wife was considered pitiful when her family had to sit down to a meal cooked by someone hired.[1] It meant the woman of the house was in some way deficient— either in health or in character. But that was one attitude Bernice cheerfully relinquished as soon as she became a married townswoman. Indeed, she said that she could not have written books without the help she had in the house from the African American women she hired: "Most of my writing was done while Mattie and Melissie were with us. Seven novels, two short stories and a book of plays were published from 1939 to 1951."[2] Herbert, although watchful of every item of expenses, could hardly object since it was the custom for *urban* middle-class housewives to hire African American women as cooks, laundresses, and housekeepers.[3] Indeed, to have hired help was a status symbol, and he enjoyed his status in the town.

For Bernice Harris, the women who came in the house and worked for her when she was upstairs writing were important. Bernice enjoyed liking people and she wanted to be liked. Of course, these were not friendships in the usual sense of the word because of the difference in power between employer and employee and because of the race of the employee, which put her at a still greater disadvantage in relationships of power with whites. However, Bernice and the black women who worked for her were concerned about what happened to each other, treated each other with respect, and felt responsible for each other's well-being.

Bernice knew she could not pay much more than other white women paid their maids lest she anger the town matrons and Herbert as well, but she did pay the highest salary in town. Even more unusual, she insisted on paying social security.[4] Bernice made sure that when she ordered a ham, there would be enough for her to give a portion to the cook. When one pie was needed, often two were baked so there would be food to share. The bounty of her garden was always offered her helpers.[5]

A woman who worked for Bernice for years and with whom she had a complicated relationship was Ethel Vassar. Mrs. Vassar's father, freed from slavery, had saved to buy a parcel of land and build a small house.[6] Ethel Vassar was determined to hold onto that land, to pay the taxes on it, no matter how hard that might become. She and her younger sister, who was lame, worked to maintain themselves and the sister's two children. It was a daily challenge. The memory of slavery was juxtaposed against the independence of owning one's own place, and so the struggle to make ends meet was a struggle to remain free. She told Bernice in an interview for the Federal Writers' Project:

> It costs a poor person to own a home. . . . Our three-room house is 'bout to fall down on us, it needs repairing so bad. The wind blowed the paper top off the kitchen this last week of March, and something is bound to be done about that. I'm trying hard to save up enough money to buy some lumber, but my wages just don't stretch far enough. I have to pay out sixty cent a month for insurance to the burial league, fifty cent a week for straight life insurance for myself, fifty a week for sick benefits for myself and Little Sister and ten cents for her two children. There's clothes and groceries and church dues. There's school tablets and books for Little Sister's family. All that has to come out of the three dollars a week I'm paid. Then there's taxes, nine dollars a year. Taxes has got to come, if the whole passel of us goes hungry! They sha'n't take our land and our roof for taxes![7]

Impressed with Ethel Vassar's management of money, Bernice concluded that even with her college education, she could not do as well.[8]

Ethel Vassar had no faith in justice on this earth—as a single black woman she had felt directly too much injustice. She was not given to jollity. She once told Bernice that she had walked with ghosts; "but I'll say this, they don't harm you like the living sometimes does."[9] One spring day, Bernice was shocked and delighted when Ethel walked in and declared, "It's so pretty outside that I pure feel like getting down and wallowing in April!"[10]

Eventually, the two had a falling out. Ethel Vassar's brother died, and she sent word for Bernice to lend her a particular black coat to wear to the funeral. In a previous conversation, she had told Bernice that in her family, people wore black for mourning. Bernice, reasoning that Ethel was too broad and buxom to fit into the black coat, sent her a larger, blue coat instead. Ethel Vassar did not work for her again.[11]

The expectations of two cultures were different here: in Bernice's way of thinking, Ethel would be standing in the cold wind in the cemetery and she would need a coat that could be buttoned up; in Ethel's mind, wearing black was a sign of respect and mourning and that was more important than being warm. Black and white women spent hours during the day working together, shared concerns, and told each other secrets. And yet part of their lives were lived in different cultures—probably some misunderstanding was inevitable. Still, Bernice, despite her good intentions, was thinking for her employee and not trusting Ethel Vassar to make her own decisions. The paternalism inherent in this relationship of white employer–black employee intruded. Still, it is remarkable that Bernice shared her clothes with her black housekeeper—that was not the usual practice.

Mattie Ferguson was Bernice's next helper. She was so competent that when she was there, Bernice could forget everything about the house and write continuously.[12] Mrs. Ferguson was an excellent chef. When John Woodburn, Harris's Doubleday editor, came to visit, he was so delighted with the meals she cooked that he threatened to move south, buy a place on the Richmond Pike, and steal her away from Bernice.[13]

But eventually Mattie Ferguson moved to Norfolk, and Bernice was working in the house alone. By this time, Ethel Vassar had gotten over the rift with Bernice, and she sent her sister, Melissa Lowery, to work for her. Bernice called her "Melissie," as did all of Mrs. Lowery's friends. College educated, she had been a schoolteacher before she decided to end her working days as a cook. She was deeply religious and talked out loud to the Lord every day. Sometimes she just sat down, quitting work as she chose, and read the Bible. Bernice understood the way words can delight, and so she did not chide Melissie: "The impact of the beauty and majesty of the passages was so overwhelming that sometimes Melissie called out to me in a kind of transport, as though she had just received some good news that had to be shared."[14] On the other hand, Melissie insisted on her standards concerning language. Bernice said, "She bore with Herbert's expletives, but not with mine. She was exacting toward me. I was permitted no expletives in my house. Let me try damning something, and I was quickly reminded I was too much a Lady to use slack words."[15]

Melissie was also keen on self-education and purposely learned new words every day. She wrote each new word down with its meaning and then used it as soon as possible to reinforce the learning experience. Bernice observed that she collected words as some women did pitchers: "There was respect, even awe, in her attitude toward words."[16] Of course, Bernice shared this delight in words. Once Bernice used the term "hors d'oeuvres." "Spell it," Melissie said. She reached into her pocket for the notebook and pencil she kept handy and wrote it down. Another time, she heard a guest at the supper table use the word "blousay." She asked Bernice about it the next morning. Bernice said it must have been "blasé." Melissie jotted that down, with the definition—"having one's taste dulled by over-indulgence." Next day, when she had eaten too much food not compatible with her high blood pressure, she remarked, laughing, to Bernice, "I reckon I'm just blasé."[17] Social class difference intruded—for Melissie, "taste" was related to food.

Bernice sometimes read to Melissie passages from a novel she was writing. Melissie was a willing listener. And when Melissie wanted an especially eloquent speech or strong letter written, she called on Bernice. Unwilling to tolerate bad grammar or malapropisms, Melissie nevertheless insisted on using the colloquial word for expressions of condolence spoken at funerals, "condolers." She frequently asked Bernice to write these. "I was careful to use words that pleased her," Bernice said.[18]

Already in her mid-seventies when she came to work for the Harrises, Melissie could not do heavy house cleaning. However, she was an excellent cook and cooked all the daily meals, and she delighted in cooking for company. She and Bernice made up the menu together, writing down each detail. Melissie always referred to her former cooking jobs as an "incumbency," and as she always did, wherever she was working, she made every experience an opportunity to learn. She would make suggestions to Bernice, such as, "We used to serve little orange cups during my incumbency in Norfolk . . . filled with seasoned sweet potatoes and topped with a marshmallow, they are compatible with either ham or chicken."[19] Bernice, an excellent cook herself, was interested.

Bernice Harris had grown up working in the kitchen with her mother, sisters, and aunts. Melissa Lowery was a kind of surrogate older sister, as they worked together in the Harris kitchen. Yet the distrust between races, as well as the unequal distribution of power between employer and employee, impinged on their relationship: Bernice's slightly condescending attitude toward the African American women who worked for her shows up in subtle ways in her private letters. Nevertheless, she expressed her respect for Mrs. Lowery in published writings. In an autobiographical account, she said, "Melissie was a treasure in ways that had nothing to do with her work, light or heavy. We shared many experiences together, and her sense and philosophy gave me balance and poise sometimes when my own equanimity was shattered. She had an undaunted spirit."[20]

In an article called " 'The Essential Northampton'—A Portrait Drawn in Affection," published in the *News and Observer* in 1947, Harris was careful to include the contributions of African Americans: "The essential Northampton is that colored man and woman of Jonesboro who made their bodies very steam engines doing public work and standing knee-deep in mud from sun to sun molding brick." There is a picture of Melissa Lowery.[21] Harris's respect for the black townswomen and townsmen she knew becomes clear when the reader looks at the historical context. Few white southern writers at the time would have included the contributions of the African American population to the county's development. In Harris's writing as in her life, she moved beyond this preoccupation with difference to make an insistent effort to understand African American women and to discern shared experiences and feelings.

A white woman, Vaughn Holoman, was another person important in her life at this time. Mrs. Holoman was a poet, but she also enjoyed plays and play production. The two women first met when Bernice was organizing local components of the Northampton Players in the 1930s. Vaughn became president. She remembered the first time she met Bernice: she was sitting in a Seaboard living room, listening to Bernice read her play *Three Foolish Virgins,* and loving it.[22]

Vaughn was married to a wealthy farmer, Henry Holoman, and

lived in Bryantown, North Carolina. Although Bryantown is only eighteen miles from Seaboard, the two friends could not meet often because neither Vaughn nor Bernice drove. Vaughn explained her own situation: "You know how it is to be dependent on even the best of husbands, when their minds are on crops."[23] And in the late thirties and early forties, Bernice had her own worries:

> If I could get over to you—! I have not ridden even on a Sunday afternoon in two months. Herbert is obliged to rest Sundays. In fact, once I feared he would not be able to work through the gin season, so alarmingly did his blood pressure go up. He takes blue pills three times a day now and other medicine frequently. He is thin. One Sunday afternoon I did breathe a wistful, "I wish I could go to Mrs. Holoman's," though actually I do plan all my Sundays at home and am happy to have him rest as he sees fit.[24]

They corresponded regularly, however. Bernice described their letters as "relaxed notes, effortless and without style, just as we talked."[25] They greatly enjoyed being together when they could arrange it. Bernice wrote in a tribute to Vaughn about their "little adventures together": "The shared impact of persons and of simple little happenings was adventure enough for us."[26] Vaughn could express to Bernice her most secret thoughts: "I think I have been too much a mixture of conscience and rebellion. I have always wanted to be good and at the same time have wanted to kick over the traces."[27] Bernice could empathize with that. She could admit that she resented going to bed by eight-thirty, but Herbert had to get up at five o'clock every morning to go to the cotton gin. She wanted to keep the house dark and quiet for him, and so to bed she went, but she made the best of lying awake: "I miss radio programs I like, but I lie there and make stories more fantastic than any of the radio series."[28]

Vaughn could express her doubts about her writing to Bernice: "I think one reason I hate to commit myself to writing is the fact that my critical faculties are so far in advance of my creative ability."[29] Bernice could articulate her doubts about her own writing and delights, as well, to Vaughn in a way that she could not talk to others. Acknowledging that they would probably never be rich and famous, she said, "But this I do believe: we will write whether we are read or not. We are that way. What makes us so? I certainly don't sing in numbers for the numbers come. Sometimes it's travail. But when a phrase, even a little phrase, breaks through in perfection of form or meaning I am confirmed whether anybody says so or not. It doesn't happen often. But it happens. You know."[30]

Vaughn had two young daughters, Judith and Mebane, who were interested in writing. Later in the forties, when Judith and Mebane were older and could drive, they would come with their mother to Seaboard for a day-long "session" on writing. In between their meetings, Bernice and Vaughn critiqued each other's work.

In 1939 Harris also began a correspondence with a young high school teacher, Richard (always called Dick) Walser. It turned out to be a friendship that lasted the rest of her life. He had had a privileged upbringing as the son of the state's attorney general. When Harris first met him, he was teaching English in Greenville, North Carolina, and bringing his students and their plays to Chapel Hill to the annual drama contests Koch had begun. Impressed with Harris's plays and with *Purslane*, he asked her to be a speaker at a literary event he was organizing. She tried to wiggle out of it but finally wrote him, "I really should decline because I am not a speaker at all. I might read a few remarks if that would do."[31]

In October 1939, she invited him to come to Seaboard to read and comment on modern poetry. He did come, and she expressed her delight in a letter to him, adding, "Mr. Harris' reaction pleased me; he was quite carried away with your reading of the poems, with your voice, etc., and wanted more poems instead of the ice cream."[32] (She could be a little wicked, too.)

Harris, writing alone in the upstairs bedroom in the house in Seaboard, always had the support of these friends in the back of her mind. By the late summer of 1940, she was nearly finished with her third novel—eventually she settled on the title *Sweet Beulah Land*, from a hymn by that name. In early October 1940, she wrote her former Doubleday editor, John Woodburn, that "the third one is named and ended."[33] In this novel, she continued to wrestle with the question she explored in *Portulaca*: at what price do we achieve connection? But now the setting is different and her protagonist is a man, Lan Holt. He is a drifter who comes by chance into an area much like Northampton County, to a hamlet she names Beulah Ridge, North Carolina.

Falling sick in the road, Lan is taken in by an old woman, Miss Partheny, who determines to nurse him to health. She needs a man to plow in order to fulfill her sharecropper's agreement with the landowner, Archibald Hart. There is only herself and her granddaughter, Sophie, on the place.

Another landowner, Alicia Donning, comes to check on Lan—she thinks she knocked him down on the road as she drove past. She looks at him now, bathed and clad in a white shirt, and notices his good looks. In spite of herself, Alicia feels drawn to him and keeps coming back to Miss Partheny's shack to see him.

Meanwhile, Archibald Hart proposes marriage to Alicia, but she turns him down because she wants an emotional relationship, not a land deal. In truth, Arch (as he is called by peers) does just want her land; the woman he desires is the voluptuous redhead, Sophie. Arch surmises that Alicia's attraction to Lan stands in the way of Alicia's marrying him. He throws old Miss Partheny, Sophie, and Lan into the road along with Partheny's clothes and furniture.

Sophie begs Lan to take her away and to love her. He refuses, saying he will stay with "The Old One," that the three of them will make a living together. Sophie leaves, angry and humiliated.

She walks down the road, turns into the woods, and encounters Arch. He promises that she and her grandmother can come back in the house if Lan leaves. Sophie happily succumbs to his seduction of her even though she has already become sexually intimate with Alicia's foreman Trent.

Lan goes to Alicia to say good-bye, but she cannot stand the thought of his leaving and offers him a job on her land. She hates the idea of his being an uneducated tramp, but she is impressed with the fairness and prowess he shows. And she loves his looks.

Miss Partheny comes to visit Lan in the cabin he shares with Trent. She is worried about Sophie and asks Lan to look after her after she dies. Lan promises.

Lan's quick thinking and bravery are demonstrated when he puts out a fire Trent started and thus saves Alicia's cotton crop and timber. She offers Lan a deal. He can buy land on a little island in the river she owns; he will become her foreman and she will deduct payments on the land from his salary. Lan is highly troubled: owning land means settling down, staying in one place, making commitments. But he is also in love with Alicia, whom he pictures as an angel. He forgets who he is—a working man and one who always moves on—so eager is he to be with her. He accepts the deal.

Alicia offers to teach him arithmetic; and as her student, he becomes a frequent visitor to her plantation house, Elmhurst. Finally he confesses he hates to leave when the lesson is finished, and she admits she does not want him to leave. He tries to please her; he senses that he must somehow fit into her life. He tries to clean up his grammar. He even plays the role of host when her aristocratic friends come to a party at Elmhurst. Alicia decides she will have him as a husband, and he readily agrees.

Miss Partheny dies. Shortly afterwards, the buzz of gossip fills his ear: Sophie is pregnant.

One winter's night, when Lan returns to the cabin he has built for himself on his small plot of land on the island, he finds something whimpering in a box at his doorstep. It turns out to be a baby boy, and he knows immediately whose it is. He dries and warms the baby and feeds him sugar water. Next morning he carries the baby to Sophie and insists she feed him and take care of him.

That day in the road when he refused to leave with her, Sophie told him that she would make him sorry. Now she keeps her promise by telling everyone that Lan is the father of the child. Alicia is enraged and breaks her engagement with Lan.

Lan builds a second cabin so he can set up a store on the island. Mostly his customers are the black sharecroppers who are working for Arch or Alicia. Not many can pay their debts to him, and so his store is run on a shoestring. Eight years go by.

Sophie's little boy, Bit, regularly comes to the store and trades pieces of glass, or whatever he can find, for canned goods. Lan wants to be generous with him and to know how he fares. But Bit is secretive; in fact, he has a cave where he hides the canned food. He plans to escape from Sophie, who regularly goes out with Archibald Hart but also has Trent (now Hart's foreman) beat him to keep him in line. Lan suspects Bit's life is hard but does not know what to do except be a friend to Bit. He teaches him to fish, gets a puppy for him, cooks for the child when he is in Lan's cabin.

Hart, anticipating the spring rains that often cause flooding on the island, has a dike built to protect his part of the land. When the heavy rains come in spring, the waters are directed by the dike to others' land, principally Alicia's; serious flooding results. Lan goes around in his little rowboat, trying to ferry people to higher ground and safety.

But as soon as the people living on the island are safe, Lan dynamites the dike so the waters can recede. For this, he is attacked at night by masked thugs and beaten severely. Just as Lan manages to drag himself up from the floor, Bit arrives at his door and tells Lan that Sophie has married Hart and given Bit to Trent. The child has run away and has sought the only friend he has, Lan.

In the morning, Alicia comes to Lan's cabin, grateful that he has once again saved her cotton and timber, this time from flood waters. She admits she made a hasty decision eight years earlier. She presses against him, kisses him, begs him to let the past fade away. She wants him to marry her and come to Elmhurst to live with her. Just then, she hears someone in the cabin's other room. Lan tells her it is Bit. She says that Bit cannot come to Elmhurst.

As soon as she goes, Lan, Bit, and his puppy leave the cabin. Lan stops at the store and takes the last few cents from the cash register and the tax documents. Man and boy walk down the road together, Lan explaining that he will keep paying the taxes on the store so that he can come back someday. Meanwhile, he will see that Bit can grow up loved and safe and away from Beulah Ridge, North Carolina.

A sense of impending danger permeates the mood of the novel, and so it is a relief when Lan and Bit walk away from Beulah Ridge. Reviewer Frederick Wight wrote that Harris "puts across a thunderstorm atmosphere, the feeling of events slowly and inescapably brewing, of a quality of suspense that is pervasive as a climate."[34]

The community—all classes and people, black and white—provides the context in which these struggles take place. There are the aristocrats, who call themselves simple farmers, who date their landownership back to the eighteenth century. They have mansions and electricity and other people to do their work. And on a deep level they know that their days are numbered. There are the sharecroppers, who desperately hang on from harvest to harvest, moving on—or being evicted—from one place to another within the area, always hoping for a better deal and always living without adequate nutrition, shelter, medical care, or education. The white working class is represented by only a few characters, such as the miller; and the independent small farm owner, the lower middle class, by the man who is also justice of the peace.

Harris's landscape is peopled by various individuals whose lives intersect at a crucial time. As in her previous novels, many of the characters in this community are based on people Harris had known; especially she drew on her work for the Federal Writers' Project. She had placed on one of the first pages of the novel: "Some of the people and incidents in this book are fictional." This use of the qualifying word "some" was certainly not the usual disclaimer. Above all, the world of Beulah Ridge is so expertly, so vividly, presented that the reader never doubts its reality.

Miss Partheny is perhaps the most memorable character in the novel. Eudora Welty described her as "a righteous wild cat."[35] Harris was remembering Miss Sis, the seventy-five-year-old narrator in the Federal Writers' Project who walked four miles in the hot sun to attend an adult literacy class. Bernice heard her read with militancy the gentle Twenty-third Psalm; indeed, she lived her life with creative militancy, Harris said.[36] In the novel Miss Partheny goes to an adult literacy class. The aspirations of Miss Partheny and the neighboring poor women to gain entrance to the world of literature and to a spiritual life are portrayed dramatically. Their song is reproduced:

> Lord, lift me up that I may stand
> By faith on heaven's tableland—
> A higher place than I have found,
> Lord, plant my feet on higher ground.[37]

One reviewer remarked about this woman: "Miss Partheny, 'the old one,' of the migratory laborer, Lan Holt, had the grand burial of her ambition half way through the book, yet her rugged influence lasts until the end, and it is largely her strength which reinforces the primitive dignity of Lan and enables him twice at gaps of eight years to retain his integrity in the face of Alicia's charm of person and position."[38]

Typical of Harris's writing style, each character, however minor, is vividly drawn. An especially unforgettable one is Old Dugger, the ninety-year-old servant to the aristocratic landowner Matt Ransom. At one point, he uses the words of the ancient Lettice Boyer, a woman Harris had interviewed: "I was here when de stars fell, when de earth shook, when de surrender was."[39] His stories about the Yankees coming, told to amuse his employer's guests, are taken from other interviews.

Yet another memorable character in the novel is the ninety-eight-year-old black woman, Aunt Lettice, whom Lan befriends. Tank Valentine Daughtry was the model for this character, and Aunt Lettice is described in the novel the way Harris first saw Mrs. Daughtry when she went to interview her for the Federal Writers' Project: braids of hair wound tight around her head, the black lace scarf, the gray outing-flannel jacket over the blue print dress, the large safety pins strung along the front like medals.[40] She moves with the quick grace Mrs. Daughtry had.

Harris had interviewed a basket maker, Eddie Davis, and could not forget him. In *Sweet Beulah Land* he appears as the character Willie, another of Lan's friends. Eddie's will to make something of his life impressed her:

> His spine did not support the frail, misshaped one-sided body. Instead of sitting to his work, he had to lie to it, his stomach across a chair and his weight on one elbow, as he assisted his hands with his teeth. From the blue denim garment, which was like an infant's long dress, his feet lay bare in the sunshine.
>
> The stark feet were not important. The malformed head set on hunched shoulders, the man's features and the infant body, the queer garment that covered his deformity were not important. For Eddie Davis was not of this deformity. He laughed and sang and smoothed off his white oak splints, exhibited his handiwork with pride, and explained to his visitor how he made baskets and ferneries and lamps.[41]

Archibald Hart is a character drawn from imagination, a villain, but a smart one: he is the new capitalist farmer, a type Harris had begun to observe around her. He intends to expand and consolidate land holdings and to drive off the sharecroppers. He will use machinery extensively and hire only day laborers, chiefly blacks, whom he can get away with paying almost nothing and for whom he will have no responsibility. Harris cannot have predicted the future in all its ramifications, but she observed the beginnings of the use of machinery to replace human labor in cotton production; she could foresee the end of sharecropping as a way of life for the majority of farmworkers.

In 1940, on the eve of the Second World War, changes in agricultural production were already taking place that would be greatly accelerated during the war. Within a couple of years, war industries drew sharecroppers to towns, where they experienced for the first time a weekly paycheck, enough for the first time in their lives to adequately feed and clothe their families. And the United States Department of Agriculture had been paying farmers to take land out of cultivation since the New Deal. Who needed sharecroppers when you could get paid for not planting?

Machinery that would decrease the need for intensive human labor would become, by the 1950s, even better technologically. The old cotton harvester had picked up too much trash along with the cotton bolls; the new machines were more efficient.[42] And the money to pay for this expensive machinery would come from the money the government paid farmers *not* to plant.

At the same time, government loans to improve agriculture were available so farmers could buy chemical fertilizers. New markets for soybeans, peanuts, hogs, and cattle would make diversification profitable.[43]

And so Archibald Hart can see what is happening and makes his plans accordingly. He is rapacious, but so is Alicia, who represents the old values. When Alicia reminds Arch that he has to take care of Miss Partheny because his grandfather promised her a home on the Hart lands, he replies that he himself made no such deal. When he asks Alicia to take care of Miss Partheny, Alicia says no. She declares frankly that she simply can't use her.

Neither Arch nor Alicia comes across as a sympathetic character. Perhaps, the complexities of Alicia's psychological makeup are not fully presented. Nor is her love affair with Lan completely convincing. Yet Harris gives her courage: Alicia makes up her mind to marry for love and not for land. And she is determined to make her plantation a success, alone if need be. Conscious of her family's long history as landowners, she is resolved to make the wise decisions and do the hard work required to continue ownership of the land. She is brave to defy the social norms of the place and decide to marry a landless drifter because she is in love with him. But one of her flaws is her inability to relinquish even an inch of the traditional lifestyle she has known; any partner she takes must conform to it. She makes Lan a landowner, corrects his grammar, molds him into an acceptable host at Elmhurst.

Individuals within this community play out their destiny: other women face in one way or another what Alicia faces. Aristocratic Fahr Courtney escapes her domineering mother and gains adulthood by running away and marrying a working man, a miller. Her twin sister, Claire, gains her personal freedom by attempting suicide and then forcing the town doctor who treats her to support her in her desire to be a nurse. Alicia is willing to challenge the community's expectations for an upper-class woman as Fahr and Claire do, but only to a point. The recklessness with which the sisters act in order to change their lives is something she cannot muster.

Criticisms of the novel centered on the main character, Lan. He seems less real than the villain Archibald Hart. Possibly the problem is that often he is someone acted on rather than acting. As a working-class man, he is often at the command of others. Only twice, when Alicia accuses him of being the father of Sophie's baby, implying that a lower-class man cannot have a sense of honor, and again at the end, when she demands that he abandon Bit, does he actively resist Alicia. When he puts out the fire on Alicia's land and when he dynamites Hart's dam, his character shows ability to take action and he becomes less shadowy. The *New York Herald Tribune* reviewer Frederick Wight observed, "The dignity of her field-hand hero is the strongest of all. Lan Holt is primitive stuff, above and beneath ridicule, captured for a season in his drifting life by the possession of land. He is introduced too nebulously, perhaps, so that he strikes the reader as a sort of myth; but he belongs to the American myth, the stock that brings an Abraham Lincoln into history."[44]

Lan almost gives up his autonomy and his identity as a free-roaming man in order to be united with the beautiful woman he loves. At the end he realizes that to be connected to Alicia, he would have to break his promise to Partheny and abandon her progeny, her great-grandchild, Bit. He would have to go against what he knew to be the compassionate and responsible thing to do. When he takes Bit away in order to save him from Trent's abuse, Lan is truly himself. He chooses his own integrity rather than the woman's love he so desires. He is no longer rootless, however, because he knows and loves a place and the people there—the working-class and middle-class whites and the black sharecroppers who have been his customers. And he is connected with the child he saves. The emotional bond with the child is satisfying to him. And so, the dilemma is solved: he has both his autonomy and emotional connection—although not in a way he could have foreseen.

Unlike any of her other novels, the principal character in this one is a man. And the man is a drifter, not the sort of character one might expect a proper southern lady to choose as hero. In *Portulaca*, the novel Harris had just finished before *Sweet Beulah Land*, Nancy could not leave—women in Harris's world could not do that—but in this novel Harris chooses a man as protagonist because he can leave and does. Lan's dilemma is one she has confronted: self-direction and love for a child or intimate union with a mate. She arranges the plot so that Lan cannot have both; he must choose. He chooses integrity, the freedom to do what he judges right for him. And he chooses to leave the place where he has a lover as well as a community so that he can nurture a child. He does not devalue connection to a community; he vows to return, but on *his* terms.

Like *Purslane* and *Portulaca, Sweet Beulah Land* is a novel about class-ridden society. The *Greensboro Daily News* reviewer captured the essence of the plot and subplots when he wrote that both Hart and Alicia passionately desire someone outside their social class.[45] Hart, crude, grasping, goes after his sharecropper's granddaughter, Sophie, seduces her, and after trying unsuccessfully to win aristocratic women, finally marries her. Alicia wants the tramp, Lan, but only if she can refashion him to fit into her aristocratic lifestyle. Plot and subplot come together when, after eight years, Hart marries Sophie, who then abandons Bit; and Lan, determined to save the child, is pushed into his decision.

There are moments of tenderness in Lan's concern for Bit. Harris's former editor at Doubleday, John Woodburn, told her that the character of Bit and his relationship with Lan was as beautifully done as anything he had ever seen.[46] The novel also has touching moments, such as, the ancient aristocrat Mr. Matt and his servant Old Dugger going to the graveyard at night to take flowers to Mr. Matt's dead wife. And there are terrible moments, such as Trent's beating Bit without mercy, with Sophie standing outside the door, listening to the blows—her only thought being that it is strange that Bit does not cry.[47]

The novel finished, Harris did not, of course, make the same choice in life as in fiction. She was immersed in her own community in Seaboard. And, as usual, she was also speaking somewhere in North Carolina at least once a month. These public speaking engagements continued to be mostly at women's clubs, and she took each occasion very seriously. Never paid, she would be invited to spend the night at a club member's house if the distance was too far for her to return home the same day. However, she kept overnight travel to a minimum so that she could be at home at night with Herbert.

Harris usually received a pitcher as a "token of appreciation" for her talk. Her hostess always got a beautiful handmade basket. Ever mindful of individuals she had met through the Federal Writers' Project, Harris particularly liked to keep in contact with Eddie Davis, the basketmaker. She gave him as many commissions as she could.

As soon as she finished this novel, she began the next. In a poem that was a public tribute to her, a Seaboard neighbor wrote that when Miss Kelly got a far-away look in her eye, everybody knew she had checked out of the conversation and was thinking about the novel she was working on.[48] But a thunderstorm was brewing, like that in *Sweet Beulah Land*. World War II began.

9

Wartime and Peach Trees in Bloom: *Sage Quarter*

The new novel Harris began working on as soon as she finished *Sweet Beulah Land* had the title *Peach Trees* for a long time—eventually it was published as *Sage Quarter*. "Peach Trees" came from an old love song Tank Daughtry had sung when Bernice visited her; it was a folk song passed down through generations—how many generations no one knew. The rhythm indicated that it was sung to the motions of a spinner at her wheel. Harris liked the romantic mood of the song, with its refrain about peach trees in blossom and a wedding approaching.[1] She heard the song in her mind as she worked on the novel: "My peach trees is all in bloom / Come, my love, and go with me."[2]

Harris wrote the novel in 1941 and 1942, finishing it in the first half of 1943. On the surface, it is the story of a woman who waits for a man, just on his promise. It is, on a deeper level, the story of a woman who gains a sense of herself and becomes so independent that she can move towards a relationship with a lover without fear and with an assumption of equality.

Sage Quarter begins with Tiny, the central character, as a child, listening to Aunt Cherry's peach blossom song. Tiny's twin sister Ruby is up in a tree, taunting Tiny with a secret she will not tell. Tiny's real name is Pearl, but she was the second-born, small baby—so small she could fit into a quart pot, as her grandmother, Nurmama, always reminded her. (When Tiny's widowed mother, Lallah, came into the house, her mother-in-law took over the twin toddlers, insisting they call her "Another Mama"—but they could say only "Nurmama.") Tiny was born with one leg weak and so the family considers her "fau'ty," a term used to refer to inferior fruit that had not matured just right. Ruby is the pretty twin, black-haired and blue-eyed. She is also the one who defies the matriarch Nurmama and gets the whippings. Tiny grieves over these whippings and tries to protect Ruby, but she stays obedient.

The twins live in the family's early-nineteenth-century farmhouse with Nurmama, Grandfather, their widowed mother, Lallah, the hired hand, Ashley, and Nurmama's unmarried daughter, Aunt Nan. Nearby in a little house lives Aunt Cherry. When things go wrong in the big house, Tiny runs to Aunt Cherry. She feels closer to this black aunt than to her white aunts, she says.

Tiny's world is peopled by Nurmama's and Grandfather's children and by their spouses and children. Nurmama tells them all how to live their lives, and they comply. They gather at her house every Sunday for dinner: the family is their community and their way of defining who they are. Nurmama has exiled from the family her own brother because he shot and killed a man—she said that "if there was a single commandment he had not broken, it was an oversight."[3] He lives close by, but no one speaks to him. Nurmama has exiled another man from the family, Jim Balk, because he drinks whiskey.

It is Nurmama who decides who shall marry whom, who shall stay together, and who shall part. The feeling in the novel is that of a dream state. The child Tiny observes everyone around her and she is conscious of their psychic pain, but she feels helpless in the way that dreamers do when they try to call out but cannot make a sound. She knows that much of the pain comes from the failure of their hopes as they obey Nurmama. Or else, they get what they want but they must cross Nurmama to get it. Tiny is aware of the sadness that comes from their resulting isolation and guilt.

Tiny has noticed the way Cousin Ashley tries to be close to her mother at the dinner table and how he watches her. When Ashley does finally convince Lallah that he could make her and the two little girls happy, Nurmama tells Lallah that she will keep the girls if Lallah tries to leave with Ashley. Ruby, who hates Nurmama but hates even more the thought of her mother happy with Ashley, refuses to go with her mother if she leaves. Lallah resigns herself to a life with Nurmama.

Ashley stays, suffering, but needing to be near Lallah, if only to sit down with her at the family's supper table at the end of the day. When Lallah dies a few years later, Ashley leaves Nurmama's house forever.

Tiny reaches outside the family. She wants to be a friend to Stonewall Williams, a boy at school, the ragged son of a sharecropper. His grammar is poor, his clothes un-ironed (his mother has died and his overworked father is ill); the children call him "Rough-dried" and taunt him. Tiny is the only one who treats him kindly. He confides in Tiny, telling her that he wants to be a doctor. She brings him one of her dead father's medical books and tells him her great-great-grandfather Sage had built a cabin to serve as an office because he wanted someone in the family to be a doctor. She explains that Sage's dream never came true, for one reason or another; her own father died young while he was still studying. On the last day of school one year, Tiny waits to walk home with Stonewall and shares her lunch—all she has left, a dry biscuit and a pickle.

Stonewall's father dies and he is taken into the home of the town doctor, Wilkes. Tiny does not see Stonewall again for eight years.

During those years, Tiny edges toward resisting Nurmama. She encounters the exiled Granduncle (the one who shot a man) and finds him likable. She secretly goes against Nurmama's orders to the family members to have nothing to do with him. Tiny identifies with him— they are both discounted by the family. At the family dinner one Sunday, Tiny gets up courage and indirectly questions Nurmama's decision to exile Absalom, a black man, a mole catcher, who is Granduncle's best friend. Nurmama has had the uncles abduct Absalom and carry him a hundred miles away. She declared, "I wasn't going to have him keeping company with color. Not even if it gave him a stroke and ended him" (126). Tiny knows how much the loss has hurt Granduncle. Nurmama's sons and sons-in-law bring up the subject of Absalom and Granduncle, saying what Nurmama wants to hear:

> "Hush about Ab," Nurmama ordered. "Don't call his name anymore."
>
> "He was a good mole catcher," Tiny said musingly.
>
> There was a sudden silence around the table. Nurmama looked sharply at the girl. Aunt Ebb held the chicken breast suspended between her mouth and plate. Uncle Batt rested his fork on the mound of cabbage he had just served himself. Cousin Simper coughed. Uncle John

passed the platter of ham. Aunt Nan said, Well, tomorrow was Monday all day long. Auntie said Wash Day at her house. (140)

Tiny's challenge rocks them back on their heels, but it is Ruby who defies Nurmama consistently. As Tiny grows up, she adores her twin, Ruby, who shows no love for Tiny. In fact, Ruby disdains her and isolates her. Tiny always hopes that Ruby will share her secrets with her. She takes pleasure in Ruby's beauty, and she is in awe of the way Ruby gets what she wants.

Tiny does not know that Ruby can hardly wait to escape the country life and Nurmama's domination. The twins have inherited from their father two stands of timber. As soon as Ruby grows up, she sells her timber and uses the money to move to the city and finance a secretarial course.

Tiny stays with Nurmama. Grandfather dies, and the two women are alone in the house, except for Uncle John (whose wife has left him because she cannot tolerate his obsequious behavior toward his mother). One night Uncle John becomes ill, and when morning comes and he is no better, Nurmama sends for the doctor. Stonewall Williams arrives: he is now a man. And at this point he is finishing his medical training. Tiny is shocked to see him grown up. " 'It's you,' she said, the direct way there would be recognition in heaven" (149).

After taking care of Uncle John, Stonewall pauses to talk to Tiny. He demands to know, "When did you do all this growing?" She reminds him that her real name is Pearl. As he leaves, he tells her he will be in town the rest of June, "I might see you again." For Tiny "all living was suddenly related to that possibility" (152).

He does come back, and he calls her Pearl. He asks if she will go to the city like Ruby did. She says she will stay on the homestead, that the place and the farming life suit her. Even Stonewall admits that he is homesick for the look of this countryside.

When Stonewall keeps returning to see Uncle John, Nurmama begins to worry about the doctor's bill that is mounting. But Uncle John gets better, gets jolly even, and asks Stonewall to come to Sunday dinner.

That Sunday, when the children announce that Dr. Williams' car is in front of the house, Tiny runs to the door: "But at the porch she halted and was breathless one speechless instant before the miracle dressed in a blue suit and looking glad in her direction. Then she said come in and have a seat" (168).

At the end of the afternoon, he asks if she will wait for him. He will practice in the clinic in the city and learn what he needs to know and then he will come back to her and set up his office in Great-great-grandfather Sage's cabin. They kiss. For Tiny, "A great brightness dazzled her, and it might be Damascus Road or the lane toward home that she was in" (171). Tiny keeps all this secret from Nurmama and the others, even Ruby. She waits.

Uncle John and his brothers and sisters worry that Nurmama is aging and not in good health (although she will not admit either fact). They have a birthday party for her, to which all the extended family members come, except Ruby. In a rage at Ruby's disobedience after she had ordered her to be there, Nurmama has a stroke from which she does not recover.

After Nurmama's death, her daughters and sons divide the belongings, carry off the good furniture, clean out the pantries and smokehouse, take the chickens and livestock, and close the house. They tell Tiny she will live with each uncle or aunt for six months at a time. Tiny tries to do their bidding—she has always been obedient. She goes first to Uncle Todd's because his unhappy wife has been taken to an asylum. (They had married on Nurmama's order, but had never been lovers.) During the night, Tiny hears him trying to pry loose the lock on her bedroom door. At first light, she leaves and goes back home.

Coming back to the lonely house at break of day, she is scared that she, a small girl and crippled, will not be up to the challenge of making a life by herself. But despite her fears, she makes a beginning:

> The sun was just rising over the rim of creek woods as she reached the lane. She rested there a little while, filling her eyes with the vitality and strength of the old house, the Office, the orchards and fields, the little footpaths. Over the hill the smoke from Aunt Cherry's cabin rose into the morning, the bare tree branches looked like brown embroidery against the winter sky, and east looked solid east again.
>
> Tiny walked on to the house. There she opened the doors to empty the rooms of stale air. The emptiness inside was at first oppressive, and she cried in the bare corner where Nurmama's bed had been. But she had come home to stay, and so began to collect the furniture that had been left and to arrange the rooms to live in. . . .
>
> Tiny, realizing that she needed food, hurried to bring stovewood into the kitchen. But there was still no match. And there was no food anywhere, only a few empty coffee cans and fruit jars on the pantry shelves.

. . . But the crocks of preserves and pickle, the molds of yellow butter and pails of rich milk, the barrels of plenty were gone; there were only spider webs and dust in the dairy.

It was there in the desolation of dust and webs that Tiny resolved, no matter what kinfolks might say, she would make good living here again, would fill the dairy with crocks and jars and barrels of plenty, would be her own woman. (203–204)

All of the uncles and aunts warn her that she cannot live alone and demand that she give up her foolish ideas. She is wicked, they say, to defy them. Tiny, having found some turnips in the abandoned garden, is cooking them her first day at home when Uncle Batt and Aunt Ebb storm in.

"Come on live with folks," Uncle Batt told her; "give up this foolishness, Tiny."

"She's got to," Aunt Ebb snapped; "we're going to make her. Pack your suitcase, Tiny."

Tiny had one refrain: she was going to live here.

"It's not safe," Uncle Batt said.

"You can't live on collards and turnips," Aunt Ebb reminded Tiny. "You'll freeze this winter and starve. Go get in the car. You're going with us!"

Tiny did not speak or move, and her silence stumped them worse than her refrain.

Impatiently Aunt Ebb grabbed her arm, pulling her toward the door. "I live on Bunker Hill," she said, "and if one way won't do, another will!"

Tiny broke away so violently from her aunt's hold that Aunt Ebb all but slipped flat on the floor. "Go on home," Tiny said angrily. The instinct of hospitality was stronger in her than anger, and she added quickly, "Or—have a seat." (208)

Tiny goes to Aunt Cherry's to ask for something to eat. Just as she used to do when Tiny was a child, Aunt Cherry shares her fresh pork and cornbread. Tiny takes the food home, thinking that she will eat her first real meal in her own home and that will give her courage to think about what to do next. That evening Aunt Cherry brings quilts and the puppy Pal and makes a bed on the floor, saying, "I'll keep you company tonight. Miss Lallah's child ain't goin' to stay here by herself" (210). The two are so content in each other's company that they end up living together.

Eventually, the relatives break their promise to each other to starve Tiny out of the house, and they bring some food and firewood. Tiny and Aunt Cherry get the house in order, finding pieces of furniture left in the barn or attic, all broken items or those judged worthless by the aunts and uncles.

Tiny discovers that in the town market, flowers sell as well as butter and eggs. Bernice had learned this from her sister Rachel Floyd, who had as a very young girl spent her hoard of pennies to buy jonquil bulbs. Bill Kelly, in despair over his daughter's foolishness, had plowed them under. But his plowshare only divided the bulbs—they doubled and came up in early spring. From then on, the flowers brought a cash income in the town market.[4] So, in the novel, Tiny and Aunt Cherry plant jonquil bulbs.

In the spring Tiny makes a good profit selling her flowers—so much so that her aunts and cousins secretly start planting bulbs so they too will have flowers to sell. Tiny also figures out that although she cannot compete with farmers raising chickens and beef cattle for the local market, she can raise sheep. Townspeople want something different, she reasons, maybe lamb for a change. She begins to make money.

Ruby comes home to inform her sister that they are selling the homeplace, which they had inherited together from Nurmama. Tiny refuses. Ruby demands, then, that Tiny pay her for her share. Tiny sells the timber on her land, pays Ruby, and gives up her dream that Ruby will come back. She accepts the reality that Ruby will never live with her and be her friend.

Ruby says that she works at the clinic, where she has met "Stoney" Williams. She sends Tiny a letter saying that she is going to marry him. At first Tiny cannot take this in: "After a pause she fastened her eyes on the lines again. Those lines became black marks on a white page. The sense of the marks beat upon Tiny's brain like the heat bubbles over the field" (232).

Shocked and distraught, Tiny just manages to get through the days after receiving Ruby's letter. Vic, a local boy who had loved Ruby but given up on her, asks Tiny to marry him. Tiny remembers that Aunt Nan had told her it was well enough for a girl to marry *somebody*. And it was clear that Aunt Nan, who had lost her first love when Nurmama forbade the relationship, had settled for "somebody," Little Hardy, and was not unhappy. Tiny had even seen Aunt Nan in moments of happiness. But Tiny decides she will not settle for just some-body—she would rather live alone. She says no.

One morning, when the peach trees are in bloom, Tiny awakens to hear Aunt Cherry's singing as she sows seeds "in neat little woman hills." When she looks out, she sees Stonewall's car in the yard. In the little house Great-great-grandfather Sage had built to be his son's and grandsons' medical office, there is a sound of hammering and knock-ing. From her window, she can just make out the black letters on the white board: "Stonewall Williams, M.D." She runs out to ask him about Ruby and about Cousin Juanita (whom Ruby said she had beaten out of the competition for him).

> "Ruby, Juanita? I don't get 'em. There's two girls I don't get at all,"
> he had declared. "They're over my head. I think they need to eat more."
> (259)

Tiny realizes that Ruby, who had always managed to get what she wanted, had created a story and convinced herself it was real. Some-how, the boy Tiny had shared her biscuit and pickle with, to whom she had given her vote of confidence when she brought him the medical book, and who had become the man she loved, had returned to her. At the end, the dim, dreamlike mood of the novel changes to the bright, clear feeling of sunlight.

Harris's phrasing is always precisely right: her sensitivity to the nu-ances of words and her razor-sharp observation of behavior in this culture are revealed on every page of the novel. She deftly conveys in this novel with a few lines of dialogue and a brief descriptive phrase the essence of particular personalities and the kind of interaction they have. Here, Little Hardy, who wants to court Nan, has risen from the table to follow her outside, saying she might stumble in the dark. Nur-mama tells him to sit.

> Uncle Batt laughed out hearty and said, "Go on, Hardy. Nan does
> stumble in the dark, sure 'nough."
> Nudging him, Aunt Ebb told him to hush his foolishness.
> "If Ebb should die, I wouldn't let womenfolks stumble in the dark,"
> Uncle Batt went on. "Me, I'd say 'Peas' to some likely girl, and she'd say
> 'Cook'em,' too."
> Aunt Ebb, watching Nurmama's expression, fidgeted.
> "Think I wouldn't shake the bedsprings out of a third honeymoon!"
> "Batt!" Aunt Ebb exclaimed.

"You womenfolks always trying to quile somebody down!"
Grandpa just looked at Uncle Batt, and he quiled down. (68–69)

In *Sage Quarter*, Harris's handling of relationships is especially beautifully done—here is the mature writer, the masterful craftsman. Tiny's walk with Grandfather, the fishing trip for the old men Absalom and Granduncle, an evening picnic with Aunt Nan and Little Hardy—these sections are remarkable for the way Harris focuses on a most ordinary moment and expresses its magic.

When *Sage Quarter* was published in 1945, critics saw the novel as a presentation of a child's world. The *Boston Globe* reviewer wrote, "Bone clean of sentimental nonsense about childhood, the novel stands as an honest appraisal of the happiness and terror of childhood. . . . It's as fine a book as there has been this year."[5] Other critics praised its careful, honest reporting of a particular culture. The *New York Herald Tribune* review followed this line: "*Sage Quarter* has a freshness and convincing localism that gives individuality to its people and the stretch of North Carolina country by which their lives are bounded. Here is a South that has neither the gentility of white-pillared plantation houses nor the sordidness of Tobacco Road."[6]

The *New York Times Book Review* concluded about the novel: "The peculiar charm of this tale lies not in its story-book plot of Tiny's love for Stonewall Williams, but in the series of little plots—the everyday dramas that touch each member in his search for happiness."[7]

In fact, each everyday drama taught Tiny something, moved her towards resistance. Each detail about childhood established her as a person who could hold herself apart, could observe, even as she loved the people around her. And Stonewall's staying out of the picture allowed her to establish her autonomy and strong sense of self. Only on the most superficial level is this a storybook romance: the romance is a framework to present Tiny's evolution from obedient child to independent woman.

Sage Quarter is, at its very core, a vision quest, a search to know one's strength, a bildungsroman like many novels about men in Western literature—but in *Sage Quarter* the hero is a woman. In vision quests with man as hero, physical prowess advances the plot, but *Sage Quarter* has a theme similar to that in novels like *Jane Eyre*, in which the girl/woman encounters psychological challenges and grows in self-knowledge and self-determination. In their critical study of women's writings, especially *Jane Eyre*, Sandra Gilbert and Susan Gubar describe this female bildungsroman as a progression of challenges the protagonist faces and overcomes as she "struggles from the imprisonment of her childhood toward an almost unthinkable goal of mature freedom."[8]

The description aptly characterizes *Sage Quarter*. Because Tiny has been so observant, she knows what people gain from insisting on doing what they believe is best for them and what they lose when they just give up and conform. She is aware of what her mother loses when she acquiesces in Nurmama's insistence that she remain single and obedient to her. She knows that by obeying Nurmama's order to marry, Uncle Todd and his wife Pinkie have made themselves unhappy. She sees the childless Pinkie secretly putting other women's babies to her breast and knows before anybody else in the family that Pinkie is sinking into madness. On the other hand, she observes that Nurmama's daughter, Aunt Nan, marries a local farmer, Little Hardy, against her mother's order and nevertheless has some moments of happiness. And even Uncle John and his wife are happy when at last they are reunited, despite Nurmama's denying their existence.

At first obedient to her family after Nurmama's death, Tiny decides she cannot be at their command when she hears Uncle Todd trying to get into her bedroom. That is the dramatic event which turns her indecision about what to do into the realization that she can take better care of herself than she will be taken care of by anyone else, but she has been working up to this all along.

With each challenge that she faces, she gets a clearer picture of herself. To Nurmama, she was so small that she could be considered of lesser importance than the others; to Ruby she was just a pest to be ordered around; to all of the family, she was the "orphan." She does not know how she looks and so she cannot tell the reader—she just knows that her twin Ruby is offended whenever someone suggests they look alike. It is not until Stonewall remarks about Tiny's robin's-egg-blue eyes that the reader has any idea of her physical characteristics except for the weak leg. And only Stonewall notes that she has grown up. But her sense of herself grows as she recognizes herself in the one who finds a stick and kills a huge snake, who can figure out how to make a living and do it, and who can transform a deserted house into a comfortable home. Moreover, she is the one who can say no to her relatives when they order her to leave her house, no to Ruby when she says they will sell the homeplace, and no to a marriage proposal when such a marriage is not right for her. With each step, Tiny becomes more and more sure of her own ability to direct her destiny. Her self-concept changes from the little, obedient girl, the "faulty" one, to a strong, self-reliant woman.

Tiny chooses to differentiate herself from the significant women in her life: she is unlike Nurmama in that she does not want power over others; she is unlike her mother in that she resists others' attempts to have power over her. She rejects her grandmother and mother as role models—even as she loves them. Nor will she be subservient to her husband. When Stonewall comes back to nail his name to the office door, it is clear that he will have his area of expertise and she will have hers—the farm. She is an independent farmer and will remain one.

Once again treating the theme of autonomy versus connection, Harris arrives at a solution different from those in her previous novels. Nancy in *Portulaca* just gives up her integrity and acquiesces—she will live under Kirke's authority and play her role according to Bonwell's expectations of a town matron. Lan in *Sweet Beulah Land* refuses to give up his identity to conform to Alicia's concept of who he must be, but in so doing he loses Alicia. In *Sage Quarter*, Tiny stubbornly does what she needs to do for herself. She insists on her autonomy and risks losing connection with everyone; but in the end she keeps both autonomy and connection.

Even though *Sage Quarter* turned out to be her favorite of all her novels,[9] Harris had trouble finishing it. When John Woodburn, the Doubleday editor, came to visit, she gave him the unfinished manuscript, expressing some doubts about it. He was critical of the second half, which she was trying to bring to a successful conclusion. He commented:

> I am afraid I left you a little discouraged about the second half of the book. I hope not, because I am absolutely sure that it is going to be a fine book, your best, so far. I tell you, it has the indigenous flavor of the country in the way that *The Yearling* repeats the folk-ways of another place. The scene by the brook [Tiny and Grandfather], the little girl [Tiny] with her flower graves—the whole reflection of place and time and thought are absolutely first rate.[10]

Harris was also afraid that *Sage Quarter* suffered from "author intrusion"—presumably meaning that the reader is conscious that the author puts her own thoughts into the mouths of the characters. Vaughn Holoman read the novel as soon as it came out: she thought it the best yet. She said she was so caught up in the lives of the characters that Bernice Harris was not on scene at all.[11]

But Harris, sophisticated about writing, was naïve about the informal workings of the literary world, and her friends did not have the experience to advise her. John Woodburn, who had threatened to steal Mattie Ferguson away from Harris when he escaped New York and bought a house on the Richmond Pike, was himself stolen away by Harcourt, Brace and Company at the end of 1942. He explained that it had happened suddenly, that he was going from "desk to desk":

> I want you to know how very much I have enjoyed working with you. I have worked with some two score authors in my editorial career, and I can truthfully say that none have been more cooperative, more amiable under suggestions, more pleasant intellectual companions. I shall miss you very much. Your contractual status with Doubleday "freezes" you, as the Government would say, for the time being, but with your permission I would like to discuss your future with Harcourt, Brace.[12]

He even made a trip to Seaboard to try to convince her; he was sure that Harris would follow him.[13] She did not.

She did have a contract with Doubleday, and Doubleday had published every novel she had sent so far. But something else might have been going on in her mind: at the time she was trying to decide whether to publish *Portulaca* with Doubleday rather than the University of North Carolina Press, Woodburn had said that she would have to make substantial changes in the novel to satisfy William Couch. Woodburn said that Couch had told him that he had to think about how the novel could be made palatable to a southern readership. Harris checked back over Couch's letters to her. He had questioned her about Nancy's defense of *Tobacco Road*. He had objected to Nancy's going to the hotel room with her New York editor, saying that this would have to be changed. (Wisely, she refused to follow his suggestions.) But Couch denied Woodburn's charge: in his letter to Harris on 6 November 1940, Couch says he may not have made himself clear to Woodburn: "We do not usually hesitate about publishing any book because it might not be palatable to Southern People."[14] Since that time, she had had reservations about Woodburn. It was a misunderstanding between Woodburn and Couch, but one which greatly affected her career. Her decision in 1942 not to follow Woodburn was pivotal, but she did not know that. She lost a sensitive editor and a powerful champion in the literary world.

Harris's new editor at Doubleday, Clara Claasen, did not have as much power at Doubleday or in the literary world as Woodburn had. She was nonemotive, but Harris could depend on her to be forthright, and so at least Harris had a good working relationship with an editor. With Claasen, it was a business relationship, but even Claasen relented a little one Christmas, and thanking Harris for the poinsettia she had sent, wrote, "You have a quality that is very rare." She added, "It has been a pleasure to know you all these years."[15]

Bernice concentrated on her writing and on the life immediately around her. While she was working on *Sage Quarter*, she was very much involved in Seaboard's response to the Second World War— possibly the writing gave her some relief from war concerns. As she had done earlier in her life, she gave herself a respite from worry by creating a different world in imagination. But while she snatched hours to write, Bernice also spent hours taking courses in first-aid and home nursing. Regularly she sat at a government desk, issuing ration and gasoline books. Once a week, she spent an afternoon in the Red Cross sewing room, "where lengths of printed and plain materials were cut into sad, ugly garments": "Sometimes we mused over the stitches and pressed wrinkles out of garments, breathing wordless prayers that the bully nightgowns and waists and skirts might get to the Russian women. With one accord we all sewed for the Russians that first year, for the besieged of Stalingrad who had our admiration and sympathy."[16]

Like all her fellow citizens in Seaboard, she grabbed the papers each day. The headlines about the increased fighting in the Solomons, the battle of Guadalcanal, the sinking of United States ships were frightening. She hoped for a report that casualties had been light, but realized these words were "agonizingly ironic." She knew, "Each casualty, every loss of life, had destroyed a world."[17]

Identification of aircraft was a crucial part of national defense in places near the coast. Seaboard was close enough to the ocean to make airplane-spotting necessary, and everybody volunteered to spot planes. The observation post was manned in three-hour shifts over the twenty-four-hour period each day. Bernice said the volunteers were "farmers who had to be up at dawn to see to the harvesting of cotton and peanuts, bankers whose heads had to be clear for the next day's figures, schoolteachers who had to ring bells at eight-thirty mornings, housewives, preachers, storekeepers, office workers."[18] Reports were telephoned to a defense center in Norfolk, Virginia.

So, Bernice went to the training sessions and learned to identify "dihedral, swept-back wings, raked tailplanes and fuselage blisters." She spotted aircraft with her friend Josephine Parker. They could call in a report such as: "Long thin wings, swept-back to tapered, four motors, nacelles extending through leading edge, oval-shaped fin and rudder, transparent nose, rectangular tailplane." Herbert, whose hearing loss had worsened but who had excellent vision, spotted planes with a neighbor who was nearsighted but had excellent hearing. Both Bernice and Herbert received Certificates of Honorable Service from the Army Air Forces on May 29, 1944.[19]

After the war, she realized she had not used half of her ration stamps—"Maybe that is a certificate of a sort too," she said. All during the war they were eating the products of their labor in a gigantic Victory Garden. And Bernice decided on her own to raise chickens so that she and Herbert would not deplete the homefront's supply of eggs and chickens. She ordered twenty-five chicks from Sears, Roebuck and Company. When Herbert saw them, he blew up. There were no building materials to be bought anywhere. But finally, he took the garage doors down to build a shelter for the biddies and found enough garden wire to make a small enclosure for them. Gradually, his anger subsided and he concentrated on feed and water for them and medicine when he thought they might need it. He started standing by the fence to "watch their cunning ways." Then Bernice observed that he would "go inside the enclosure and sit with the biddies, pet them."[20]

But biddies grow up to be fryers. Herbert told Melissie to kill one of the pets, "Big Un," for Thanksgiving—William Olive and his family were coming. When the platter of fried Big Un reached the table, Bernice burst into tears. Herbert tried to eat a drumstick with relish, but Bernice saw the look in his eyes that suggested he felt awful. William Olive, Mary, Gordon, and Alice Jo did not know whether to eat out of politeness or apologize for being "the occasion of the slaughter."[21]

Bernice and Herbert lost all taste for chicken. Finally a weasel destroyed all their chickens but two. Herbert asked Melissie to take the two home and keep them for egg-laying, but all three realized these chickens could not live forever. Bernice told Melissie, "Go ahead and do what has to be done. But never let us know."[22]

Bernice tried to find time in the war years to do her writing and her war work and also to keep up a correspondence with friends overseas. Dick Walser, now a navy lieutenant on a ship in the Pacific, wrote,

> My Dear Mrs. Harris:
> I've put your beautiful little letter among those few I allow myself to keep during this nomadic life I'm leading. I read it over and over again, and you were so clearly before me.[23]

When *Sweet Beulah Land* was published in February 1943, there were many letters of congratulations. She especially treasured praise from her mentors J. O. Bailey[24] and Frederick Koch.[25] She was thrilled to get letters from men overseas who had managed to get her books. She had a copy of *Sweet Beulah Land* sent to Walser, who replied, "*Sweet Beulah Land* survived the twelve thousand miles and reached me several days ago. Oh, how I love it! How I enjoyed every line of it. And most of all, how close it made me feel to the North Carolina you and I love so much. I'm personally grateful to you for writing it, even if it did make me homesick."[26]

Sometimes the books went to the bottom of the ocean. But the copy of *Sweet Beulah Land* she sent across the Atlantic to a journalist, George Butler, now a technical sergeant in a bomber group in England, reached him. He wrote to her that his copy was getting "dog-eared so many GIs are reading it."[27]

The generally positive reception of *Sweet Beulah Land* cheered Bernice, but she still worried about Herbert's health. And Herbert also worried about his high blood pressure so much that even he relented occasionally and took a break from work. A neighbor, Reece Bullock, the little boy next door whom Bernice had taught in school, had grown up and married another of her students, Elizabeth "Lib" Bottoms, now a schoolteacher herself. Reece and Lib came one Sunday to take Bernice and Herbert for a ride to the coast. They dressed up like they were going to church, even wore hats, although they planned a picnic on the beach. When Lib announced that she was going into the water, Bernice pulled her dress up above her knees, and still wearing her hat, waded in also. When she saw Herbert roll up his pant legs to wade in the waves, she could not stop laughing.[28] And sometimes Bernice and Herbert would manage to get enough gasoline to go to the beach for a few days' rest—they had never taken vacations before in their nearly twenty years of married life.

For Bernice, in 1942 and 1943, life was agreeable: she was having some good times with Herbert, enjoying close friends, receiving positive reviews of *Sweet Beulah Land*, and working on *Sage Quarter*. She also sold a story, "Yellow Color Suit," to *Colliers Magazine*—it was a feat to break in there, because *Colliers* had a nearly closed group of favorite short story writers. Mass-circulation magazines paid well, up to $2,000 for a story. As she did when she received the check from the *Saturday Evening Post* for "Bantie Woman," she said about the check from *Colliers*, "It sort of sealed our partnership."[29] But as earlier, that was more a wish than a reality.

In spite of good things happening to her, Bernice was losing creative energy as she finished *Sage Quarter*.[30] Times when she had no interest in anything, when she felt "flat," had begun to occur two years earlier, but now these bouts were more frequent and lasted longer than before. She had, with *Sage Quarter*, worked out one answer to the question so important to her about whether a woman can have both autonomy and connection—Tiny has both. Writing the novel had given Harris much pleasure and she was reluctant to end it. With its end, she had to face what was happening to her emotionally.

10

Against the Grain: *Janey Jeems*

Although *Sage Quarter* was in final form early in the fall of 1943, it was not until 1945 that Doubleday published it. Just as she finished the novel, Bernice increasingly experienced feelings of depression. She felt that she could not write. She became so depressed finally that death began to occupy her thoughts. She wrote to Vaughn Holoman:

> Vaughn, my dear: I have just taken a teaspoonful for "weakness and nervousness" and will add a page to you. So much of the time lately I have been under normal and terribly depressed. I'm fighting, though, and this morning I enlisted Dr. Parker in the conflict. Well, we're middle-aged but once. Recently in a mood I told Herbert to save what I had written and give it to you if it should remain unfinished: you would know what to do with it.[1]

The teaspoonfuls of bootleg whiskey she was taking each day helped only for a little while and not much even then. She was placed in a hospital in Norfolk for treatment. The actual medical diagnosis is not available, but she named depression to Vaughn. And she also hinted that this was just a crisis of middle age, such as women ending menopause were expected to have—she was fifty-two. Although that was the conventional wisdom at the time, research results at the end of the century indicate that depression in middle-aged women is not necessarily caused by hormonal changes. Emotional distress figures prominently in theories of causation, as does hereditary predisposition.[2]

Few people, even those close to Bernice, knew anything about what was happening to her. In southern families at the time, you could talk about physical ailments, but you could not admit to psychological problems. Such an admission would jeopardize the family's standing in the community: it was like a confession of a weak strain in the moral life of the family. Consequently, the generations in Bernice's family living now do not know or cannot talk about these troubles.[3]

What treatment was given to Bernice Harris is not known. Was it the standard treatment of the time, electroconvulsive therapy? Patients would be taken to a special room in the hospital, where they would be strapped to a table and administered electric charges. The patients shook violently, as with a convulsion. Short-term memory loss would result, but psychiatrists thought this was a good effect because the obliteration of memories caused by the shock treatment would include the thoughts that had made the patients agitated.

After her hospitalization, at home again, Bernice wrote to Vaughn, making it clear that to her the worst part of the hospital was "That Room." She put "Hospital" in parentheses beside it so there would be no mistaking her meaning:

> Whenever I think of you across not so many—how many!—miles I am lifted in spirit. You are so steadfast and sure and—there. If I need you in an emergency I know you are there, and it gives me strength and assurance. Almost I could ask you to go with me to the door of That Room. (Hospital) I probably shall not, but it will be a comfort to know that I could. With returning strength I think I'm gaining courage. I am not sure.[4]

She did regain courage, and she did it by immersing herself in her writing. As long as she was writing, she could see her troubling thoughts expressed in a safe context, or else escape them. She told her biographer Dick Walser that once she was so far down she did not think she could ever come back, but that at the end of that siege of depression, she began the novel *Janey Jeems*.[5] It is interesting that while *Sage Quarter* and *Janey Jeems* are both stories of mature, happy love, *Sage Quarter* presents the story of a woman who achieves independence; but *Janey Jeems* is the story of a woman who stays happy in a marriage where she is the dependent, obedient wife. It is the latter theme that Bernice Harris turned to now and which she wrote as she came out of the depression.

In *Janey Jeems* she put herself into the mind and emotions of a black woman, her heroine. She drew from her relationships with the black women she had known in childhood as tenants on her father's farm in Wake County, visited in cabins with the Northampton County home-demonstration agent, interviewed for the Federal Writers' Project, and worked with in her kitchen in Seaboard.

In *Sage Quarter*, Aunt Cherry was modeled on the real Aunt Cherry, who had been a tenant on Harris's father's farm. Now *Janey Jeems* gave Harris the chance to portray another woman very much on her mind: the main character Janey was inspired by a farming woman, Lucy Ivory, whom Harris had interviewed for the Federal Writers' Project. Although Mrs. Ivory had little education, Harris described her as "genteel." Often Harris found her narrators lovable, but she felt particularly drawn to Lucy Ivory.[6] In the novel, the character Janey's practical sense and loving ways, as well as her stubbornness and jealousy, are characteristic of the persona projected in Lucy Ivory's narration. She told Harris that when she married her husband, she really went to work:

> He had bought a little place on credit, and I aimed to help pay the debts off. "I didn't marry you to set down on you," I told Honey soon as we was married. "Let's put our heads together and study up how to make a living and get something ahead."
>
> While he was doing public work off from home to help pay for this place, I worked in the field and the brick hole. I stood in mud knee-deep making bricks, dipping my molds in the ground clay, and then laying them on the table to be burnt. When I wasn't at the brick hole, I used to grub all day and into the night clearing up land for us to farm on. Honey would come home from public work and see what all I had done and say to me, "Pig, it won't do for you to work like this." But I wanted Honey to come home and stay, bless his heart.[7]

Harris was touched by Lucy Ivory's strong love for her husband and by the way they had made themselves a team.

She was also impressed by Lucy Ivory's wisdom and sense of humor. Ivory related the story of how her husband had forgotten he was supposed to meet her at a certain place. When he came home and saw her, he realized that he was at fault. She said, "Then I saw in his face that he remembered his unremembrance. You know what that fool man done? He scolded me for doing exactly what he told me to."[8]

She knew his faults but loved him still: "I love his bones in the grave," she declared.[9]

Lucy Ivory and her husband did get clear title to their land and bought two more farms as well. Bernice wanted to understand what land meant to them and to contrast that with what land meant to the Harris family. She suspected they were not the same meanings. She thought about how much it meant to Herbert to keep the land purchased by his English ancestor Michael Harris in the eighteenth century. But unlike the Harrises, Lucy Ivory wanted to pass the land down to children—she was not accumulating wealth to have power over others. When Bernice plotted the novel, she was clear what the land would mean to Janey and Jeems: "The desire of Janey and Jeems was not to be for land per se, but rather for the continuity it symbolized. . . . Title deeds were their means of passing on the composite beauty and mystery and aspiration of humanity."[10]

Tank Valentine Daughtry, another African American woman, one of her favorite narrators in the Federal Writers' Project and the model for characters in several of Harris's novels, sang the song that was the inspiration for the lonely character Valentine: "I'll build me a eyrie / in the mountains so high. / Where the wild birds will see me / as they pass by."[11]

The plot of *Janey Jeems* is simple: it is a life history of Janey West, farmer. Janey's life story begins about 1870 and ends in the early 1940s. As an orphan, not yet fifteen, Janey feels attracted to a farmer, James West, who lives near the family she works for. He has worked overtime at public work and saved and managed to make a down payment on some land. Janey likes to follow his footsteps in the field, putting seeds in the ground he has prepared. When the family that had let Janey live with them and work for them loses their sharecropping agreement, they have to move on. They tell Jeems to marry her and take her into his house because there is no place else for her to go.

Janey's marriage to Jeems becomes a love match for both, a passionate, sexual relationship and a solid friendship despite their occasional differences. Janey gives birth to ten children, and she and Jeems take in three orphans. Her aspirations for her children are not realized—they have their own aspirations. And the hard work and vexations they bring she voices in a prayer that is a question: "Lord, did you ever have a family?"[12] Janey and Jeems build a community when they get a one-room schoolhouse started, and they even achieve their dream, the erection of a church with a white steeple.

Against Janey's conventional life as a married farming woman is juxtaposed the nonconventional life of the solitary woman Valentine. Again, Harris explores the issue of autonomy versus connection, for Valentine is the antithesis of Janey: Valentine is not connected to anybody. She is defined by the community as strange, and she learns to act the part. As a woman living alone, she is seen by the other women as a threat. They totally reject and isolate her. There is no one's kitchen that she can walk into; there is no woman's door she can knock on to ask for help. Even the daughter she gives birth to does not call her mother. Indeed, Valentine names her child Bird, from the song she sings to the baby about wild birds (quoted above).

In old age, Valentine is a crazy woman who tries to lure boys into her cabin. She wears a red hood like the dead ancestor from whom she inherited her land. The neighbors are aware from time to time of a red-hooded figure moving stealthily through their lives, watching them, but they think it is a ghost. She is that much outside of their world.

It is hard not to have compassion for Valentine, this underdog the community punishes because she is alone and autonomous. Her condition makes more convincing Janey's need to live the life of a woman connected to family and community.

Near the beginning of the novel, there is a reference to slave ancestors. At the end of the novel, when Janey and Jeems are old and Jeems is dying, the doctor tells Janey that he has done as much as he can for "Uncle Jeems." "Auntie," he says, "he needs treatments I can't give him."[13] This is the first direct indication that the main character is an African American woman and that all these people are black, except for the white doctor. It is an eloquent and convincing argument for relegating skin color to the level of importance of eye color or size of hands or shape of ears because readers have already identified with Janey in all the aspects of living that matter.

Harris does not deny the importance of culture, but there is no condescension here and no idealization. Farming life in this African American community is seen as abundant of self-sacrifice and of noble deeds as well as destructive behavior, of struggles and failures, and of both aesthetic pleasures and the drudgery of constant hard work.

A few critics understood that *Janey Jeems* was a history of a black family, but many critics missed the point—they thought she was writing about a poor white family in Appalachia. At first Harris was disappointed. "Then," she said, "I realized that I had made my point after all. Janey and Jeems were human beings, whose universality made locale and color essentially unimportant."[14]

In novels by African American authors, the black heroine was often portrayed as a light-skinned person; a present-day scholar, Vashti Lewis, argues that in this way the writer produced a heroine with whom the predominantly white readership for novels could more readily identify.[15] And often the light-skinned heroine would have a sad life. In Ann Petry's novel *The Street* (1946), a naturalistic treatment of a single black mother trying to raise a child in a city, the heroine has long, straight hair and brown skin. Her destiny is tragic.[16] On the other hand, Janie, the black heroine of Zora Neale Hurston's *Their Eyes Were Watching God*, published in 1937, is a mulatto—her white ancestry is described early in the novel—but she is not a tragic figure.[17] She meets challenges and experiences loss, but she grows to mature womanhood as a directive, strong person. (There is no evidence in Harris's letters or writings that she had read Hurston's novel; it is probable that similarity in the heroines' names is coincidental.) Like Hurston, Harris presents a way of life in an African American community which has both its joys and its tragedies. Like Hurston's Janie, Harris's heroine is not tragic—she is successful in ways that she chooses. But Harris's approach is different: there is nothing of white ancestry in her heroine's background. Harris expected the reader to identify with Janey on the basis of shared experience.

Although this is an exploration of life in a rural African American community and nearly all the characters are black, the presence of the white world outside is felt. Ovid Pierce, reviewer for the *Dallas Times-Herald*, noted that all around this community is "the wall of the white man's world." He wrote, "White people do not enter the story, but their governance and authority is as strong as if they stood upon every page."[18] It is to the white man's world that Janey must go to earn extra money making bricks; it is to the white man's world that Jeems must go to work in the lumber industry to make the money to build his house. Both feel safer when they can return to their own community. But the threat of the "Law," the white man's power to judge and punish, is always there.

The novel is naturalistic in style, but it has another dimension as well. Pierce's review of *Janey Jeems* was titled "Dark Mixture of Religion, Superstition."[19] Indeed, it is on one level a ghost story. Harris dedicated the novel to her professor at the University of North Carolina, Frederick Koch. And in this novel, she does what Koch inspired his students to do: look closely at the lives of people around you, at the ways they interpret experience, at the language they use to convey their meaning-making.

Harris did not discount her Federal Writers' Project narrators' interpretations of the impingement of something mysterious in their lives. In childhood, Harris knew stories of haunted houses, and in one of these houses she was convinced that she herself had heard ghost steps. And she had seen an apparition.

In the Federal Writers' Project interviews, she had listened to stories of people having visions, of having witches ride them, of being put under spells, and of encountering ghosts. A common belief was that if a person had been born just before dawn or just before dusk, she could see things others could not. One narrator, Mrs. Dugger, explained her daughter's visions: "Folks born between lights can see things."[20]

Someone could put a spell on another person, could "conjure" him. This belief in conjuration was an important component in African American folklore.[21] Tank Valentine Daughtry told Harris that when she had reported to the church an improper advance by a lay preacher (a "jack-leg preacher"), his mother-in-law was angry with her and tried to put a spell on her. The woman put something magical in Tank Daughtry's snuff, but she protected herself:

> Soon as we got to the bridge, Mr. Jenkins told me to throw the whole thing in the branch. If you throw conjure in runnin' water it won't hurt you, but will trick the one that tried to harm you. . . .
>
> I'm tellin' you, honey, it wa'n't long 'fore that woman went away from here! They's other ways o' conjurin' besides puttin' it in your somethin' t'eat and drink. Some puts roots and one thing or 'nother in the path for you to walk over. Don't ever let nobody ever get your hair combin's; they can kill you with them.[22]

A preacher told Harris that people who sell their souls to the Devil can get the power to put evil spells on other folks: "Now white folks is not as easy to conjure as the colored; they have a hole in every hair in their head; so the trick can work out through the holes. But colored folks's hair is in a kink, and the trick can't work out till it's took off."[23]

In addition to discussions about conjuring, narrators often told stories of people returning from the dead. In many of these stories, the deceased has a mission. Mrs. Daughtry described the way John Jenkins, her first and most-loved husband, came back after death to visit her. She had folded his clothes after he died and put them away with his shoes and hat. Although her "feet was on the ground," she would not use his shoes. He appeared one night and told her, "Honey, go on wear my shoes. And give my clothes and hat to somebody that can wear'em. I shan't need'em no more."[24]

Narrators told Harris stories about a haunted house and a ghost with a mission, a common story in both European and African American folklore.[25] They talked about glimpses of ghosts; these spirits seem to be restlessly roaming rather than purposeful. Mrs. Dugger said she had heard a woman with high-heel slippers walk through her door. And she would hear at night a straw broom go *sweep-sweep, sweep-sweep,* but she could see nothing.[26] Another narrator described an encounter:

> And the dead come back; I've seen one. One night near dus' dark, when we child'en was comin' from the field, singin' on our way home, a woman suddenly appeared out of the side woods and walked along the edge of the woods near the road. She had a shawl over her head, and her arms was folded over her chest. We knowed her; she was one of Mama's friends that hadn't been dead long. She went through the briars near the woods without makin' a sound and followed us almost home; then she disappeared.[27]

In addition to belief in ghosts, a common notion was that if a person felt strange or behaved in a strange way, witches were riding him. Mrs. Dugger described for Harris the way her daughter Hattie Belle would lie "in a quare fix" some nights. Hattie Belle said, "It's de witches ridin' me." Her mother said that her blood slowed down in circulation after her automobile accident and that was the reason for her spells. Hattie Belle persisted, "How come I gets all right soon as I puts a fork under my pillow?"[28]

It seemed right to Harris that she would use magic, spells, and contact with the other world in this novel of rural life, as she had done earlier in *Purslane*. She gave prominence to folk beliefs about the supernatural in *Janey Jeems* because she understood their importance in the community she was writing about: they were the way people explained some of their experiences. With all of their Christian beliefs, they felt that some things were just not covered.

The plot of *Janey Jeems* incorporates a curse. When Valentine came to the neighborhood, her purpose was to claim land fallen to her by inheritance. The land had belonged first to a white master, who left a portion of his estate to his slave, Cat Brown, Valentine's ancestor. Cat Brown built a grave house to shelter her coffin and declared she would curse anyone who tried to live on the land within a period of ninety-nine years after her death.

Jeems forbade his family to give any credence to such a superstition, and Janey tried to honor his wishes. But her adopted daughter Delzora (whom Janey calls Zora, for short) went too near the Cat Brown place and began having spells and seeing visions. Or was it epileptic seizures? Valentine was dogged by ill luck in love and became quite mad at the end because she had defied Cat Brown, who had ordered her heirs to stay away from the house. Or was Valentine's madness due to the isolation that the community imposed on her? She started wearing Cat Brown's red hood and sneaking soundlessly around the community; she seemed to be in touch with spirits. Indeed, she was like the apparition the narrator described above as being a silent ghost with shawl over her head and arms folded over her chest. Or was she just playing the role assigned her by the community as an evil, quasi-supernatural, powerful being? Janey's adopted daughter Swannie in a frenzy embraced a pine tree. Was a witch riding her, or was it the need to experience her body as it had changed in adolescence? Janey felt the presence of the dead Nellie when the ghost was not pleased with the way Janey was taking care of her children. Or was it Janey's conscience making itself felt?

Two of the churchwomen have had animosity between them; Fairy asks Idonia to dip snuff with her, but Idonia, suspecting this is a conjuring, refuses. Later, Idonia thought her own snuff box contained more snuff than it had previously, and so she threw the whole box into running water. Next day she felt fine—to Fairy's consternation. Or did she convince herself that her observations were real?

Still, Delzora's visions did come true. And Valentine did seem to have some kind of power. Especially, Janey feared that Valentine drew Jeems to her as if by magic. These dark mysteries were present in Janey's mind as she went about her normal, daily tasks.

And evil slid along in the shadows beside lighted innocence. Janey's beloved first-born son, Davy, fell in love with Bird, Valentine's daughter. Jeems, at Janey's insistence, forbade Davy to see Bird. The two young people contrived to meet in the only place they could be alone—Cat Brown's grave house. They sat on the wooden coffins to talk and kiss. The last evening before Davy was to return to college, a storm arose, and Janey would not let Davy leave the house. He had to return to college without seeing Bird. Bird had forbidden him to write to her, and so he had no news of her. When summer came and he returned, he found that Bird had died of pneumonia. In a quarrel with Valentine in her cabin, he struck her. (Apparently, Valentine wanted him to marry *her*.) Believing he had killed Valentine, he ran away and remained a fugitive for fourteen years. The heartbroken Janey heard nothing from him. Extensive contact with Cat Brown's remains had fated Bird and him for tragedy, it seemed.

The story is told appropriately in a simple, unpretentious style. The dialect is rendered just to the degree that the reader hears it; the rhythm of the speech is maintained even in the narration. Some expressions are at first difficult for the modern reader, such as food being referred to as "t'eat." But there is a ring of authenticity. Nash Burger, reviewer for the *New York Times Book Review*, concluded, "Perhaps no writer has caught the idiom of rural Carolina more exactly than Mrs. Harris."[29] More precisely, this is like the speech of the African American culture in the northeastern border counties of North Carolina—as Harris wanted her readers to hear it, but it is not an exact rendition.

And in this novel as in her earlier ones, Harris is characteristically master of the vivid, succinct descriptive phrase. The reviewer for the Quincy (Massachusetts) *Patriot Ledger* remarked, "What better way to characterize a mean woman than to say, 'She is so grudge-hearted,' or to speak of a fine man as 'on the exact balance'?" When Janey walks on the land to which she and Jeems have title, she walks "stiff-starch proud."[30]

Never explicitly describing sexual intimacy, Harris still presented sexual desire in a vivid way. On the way to Rising Star for her baptism, Janey thought about the past few nights:

> On the wagon seat by her husband Janey held herself away from the touch of his arm against hers. Before daybreak she was be-bound she'd lean toward him and crush her side against his arm and go through that rush of need that his nearness always brought. Before the sun should come up she would savor that need and know his want of her.

All night whenever she had moved near him he had withdrawn from her touch. Once when she had whispered in the stillness, without pride, he had said, "You're going to be baptized today, Pig."

"I'm me, just same," she had said.

"Not quite." And he had denied her.

He had denied himself these last nights. Janey knew he had punished. She glanced toward the east, still dark except for starlight.

She breathed deep of the starry morning. It was all a sweetness in her nostrils—the smell of plowed ground and of dew on young crops and woods flowers, of the stable warmth of Jeanette and of starched clothes and Sunday-go-to-meeting worsted. Living was a thing to do; she was sorry for the dead they passed at Shepherd Oldfield, for they had only gone to heaven and she was on her way with her husband to Rising Star.[31]

To be with him was better than heaven. The terms used to describe sexual desire and the anticipation of sexual connection are juxtaposed against words for the journey to a place called Rising Star and baptism—a new life. One experience intensifies the excitement of the other.

When Janey longed for a white tablecloth for her table or for her son to be a minister, her aspirations were characteristic of any rural poor woman. In fact, Janey was a most conventional woman—like Bernice Harris. She married a man and followed his lead. She worked by her husband's side as his partner—as Bernice also wanted to do. She supported the church, as Bernice did; faith was necessary for her sense of well-being. Janey had differences of opinion with her husband and questioned his pronouncements without openly challenging him. Harris referred to Janey as "wise," and she wrote once after Herbert had criticized her, "Like her [Janey], too, I felt oddly cherished when he ranted most."[32] Janey is more like Dele in *Purslane* than like the aristocratic Alicia in *Sweet Beulah Land* or the urban, middle-class Nancy of *Portulaca* or the independent Tiny in *Sage Quarter*.

Janey's opposite, the wild, autonomous Valentine, comes to a sad end; the reader could take this as a moral that it is bad for a woman to be unconventional. *Janey Jeems* might be derided by the modern critic for setting up a dichotomy between the defiant and the conventional, yet Janey is the farming woman Harris knew well early in the century. And Valentine's type—a wild, unpaired woman—was suspected at the time. There is historical accuracy in the portraits. Diane LeBow, a present-day critic, analyzed heroines in the novels of selected black and white American women. She looked for a female protagonist who chooses nontraditional rather than the expected female roles, who grows in her sense of herself and survives.[33] Harris's heroine, Janey West, follows the traditional female role but grows stronger in her power to master life's challenges. Janey lives to an old age, content with her world and herself.

It was not the sympathetic portrayal of a conventional woman that drew down criticism upon Harris's head, however, but her choosing as the heroine a black woman. Although near the end of her life Harris threw away most of the negative letters she had received, enough remain to give an indication of the chiding tone. Many readers did not understand her intention and thought she had played a trick on them by not emphasizing skin color. She would have to reply over and over again, "I deleted all reference to color and race, not with any wish to mystify or deceive readers, but rather to point up the essential oneness in the human experience, in happiness and tragedy and in love and hate."[34]

Later, in the 1950s, when she was at a North Carolina Writers Conference, she was criticized for writing *Janey Jeems* probably because her heroine had both black skin and true nobility. Harris wrote a brief account of the incident: "Twice when I was a panelist certain objections were voiced by a college professor and an established writer (Inglis Fletcher) because of my obvious liberalism regarding racism." Two people followed her outside one meeting and continued to hound her.[35]

Janey Jeems is a strong argument against racism. And the date of its publication—1946—makes it remarkable in literary history. It is clear that Harris intended the novel to be provocative. It is consistent with her way of being soft-spoken and conventional in her public behavior but exploring in her writing basic problems in society. In this novel she uses all her skill as a novelist to inspire readers to feel as well as know intellectually the effects of race prejudice inside themselves.

Another southern writer, Lillian Smith, had published her novel *Strange Fruit* in 1944. It was a story of an interracial love affair.[36] Smith's aim was similar to Harris's: Smith said she hoped that her book would "arouse their [readers'] imagination so that they will think of our people, white and colored, as human beings, not as 'problems.' "[37] Smith's biographer, Anne Loveland, thinks that Smith intended her work to be a psychological preparation for moving toward a more just society, toward desegregation.[38] Probably that was Harris's aim as well, up to a point. But while Smith was clear and public in her advocacy of desegregation, Harris was more concerned about clearing away injustices she had witnessed—such as giving a one-legged man a job digging ditches because he was black. Harris would confront her own fear of rapid change, of the social and cultural integration of races, in the late 1950s and early 1960s. Only then would she question and discard the "separate but equal" belief she had learned as a child.

Earlier, in the twenties and thirties, another white woman, Julia Peterkin, also identified closely with the African Americans she wrote about in novels. Her book *Scarlet Sister Mary*, which won a Pulitzer Prize in 1929,[39] is like *Janey Jeems* in that both stories have as a main character an African American farming woman. Situations were different: Peterkin's characters were workers on a South Carolina plantation; Harris's were yeoman farmers living on individual small farms in North Carolina, near the Virginia border. But both authors wrote from a position of friendship and admiration for the black women who were the models for their books; their intention was to help the reading public understand these lives. However, the perspectives on the black woman and her relationship to her community are entirely different. Peterkin's Mary is an independent woman, free of sexual restraints, and defiant of her community. Peterkin's biographer, Susan Millar Williams, believes that Mary is a projection of the free spirit Julia Peterkin wanted to be (and was, to some extent).[40] Janey is the projection of an author with a different personality: Janey is a conventional woman, subordinate wife, and community-dependent person such as Harris knew herself to be—the kind of woman Harris believed could endure.

Janey Jeems presents an era Harris knew well growing up; undoubtedly writing about it gave her comfort. She liked thinking about this lifestyle, in which "there was no sharp line between living and making a living." This would change irrevocably for Jeems's and Janey's children. But for all times, Harris's pleasure in Janey and Jeems is revealed. In a talk about the book, in which she defended her choice of heroine and hero, Harris said, "They're really fine people whom I love and respect as much as any that it has been my privilege to present."[41]

11

Community Denied: *Hearthstones*

In early 1945, Bernice Harris was hard at work on the novel that would become *Hearthstones*. And, as always, she was thoroughly immersed in Seaboard life—teaching Sunday school, entertaining ministers, serving on church committees, working for the Woman's Missionary Society, singing alto in the choir, going to social events such as bridge parties and wedding and baby showers, and speaking to various clubs about her novels and the craft of writing.

Bernice had many personal friends both in Seaboard and around the state. Just on her block in Seaboard, there were very close friends, such as Edith Bradley and her sister-in-law, a young mother, Maria Bradley, and Elizabeth Smith Bullock, an elderly widow confined to a wheelchair, whom Bernice visited every day.

Josephine "Jo" Parker, Bernice's partner in spotting airplanes during the war, often drove Bernice to speaking engagements. She was the wife of the local doctor, John Wesley Parker, and both were close friends of Bernice.

Parker had come to practice medicine in Seaboard in 1928. He soon had a thriving practice—so much so that it was rare for either doctor or doctor's wife to get a full night's sleep. When his patients could not pay for prescriptions, he paid for them at the local druggist's. When they could not pay his fees in cash, they paid Parker in goods, such as chickens or eggs or potatoes, and sometimes the doctor just jotted fees

down and left it up to the patient to pay if he ever could. John Wesley
Parker played Santa Claus at Christmas, pallbearer at funerals, wit-
ness to death-bed wills, consultant in marital disputes, and go-between
in loan agreements.[1] For twenty years, he was chairman of the county
board of education, and he often consulted Bernice about decisions
concerning education.

Jo Parker liked to go places and enjoyed social occasions. She was
an attractive woman, petite, with a round figure. Outgoing and self-
confident, she had a lively personality. Her driving jaunts with Bernice
possibly gave her an identity which was separate from that of wife of
busy country doctor. Often a thank-you letter from a woman's club
after Bernice had been the main speaker mentioned how much the
members had enjoyed Bernice's and Jo's company.

Herbert's second cousin Elizabeth Harris was also a good friend at
this time (they became very close friends in the 1950s). Elizabeth had
been a schoolteacher but had come back to Seaboard to work in her
father's bank, eventually becoming executive vice-president. She was
more than twenty years younger than Bernice, independent-minded
and adventurous. Her chief love was international travel, but she also
enjoyed driving Bernice around the state, especially to cultural events.
Often Bernice received an invitation saying, "Can you and Elizabeth
come?"

Sometimes Bernice took the train to Raleigh to visit her family and
to attend meetings of The Strugglers. Occasionally William Olive
and Mary, with Alice Jo and Gordon, came to visit her for a weekend,
and they always came at Thanksgiving. Bernice would serve ham
(sliced paper thin), Brunswick stew, turkey, exquisitely seasoned
greens and potatoes, her garden's butterbeans she had canned, and
several kinds of pies and cakes. Next day, the family, with Bernice,
would go to Richmond to shop. When they returned to Seaboard at
the end of the day, they always dumped all the packages on the bed so
that everybody could see what choices had been made and could talk
about the treasures.[2] Bernice reveled in these family activities. Herbert,
with his hearing difficulty, talked as best he could with William Olive
about crops and the cotton gin business. Gordon and Alice Jo knew he
did not enjoy children but felt they could depend on him to be kindly,
if distant.[3]

Older children and adolescents came to "Miss Kelly" for help with
homework. Grown-ups came with difficult letters they needed help

writing. And she still wrote obituaries, church news, and accounts of weddings for the papers. She kept up a stream of letters to correspondents—family members, friends from the past, groups wanting her to speak, and fans. And she somehow found precious hours to work on her novels.

But it was to Vaughn Holoman that Bernice wrote thoughts she dared not confide to anyone else—including what she really thought about the church activities she was so much involved in, how she reflected on what preachers were saying. Sometimes, she revealed how much she felt like rebelling, as in this letter to Vaughn:

> Dr. Kincheloe is preaching, and he . . . gives instances after instances of his winning hardened sinners during his revivals. He told of a community to-night [sic] that would not let any of its citizens go to hell. There's an idea. We were requested to turn and shake hands with those sitting to our rear. I was on the back seat, but I was somebody's rear. The handshaking was as spontaneous as Mr. Trueblood's: "Let us now pray the Lord's prayer . . . All right." (Left-right, left-right) I wish you could attend one service and study Mr. Trueblood's face. You wouldn't believe me. I like that community that refused to let anybody in it go to hell. Just for pure stomp-down cussedness, I'd show 'em—[4]

The Reverend Mr. Trueblood is the one who, when Bernice offered to bake pies for a church function, remarked that a sacrificial offering would be better.[5] It was snide of him, but he knew she liked to cook and also that Herbert was reluctant to let go of actual money.

And Herbert was a Methodist—he did not go to the Baptist church with Bernice. In her church, Bernice was not part of a couple as much as she was an individual. Her opinions were listened to; there was some talk of making her a deacon even though at the time women deacons were exceedingly rare.

But it would seem that sometimes the compulsion to believe whatever the preacher said aroused her ire; and her own habit of observing her fellow humans, including the preacher, did not bring reassurance that all was well. Yet judging others was something she was not comfortable doing. In later years, a letter from a former pastor of the church in Seaboard, E. S. Morgan, testifies to her support of those struggling with her to lead the "good life": "Your genuine Christian character, your culture, your refinement, and your wisdom will remain with me as long as I live. Your encouragement while I was your pastor cannot be forgotten."[6]

She believed in the Baptist church as a positive force in general—an institution so much a part of her way of life since she opened her eyes in this world that to be out of the church would have been unthinkable. But she was never sectarian: she gladly worked on the history of the local Methodist church; she quoted Jewish writers in her Sunday school class.

She wrote plays (no longer extant) dramatizing biblical characters and their struggles. But from occasional references to the plays, it seems that it was the human stories in the Bible that caught her attention and engaged her imagination.

Poet and critic John Crowe Ransom thought his contemporaries used religion for its ritual, which is a stabilizer, a rock in a confused society, rather than for its doctrines.[7] Indeed, ritual was important to Harris: she enjoyed the services that marked the seasons. But she believed in specific doctrine, and beyond that she seems to have had a deeply felt conviction that there is an order in the universe, an all-knowing God compassionate toward humans. With this, her Christian belief system was in concordance. This and her childhood upbringing provided the code of ethics that ruled her way of being in the world. It is indicative of her emotional attachment to this belief system that "Faith of Our Fathers" was her favorite hymn: "Faith of our fathers, living still in spite of dungeon, fire and sword . . . Faith of our mothers, we will love both friend and foe in all our strife and preach thee, too, as love knows how, by saving word and faithful life."

She did not allow herself to be sidetracked by doctrinal controversy. Nor was she given to public display or to public pronouncements about the power of faith in her life or to insinuating even in private letters that she had a special connection to God—religiosity was not something she would indulge in. When her close friend Elizabeth Harris was asked why Bernice rarely talked about her religious beliefs, she replied, "She lived them."[8]

She felt expansive sometimes, and in one letter she wrote to Vaughn Holoman, she asked, "Will you come along to New York and Cuba with me? I do need to get out more, to read more, to study. Will I ever?"[9] She had been invited by a national artists' association, the Pen and Brush Club, headquartered in New York, to become a member and to speak to them. The organization kept writing to ask when she would come to New York.

However, Bernice did not get to travel far: she worried about Herbert's health, and also she had no experience of traveling alone. She became even more caught up in the life of her town. She and Elizabeth Harris revived the Woman's Club in Seaboard—it had been started earlier and had been chartered and affiliated with the national organization. According to the rules, anybody at all could join; you had only to ask a club member to put your name on the list and the membership would vote you in because they needed all the help they could get. They worked: they had various fund-raising events and used the money to buy needed equipment for the school or town. Elizabeth was president. She said Bernice did not have to be a leader, did not especially want to be, but she liked to work and to be involved. Elizabeth added that Bernice never did sloppy work of any kind.[10]

In the midst of all these social relationships, this feeling of being so much a part of a community, Harris was writing a novel testing what it would be like to live without community. She was thoroughly engrossed in it. Her neighbor Maria Bradley said that when Miss Kelly was writing a novel, she would be so much involved that she would address anybody talking to her by the name of the main character whose head she was in at the moment. Bradley herself had been called Janey while Harris was writing *Janey Jeems*.[11]

Hearthstones, the new novel, is a strange one. Its evolution from the short story "Yellow Color Suit"[12] to novel is easy to trace: unlike the short story, however, the novel extends back to the Civil War era and brings in the romantic love relationships in the generations. However, the gist of meaning is the same in short story and novel.

It is, on one level, an assertion of the human costs of war: it is a woman's reaction to war. And indeed by the spring of 1945 when she began the novel, she was heartily sick of deaths in war. She turned her attention to the Civil War—a war very much present in her childhood when she sat at table with her Grandfather Poole and listened to him talk about his experiences fighting as a Confederate soldier.

In adulthood, she had serious questions about that war. In searching church records from the period of the Civil War, she found a petition from a man who had been expelled from the church for refusing to fight and now wanted to be reinstated—"23 April 1864, John H. Renfro expelled for sin of desertion of the Southern Confederacy."[13] The church members refused to reinstate him, which meant that he and his family were cut off from human society. In her novel Harris recreates this event and explores what expulsion from society could mean to a family. And so on another level, *Hearthstones* is an exploration of the effects of isolation from community.

Her concern with loss of life in the war she was living through, her rebelliousness against forced conformity, the information about the hardships of the Civil War she had held in her mind since childhood, the questions she had about that war and all wars—all infuse the plot of the novel *Hearthstones*.[14] The story begins with the little girl Henrietta Day listening to her mother call her deserter father, "You want to come out, Caje?" Her father comes out of his hiding place during the day only to eat. At night in the moonlight he tends the crops. Henrietta, who has been taught not to lie, observes her mother lying when neighbors ask her where her soldier husband is. The world becomes a strange place for Henrietta.

When neighbors come to invite her mother, Lalla, to move over to their house because they believe her husband is away fighting in the Confederate army, Henrietta knows to keep silent. Then the mistress of the nearby plantation Seven Hearths, Camilla Allison, whose husband has been killed in the war, arrives at Lalla's house. She demands that Lalla bring her children with her and come every day to the plantation to spin and knit for the soldiers. Lalla protests but knows she must go, lest the people in the countryside around think that she is not with them in the war and suspect that her husband has deserted. In fact, like her husband, Lalla is not in favor of slavery, and because she sees the war as a defense of slavery, she cannot be in favor of it either.

At Seven Hearths, while her mother works in the sewing room, Henrietta and the other children are ordered about and drilled by Camilla's young son, Freddy. Henrietta alone stays in the strenuous game with him. He is pleased with this little playmate and even promises to let her ride his pony. Tiring of the games they know, he wants a new game. And Henrietta, afraid he will tire of her also and not play with her anymore, tells him to hide and she will call him three times, "Do you want to come out?" Freddy's grandfather hears her and guesses that her father has been hiding. He sends a posse to round up the deserter, but Caje manages to escape to a cave on deserted Urahaw Island—a wilderness he owns. Lalla is turned away from the sewing room. When Freddy brings his pony to Henrietta's cabin to let her ride, Lalla orders him to leave. Henrietta does not see him again for years.

After the war is over, Camilla takes her son and daughter, Carrell,

to her family in South Carolina. Lalla persuades Caje to apply to the
church for reinstatement of membership because she fears that total
isolation from the community will be bad for the children. His request
is turned down, and the family lives on its own from then on: the only
contact with the outside world is Caje's annual trip to town to sell cotton and buy needed goods at the store.

Lalla gives birth to more children, hoping they will provide company for one another; of these births, only three girls survive—Lollie,
Eveline, and Ailey. Henrietta and her three sisters know that something their father did caused their isolation, and bits and pieces of conversation bring them to the knowledge that he was a deserter. Caje
Day becomes a strange man, silent and withdrawn—they don't like
being around him. Their mother seems tired and often ill. The girls
know that they can depend only on each other, and so they grow up
learning to be self-sufficient farmers and to be content with the company of sisters.

When her father becomes ill, Henrietta, a teenager now, goes each
day to the deserted Urahaw Island to tend to the animals stabled there
and to clear land. Thinking herself alone as always, she is shocked to
hear a bullet whiz past and see her father's pig fall. A man comes riding from the woods—it is Freddy. They recognize each other immediately. He offers to replace the pig he has shot and to help her with
clearing the land for the next crop. She shares with him the lunch her
mother has packed for her.

Freddy comes every day from then on—he seems not to be able to
stay away from her. Henrietta is excited and confused, but alive in a
way she has never been before. One day when he does not come to
their tryst, she thinks he will still come another time. When she takes
produce to the store, she learns that Freddy's family has left again. She
is emotionally devastated and at the same time becomes physically ill
and for several days runs an extremely high temperature. From the
time of this loss of Freddy in her teen years, she is not consistently
lucid. Sometimes she seems like a child to her family.

The Day family moves to the island, and the three sisters with Henrietta continue to farm after the deaths of their parents. Lollie is the director, the one who says when they will harrow, when they will plant,
and even what tasks each will do on a daily basis. She is the one who
takes their crops to the store once a year, by mule and cart. Eveline
plays her mother's role, thinking up new recipes to try out to provide

the family with little surprises. Henrietta obeys Lollie as best she can, but sometimes her mind wanders to the past. Ailey, the youngest, balks at Lollie's bossiness. She is deeply offended by the way Lollie intrudes into her life, even demanding that she show menstrual stains to prove that she has "nature" when she is supposed to. Ailey does not want anyone to touch her. She tries to run away, but Lollie catches her and destroys the bridge that connects the island with civilization. From then on, the creek can be forded only when the rains have been scarce.

The sisters grow old; Henrietta reaches eighty, and her sisters, their seventies. Ailey, well past menopause, still bloodies cloths and leaves them for Lollie to see. If anyone comes on the island, Lollie gets the shotgun out.

The sisters know that the country is fighting World War II: Ailey learns that news when she has to drive the mule cart through the creek and on to the store to get medicine for the ailing Henrietta. Ailey contrives to go back to the store many times because the store owner gives her things to read, such as testimonies to the efficacy of tonics. She reads these revelations out loud, and the sisters become interested in the women who tell of their lives in the tonic advertisements. The sisters study the pictures. They worry about these far-off women: will they stay well?

One day Ailey comes into the house to show her sisters that the cow has little milk left. Other strange things happen. Lollie had gotten Caje Day's boots and clothes out and put them on the line to air, thinking she would wear the boots and Eveline could make garments for her sisters from his clothes. The garments disappear from the line. The sisters begin to think some creature is living on the island, and they are very much troubled. One night, they hear a knock on the door. They refuse to open it, but at dawn Henrietta goes out and finds a young man in her father's clothes lying on the porch. She notices that he has yellow hair like Freddy's. He is obviously ill. Henrietta makes the decision to take him into the house; and the sisters, amazed that Henrietta can make any decision, go along with it. They reason that the man is so sick and weak he cannot do them any harm.

He tells them his name is Billy and that he has run away from the army. The sisters decide they will nurse him back to health so that he can go back to his army. Billy is touched by their concern for him—he has no family and no one has cared for him before. He begins to love the four strange old women, especially the whimsical, childlike Henrietta.

Camilla Allison's daughter, Carrell, now an old woman, returns to Seven Hearths, bringing her granddaughter with her. Allison, the granddaughter, is a sophisticated young woman; she knows the family has no money left and that she will have to make a living. Her father was killed in World War I; her mother has died. Her great-uncle Freddy has been killed in a fracas. She resolves that somehow she will manage to keep her grandmother comfortable at the homeplace, Seven Hearths. She gets a job keeping the books at the nearby army commissary. And she longs for the boy she had met—a baseball player, tall and yellow-haired—who had gone away without explanation and never contacted her again.

Allison learns to spot airplanes for the army, and she decides that she will do even more for the war effort: she will organize the women who cannot come to the Red Cross sewing room to knit in their homes for the soldiers. She learns that there are four sisters on Urahaw Island who not only sew their own clothes but make the cloth itself. She resolves to enlist their services for the country. When she drives through the creek and over a narrow dirt road to reach the old house, she is startled to find sitting on the porch the man who has been so much on her mind.

Billy is equally startled to see Allison. They are both troubled by this chance meeting. Allison leaves the yarn and patterns for the sisters to knit sweaters for soldiers. At first, the sisters are dismayed when they learn that someone else has come to the island, but they want to do something for the soldiers, and so they begin to knit.

Allison returns and tries to see Billy. He is reluctant to encourage the relationship: he tells her he is nobody, just a deserter, a man who has not been able to stick to anything. Allison, however, persists in her determination to have time with him.

Meanwhile, he gets well enough to help the sisters do farmwork, and finally he decides he will go back to the army. The sisters are heartbroken when he leaves, but they support him in his decision. On an unconscious level they feel redeemed: by sending their loved one to the army, they pay back society for their father's desertion. They build a bridge to the mainland so that he will have an easier time returning to them, and they live for his letters to them.

The army punishes Billy for desertion by putting him in jail, but after serving his jail term and probation, he is reinstated. When he gets leave, he returns to the Day sisters. At the last meeting with Allison, he says that he will have to prove himself to be worthy of her before they can ever be together.

Billy goes overseas. When the war is over, he returns to Urahaw Island and takes up the farmwork for the Day sisters. They tell him they have made him their heir. Although he works determinedly during the hard, long days, the sisters sense that he is sad. They wonder if they are doing something wrong. Henrietta says it's boy-girl trouble, that she knows what that is.

Henrietta thinks that because of his connection with them—the daughters of a deserter—Allison has turned away from him. She knows what kind of pain the loss of a love brings, and so she walks the miles to Seven Hearths to make things right for him. When the maid finally lets her in, Henrietta finds that Allison is not at home. Consequently, she identifies herself to Carrell, telling her that she is the daughter of the deserter Caje Day. She insists that Billy is not kin to them, that he has no connection, that he will not live with them again. Carrell is enraged that a daughter of a deserter would enter her house and orders Henrietta out.

Henrietta thinks that she must let Billy go away so that he will be able to win Allison. Somehow, she will protect him from the terrible pain that the loss of Freddy had caused her. When Henrietta gets back to the island, she tells Billy to leave. He is dumbfounded. Angrily, he throws the hoe down and stalks back to the house to get his clothes. He starts down the dirt road that leads away from the island. The sisters are horrified.

But he stops at the bridge and thinks over what he is doing—quitting again. He wants to prove to himself, to the sisters, and to Allison, that he is not a quitter. He wants to be a part of the family of sisters. He thinks about the car he has dreamed of buying so that he could take them for a ride:

> In the ditch, among the peanut shocks, over the shrubs, he had been so full of chuckling delight at the prospect of driving those women round different parts of the country, seeing sights they wouldn't believe except they saw, buying them ice cream and Coca-Colas and maybe pretty dresses with lace collars, piping water from the spring to save them steps, cleaning up the grave-yard, maybe putting a stone over Caje Day. . . .

> He had thought of the girl too. But more he had thought of the Days.
> Standing on the bridge, the last link with the island, he thought back over his twenty-eight years and realized that whatever first class was in him now he owed to the Day sisters. He had been a spender, a quitter, a deserter. . . . The stout, solid bridge, crude and old as patterns of bridges went, was a symbol of those old unflagging women. The trees cut down and dressed and notched, the heavy logs rolled into place under their scarred old hands. (272)

He walks back to the island. He sees Lollie first. "William," she blurts out, "stay." And he says, "On any terms, I'll stay." She says there are no terms. The story ends with a redemption for all: the Day sisters have reached out to someone outside themselves, have recognized the need of connection to others; the deserter has realized his aim of staying with a task and of knowing the love for others that makes the task easier.

Caje Day's daughters had left his grave unmarked. In fact, Henrietta spoke for each sister when she said she would not be buried in the family plot with him, but by the end of the novel, she has changed her mind. Loving the deserter Billy, the sisters begin to think better of their father. A man could have understandable reasons for deserting, they realize. When Henrietta goes to Seven Hearths to declare to Carrell, "I am Caje Day's, the deserter's, daughter," she owns her father before the world.

Hearthstones is not so much a justification of desertion as a demand for understanding. The novel is Harris's plea for compassion for those who think and feel differently from the community. And at the same time, it is a testimony about the importance of community in an individual's life.

Contemporary critics did not see the novel as a protest against war—and indeed, it is more a lamentation than a protest; but neither did the critics note the strong plea for compassion for those who have their reasons to turn away from war. Certainly it is not a glorification of the Civil War: Caje and Lalla Day cannot support a war whose victory would continue slavery. Nor is there a brave hero who comes back to a postwar world that is in rapid change and is experiencing a decline of old values—a theme often found in novels about the Civil War.[15] This is indeed a different kind of Civil War novel: the heroic actions are undertaken by four old women, and in their isolation, they maintain their world unchanged.

The Day sisters, like Lan in *Sweet Beulah Land* and Tiny in *Sage Quarter*, can make a life by themselves. They can remain unconnected to community. For decades of the sisters' lives, they are entirely self-sufficient. In their world of women, they can do all the tasks necessary to survive. They can know the joy of the seasons and the beauty of the natural world; they can know the satisfactions of the beauty they themselves create. And yet, having Billy to love as their own family makes the difference: being connected to the community outside themselves—a community of which he is a representative—gives a dimension to their existence they had not glimpsed.

And Harris's conviction that women and men need each other is nowhere more convincingly stated than in this passage near the end of *Hearthstones*, when the sisters feel lonely for the soldier Billy after he has gone back to the army when his furlough has ended:

> For a fundamental need of their own had been met. Their womanliness had become a stunted, deformed thing that made them queer not only as women but as human beings. Henny had been their appeal toward tenderness, though her affliction was so old and tiresome that protectiveness toward her had become mechanical without feeling in it.
>
> They had all been too much of a piece, too unpitted against specific outside relationships to be aware of tenderness for one another much more than for inanimate things on their parcel of earth. The maternal had scarcely been challenged. Stirred at all, it had twisted into strange and morbid channels. In Lollie it had become matriarchal despotism, rarely relieved except within the province of boss. In Eveline it had hovered near bovine, placid contentment to supply pap, to rid herself of its fullness; even the surprises, so dreamed about and elaborately accomplished, were artificial stimulation, not of need except her own. In Ailey it had become a crazed, desperate thing, inarticulate and animal, that fought itself and kept her a battleground. In Henny it was always just under a mist, beyond which she remained child.
>
> William had released the maternal in each woman from its thwarted, devious course, and their response toward his need and helplessness had given them an aware tenderness for one another. Even Henny had become more motherly than childish at last, advising and prompting sisters all younger than herself. (255–256)

And so, Harris expressed in *Hearthstones* her belief in the necessity of community to be fully human and the necessity of both genders to be together so that each can fully develop as individuals. *Hearthstones* is not about men and women as mates, however, but about community of men and women of different ages. It is community, Harris implies, which enables us to play different roles and experience different kinds of emotional bonds.

For Bernice Kelly Harris, involvement in community was necessary and immensely satisfying and she has her main characters experience this. In *Portulaca*, Nancy puts her place in the community above her own integrity. In *Sweet Beulah Land*, as he leaves his store and cabin, Lan declares he will come back and reclaim his place in the community. Harris contrasted her own involvement in her community with the isolation of the four women in *Hearthstones*. And yet Harris compelled her readers to see that the community must recognize and tolerate differences. She expresses in this novel a variation on the theme of individual freedom versus connection which she had explored in other novels. Consistently she asserted the need for connection to another and to a community, but she also insisted that the community cannot override individual conscience.

The community is not a monolithic entity in her mind, however. Harris is always aware of class antagonism as well as fears and injustices based on racial differences. In *Hearthstones*, as in earlier novels, she exposes class structure in a rural setting. It's obvious that her sympathies were not with the slave-owning rich, such as Camilla Allison represents, but with the yeoman farmer, Caje Day.

When *Hearthstones* was published in 1948, Nash Burger in his review in the *New York Times Book Review* pointed out the juxtaposition of social class in *Hearthstones*: "It is a conflict that, as here represented, brings to a head an underlying antagonism between two ways of life: of the small farmer who works his own land and of the plantation-owner whose land is worked by slaves." Burger thought the "complications of plot take precedence over the rich store of setting and character." However, he praised the novel: "The agrarian, workaday world of the small farmer Caje Day, his wife and children; the slow movement of the seasons with the resultant variations in jobs to do and pleasures to be enjoyed; the relations of the self-reliant, yeoman Day family with the slave-owning Allisons of nearby Seven Hearths plantation—these things, as Mrs. Harris can project them, contain sufficient elements of struggle, suspense and accomplishment to hold any reader."[16]

Generally, critics reviewed *Hearthstones* favorably. The review in the *New York Herald Tribune Weekly Book Review*, titled "Not His War," also stated that the novel "holds the reader's attention through the last chapter." It's a work "off the beaten track," the reviewer said, but entertaining.[17]

Margarette Smethurst reviewed the novel for the Raleigh *News and Observer*, concentrating on Lalla's plight: "Lalla, learning in her youth that there are worse ways to lose a man one loves than through death; Lalla, shielding her deserter and weaving for the Confederacy, Lalla frozen in the hope that Caje has sensed the shame, too, and has voluntarily returned to the Army; Lalla, hot with dispair [*sic*] in the fear that he has left his hiding place in the smoke house for the safer haven of Urahaw Island, is real and fine and good in the dignity of genuineness and piety."[18] She found the four old women no less real in "their superhuman efforts to push out the thought of their family's shame." But she thought the people at Seven Hearths were less believable. However, Smethurst concluded, "Nowhere . . . has the stigma of desertion been made more real, the blight more devastatingly complete."[19]

Harris finished *Hearthstones* in 1946; the Second World War was over—ration books, airplane spotting, even desertion, were fading from people's memories. She began working on her seventh and last published novel, *Wild Cherry Tree Road*, once again returning to the world of her childhood, bringing before her the characters who had made such lasting impressions on her and affirming the values she had learned from them. She may have sensed on a deep level that all her strength from this formative period of her life would soon be needed.

Photograph taken for publicity on the occasion of the
publication of Harris's first novel, *Purslane*, in 1939.
She is forty-eight.
*Courtesy North Carolina Collection, University of North
Carolina Library at Chapel Hill*

Herbert Harris. The date of the photograph is unknown.

Courtesy Alice Jo Kelley Burrows

Bernice Kelly Harris's house in Seaboard, North Carolina. Photograph taken by Richard Walser in 1953. The porte-cochère she nicked while driving Herbert's car is on the other side of the house, away from the camera's angle.

Courtesy Southern Historical Collection, CB#3926, Wilson Library, University of North Carolina Library at Chapel Hill

The Seaboard Baptist Church
Courtesy Gordon Kelley

Bernice Kelly Harris at her typewriter in the front upstairs bedroom of the Harris house in Seaboard—she always referred to
this space as "my corner." The picture was made by her friend
Bernadette Hoyle in the mid-1950s when Bernice was in her
early sixties.
Courtesy Southern Historical Collection, CB#3926, Wilson Library,
University of North Carolina at Chapel Hill

Richard Walser in 1953. This was about the time
he went to Seaboard to spend a week interviewing
Bernice Harris for the biography published in 1955.
*Courtesy North Carolina Collection, University of North
Carolina at Chapel Hill*

Mary Sullivan Kelley. Photograph
made in the early 1960s.
Courtesy Alice Jo Kelley Burrows

William Olive Kelley. Photograph
made in the early 1960s.
Courtesy Alice Jo Kelley Burrows

Left to right: Mebane Burgwyn, Virginia Harding, Bernice Kelly Harris, Thad Stem. Bernice was in her late seventies; here she proudly poses with her student Virginia Harding who had just published a novel, *The White Trumpet.*
Courtesy Alice Jo Kelley Burrows

12

The Troubled Late 1940s

On Christmas Eve in 1946, Bernice was in the kitchen most of the day, working with Melissa Lowery. She answered the doorbell several times—someone soliciting for a widow whose store had been burned in the general fire in Seaboard the day before, a war veteran asking her to subscribe to *Collier's Magazine*, a friend bringing holly, a neighbor who wanted her to type a letter of recommendation for a job. Bernice obliged each caller.[1]

She helped Melissa finish icing a chocolate cake for her own Christmas dinner. Bernice spread her best lace tablecloth on the dining room table. Melissa's headache got worse, and Bernice went upstairs to get aspirin for her. They finished the Christmas cooking.[2]

Just after Melissa left to get her house ready for Christmas, Bernice saw their friend, Reece Bullock, drive Herbert's car to the house. Herbert was sitting in the front seat.

Reece called out to her, "He's not feeling at all well. He thinks he's had a stroke." Reece pushed her aside and carried Herbert into the house and laid him on the davenport. Bernice dashed upstairs to get the nitroglycerin to put under his tongue as Dr. Parker had instructed her.[3]

Herbert was trying to talk. "I knew I was going into the ditch but there was nothing I could do about it."

Bernice told him to lie still and went to call Dr. Parker. Meanwhile,

Reece drove off to get Melissa, who was in the woods searching for a Christmas tree.

Dr. Parker came over right away. He listened to Herbert explain, "You know the first thing I thought of when I came to myself? My father died fifteen years ago tonight."

The doctor motioned Bernice to step a little to one side with him. "It won't show up completely until morning, Miss Kelly, but I think it's a cerebral hemorrhage, just like President Roosevelt had down at Warm Springs, remember? This is just the beginning." Bernice closed her ears to the rest. When she saw Melissa through the window, she slipped away and went out to her. "Our arms were around each other. I felt stronger already with Melissa in the house."[4]

Later Dr. Parker came back with two strong men to help him carry Herbert to his bed upstairs. Tonight he had to rest. Worried friends stopped by. A neighbor, Edith Bradley, offered to stay the night, but Bernice declined, sensing there would be nights to come when she would need to accept this offer. Covered with a blanket, she sat in the chair beside Herbert's bed. Melissa Lowery lay down on the sofa in the study in the next room. Bernice waited, feeling like death was everywhere. Even the street outside seemed a place where people died, not lived.[5]

Christmas morning in the house, there was no opening of packages. Bernice heard someone talking downstairs. It was Melissa praying in the kitchen, "I was asking the good Lord to give us strength to do all we can and then for Him to take hold where we leave off." That Christmas day was a day of nitroglycerin, sedatives, and fruit juices, but also of a "steady stream" of gifts and expressions of support from neighbors.

A surprise awaited, however. The furnace quit. Melissa stood by, nervous but loyal, begging Bernice not to fool with electric gadgets like the starter. Both feared it would blow up, but Bernice had to start it. Sometimes in the next three weeks Bernice could get it to run for a few hours at a time. Friends came in and tinkered with it. Finally, however, Bernice just tried to keep Herbert's room warm with a space heater.[6]

Herbert got a little better. He started looking better than Bernice, in fact, who was worried and tired. Even his blood pressure went down. But then the big stroke came, as Dr. Parker had predicted. In early 1947, Herbert was paralyzed on one side. He did not want to see the doctor; he refused to have a nurse. Melissa helped Bernice take care of

him, and at times he railed at Melissa. But he gradually improved.
Some days, he even managed to walk downtown.

One day, he went out to supervise the grass cutting and stayed in
the hot sun. His blood pressure soared, but Bernice convinced him to
lie still for three days afterwards and the crisis passed.[7]

When he began to get better, she returned to answering letters from
correspondents. Letters about *Janey Jeems* abounded. Some scolded
her for not being clear about the race of the characters. She answered
all letters. She wrote to her friends with the wry wit she always had. A
journalist George Butler remarked in a letter to her, "Your letters are
a delight. . . . Your savory language makes me hesitant to pen my pro-
saic replies."[8]

She had hoped Herbert would get back to being himself and she
could travel a little. She and Vaughn Holoman had a dream of driving
over to Chapel Hill to visit J. O. Bailey.[9] She even thought of going to
New York when Herbert recovered.

From time to time, Herbert's brother Jethro would stay with Herbert, and Bernice could go to dinner at Warren Place, the plantation of
Gilbert and Grace Stephenson. Vaughn's daughter and son-in-law,
Mebane and John Burgwyn, would be there, and the talk would be
about cultural developments as well as crops in eastern North Carolina. Gilbert Stephenson, a retired banker, had returned to Warren
Place, where he had been born. He had written seventeen books on
banking and finance and now was devoting his time to memoirs and
community affairs. Grace Stephenson was also a church and community leader.

In 1947, Gilbert Stephenson organized a conference of area writers,
artists, musicians, and patrons of the arts. They named themselves
"the Roanoke-Chowan Group" and decided to meet annually during
summer. Times with the Stephensons and these summer meetings of
people in the Roanoke-Chowan area who loved the arts were bright
moments for Bernice.

In the summer of 1947 Herbert was feeling better. Reece Bullock
and his wife Lib often came by after supper on Sunday evenings to
take Herbert and Bernice for a ride.[10]

For Bernice, even in the midst of caring for Herbert and hoping for
time to write, that summer brought its own tasks that would not be
delayed. By September, she complained to J. O. Bailey that she wanted
to work on her next novel but that she was "shackled" by revival

meetings at church and canning the garden produce. She said she was determined to "shed this domesticity" or the book "would not materialize." He replied, "I've an idea that the book was really 'materializing,' where materialization counts, in your mind, during the revival and the canning routine."[11]

In 1948, Herbert had another stroke. Sometimes, in letters to close friends, Bernice confided her loss of hope. Her friend Charlotte Hilton Green, a nature writer for the *News and Observer*, answered, "I know as well how you feel when you write about watching a mind deteriorate, reasoning power worsen steadily."[12]

In an odd hour now and then, when Herbert was sleeping and the house was quiet, she wrote. The novel she had been working on before Herbert's first stroke, *Wild Cherry Tree Road*, was going slowly but was a great source of contentment. And Richard Walser had just published his collection of short stories by North Carolina writers, which included her story "Bantie Woman."[13] He wrote that the *Durham Herald* had singled out her story for praise and quoted the review: "Mrs. Harris' 'Bantie Woman' is as tender as it is knowing. I think this story is a reminder that we Tar Heels have not afforded Mrs. Harris the credit she deserves."[14]

But it was not easy to find even a small block of time to write; there were only scattered periods, and even these were not without the threat of interruption. She confessed to Mebane Burgwyn, "During the intervals I have, I have been trying to get some work underway. It is difficult to coordinate mood with the bits of time available."[15] Later, she told William Olive and Mary, "My editor writes this morning, wanting me to get to work on the next novel." She added hopefully, "I worked on a story last week. It's one more for the collection I am accumulating. I'll probably work them into something sometime."[16]

But 1948 was a year too full of sorrow to write much. Vaughn Holoman became ill. Her daughter Mebane thanked Bernice for writing to her, "Your letter came last week and I did appreciate so much the beauty and sincerity of your sympathetic understanding."[17] Vaughn rallied, wrote to Bernice, and then had another bout with illness. In March 1948, Mebane sent news that her mother had been desperately ill for four weeks. She enclosed a card her mother had written to Bernice—one of her last attempts at writing. "I thought you'd like to know," Mebane said, "that she thinks and speaks of you quite often, and that her friendship with you is one of the lovely things in her life."[18]

Bernice's sister Rachel Floyd became extremely ill early in the year. Bernice was very close to this sister who had been widowed early in her life, when her son Carey, the oldest child, was only fourteen. Rachel Floyd had continued to farm with the children's help and was so respected in the community that she became a deaconess in the Baptist church (a rare occurrence at the time). Bernice managed to get to Durham to visit Rachel Floyd one last time in Duke University Hospital, shortly before she died at the end of February. Bernice attended the funeral, but afterwards broke down completely.

Herbert's illness, Vaughn's illness, and now her sister's death were too much. In apologizing to Mebane for not writing, she described the state she was in: "I had a nervous collapse or something. Anyway, for three weeks I have been unable to do anything at all and had to stay in bed to rest and take vitamins, shots and sedatives. The year had been too heavy—Herbert, then Vaughn, then my sister. And of course too much steady work."[19]

Only a few months after Rachel Floyd's death, Bernice's brother, Elwood, had a heart attack. Even though she hated to leave Herbert, she was determined to go to the hospital to see her brother. It was their last meeting. He clung to her hand; for weeks, she could not get this gesture out of her mind. She counted every day since she saw him, every day since his death. She confided to Mebane Burgwyn, "Every day in the week is still related to his last hours, try as I may to fill the time with ordinary and pleasant things."[20] But soon after, at Easter, the death from a heart attack of the husband of her much-loved niece Rosalie shocked and distressed her. Then in August the death of a brother-in-law had to be endured. A terrible sense of sadness, almost unrelieved, dogged every step of her daily living that year.

She desperately longed for her family when the holidays came. William Olive, Mary, Alice Jo, and Gordon were expected for Thanksgiving, as usual, but those plans had to be changed. In a letter to them in November in 1948, she said cheerfully, "Herbert is dressed this morning and sitting up, though of course he feels pretty weak." She hoped they would still find some way to come for Thanksgiving. "Your coming will help me a lot, shut in as I am."[21]

They promised to come at Christmas—William Olive and his family, as well as Bernice's niece Rosalie and her daughter Sandra. She remembered the card games they had played the year before and looked forward to the relief of games again. She wrote Alice Jo, "Shall we GO FISHING?"[22] Their visits put "zest" back into her life, she told them.

Alice Jo said that, as a child, when she had to leave Seaboard to go back to Raleigh, she would go around the house, kissing the walls, to say good-bye—perhaps by this ritual she would ensure that she would come back to her happy times there. Whenever she could not get to sleep, she would imagine being in the Seaboard house with Aunt Bernice. Then she got a pleasant feeling and could drift off to sleep.[23]

Even with her preoccupation with Herbert's illness, Bernice continued to be very much concerned about each person in the extended family, fretting when someone had car trouble, expressing dismay when someone's hopes for something were denied. In her letters she asked about the details of their lives. She wrote to her niece Alice Jo, "I have your picture on my desk where I can see you daily."[24]

Her sister Pearl began to spend long periods of time in bed; there was no diagnosis of a physical illness. Eventually she got up only for brief intervals, staying in bed nearly all the time, mostly reading magazines. She was pleasant to talk to, but she kept a shotgun by her side.[25]

Bernice worried about her sister, but she was concerned about her father especially. She feared that he and Miss Myrtle worked too hard for their age and chided them.

Bernice continued to be puzzled by Herbert's family members' behavior. Herbert's brother Jethro came by occasionally, but no one else visited the sick man. She confided in a letter to William Olive and Mary one Monday morning, "I haven't seen Jethro since Wednesday afternoon. I thought some of them might drop in yesterday afternoon. Nope. I've stopped writing them now." She added, "He lies there whispering, whispering."[26]

At the beginning of the year in 1949, she wrote William Olive and Mary that she had had a good weekend. Her friends Josephine Parker and Pearl Long came to see her Saturday night and visited until after ten. But on another occasion, when friends were there, Herbert got up, put on the heaviest shoes he could find, went into the guest room upstairs and stomped over their heads. They left. Bernice commented in a letter to William Olive and Mary: "Herbert does that invariably and invariably folks rise to leave. I've explained the circumstances, and I've belabored Herbert about it. But it's wasted breath. I've tried to find a key to lock the guest room, so that he can do his stomping somewhere else than over our heads, but have not succeeded. It tickles me, because he really thinks he has found a way to make me come back upstairs."[27]

One Sunday afternoon in January 1949, Jethro came to drive Bernice and Herbert to the Harris homeplace in the country. The married brother, Otis, and his wife, May, had come from Norfolk, as well. Bernice described the interaction:

> Anna sat in her corner behind the stove, not moving from her seat till the time of leave-takings. The room was quite hot, since the heater is a good one and since the afternoon was warm anyway. The Norfolk folks kept cracking the door for fresh air and going outside to cool off. Anna rose (yes, that once) and got her coat. She said she was cold. Someone commented on her broken tooth, asking why she didn't have it capped. She said it was the way she wanted it. As we were about to leave, she slipped up to Herbert and asked, "Hub-but, were you bad-off?" Herbert was so glad to see them that he walked all the way over to her corner and shook hands with Anna. She laughed and said, "Hub-but shook hands with me!"[28]

Often in 1949, Herbert would be too weak to do anything but rest or sit in a chair in his bedroom. For some diversion, Bernice tried to interest him in the radio. He listened to the news so that he could "check on those spenders in Raleigh." He was also able to check on their own wood supply and declared they were burning too much.[29]

Bernice and Melissa Lowery had been cooking on the woodstove, summer as well as winter. A town merchant offered to sell Herbert and Bernice an electric stove at the wholesale price. Herbert agreed; but when he realized that it would cost sixty dollars to update the house's electrical system in order to install an electric stove, he was irate and canceled the order for the stove.[30] And so, Bernice and Melissa were obliged to fire up the woodstove even on the hottest days during the 1949 summer because the garden harvest had to be canned. She described this June day in 1949 to her "Dear Folks," William Olive and Mary:

> I was in the garden gathering snaps at five yesterday, in order to get that canning off and ease my mind for other things. Our one row was hanging full, and of course we can't keep the beans eaten, so something had to be done. I thought of giving the surplus to nieghbors [sic], but snaps are too hard to gather to go in for that extensively. I picked six quarts—six canned, rather. I may have one more canning later this

week. I hadn't really wanted snap beans in the garden this time, but Je-thro planted them, and now they are on hand. We'll have squash by the end of the week. . . . I do want to put up preserves and pickles.[31]

Melissa would stay the night to give Bernice a chance to sleep when there had been no sleep in the house for several nights. Herbert took out his frustrations on Melissa: one time, he delivered such a loud ti-rade against her that she threatened to quit the job. She said she didn't have to take such insults. Bernice convinced her that because of Her-bert's stroke, there were areas of the brain that were damaged and that was the reason he said such "bad things."[32]

Soon afterwards, Melissa Lowery was diagnosed with tuberculosis. She kept hoping she would get better and could come back to work. When Bernice realized how sick Melissa was, she was staggered. Melissa died in July 1950. Bernice wrote the testimonial to be spoken at her fu-neral. "I tried to use words that would have pleased her," she said.[33]

Bernice's dearly loved friend Vaughn Holoman's health grew stead-ily worse. Bernice wrote to her daughter, Mebane Burgwyn, "It has been deprivation beyond my powers to express to have been without her through these months, to have had to speak half truths and euphe-misms when we always based our friendship on complete honesty. But deception can be loving and tender. I have had to practice it for the past year until I am a skilled liar!"[34]

Vaughn Holoman died at the end of 1949. Characteristically, her daughter Mebane Burgwyn wrote to Bernice to console *her*. In reply, Bernice said, "I loved her, I love her. She seems quite near, quite in the present tense to me. The greater sorrow to me, I believe, was in her suffering, in her own knowledge of the confusions that sometimes in-truded, and in my own helplessness to be of any use to her." She added, "Spiritually, you are most her child."[35] She asked Mebane, "Please let me be your Mother, in the limited sense that I can, when you want a reaction on some of your work. . . . It will please me—and Vaughn, I think—for you to bring me questions."[36]

Saddened by this loss, Bernice had still to confront daily Herbert's steadily worsening condition. He continued to suffer small strokes, which finally paralyzed his throat so that he could not speak. When she tried to leave the room, the expression in his eyes showed such distress that she felt she could leave him only if it was absolutely necessary. Wil-liam Olive and Mary came to see them. Bernice told them, "Let me say again your coming tided me over a bad time. It gave me a sense of strength for you to be close, and that is the truth."[37] Her much-loved niece Rosalie Upchurch stayed a week with her. Mebane and her father came to visit. Neighbors—Edith Bradley, Maria Bradley, Lib and Reece Bullock—and her friends Elizabeth Harris and Josephine Parker tried to help. She was also grateful when a young widow, Magdeline Faison, an African American townswoman, came to work for her.

In odd moments, with Mrs. Faison's help in the house and in caring for Herbert, Bernice would work on her novel *Wild Cherry Tree Road*.[38] It provided a way for Harris to reflect on her original family and rural life. At the same time, the novel-writing must have also offered an hour's respite sometimes from the daily worries about Herbert's condition. But in late 1949, Herbert had another major stroke, and her writing came to a stop—it would be months before she could finish the novel. People praised Bernice for the constant loving attention she gave Herbert. That seemed odd to her. She thought, "It seemed myself I ministered to." She compared their life together now to the life they had had when they began: "There was mysticism in our union now that he required an infant's care in a sense there had not been when he was lover."[39]

He died at dawn on July 13, 1950. He was sixty-six; she was fifty-eight. She said simply, "I knew there was no going or staying that we were not in together." She felt like a part of them had died and a part of them lived.[40]

13

A Solitary Life: *Wild Cherry Tree Road*

With Herbert gone, Bernice did not feel like herself. "I became bewildered and insecure in identity," she said.[1] She could not bear to be in the house alone. Magdeline Faison's daughter, Shirley, a high school girl, stayed with her at night, sleeping in a bed beside hers. During the night, she could hear Bernice crying.[2]

The Harris family lawyer began the legal arrangements, referring to Bernice as "widow of the decedent." She found this term foreign. "As 'widow of the decedent,'" she realized, "I was a stranger to myself."[3] She was named administratrix of the estate, and she asked Herbert's brother Jethro Harris to be coadministrator, since he had been kind to them during Herbert's illness.

While Bernice was still feeling the shock and grief of Herbert's death those first weeks, suddenly life became even more strange. One day she went to the post office box to get the sympathy cards that came regularly and opened the letter that told her clearly what "widow of the decedent" meant. As she read the letter, she began to tremble.[4] The cold legal statement informed her: "Estate Counsel had talked with the spokesman for the collateral heirs. He feels that the residence on Gay Street is more than you are entitled to."[5]

Many times during their life together she had asked Herbert to make a will. During his illness, at one point when he was lucid, he had said, "Bernice, I want to fix up my business as soon as I am able. I want you to be satisfied, and I want them to be satisfied, too." He began to cry.[6] But he did not make a will. There were more hemorrhages, and any possibility of attending to business ended. He had another brief lucid interval, however. He said, "Bernice, I'm sorry for you." And he sobbed.[7] He must have realized that he, one of the richest men in Seaboard, had left his wife without sufficient means to sustain her life. But he acknowledged this only at a time when he also knew that he could do nothing about it.

Now she realized that "he must have lived with a sense of conflicting loyalties." Having "broken the bond of blood" by marrying, he could not bring himself to diminish his family's wealth in any way.[8] Like his elder brother Whit Harris, Herbert made the decision that he would have no children. And like his brother Whit, Herbert could not bring himself to make a will giving a wife a portion of the family's worldly goods. His brother Jethro had avoided the decision by dating a woman for over a decade and never marrying her. Only one family member, the youngest brother, Otis, had moved away from the family, married, and had a child. Bernice felt the immediate and bitter meaning for her of Herbert's family's value system.

Because Herbert died without a will, according to North Carolina law at the time, all his heirs within a certain degree of kinship were legally entitled to a share of his possessions.[9] In 1950, concerning dower's rights, the law stated: "Every married woman, upon the death of her husband intestate . . . , shall be entitled to an estate for her life in one-third in value of all the lands, tenements and hereditaments whereof her husband was seized and possessed at any time during the coverture, in which third part shall be included the dwelling house in which her husband usually resided."[10]

The book royalties and salary for newspaper and magazine articles Bernice had earned had gone into Herbert's businesses and his bank account and were now considered Herbert's assets to be divided among all his heirs.[11] Worse for her, her own personal things were inventoried and prices assigned: "Personal possessions that had been integrally of life and love for a quarter of a century became items to be evaluated for pro-rata shares of collateral heirs—when the bed and table and sofa I had so clearly known for my own that day in the Norfolk furniture place became second-hand furniture I was asked to put a price on."[12] Home now had to be seen as a piece of property to be divided, just like the cotton gin, farmhouses, land, timber, mules, and farm implements. And the family's lawyer demanded that even her diamond engagement ring be figured into Herbert's assets.

The problem was that Herbert had been in various partnerships with his brothers, and his holdings were almost inextricably bound up with theirs. Much depended on an honest accounting from them, of course, but figuring up precise market value for every item could not have been easy. Their lawyer came up with the formula that Bernice's portion was to be one-half of one-sixth of these investments, since Herbert had been one of six siblings.[13]

In desperation, Bernice risked incurring the displeasure of Herbert's family by hiring her own lawyer, a Mr. Midgette in Jackson, North Carolina. She was hopeful when she wrote to Mary and William Olive about keeping her home: "Mr. Midgette came over to talk to me, and he assured me that we are in the best spot now we have been in. We offered a fair trade and those greedy rich Harrises think I am not entitled to so much real estate(!!) Now, we take the offensive."[14]

In the end, the "widow of the decedent" kept the home and "second hand furniture" and her engagement ring. (The furniture and diamond ring were not included in the inventory of property deposited with the clerk of court in Northampton County, and so apparently Midgette persuaded the other lawyer not to figure these in.)[15] All other real estate went to the family, and she had to relinquish all interest in the income from the cotton gin and other small businesses, as well as timberland, farms, mules, equipment, and so forth. Possibly the house was overvalued in its market price and the businesses were undervalued in market price, but this is not clear.

Herbert had savings bonds with his name only on them, maturing at different times in the 1950s—there were none with both their names even though he had invested her money earned from her writing in them.[16] The family agreed that she could receive the annual interest on one-half of the bonds: the inventory indicates a total value at maturity of $39,000; interest was calculated at 4 percent, or about $780 a year.[17] Herbert had money deposited in checking accounts in six banks amounting to $27,580.16.[18] If she received one-third—as the law at the time gave the widow to get her through the first year of widowhood—she would have realized $9,193.39; but it is not clear that she did get any of this money at all. She said only that she received one-half of the interest on the bonds. Considering that in the Northampton County area a beginning schoolteacher's or minister's annual salary at the time was about $3,000 (although this was hardly a living wage), she could have struggled along for several years on one-third of the money in the bank. However, Bernice lived twenty-three years after Herbert's death.

Still, in public, she took care to say nothing negative about Herbert's family. In the silence and privacy of her bedroom, she wrote out her anger, folded the sheets, and placed a caution on the front, "Burn this! Do not read!" Her nephew, Gordon Kelley, found the papers after her death and did read, of course, before he burned them.[19]

It was inevitable after a period of intense grieving that she would have to think through and come to terms with the life she had shared with Herbert. One Sunday afternoon, she went for a ride with friends (who, no doubt, meant to offer companionship and diversion to the recently bereaved). They drove to the nearby springs. While her friends went down to the springs, she stayed in the car. She remembered gathering wildflowers here for her classroom when she was teaching. Then she was jerked back into the past when she and Herbert had gathered Christmas greenery together the first Christmas of their marriage. She remembered the happiness she had felt then. She left the car and moved toward a rock they had sat on. And then she thought about the first day of their courtship, when Herbert had come up the hill bringing violets he had picked for her. "It had been moving to me then to think of the strictly business man stooping to pick wild flowers for me."[20]

But thinking about the way he had disinherited her, she began to doubt his love. "What was the reality of Herbert or of myself?" she thought. "What had begun here? What had I had of it all?" She thought she had stopped the dreaded trembling that began with the first legal letter at the post office, but she felt herself trembling now.[21]

In the days after his death, she had reasoned that she would be able to go on, "In the light of my faith in the continuity of love I had the will, even at the crisis of grief, to live positively and to reflect in my living something of the bounty of what I had had."[22] But now she questioned her own reasoning. Was this really a love relationship between two equally trusting and committed people? "It had not been material insecurity or the necessity of contriving ways and means to pay the bills that had shaken the positiveness," she wrote. "The implications of dispossession cut beyond that."[23] Her friends returned and stopped her agonizing for the moment. Always the lady with good manners, she felt she had to be sociable on the drive home.

But she continued to wrestle with the question of whether he had indeed loved her and, if he had not, how she could go on. Now the characters from her writing—many of whom she had known in real life—came back to save her. She remembered Miss Partheny in *Sweet Beulah Land*, who declared she would not make a mess of living or of dying (and of the widowed teacher in the teacherage when Bernice was single who first said that to her). Kalline in *Wild Cherry Tree Road* asserted her identity as a strong woman, even when she knew she was alone. Tiny in *Sage Quarter* started from nearly nothing, repairing the broken furniture no other heirs wanted and working the land.[24] Dele in *Purslane* ordered that her dying son Calvin's wish to be left in peace be honored. "Resolutely, through her own anguish she had willed peace," Bernice insisted.[25] She made up her mind that she would give Herbert and herself peace. "I willed to will positively," she said. She was determined that by her efforts now, she and Herbert would not make a mess of dying or of living.[26]

She read again the sympathy letters she had received. One was from a former teacher at Meredith. She wrote simply of the loss of her own husband, "We had what we had."[27] Bernice mused over the statement. "It was not what I had or otherwise, but rather what Herbert had had."[28] She realized that Herbert had lived his life as he chose, according to his values. She had made herself fit into his scheme. He had had a life, but had she?

That realization tore into her. She did not see that she could teach or write now. "Out of what vitality could I impart, I had asked myself, what interpretation give to literature and life without the validity of love and truth firm in myself?" She continued to agonize, "If love as I had known it had not been valid, then how could I make affirmation?"[29]

The resolution came as she realized that Herbert was simply a different person from herself. She reasoned that his motivations had been rooted in a different ideal, that there must have been for him a truth in it. She did not have to understand his version of truth, but she could accept it as truth for him:

> The challenge and the questionings were resolving. The resolution was so simple after all. The crux of it, I knew now, was not that I had

had or otherwise. It was rather that he had had. He had had my love, the grace and wideness of its integrity. That was the validity of love, the ultimate truth.

Herbert's ideas about trees and land, still unclear and mysitfying [sic] to me, nevertheless had somewhere in it a reach toward excellence I did not have to understand, had in it a facet of truth indeed. However obscure or erratic they might seem to outsiders, Herbert's motivations had been rooted in an ideal. My love had served it. The service was forever mine.

So was there love. And truth. And so could living, in any decade, be positive and forward-looking. So could there be imparting, affirmation.[30]

The certainty for her was that *she* had loved him. About that, she could make the affirmation which would allow her to go on with her life.[31] Love and loyalty were *her* values and she had lived them.

And so, somehow her love had to make things right, in death as in life. In the published autobiography, she wrote simply—"Forever we had what we had had."[32] She always referred to herself as "a woman who had been happily married." That was something she needed to believe, and in widowhood—as in her life with him—she made that her truth.

Now she lay awake night after night trying to figure out how to maintain her home, how to keep herself fed and clothed, and how to pay for necessities like medical care and taxes.[33] Her way of making a living was as a writer, but a writer's life is precarious, with occasional windfalls, routine rejections, and occasional small remittances for newspaper articles. The windfalls she had deposited in Herbert's account, as a dutiful wife would have done at that time. Only a fraction of those earnings were available to her now.

Her last novel, *Wild Cherry Tree Road*, would soon be published, and a few earlier novels were still in print. But books go out of print; and her first three books had gone out of print quickly because they were published during the war, when the paper shortage dictated a limited run. Now Doubleday made no effort to reprint those of her novels for which there was popular demand, such as *Janey Jeems*. Harris was probably no longer certified to teach school. She wrote articles for the Raleigh *News and Observer* and magazines, usually publishing eight to ten a year in the fifties and sixties; these paid between $25 and $50 each. Upon her father's death later in the decade, there was a small inheritance of a few thousand dollars. She made $450 for a television script, and she received royalties on two Christmas books for children published and reprinted in the late fifties and early sixties. In the 1960s she took in as boarders the women schoolteachers who came to Seaboard for the nine months' school term. In 1963, she began teaching non-credit creative-writing courses for Chowan College, a course a semester, making about $125 a month.

As the fifties wore on, her financial situation became very difficult. While not fully aware of the extent of her need, her nieces Alice Jo Kelley and Rosalie Upchurch went to see Herbert's sister Zenobia Harris to ask if she would be willing to help. Zenobia relented and from time to time sent a small check—never large enough to relieve the situation.[34] In the sixties, when her nephew Gordon Kelley was on a business trip in the area, he stopped by to see Bernice one bitterly cold winter night. There was no money to repair the heating system; she was living in her upstairs bedroom, warmed only by a little space heater.[35] By this time, any donations from Zenobia had long since ceased.

Bernice preferred that no one knew about her financial straits, not even her family. "She was always so proud," a neighbor said.[36] She wanted to continue to be a gracious hostess and generous neighbor. "Living alone, I yet had to carry on the semblance of family routines," she thought.[37] Not to do so would be to announce that hers was an aberrant lifestyle, to set herself off from normal living in the community. And if she let people know of her financial situation, it would be an announcement of Herbert's lack of foresight or lack of concern for her.

The months after Herbert's death were even more difficult because she was exhausted emotionally and physically. She wrote Mebane, trying to tone down the expression of her feelings: "I shall try to meet the situations with acceptance and sense, though I do feel the weight of the past two years' suffering and loss."[38]

When she went to William Olive and Mary's house in Raleigh and then returned to her empty one, it was the "most anguishing experience yet."[39] Indeed, she was unused to a solitary life—there had always been people around her. She had grown up with brothers, sisters, uncles, aunts, cousins, and grandparents in the house or nearby. At Meredith, her friends and fellow students were heard everywhere in classroom and residence hall. As a schoolteacher, she had boarded with families and later she lived with other teachers in the teacherage.

She turned to writing to keep her sense of discipline, she said. Probably she also needed to recover her sense of herself—she might be this strange thing "widow of the decedent," but she was still a writer. When Herbert died, she had stopped writing in her daily journal, "My Day," a kind of reflective writing she had done since the 1920s. Now, she started a short story in which the main character begins by describing loneliness. She knew the feeling.

> The silence is deafening. The empty house creaks and I'm as lonely as a cedar in a cemetery. I walk out on the front porch, ringing the door bell as I pass to create a little sound, and I sit staring at an almost empty street. The cars that pass are the slow traveling ones of the older generation. I take a look at the thermometer and the mercury points to eighty-eight degrees. It's a quiet, still, hot autumn day, perfect for boating or skiing—but not for just one person. The sun shines on the half brown, half-green grass and I think—the lawn doesn't even need cutting.
>
> I walk about the yard, aimlessly inspecting the flowers and shrubbery. The zinnias are faded and past their colorful glory and the pyracantha berries have not yet reached their winter's crimson. I feel something winding around my legs and look to see Missy, the cat, purring forlornly. I go into the kitchen and find some food scraps for her and as she eats I listen for something. I know not what.[40]

The short story fragment ends as the woman telephones her married daughters. Did Harris think of the comfort grown-up children might have been to her now?

She picked up the manuscript of her last novel, *Wild Cherry Tree Road,* and resumed work. The novel has no plot and no central character the reader can identify with. Rather, *Wild Cherry Tree Road* is a study of a community: any one chapter could be an essay on some aspect of life in a farming community at the turn of the century. While it is not as engrossing as earlier novels, this book's graceful prose style, startling descriptions, and insightful commentary are seductive.

If there is no plot, there is nevertheless a bright thread that runs through the cloth: it is the story of a family, the mother Hannah Gowen and father Sim Gowen, and their children—Lucy, Neva, Anne, and George. Living around them on Wild Cherry Tree Road are near and distant kin, each with aspirations and tragedies that affect everyone else.

The novel begins with Hannah taking her little son, George, to see a new baby, Daphne, who is more beautiful than anyone in the community has ever seen. They also visit new neighbors, who have inherited land in the neighborhood, and see their baby, Penny—so ugly Hannah is at a loss for polite words to say.

George and the little girls grow up and go to school together. Daphne is lovely to look at and pleasant in manner; Penny is not pretty, but she is resourceful and independent-minded. By the time of their high school graduation, it is assumed by the community that George and Daphne are meant for each other, and George begins courting Daphne as they near their late teens.

Daphne insists on taking Penny with them on a picnic by the river. Penny saves George's life when he is bitten by a rattlesnake: she sucks the venom from the wound. George realizes that it is Penny who is the interesting and adventuresome woman, and he begins to arrange to see her. At nineteen, he is straining to establish his independence, build his own house, and choose his wife. Daphne seems more like his parents' and his community's choice—Penny, his choice. But Penny's parents have higher aspirations for her than marriage to a small farmer; they arrange for her to leave Wild Cherry Tree Road. George drives his carriage to the station where she is waiting to board the train and persuades her to elope with him. Daphne assumes the role of the beautiful, injured woman in the community.

Appearing throughout *Wild Cherry Tree Road* is the homeless woman Kalline, who had been on Harris's mind since childhood. As mentioned earlier, Kalline had appeared in one of Harris's plays and in her first novel, *Purslane*. Harris was fascinated by Kalline's courage in surviving a homeless condition. It is Kalline who announces in the beginning of the novel that Daphne is about to be born. Near the end of the story, it is she who takes George's letter, intended for Penny, to Daphne and so causes Daphne to realize she has lost George.

Kalline's honest, unvarnished, direct pronouncements are in contrast to the niceties the married adult women perpetrate. In this exchange her kind of wit is demonstrated:

> Kalline left the dinner table to do the churning. Simultaneously as she moved the dasher up and down she began shelling corn for the chickens.
>
> Hannah hastily stopped the churning. "One thing at a time and that done well," she quoted, precept for the children's ears as well as for Kalline's, "is a very good rule as many can tell." Hannah placed a clean towel over the churn and pushed it out of Kalline's reach. "You can't do

two things at a time, Kalline!" It was going to take precept upon precept, line upon line, to make the creature tolerable, Hannah reflected. "Just remember now—"

"You can do three things at a time," Kalline murmured. "You can fizzle and fart and drive a oxcart."[41]

Near the end of the novel, Kalline is made to go to the poorhouse. She throws a fit but to no avail: "When finally they managed to get Kalline into the surrey, a harassed and beaten little woman, her protestings and lamentations suddenly ceased. For the first time in her life she had given up. The worst had happened. It was as though no despair could touch her further" (255).

George is so affected by Kalline's tragedy that after he says good-bye to her, he goes home feeling melancholy. Penny suggests they build a house for Kalline on their land. Now the neighbors, tinged with guilt, come to George to contribute something for a home for her. But when Kalline comes to visit months later and George and Penny show her her house, she tells them her home is in town, where at the County Home she has electric lights, steam heat, and friends to enjoy it with— and no pesky roosters waking her up at dawn.

It is Kalline that Bernice saw as the protagonist in this novel, but when she sent the manuscript to her editor at Doubleday, she received a positive but unsettling reply, as she told J. O. Bailey: "Miss Claasen wrote me after her first reading of the manuscript, that she liked it very much, particularly the second part which deals primarily with the love triangle, a tenuous one at best, I'm afraid. I counted on her seeing through the underbrush to the heart of the book—to Kalline who is the toughness of the human race. I like my love story all right, but I consider it unimportant except as it helps to interpret Kalline."[42]

In *Wild Cherry Tree Road*, it is Penny, whom the community defined as ugly, and Kalline, who was treated with scarcely disguised disdain, who get the happiness they want. In Harris's novels, those who are least favored by the community triumph. Tiny, the "fau'ty" twin in *Sage Quarter*, wins the man she loves. Lan, the drifter in *Sweet Beulah Land*, is happy in the end when he is connected to a child. The orphan Janey in *Janey Jeems* marries the man she loves and makes the home she wants. The ancient women in *Hearthstones* are happy in their love for Billy and his love for them. Harris empathized with the most vulnerable people in society—these are the ones she as God/

writer gave a fortunate destiny. She does not let the community define the individual.

In this novel, she again draws on people she had known in her childhood, just as she did in *Purslane*. Wild Cherry Tree Road is her old neighborhood, Poole's Siding, in Wake County, and characters like the moocher Cousin Sell just switch novels from *Purslane* to this one but keep their roles. The grandfather, Ashley Neal, is Bernice's grandfather Calvin Poole. Events from her childhood appear in *Purslane* and reappear here.

Harris continues her critique of the society she had known: she explores the attitudes that troubled people in this kind of white, farming neighborhood. One was racial difference. The distrust that existed between the white and black communities was played out when the local scholar and would-be gentleman Archibald Holt interpreted attempted arson at the school as the beginning of a murderous rampage by blacks against whites. He led the white women and children into the woods to hide. Actually, *he* had made threats to the African American Ishmael that whites were going to punish blacks. While Hannah and the other mothers were hiding with their children in the woods, they saw a group of black families pass. The white people heard the black mothers talking about seeking a place to hide from murderous white families, repeating Archibald's threats that the white people were going to punish them severely for their insubordination.

Unreasoning prejudice of whites against blacks is shown several times. Nevertheless, the reader sees an injustice against Ishmael righted. It's a particularly rural incident and an example of the discretion concerning the law a local justice of the peace like Sim Gowen could have. Ishmael comes to Sim to complain that Archibald is stealing his tools, including his prized shovel. Sim says that white men do not steal, and so Ishmael is helpless to get his tools back. When Archibald leaves town for a few days, he tells Ishmael to take care of his farm animals. Ishmael owns his cabin and small plot of land and is not legally Archibald's tenant, but Archibald just assumes that a black man has to do what a white man tells him, whether he wants to or not.

Archibald has three healthy pigs; Ishmael has five sickly ones. While Archibald is gone, Ishmael has a barbecue for his friends and shares the pork with his white neighbors, as well. When Archibald returns, he discovers he is missing a pig. He goes immediately to Sim, determined to swear out a warrant for Ishmael's arrest for slaughtering his pig for the barbecue. Ishmael says one of Archibald's pigs became ill and died and he buried it. He swears that he barbecued one of his own pigs: sure enough, Sim counts Ishmael's pigs and one is missing. Sim suggests they dig up the carcass of the sick animal to see if it's Archibald's red Duroc pig or the thin razorback Ishmael owned.

Archibald is enthusiastic about this plan and runs to his barn to get his shovel. When Sim sees it, he recognizes it as Ishmael's shovel, and Archibald realizes he has betrayed himself. Suddenly Archibald changes his mind about a warrant for Ishmael's arrest. Sim says, "I don't want to hear any more accusations from either party" (53).

It was a culture in which people feared not only black-white differences but "strong drink" and their own sexuality. Hannah and Sim are ashamed that Sim's sister has married a tavern keeper in town. However, they do not protest when the tavern keeper lends them his fine carriage when they need protection against the rain on their drive home. And when Hannah is not there, Sim has more than a taste of his brother-in-law's whiskey and gets lost on the way back home.

Hannah is distressed over Cousin Sook's visits because Cousin Sook is a symbol of feminine sexuality—this is the way Hannah sees her:

> But she had those monstrous breasts. They stuck out in front and cascaded over her waistline so that she had to pin her belt low in order to have any shape at all. During the months since her last visit the monstrous size of the woman's front had receded in Hannah's thinking, and it was something of a shock to walk in on a bosom as big as ever.
>
> When circumstances forced a public appearance with Cousin Sook, Hannah had always mused on how much better it would be to keep her at home, where she and her big breasts could be handled privately. Today Hannah was not so sure. Any wife hated for her husband to have to sit and look on such evidence of woman flesh, just as a mother disliked the wonder and speculation lurking in children's eyes. (76)

Hannah, but for this obvious evidence of woman's sexuality, might have been able to keep such a topic out of her thoughts and away from everybody's awareness, as well. A similar fear of sexuality is expressed in Daphne's mother's advice to never let George kiss her or touch her—the consequences would be the loss of his love. Too late, Daphne realizes he cannot understand her refusal of a kiss. She knows her coldness toward him in refusing one kiss has caused the moment when they might have come closer together to slip away forever.

Obviously Bernice Kelly Harris was examining the beliefs that had shaped her own thinking. Although her gaze into the past and the people in that distant world was compassionate and affectionate, she nevertheless subjected their behavior and beliefs to scrutiny. What resulted for her was renewed acceptance of the people—in spite of the shortcomings she brought to the fore. She felt pleasure in recalling their individuality as well as their commonality.

With *Wild Cherry Tree Road*, she continued to place her novels in either a small-town setting or a rural setting; the two unpublished novels she wrote in the mid-fifties have these settings, as well. She was not trying to argue that the rural way of life is morally or aesthetically superior to modern, urban society.[43] She simply had little experience with big-city living, and she liked writing about a situation she knew well. She probably assumed that her observations of human behavior, her main focus, would be interesting and relevant to readers, that they would delight in these characters as she did. But certainly the evocation of setting and characters from her childhood comforted her when she needed comfort most.

When *Wild Cherry Tree Road* was published in 1951, reviewers liked it: the Wisconsin writer August Derleth gave an especially positive review for the *Chicago Sunday Tribune*, addressing the problem writers who wrote consistently about one region encountered: "The regional writer is always in danger of remaining merely regional, of writing stories too narrow in their application to command a wide audience. Mrs. Harris's novels, however, have a universality which transcends mere regionalism. Her characters are people who, tho [sic] indigenous to the near south, might be found in any community; the events of her novels are those of life in any community; and she somehow manages to invest the commonplace with an aura of the unusual without once departing from reality."[44]

The reviewer for the *Greensboro Daily News* called it a "Hardyesque Gem." He wrote, "She has in her people something of the tenderness and basic reality of Thomas Hardy's characters. She has some of Hardy's rural and natural sense of proportion." But he argued that "where Hardy used atmosphere to enmesh people, Mrs. Harris permits her characters to work their own way."[45]

That must have been a swallow of energizing tonic, for she was already thinking about the next block of writing—even while she was having the wrangle with Herbert's family over the inheritance. The loneliness did not go away, but it was mitigated by the presence of good friends in her life. She became even closer to Mebane Burgwyn, who would come to spend a day with her and invite Bernice to visit her and stay overnight. Bernice was impressed by Mebane's ability to care for her four young children and still write: "I marvel that you manage all the courtesies, which you do so beautifully, when I with a family of one find all the time taken in household matters."[46]

Mebane wrote novels for young teens. Her first, *River Treasures*, was published in 1947, and a second, *Lucky Mischief*, followed in 1949. Bernice read everything Mebane wrote and gave her enthusiastic support. When *Penny Rose* was published in 1952, Bernice was delighted and wrote to Mebane, "Implicit in it is the reminder that security is within one's own will and spirit and not without. . . . I am so proud of your talent and loveliness and charm and integrity. You will not be moved—so like your mother in the steadfastness that counts."[47]

About Mebane's attending an important dinner, Bernice commented in the way a mother would: "Are you going to wear white? You looked so exquisite in white at Mrs. Long's tea, though I think you are beautiful in anything."[48]

Mebane was a loving and supportive friend to her as well. Bernice treasured her letters, as she wrote to Mebane: "Your letters are exquisite. I reread them, over and over, for the sense of warmth and affection they give. Bless you! I seem to be getting to the stage that I want to bask in what you are doing—rather than do myself. I do feel so proud and so *satisfied* with your accomplishments."[49]

Mebane would drive over to Seaboard from Jackson (about ten miles) to talk about writing. Sometimes they were joined by two other writers: Charlotte Hilton Green and Margarette Wood Smethurst. Both lived in Raleigh; Bernice had met them at meetings of The Strugglers in the late thirties. Green was a world traveler—her friends called her "Mrs. Columbus." When Bernice met her, she was a white-haired widow who was following her passion for research and her love of nature. She published *Birds of the South* and *Trees of the South* in the fifties and continued to write and publish articles for various magazines. In addition, she wrote a weekly column for the *News and Observer* called "Carolina Out-of-Doors."[50]

Margarette Wood Smethurst, the widow of *News and Observer* editor Frank Smethurst and mother of a journalist as well, Wood Smethurst, had been writing columns for the *News and Observer* since 1919.

She was known in North Carolina as an outspoken person, "a first-class fighter."[51]

When Charlotte and Margarette came to Seaboard, they would spend the weekend, and Mebane would come over for their day-long workshop on writing. Each of the four would read a work in progress, and the others would critique it. Mebane would go home to her family in Jackson at the end of the day; but Charlotte, Margarette, and Bernice would stay up late at night, reading from their manuscripts and talking.

The four individuals in the group became very close friends, corresponding regularly, giving each other support with writing. Charlotte wrote to Bernice, "Do you wonder I think friendship is one of life's greatest glories? And understand why I treasure our friendship (yours and mine) so much. And of what our "Four" meeting—you, Marg., Mebane and I—meant, and how I look forward to others."[52]

Charlotte and Margarette, even though they had seen much of the world, rather liked Seaboard. Margarette gave it a positive review in her letter to Bernice, "I'm still in a 'glow' from my visit. I hope we didn't wear you completely out and that I didn't talk you slam to death." She continued, "Your town, your friends, and your *place* in the hearts of your people (not just your 'position,' Bernice, but your *place*, earned by your life and example and understanding) all inspire me to be a better person. Don't ever leave it, my dear. There's nothing in a bigger town to match it and nowhere could there be a finer thing. It's wonderful. I loved being a part of it for a brief spell, but even more I savored and relished all that it means in reality and implications."[53]

Whenever Bernice was in Raleigh, visiting William Olive and Mary, she would go to Charlotte's to have lunch with her and Margarette. And Bernice went to Raleigh often after Herbert's death; she seemed to need to be with William Olive, Mary, and Alice Jo. They came to spend long weekends with her in Seaboard, bringing with them Bernice's and William Olive's niece Rosalie Upchurch and her daughter, Sandra. (Rosalie was the little blond niece who had helped unpack Bernice's trunk when Bernice was a teacher.) Rosalie had lost her mother Rachel Floyd as well as her husband in the late forties. Widowed at thirty-eight, with a young daughter to raise, Rosalie had returned to college to prepare to be a teacher, and so she had much to discuss about education with Mary, William Olive, and Bernice. She had always been especially loving with Bernice, who referred to her as "my daughter, practically."

William Olive and Mary would pile the whole group of six into the car for a trip. Their first excursion was to the mountains, but Bernice, having lived her life on land of low, rolling hills in Wake County or utter flatness in Seaboard, kept her eyes closed most of the time. She would open them long enough to say, "Isn't this beautiful?" and close them again tight.[54] She was comforted by being with her family, though, and the six often went to the coast, to Wilmington, to see her brother Darwin and his family.

Bernice spent every Christmas with William Olive and Mary in Raleigh, but Christmas Eve they went to the homeplace, her father's farmhouse in the countryside east of Raleigh. The extended family would be there—four generations. There would be a feast. Her father, now in his nineties, would tell funny stories, and he would be joined in story-telling by his children and grandchildren. They would play "Pollyana," exchanging humorous gifts anonymously. Often attached to the gifts there would be a little poem. On one occasion, a niece's husband cleaned out a cold-storage room in Raleigh and found fur coats that had been there for decades. He gave one to Bernice as a gag gift; she posed in it to have her picture taken—just before it disintegrated.[55]

Bernice's nephew Carey Coats (Rachel Floyd's son) was now a grown-up and directed the fish fries the family liked to have in the fall when crops had been harvested. Sometimes these were held in the yard at the homeplace, sometimes at nearby Rocky Branch. He would buy thirty or forty pounds of fish and fry the fish outside in a huge iron skillet. Nearly fifty people would come. Bernice quite forgot everything else as she played with the children.[56]

Summers, Alice Jo and Sandra came on the train from Raleigh by themselves to visit. Bernice enjoyed these visits with her niece and grandniece. As young adolescents, the girls' favorite activity was sliding down Bernice's bannister. Rather than chide them, Bernice used wax paper from her kitchen to rub on the bannister to make it more slippery. She would invite the girls in the neighborhood for a party under the trees in the back yard. Best of all she gave her nieces independence: even when they were nine and ten, they could walk to the drugstore and dimestore by themselves. Seaboard was a safe place to be.[57]

Bernice began to travel farther and more often than she had done when Herbert was living. In the fall of 1951, she went with J.O. Bailey and his colleagues in the English department of the University of North Carolina to Atlanta for the conference of the South Atlantic Modern Language Association. She spoke at a session on the "Literary Use of Folklore."

In the spring of 1953, Bernice went to New York for the first time in her life. Elizabeth Harris, Mebane Burgwyn, and Mebane's son, Johnnie, went with her. During their three days and four nights there, they saw six shows—among them, *Time of the Cuckoo* with Shirley Booth and *Wonderful Town* with Rosalind Russell. But *Picnic* was the one Bernice liked best of all.[58] And she paid a visit to Miss Claasen— she thought the New York editor would want to see the "quaint" woman she'd been working with. Riding the subway and tramping along the New York streets in April, she thought of herself in a context from her fiction:

> I was a little like the Morehead excursionists, on their first ride to the ocean. I identified the strange with the known and familiar. Persons and prototypes from the novels rode with me to the city. A venerable colored woman across the aisle from me was Janey Jeems, on her way to Harlem to visit children and grandchildren. Would she get homesick, as Janey did, for the sight of a cotton patch among the steel and concrete? The lovely aloof passenger was Alicia of *Sweet Beulah Land*. I saw little Henrietta of *Hearthstones* in the gentle child with the dark fringed blue eyes. There was Calvin of *Purslane*, only he wore a soldier suit. We ourselves were tourists from *Portulaca*, off to see some shows in the big city.[59]

She told Mebane that the trip was "a grand time" and helpful, too: "It was a very satisfactory trip. I received help that I could not have had through letters, and I am convinced that the suggestions for development were good. When I shall begin work will depend on circumstances. Now it is garden peas and strawberries."[60] To J. O. Bailey, she said, "I love the South, but I'm glad there is a New York."[61]

Her longest trip was to Niagara Falls in the summer of 1954, with William Olive, Mary, Alice Jo, Rosalie, and Sandra. She was funny, her niece remembered, and fun to be with. But going back into the house in Seaboard alone was still a wrenching experience for her.[62]

And yet, there was support around her. In the mornings, Seaboard women worked in their houses; but in the afternoons, after lunch and a little rest during the hottest part of the day, they bathed to get cool, put on freshly starched dresses, and visited each other on porches. In the late-summer evenings, they sat outside on their lawns or stretched out on porch recliners, swatting mosquitoes, telling stories, swapping observations about current events, and comparing reflections on a book making its rounds.[63] Bernice's neighbor and friend Maria Bradley was a story-teller and an avid reader, with a library that she shared.

Maria Bradley's two daughters, Ann and Betsey, and two other neighborhood children, Sandra and Linda Lee Gay, engaged Bernice in their playtime. They enjoyed playing "dress-up." She would help them find interesting clothes for this.[64] Once, when nieces Alice Jo and Sandra came to visit, she allowed them to borrow particular clothes so they could pretend to be Charlotte Hilton Green and Margarette Wood Smethurst. Bernice thought the imitations were hilarious.[65] She began an annual event: each summer she coached the neighborhood children in a play they would present in somebody's back yard.

During the day, her door was unlocked. The children came in and yelled up the steps. (All of the children had pet names for her—many called her "K. K.") She would tell them to come up. She would be sitting at her typewriter by the window in the upstairs bedroom that faced the street. She would let them bang on the typewriter and jump up and down on the bed. She kept cookies in the kitchen pantry, so they could depend on having a treat. When she needed to get back to her writing, she would say so. Betsey Bradley remembered, "She would tell us when it was time to go, in the most genteel manner."[66]

One day, Betsey and Ann Bradley had made a snowman and were ready to take its picture when they realized it had no arms. Bernice came out and got down on her hands and knees behind the snow man and stuck one of her arms out on each of its sides. They made the picture.[67] When one little boy was asked, "How old do you think Mrs. Harris is?" he replied, "About my age."[68]

Bernice enjoyed play, whatever the game. All through the fifties and sixties, there were the bridge parties, indulged in by the ladies among the gentry. Afterwards, a write-up in the Northampton and Jackson newspapers would inform the public about such details as colors, theme, and guests.[69] Indeed, the guests deserved a write-up. They would arrive in a cloud of perfume, dressed as if they were going to the governor's mansion for cocktails. Bernice indulged.

One time Betsey Bradley heard the players asking Bernice what she would write about next. She replied that she would write about the town, of course, and how fortunate she was to be there.[70]

There were also good times for Bernice with Seaboard friends like Jo Parker and Elizabeth Harris. Jo Parker would invite Bernice and Elizabeth, as well as Mebane and John Burgwyn and Grace and Gilbert Stephenson to sumptuous dinners in the large house on the farm where she and Dr. Parker lived.

In the company of family, friends, and neighbors, the long year and a half after Herbert's death passed, and the spring of 1952 began. Bernice had a great fear of being alone; at night her active imagination brought visions of horror, so that she often had someone else sleep in the house. But she was also afraid of emotional loneliness, of being attached to no one; she had thought earlier in her life, when she was in the company of widows, that no one could imagine their loneliness. She said those who were married knew that in old age they would be dear to somebody—implying there is a rock-bottom emotional security in that. And she had conjured up Kalline again and again, fascinated by the homeless, lone woman. But Bernice Harris had kept her home, had even managed (for the time being) to have the necessities living demands. And loneliness was mitigated by all kinds of relationships. Like Kalline, she faced the thing she most dreaded and found it not so bad—indeed, she had moments of laughter and many good times.

Probably her letter to Mebane about her garden in August 1951, when Herbert had been dead a year, best expressed the happy feelings she sometimes had now: "I have really farmed my little acre, and there have been beautiful garden vegetables, beautiful and the tastiest that ever were. None can say I haven't done well, with very little help from any source. But I must not start ranting about the garden project, as unordinary as it has seemed to me this time."[71]

14

A Writers' Community

Bernice Kelly Harris had a community in Seaboard, and yet sometimes when she wanted to commiserate with a fellow writer, she felt very much alone. She wrote to Mebane Burgwyn, "It is a lonely thing to be the only one around who writes a book: the fellowship with other authors is a great consolation. There are times consolation is indicated."[1]

In the 1950s, she found a second community among her fellow writers, many of whom she met at meetings of the North Carolina Writers Conference. The next two decades of her life were characterized by the role of friend and supporter, which she gladly played in the writers' community and by the role the writers assigned to her—Grande Dame of North Carolina Literature.

The Writers Conference in North Carolina was organized on the spur of the moment and almost by chance. In the summer of 1950, the outdoor drama on the coast, *The Lost Colony* written by Paul Green, was not getting good attendance or much publicity. Novelist Inglis Fletcher decided to call some writers she knew to ask them to meet at Manteo and attend the play. She thought she could persuade them to go home and write about it, and thus the play would get a lot of free publicity. About twenty people attended. They turned the informal meeting into a conference, and they made plans to meet every year and to vary their meeting places so they could cover the state. As playwright Paul Green said, "Barbers and sheriffs and plumbers meet annually to talk over their mutual interests—why not writers?"[2]

With a general aversion to bureaucracy, they decided they would have none, but they soon realized they would have to have a permanent chair who would start the organizing process each year. They elected Richard Walser. There were restrictions on membership: a member had to be a published writer and a North Carolinian by birth, by choice, or at least be writing about North Carolina.[3]

Bernice attended her first Writers Conference when it was held in the mountains at Cherokee, North Carolina, in 1951. For Harris and for all of the writers, it proved to be not just an opportunity to discuss writing and publishing in sessions, but also a way to talk in spontaneous meetings with a few people late into the night. Harris described the Hatteras conference in 1954 to Walser, who could not attend: "We were in on a little post-meeting gathering Friday night. There was good talk, scintillating and a little ribald in spots. Saturday night the party moved on into our room and did not break up till after three. I enjoyed all of it. Next morning my roommates laughed when I observed, 'Last Sunday morning this time I was getting right to teach a Sunday school class, and here I am now gathering up whiskey bottles.' "[4]

From 1951 to 1964, she never missed a Writers Conference.[5] It was at one of these meetings that she first met novelist James (always called Jimmie) Street. He had grown up in a working-class, Roman Catholic family in Mississippi, left school when he was in the tenth grade, and floundered until he got a job as a reporter. At nineteen, he married the daughter of a Baptist minister and became a Baptist minister himself. At twenty, he was a pastor whom crowds flocked to hear. He thought he was just a showman: "Then I suddenly realized that people listened to what I said and I didn't know what I was talking about. It frightened me. I held two more pulpits—one in Missouri and one in Alabama and then I quit. I just didn't fit."[6]

He then got jobs as press agent for politicians and began to write feature stories for newspapers, ending up working for the *New York World Telegram*. His first novel, *O Promised Land*, was published in 1940.

When Bernice met Jimmie Street in 1951, he had already written eleven novels, some screenplays, many short stories, and several nonfiction books. He was just finishing an historical novel, *The Velvet Doublet*, which Doubleday published in 1953. He was a hard drinker, fearless and witty, who used profanity as naturally as he breathed. Bernice had never known anyone quite like him; but he became very dear to her, and she would sit beside him in meetings whenever she could. She wrote in notes at the end of her life that he "gave vastly out of his own experience and sound sense."[7]

In 1952, Bernice's second time to attend the conference, the writers met at Edenton, on the coast, during the hottest two days of the summer. The first night, it was so hot that poet and novelist Frank Borden Hanes went out into the square with the intention of lying down on the grass to get a breeze. He stopped by a Confederate monument and just missed stepping on Jimmie Street, who had gotten there first, stripped, and stretched out. Street, glad to have missed being stepped on, remarked, "Now I know what a goddamned Confederate monument is good for."[8]

The next night, in the suffocating heat, the writers met at Bandon Plantation, the home of novelist Inglis Fletcher. After dinner, in the grand living room, she began reading from the manuscript of a novel in progress. Suddenly an electrical storm arose, wind whipped through the room, and the power went out. Inglis Fletcher lit candles and continued reading. Her listeners forgot about the storm and the heat.[9]

Although the writers were enthralled, including Bernice Harris, she was also troubled. She kept on good terms with Inglis Fletcher—they worked together helping Gilbert Stephenson organize the Roanoke-Chowan Group—but she disliked the myths about the South she thought fiction like Fletcher's perpetuated. The South, in Bernice's view, was not about great mansions, lovely ladies, grateful slaves, and so forth. She deplored the trend to go back for "Persons and settings," if the result was "to create out of the Old South the American Eden, with antebellum plantation in springtime" and "Old Marse as Adam, Eve as goddess in crinoline," and "a garden with no apples, just magnolias, and no snakes."[10] In notes for a speech about literature, she declared:

> We who read and write and live will not be beguiled by crinoline and broadcloth of Technicolor gentry, or by fly bonnets and linsey-woolsey of the folk either. We will not let authors palm off second-rate writing on us just because their people ride to the hounds on vast estates, or for

that matter pitch lowly horseshoes in cramped little yards. We will sift through the external and incidental and focus on human relationships and motivations and behavior. We will not be confused by trends that bear toward the pseudo. We will see the apparent chaos in the literary world and human society in human perspective.[11]

Nor did she glamorize the Civil War and blame the South's poverty on that defeat, as many of her contemporaries in the first half of the century were wont to do.

Inglis Fletcher gave Bernice a hard time at a Writers Conference about being too liberal about race in the novel *Janey Jeems*.[12] However, Bernice never missed an occasion to write Inglis a letter of congratulation on an honor or the publication of a new book. When Bandon Plantation burned in 1963, she expressed to Inglis her distress and deep regret.[13] But the two were never close friends.

A writer who did become dear to her was poet Sam Ragan. Harris met Ragan shortly after World War II ended when she spoke at Meredith College, but the Writers Conference was the context in which Harris began to know him well. Ragan, who was then an editor at the Raleigh *News and Observer*, was a gracious, kindly man with impeccable manners and a ready generosity toward other writers. Sam Ragan and Bernice were friends for over twenty years; he told her, "I always feel that I have new insight into things after we talk, even if briefly."[14] He enjoyed her company and he and his wife, Marjorie, often visited Bernice in Seaboard. He said that when they arrived, she would have to take them on a tour of the town—it would have been short except that he had to stop the car and get out to be introduced to every soul they saw.[15]

Ragan often sent her a poem he had finished, just from an urge to communicate it to an empathic reader. She would not critique it—she realized that was not what he wanted—but acknowledged the sharing of it graciously.[16]

She also met another poet, Thad Stem Jr., through the Writers Conference. He had a fine sense of humor—he also suffered from depression and diabetes. Bernice enjoyed his company, especially his off-the-cuff observations about writing. She listened to him with "absolute glee on her face," another writer said.[17] His letters to her brought her much delight, and she, in turn, empathized with him and encouraged him in his writing.

Thad and his wife, Marguerite (or Dety, as she was called) lived in Oxford, North Carolina, where he wrote editorials and articles for the *News and Observer* and worked as a Veterans Service officer for Granville County, but he classified himself as a full-time poet.[18] He and Dety often visited Bernice in Seaboard. In a letter to her about a speaking engagement nearby, he told Bernice he agreed to speak so he could come and see his "sweetheart." Sometimes Thad and Dety drove miles out of their way to pick her up and take her to a writers' meeting when it was held on the coast.

Thad Stem liked to shock. Once, at a Writers Conference on the coast, he galloped past Bernice with a group going to the ocean to swim naked in the moonlight. Bernice was standing on the beach, fully clothed. He paused long enough to hold out his watch and keys for her to keep for him. She gravely obliged.[19]

Stem also sent Bernice his poems, reviews, and short essays. And often he told her things he could not tell anyone else, such as the time he confessed, "I feel as if I am an old dish-rag, rung [*sic*] out one time too many."[20]

Thad and Dety's affection for Bernice lasted all her life. He wrote to Bernice once, "On my part, at least, we have a flaming love affair whose poetic wonder is not obviated one whit by the mere physical difference of a few paltry years."[21] (The paltry years numbered twenty-five.) The dedication to his book *The Animal Fair* in 1960 read:

> For my girl friends—Sallie Hamilton Tarry who is three,
> And for Dety, again, and Bernice Kelly Harris
> Who are a little bit older.[22]

While Bernice Harris did not go swimming nude with Thad Stem and the group, she did believe that she had to give cocktail parties in the late evenings because every member did this. Not to reciprocate in a social exchange was unthinkable to her. Once she and Mebane stopped by a store on their way to the conference to buy liquor for their party. Bernice wondered if she should buy a pint. That amount probably lasted her a long while because the daily toddy she had had since the forties, when Dr. Parker prescribed this for nervousness, used only a small amount. Mebane said they should buy at least a fifth. They bought the fifth; but for the crowd who came, that was merely a drop. After that, she enlisted the help of Chalmers Davidson, a professor of history at Davidson College and an author, who advised her on what to buy and stood beside her and mixed the drinks for her guests. He jokingly said his only claim to fame was his title, "Bernice's Bartender."[23]

After one of these parties, there were so many bottles in the room that she and Mebane were afraid the hotel staff would think they had drunk all that alcohol themselves. They rose early, tiptoed out into the hall, and divided the number of bottles, putting a discreet few by each door for the maid to collect.[24] Bernice, despite her strict Baptist upbringing, got so proficient in entertaining in her fellow writers' way that when Walser told her he had been awarded $22 and did not know what to do with it, her reply was quick: "Buy bourbon."[25]

Much as she enjoyed the parties, Harris wanted more organization in the formal meetings—a topic and a panel to start the discussion and a workshop leader to keep it focused. She had influence in making this happen.[26] Usually she was on a panel, and her role would be that of the "talk-starter." For the New Bern conference in 1957, Mebane Burgwyn was chair and convenor. She insisted that Harris give the opening night address. Harris chose as her subject "Book People," and she began by saying, "People remain a marvel . . . the unexplored treasures . . . there is mystery that if traced to the essence would still remain a mystery." She admitted that she took her characters from life: "Yet, within limits, I created, I illuminated the facts. They are my creatures. Through these people I have confirmed something of the complexity of life, the dignity of man, the triumph of the human spirit."[27]

Her listeners were captivated—Mebane Burgwyn thought it set the tone for the entire conference.[28] Frank Borden Hanes thought it was the best talk they had ever had.[29] Journalist and photographer Bernadette Hoyle described the effect this speech had on her: "I do want you to know that to see you and hear you that night was an experience that will always live in my memory as one of the most exquisite I have ever known. You held us all spellbound—in you we saw what we all wanted to be—your insight, your understanding, your ability and your creativeness, have never been more deeply appreciated."[30]

The assigned topics for discussion at the writers' conferences were serious. One time they debated whether television would end novel reading: playwright Paul Green argued that because good books would be televised, television would stimulate reading. The writers exchanged anecdotes about personal experiences with publishers, debated the directions the publishing business was taking, and gave each other tips on ways to handle public speaking engagements and editors. When an editor insists he can pay only the standard fee for a story, Street advised them to increase the list of expenses.[31]

Another time, a hotly debated topic nearly divided the group permanently. The North Carolina legislature, at the height of the McCarthy era, enacted a law stating no Communist could speak at a state facility. It was obviously an abridgment of free speech—a matter of serious concern for every citizen and especially for writers. At the conference, several writers, including John Ehle, wanted to go on record as opposing this Speaker Ban Law. However, Richard Walser said the leadership of the Writers Conference had decided not to take a stand on any political issue. Ehle persisted and did get enough support for the writers to go on record against it.[32] Harris was silent on this issue in her remembrances of writers' conferences; witnesses living now could not recall that she took a stand at the conference either.

The conference participants were all white in the 1950s and 1960s. When dramatist Paul Green and journalist Harry Golden told the writers that it was time to do something about racism, there was heated discussion, but no conclusion was reached.[33] And although women were welcome, there was an ethnic sameness. The exception was Harry Golden, a Jew and editor of the newspaper the *Carolina Israelite.*

Golden was egocentric and sometimes gruff, but he had an engaging wit. At one session Golden talked about great writers but mentioned only the Jewish ones. Finally, Jimmie Street remarked, "You talk about no one but Jews, Harry, tell us what you know about Gentiles. Tell us what you know about Shakespeare." Golden, with a twinkle in his eyes, replied quickly, "Shakespeare was a jew-el of a writer."[34]

Golden had grown up in poverty, making a living on the streets of New York, and had known people from many ethnic groups and all classes. He had developed a liking for plays, concerts, and operas, and he read a wide range of newspapers. Largely self-educated, he was erudite and cosmopolitan. Bernice wanted very much to be his friend.

One time when Golden was speaking at the Writers Conference in Greensboro, jealousy crept in—unusual for this group, because they were generally supportive. Thad Stem had told Harris confidentially in a letter, "It doesn't perturb me that he [Golden] owns North Carolina,

lock, stock, and burned collards, but the fact that he dangles his tro-
phy on the end of his watch chain is mildly irratating [*sic*]."[35] Harris
described the occasion when all the resentment surfaced:

> It always seemed as natural for talk to radiate around Harry Golden
> as for the earth to revolve around the sun. That night in Greensboro one
> observer noticed how the earth turned toward the sun, how all of us sat
> at Harry's feet and glowed from the reflected light and warmth. A little
> conspiracy suddenly formed at the circumference of the circle. A whis-
> per to Richard Walser was passed on to Margaret [*sic*] Smethurst and
> from her to another, and presently little sparks of talk kindled into a
> glow that deflected the light and warmth across the room. His Honor, as
> Harry Golden has sometimes been referred to since his meteoric rise to
> fame, looked a bit baffled when none remained to listen to him except a
> writer with defective hearing.[36]

Harris makes no judgment on this behavior in her account of the Writers Conference.

However, an incident occurred that upset her so much she later
wrote about it when she was reviewing her life. Jonathan Daniels
(owner and executive editor of the Raleigh *News and Observer*) referred to the time Harry Golden had spent in jail for fraud connected
with the sale and purchase of stocks. In a conference session, Daniels
rose and said, "All right, Harry Golden, jail bird, get up there and tell
us about how it is to be a writer in a prison . . . [Tell us] if you would
have been a successful writer if you had not learned to write in jail."[37]
Everyone in the room stopped breathing.[38] Golden was shocked and
could not reply; the audience was angry with Daniels. Harris, usually
so slow to feel anger, so reluctant to judge, burned: "I was one of the
fans who stared open-mouthed at friends across the aisle." She said
she realized it was time to protest—but she objected only in personal
letters.[39] She probably did not realize the influence she had, but in any
case, she disliked public confrontations and shrank from entering any
fray.

Bernice Kelly Harris, Frank Borden Hanes declared, was the queen
at these conferences. "We were the Knights Errant and Erring," he
said jokingly.[40] In the 1950s, when she was sixty years old and more,
she was straight and tall and fairly trim. Her hair was white; she wore
rimless glasses that showed the clear blue color of her eyes; and she
had a pink schoolgirl's complexion.[41] Often she wore a hat and gloves,

and she carried herself with dignity, as southern ladies of her generation were supposed to do. Sometimes she wore dark sunglasses and
looked rather chic. She seemed comfortable with herself and at ease,
even folksy, with others, so that new acquaintances relaxed and enjoyed her sense of humor.[42] There was a reserve about her, however.
Hanes described this as "a certain solemnity about her, maybe derivative of sadness."[43]

Sam Ragan said that she would sit in the middle of the room and
writers would come up and talk to her about their work. "Harris had
a gentle way of steering conversation, keeping it on writing," he said.
He added that she was quiet about her own writing: "She did not like
to talk about herself. She would say something like, 'Have you read
this last book of Mebane's?' I'd say, 'No, but I'd love to.' And she'd
drag it out and say, 'You take it.' No, she didn't like to talk about herself at all."[44]

Part of her reluctance to talk about herself came from an attitude
she had learned as a child and described in *Purslane*: Dele would get
anxious when teachers bragged about Nannie Lou. One could create
too great expectations and draw too much attention to oneself. Some
danger lurked therein, for everyone had heard "Pride goeth before the
fall." And while it was considered acceptable for a man to boast, a
southern lady's behavior would be thought unseemly if she called attention to herself. But also, Bernice Harris was a very private person,
for all of her sociability. She was highly selective in what she chose to
disclose; she was uncomfortable when she sensed she might not have
control over the process of disclosure. And her passion was writing:
she loved talking to others about writing and kept the conversation focused on it—she always felt she learned, and she enjoyed the role of
nurturing other writers.

Indeed, she encouraged all the writers she knew. Even when she was
critiquing a very bad manuscript, she would think of something to
say—along with the negatives—so that the neophyte writer would not
be discouraged. Journalist Roy Parker Jr. said Bernice insisted that
there is nothing more important or satisfying than writing.[45] For her,
writing heightened the experiences of everyday life, and made it possible to live consciously and fully.[46]

Mebane Burgwyn asked if she should take a correspondence course
in writing. Bernice replied, "Don't worry too much over outside help.

You have help within. Go ahead and write."[47] When a serious critique was needed, Bernice did not hesitate, as in this letter to Mebane:

> Your story is lovely, Mebane. . . .
>
> As you suggested, there might be needed further development, more background as to why "I" hadn't loved my neighbor as "myself." The only lack I found at all was motivation. It was too pat, too obvious for the girl to fall for the charming preacher, perhaps. It's cute the way she started loving her neighbors and logical, since love spills over on others than the object inspiring it. I think that's what you meant. Yet some little conflict right in there to suggest more of her outlook on life before the minister changed it might help.[48]

She encouraged Thad Stem to follow his bent to write prose as well as poetry:

> I truly think you have things to say in prose. Actually, the poet will be reflected. Wasn't that true of Wolfe? Tell me about it when you come. That is, tell me as much as you think wise. I believe too much telling hurts the writing. The creative impulse is spent when the story or the message is told too often. The creator talks it out. But talk to me about it a little anyway. And what I have to offer by way of reaction or advice is yours, as you know.[49]

And to Harry Golden, whom she kept inviting to Seaboard and who kept promising her he would come but did not, she expressed her gratitude for enlarging her world: "I read with great interest and appreciation your article on Jewish literature. Thank you for sending it to me. I stand in respect before your erudition no more than before your human understanding and your ability to say something to such varied individuals who compose your acquaintance and friendship."[50]

She read all his writings; this letter must have pleased him: "You might be surprised to know how often I quote you in my teaching my Sunday school class. Yesterday I applied effectively, I hope, your last essay in the book to our study of Judges."[51]

To Frank Borden Hanes, to congratulate him on his book *Fleet Rabble* (1961), she said, "It has been a long time since I've had any tears for book people, but the Real People in your book moved me to that point. I was equally moved by your artistry, by the wonderful beauty of your writing."[52]

Throughout her correspondence files, letters supporting her fellow writers abound—and their replies in appreciation of her encouragement. The list of her correspondents reads like a Who's Who among North Carolina's writers at the time: John Ehle, Ovid Pierce, Paul Green, Julia Street, Wilma Dykeman, Noel Houston, Chalmers Davidson, LeGette Blythe, Elizabeth Boatwright Coker, Inglis Fletcher, Frances Gray Patton, Tom Wicker, and Manly Wade Wellman. She was especially fond of several young journalists: Holley Mack Bell (the *Bertie Ledger-Advance* and later *Greensboro Daily News*), Roy Parker Jr. (editor of the *Jackson News*, Washington correspondent for the *News and Observer*, and later editor at the *Fayetteville Observer*), and near the end of the decade, a young mother and newspaperwoman, Betty Hodges (*Durham Herald*). Bernice followed their careers, reading their columns and writing them her comments. Parker said that she would call him up and say things like, "You told that just right."[53]

Bernadette Hoyle, a journalist and photographer, sent her chapters from a book she was writing as well as important letters, asking her to mull them over and advise her. Hoyle wrote Bernice: "I know you are the dearest person in the world to be so good to me—without your encouragement and your faith I'd have junked this long ago."[54]

Ovid Pierce, a novelist who taught in the English department at East Carolina Teachers' College (now East Carolina University), had been a friend since World War II, when Bernice wrote to Private Pierce at an army camp in Texas. He told her, "I think of you frequently and often wish I could drop in for a talk. The sense of direction that I've always gotten from you has been one of the rare things of my life."[55]

Generally the writers tried to help each other with invitations to speak—opportunities to receive fees, but more important, to make their work known to the public. When one of them was on a committee to award a prize, he or she unabashedly advanced the cause of a friend. That was unfair, of course, but that was the way it was done—whom you knew counted. But also the quality of the work counted. And undoubtedly when Harris praised a work, she had influence because she was a member of the North Carolina Literary and Historical Association as well as of the Roanoke-Chowan Group, which gave an annual prize for poetry.

In 1952, she made a motion in the meetings of the North Carolina Literary and Historical Association that the Sir Walter Raleigh Award be given to her friend and fellow playwright Paul Green.[56] She nominated Thad Stem's book *The Jackknife Horse* for the Roanoke-Chowan Poetry Award in 1954. She called the attention of the North Carolina Literary and Historical Association in 1961 to *Animal Fair* by Stem.[57] Harris made sure Mebane Burgwyn's *Penny Rose* was entered in the contest in 1952 for best fiction sponsored by the North Carolina Literary and Historical Association.[58] Frank Borden Hanes was sure Bernice Harris had a lot to do with putting his work forward when he won an award from the Roanoke-Chowan Group.[59]

Harris's fellow writers reviewed her books, published articles about her for the newspapers, and sent her letters in praise of articles she had written. In 1957 John Ehle, then a faculty member at the University of North Carolina's Department of Radio, Television, and Motion Pictures, came to see her play "Yellow Color Suit" and advised NBC to televise it.[60] In his letter to the agent, he estimated the impact of her work: "All of us have a high regard for the real thing in every area she carved out for herself some few decades ago. Mrs. Harris is the first voice, the final word, and the best."[61]

Bernadette Hoyle wrote an essay about her for her book on North Carolina writers, *Tar Heel Writers I Know*, published in 1956. Hoyle gave Harris the chance to publicize her own ideas about writing by beginning with a direct quotation from Harris's conversation with her. The question was why people write:

> The motive varies. . . . Do we like people or enjoy them so much we want to share our slants? Those who say they write for money are only telling half. For fun? Half, too. To entertain? To instruct? To voice anger against injustice? I could write a theory, an analysis, but an area still would be unreached.
>
> I think the urge is rooted in something finer, more mysterious even, than writers admit. The creative impulse somewhere along the line is at least related to a force beyond the motives named.[62]

Bernice once told her mentor, J. O. Bailey, "It seems that people happen to me more than events."[63] She was aware that she was not well-traveled, and she thought that she had not done spectacular things. When she got a letter from Dick Walser, saying that he intended to write a biography of her for his series on North Carolina writers, she was troubled. Since she did not like to talk about herself, this prospect evoked much anxiety. But Walser insisted, and for this biography he wanted to come to Seaboard to interview her over several days. When he arrived, she greeted him at the door with a disclaimer: "I want to help you, but you've got a hard job. I've never done anything interesting, and I don't for the life of me see how you're going to make a book—even the smallest one—out of me."[64]

Bernice arranged a picnic for him the evening he arrived in Seaboard, the summer of 1954. Magdeline Faison cooked with her, and Bernice's nieces, Alice Jo and Rosalie, and her grandniece Sandra, who were visiting, also helped. Mebane and John Burgwyn came over. They went to a millpond and spread the picnic under an evening sky in June. It was a magic night.[65]

Next day the work began. When her family went home, Bernice had a problem: according to the social norm in Seaboard it would not be acceptable for a widow to stay alone in a house with a bachelor. Bernice was over twenty years older than Walser and he wasn't interested romantically in women anyway, but actual circumstances did not matter. Reece Bullock left his family and stayed at night with Bernice and Dick. She said, "Reece solved an immediate problem then and through the years."[66] Reece knew her well enough to know she would have been troubled by any appearance of impropriety.

As Bernice Harris and Dick Walser talked, he expressed curiosity as to why she published books with a New York firm for over a decade but never went to New York until the fifties. She said she had wanted to go, from time to time. And then she added, "But it doesn't make any difference. You see, I've traveled far—much farther than New York."[67] He said that by the next day, he knew what she meant:

> It was utterly true that Bernice Kelly Harris had never been a missionary to China, nor had she had a half dozen Mexican divorces, nor been in any literary quarrels or airplane smashes; but as the hours passed, I knew that, for me at least, there was a modesty, an honesty, an integrity and an artistry in this woman which did not demand anything of the sensational in the telling to make it interesting—*interesting*, you see was her word, not mine.[68]

Back in Raleigh, Walser confided to her the fears he had had about the trip to Seaboard:

> Of course, I knew that the most pleasant part of this little stint I'm busy with just now, would be those day[s] when I would be working directly with you. And so it turned out. In Seaboard I felt so very placid—as I told you. Does the place do that to everybody? And the hours just skipped away. But really, we got quite a lot done. . . . I shall never forget the helpfulness you gave all the time, nor shall I forget the

unabashed hospitality at your house and everywhere we went. Mainly I think I shall not forget the meals, nor you in the garden. I admit just now that I was a little afraid of Seaboard. I was afraid I wouldn't fit in— for four or five days in a row—or that I wouldn't be allowed to fit in. However, I think I did. I liked everybody, and if folks didn't like me, they were kind enough not to show it.[69]

From this time on Bernice felt closer than ever to Dick Walser. Since their first correspondence during World War II, when he was in the navy in the Pacific, she had regarded him as a friend. Now she asked his advice and she would sometimes share her secrets with him. She wanted him to be her literary executor; he agreed and took the responsibility very seriously, keeping a "fat file" about everything she wrote or someone wrote about her.[70] She sent him her manuscripts to critique and teasingly addressed him as her "lit. ex." However, the friendship was not consistently rosy. In reply to a letter from Mebane, she referred to Dick's saying something "snide," and said, "Isn't he a spoiled brat? I love him."[71]

But in spite of little negative interactions sometimes, she appreciated his talent for critiquing a work, his honesty, and his concern for her. In later years, she told him, "You have always been a great good friend."[72] She helped him when she could. In 1959, he asked her to read the biography he had written of the slave poet Moses Horton and write the editor at Henry Holt Company.[73] She liked the book and was glad to do that.

The biography, *Bernice Kelly Harris: Storyteller of Eastern Carolina*, was published in 1955 by the University of North Carolina Library. When she read it, she told J. O. Bailey, "It really is an amazing thing that I became a writer."[74] She was pleased with the biography and sent her congratulations to Walser:

> I declare it's good reading. It's amazing that even you [meaning you who know me so well] could make it so. I am very pleased, delighted, relieved. When you wrote that I'm not to mind the uncomplimentary parts, I began to worry. I really was bothered. I know so much that is uncomplimentary, but I've tried to keep it hidden the best I can. I concluded your quick and nimble mind had ferreted out all the thorns and as biographer you honestly felt you had to record the thorniness. What a relief! I didn't find a thing to mind in the least.[75]

Her mentor J. O. Bailey had a different view:

Now, I have an idea that Dick Walser put down faithfully everything you told him; but you didn't tell him enough about yourself. It is good that his book should have thoughtful criticisms of your novels and stories, but people will want to know a great deal more about the author of them. I know the trouble, your modesty. But this is at least a part of your record for the future, and if I may borrow a phrase I think you have used, you should "tell all." For any second edition, which I hope will be demanded, tell more. I think, for instance, of the many times you have written me about being in the midst of a novel, but bogged down and delayed because you had some manuscript of a would-be writer to read. I do not know the details, but I can imagine a great deal of your time and effort devoted to helping. It is a good, kind thing to devote so much of your time to so many people, and I think you should give your biographer the story, and let him appraise it.[76]

The constant interruptions that Bailey refers to in this letter continued. Harris started a new work soon after finishing *Wild Cherry Tree Road,* but she was not happy with it. For one who had always finished a novel, sent it off, and gotten it published, this was troubling. But through the decade her friendships with other North Carolina writers sustained her even in the midst of disappointments with her writing. Especially Bernice's friendship with Mebane was a constant satisfaction in her life.

Just after Mebane Burgwyn's book *Moon Flower* was published in 1954, Mebane felt jittery. Bernice tried to comfort her:

Writing a book is not lonelier a thing than waiting through the launching. It's a suffering kind of interval, right after a book is published—a suffering with joy sometimes and with uncertainty and wonder at other times. The exhilaration is no more easily contained than the doubt, and yet writers must contain it or non-writers will withdraw the fellowships there are. . . .

Moonflower is your best book. How readers are going to love it! More important than story or style is the characterization. You have interpreted people so beautifully and so wisely without flourish or exaggeration.[77]

In reply, Mebane thanked her: "There has been a month of wondering about the book. I was still too close to it as I read it and so much of the heart in it has been cut that I couldn't judge. The only two reviews have really said nothing. I had almost resigned myself to anything that might come, but your letter melted my resolution and you, in your wonderful generosity, have made it seem worthwhile."[78]

On New Year's Eve in 1954, Mebane reflected on the year just ending, "In spite of our discouraging crop year the scales weigh heavily on the good side for us. And so many of the good hours have been shared directly or indirectly with you."[79]

Often in the 1950s and 1960s, Sam and Marjorie Ragan and Thad and Dety Stem came to spend a weekend with Bernice. Clara and Holley Bell would drive from Greensboro to visit Mebane and John Burgwyn and Bernice. Bernice would get a note from the Bells, "We're coming to see you and Mag [Magdeline Faison]."[80] Writers Manly Wade Wellman and Frances Wellman also visited. After one of these dinners together, Mebane expressed her close identification with Bernice: "I wish I could tell you—really tell you—how much I appreciated and enjoyed the wonderful dinner and the visit with you last Friday night. You are a lovely and gracious hostess, and the delicious meal you served will long be remembered as one of the best. Manly and Frances sang your praises after we left, and John and I joined in, although I think we both felt the sort of glow that comes only with the feeling of identity—as though you belonged to us somehow. You know?"[81]

Feeling in touch with all these friends in North Carolina was immensely satisfying, but Harris did not make friends among the national literary elite. The forties, when she was publishing a novel every two years, would have been the time to build on favorable reviews around the country to establish a national reputation. She sought rather the full life she led in Seaboard, and she carried out her responsibility toward Herbert. She simply had no ideas about how reputations were built, and there was no one to advise her about the literary world. The writers she was in contact with were well known in North Carolina but not as much known elsewhere, with some exceptions, such as Paul Green, Harry Golden, and John Ehle. Acquaintances had best-sellers, like Betty Smith's *A Tree Grows in Brooklyn* and Frances Gray Patton's *Good Morning, Miss Dove*, but these writers were not close friends. Still, in the fifties Harris very much enjoyed the writers' friendships she had—perhaps this was what she needed.

Indeed, the emotional support of her fellow North Carolina writers was of crucial importance to her at this time in her life. She felt she was part of a community of writers; the fact that they were in different parts of the state did not matter. Harry Golden had written to her from Charlotte, "You are there; Clara and Mack [Bell] are in another part of the state and I am here, and somehow I have the feeling that we are constantly aware of these very simple facts, and regardless of how seldom we see each other or write to each other I have the feeling that at any given moment, in the dark of the night even, we can call upon each other for a word of kindness and friendship." She repeated the words to Golden and told him, "Those words you wrote on April 8 have grown in meaning and beauty during this interval. They say it. I sign my name to them."[82]

15

Struggling to Be Both Writer and Person

The new work Harris started soon after finishing *Wild Cherry Tree Road* was not coming along as she wished. For one thing, her writing suffered from lack of uninterrupted hours to devote to it. On April 9, 1952, she wrote her mentor J. O. Bailey about this manuscript she had entitled "Seven Angry Men":

> My work has been sporadic. For one month I worked with fervor on the mob story, a story in which the mob is the hero—or villain. Actually, the seven men who are the components of the mob are not villain, but ordinary men involved in extraordinary lawlessness strange to them. My problem is that the story seems diffuse, since the seven component parts are followed through motive and action and consequence. I might solve that by using a central character, around which the other members of the mob revolve. I don't want to do that; I want to show motive, action and consequence through seven men. The lawyer for the defense more nearly unifies the action than any other, but he is inadequate still. So, for a month now I have rested on the material, and my fervor has waned. I feel inclined to start another, as indeed I have tentatively done.[1]

By the fall, she was working on the new novel, as she told Mebane Burgwyn on September 29, 1952: "For the past week I've scribbled at the intervals I've had, but as yet it's a chore and no brightness in the days. I have the pages accumulating, and that is what they are—pages. There has to be a spark soon."[2]

By mid-November, there was some hope, but not a lot, that the new novel would be developing. It was titled "Bevvy Lamm." She described it as "the story of a girl who translated her romantic dreams into very practical exigency." She told Mebane, "I have been literally swamped. Not all trivia. But it has been interrupted. I wrote on Bevvy (her present name and she's stirring under it) yesterday for the first time in two weeks. Six guests over the weekend, a party and a church bazaar later this week, with a cake and pie to bake and so on."[3] She said she had given herself five years between books and "apparently it will be all of that." She added, "I'm living it up. That's important, too."[4]

But she still felt apologetic about letting social engagements and requests for help interfere with her writing time. In a letter to Mebane in 1952, she admitted: "I've planned to write you, but days have been cluttered. I do not know what happens with time. It goes, and so little is actually accomplished. At least, in my corner. I must stop saying yes. You know how a writer cannot be a person and get writing done. I'm months behind, being a person of a sort."[5]

Margarette Smethurst said that at the Writers Conference at Cherokee (1951) someone asked Bernice "if she had found a way to write without interruption, if she had trained Mag [Magdeline Faison] to ward off interruptions during her working hours. Bernice replied, 'No, I work until I am interrupted . . . and then I go back and start again.' "[6]

Magdeline Faison tried to get Bernice to slow down and take better care of herself. At one point, Faison was so exasperated with Bernice's working so constantly that she said, "All right, kill yourself. And people will soon be saying, 'Miss Kelly was a good old lady.' " She did make an impression—Bernice admitted this startled her.[7]

But she was startled only temporarily. Indeed, not only did she allow interruptions from people who wanted help with an important letter or a speech or a news item for the local paper, but she also helped neighborhood teenagers who were struggling with term papers.[8] She read entries in literary contests, with no remuneration, of course. And she still could not turn down a request to speak before a woman's club. Typical of the thank-you letters was this one from Greensboro, where Bernice and Jo Parker had driven one cold February day in 1959: "Thank you for the inspiration your fine talk gave us for more courageous, as well as adventurous, living. You saw for yourself what a responsive chord you struck—we shall remember you and your words a long, long time."[9]

When Bernice did get a chance to write, she worked with intense concentration. When Bernadette Hoyle asked if she kept regular writing hours, she said, "I should have, but I haven't." She explained, "I write all day and sometimes into the night when I'm going good, but scarcely a pause for lunch. It's a bad business. I wear myself out and then lack zest to start the next. A writing schedule is the thing, and my aim is to start one and hew to it."[10] But she did not establish a writing schedule.

The mid-fifties brought another dilemma: she confided to Walser that a suitor had made a proposal. She refused to give the man's name, so the identification can only be surmised. There are letters from Frank Parker, a widower, who had been married to one of Bernice's cousins; Bernice probably saw him at the Mt. Moriah Church after the death of his wife in 1954. In a letter in July 1955, Parker told Bernice: "Really I was plumb glad to get your letter yesterday. . . . I have needed a kind of consolation and understanding, from someone whom I knew understood. I must therefore be careful lest our wonderful relations be dampened and even discontinued." He ended the letter, "Sincerely and then some."[11]

They talked on the telephone. In August 1955, he wrote to ask if they might get together. He admitted, "You are getting in my hair lately—beginning to have you in mind too often. Your letters seem to be too much the bread of life. Is that the signs of love?"[12]

On August 13, he wrote again, saying he had seen a friend of hers from her college days at Meredith: "I mentioned that you are Belle's cousin, and had encouraged me regarding writing. That you are a grand person, but inclined to be too serious or reserved or otherwise self contained." He signed the letter, "Good night and good luck, Lady Fair. As ever—you say, but I want to say more. F.P."[13]

Bernice confided this interest to her "Dear Folks." They teased her—which she did not seem to mind.[14] And she told Mebane and Charlotte about it. Then in early fall, she wrote Mebane, "I've never finished telling you the story. There isn't one now. Sometimes I know I decided right, then again I wonder. At any rate I've had peace of mind lately."[15]

Mebane wrote to her on September 28, 1955: "I do want to hear your story—the personal one. I am sure that peace of mind is worth most any price. I had hoped that you might find a rare and lovely happiness through this experience, but if it wasn't to be that, then surely you have made the right decision."[16]

The next January (1956) Parker wrote to her, "You're my friend for life. . . . If you have such [weaknesses] you conceal them well—too well to be really human. That is what I was puzzled about you. (Mystery)."[17] Friends they had become—he married the next month.

Meanwhile, there were the joys and tragedies of people around Bernice in Seaboard. At one point, a neighbor went berserk: "All day and night he raves, curses and threatens to kill everybody."[18] Bernice sat up, awake. It was not until the next morning that he was taken away. On the other hand, the brides in the neighborhood stored their wedding dresses in the closet in her spare room and dressed the day of their marriage in her house. And because she was a good listener, people told her their troubles.

Deaths of friends grown old caused her much concern and sadness; deaths in the town she referred to in terms of "we" and "our," as in this statement in a letter to Mary and William Olive: "We lost our Mrs. Maddrey."[19] The inevitable day came when Elizabeth Harris's mother, who had suffered a long illness, lay dying. Elizabeth asked Bernice to come. Bernice, who was in bed with a bad cold, got up and went to the Harris home and stayed into the night. "It was an awful day, just sitting there waiting," she said. Dr. Parker came in all through the day to help turn the patient in the bed, but there was little else anyone could do. "The dying was hard," Bernice wrote William Olive and Mary. "Elizabeth was very brave until the end."[20] How well Bernice understood this kind of terrible watch.

Just as she had taken Mebane "under her wing" after her mother's death, now Bernice became a second mother to Elizabeth. In later years, after a birthday celebration Bernice gave her, Elizabeth wrote, "You really out-did yourself in this latest gesture of friendship (of which there have been so many). . . . You have filled a place in my life that would be void otherwise and I realize that part of my heritage from Mama and Daddy was your love for them and I am eternally grateful."[21]

Somehow, Bernice found bits of time to write. She finished the manuscript "Bevvy Lamm" in 1953.[22] The novel begins with Beverley Lamm (called Bevvy by her family) as a twelve-year-old girl who lives on a small farm in the pre–World War I South with her mother, Amelia, her father, Jim, and her little brother, Jimmy. Bevvy knows there is tension between her mother and father. Amelia wants the family to be landowners; she cannot stand the thought that she is the wife of a landless laborer. Jim simply wants to follow the work of the sawmill. He has acquiesced in his wife's ambition and helped her save enough to make a down payment on land. But he hates the uncertainty of income from farming and likes the security of the sawmill paycheck. Staying with the plow in the field when he hears the whirr of the sawmill is hard for him.

Bevvy, working in the field beside Jimmy, sometimes sees her father slip away to the woods; one day when Jimmy steals away also, she follows him and finds her father instead, working at the saw, his eyes bright.

She knows that Jimmy tries to get away and go to the sawmill to play with a strange boy named Doll, who lives in the workers' shanties. When her mother asks where her father and brother are, Bevvy tries to cover up for them; yet she has empathy with her mother as well. She does not know who she is—her mother's ally? her brother's protector? her father's friend?

Her family is distant from the sawmill people, but distant from the farmers around as well. Bevvy finds a way to escape from the elusive conflict within her family and the sense of isolation from others. She creates a world of her own:

> To begin this adventure, Bevvy would scoop out dirt, lay wild flowers and berries and ferns in the little graves and place over them chance fragments of window pane, lightly covering the glass with dirt. Then later, after she had made herself wait awhile, she would slip to the shadowy graves, uncover the glass and have her breath-taking view. Even the dusty goldenrod and morning glories and fennel and chickweed, so near and common, would look remote and rare under glass.
>
> Like the sawmill people she sometimes viewed from her secret slope in the woods: it was as though she saw them under glass, and they seemed as remote and uncommon as the wild flowers. Doll, the sawyer's son, who had taken to coming up to the yard palings to look for Jimmy until Amelia had ordered him away, seemed even more remote than the rest.
>
> People, Bevvy's senses cried out sometimes, to know the manner and make of people, to sample people like cake and pie! As often as Jimmy cried out his longing to be a saw mill hand, so often had her senses cried

out she wanted to be real people, to be with people out from under glass, to be Bevvy Lamm. (F146, p. 8)

Amelia tells Bevvy stories about her own childhood, of how she was Amelia Hardy, of how her father had sided with the Gray family in a feud between Hardys and Grays, how the Hardys disowned them, and how she was taken in by the Grays when she became an orphan. She grew up, she tells Bevvy, in the plantation mansion, Anchor House.

The aristocratic landowner Randall Gray had built a schoolhouse for his daughter-in-law Miss Rosemary, and there she taught the extended family's children, including Amelia. Now, Amelia teaches Bevvy the Latin Miss Rosemary had taught her.

Bevvy senses that her mother was made to leave Randall Gray's Anchor House, and only through occasional inferences does she understand the reason—her mother fell in love with the sawmill worker, Jim. Amelia desperately needs to disprove the Grays' predictions that she and Jim will always be lower class, landless laborers: she names the little farm she and Jim buy "New Anchor."

One day, working in the field, Bevvy notices that Jimmy is edging away in the direction of the sawmill. Her father comes looking for him, and Bevvy tells him where she thinks Jimmy has gone. Jim arrives just in time to see his son mangled to death by the saw. In trying to stop the machine, he also gets fatally cut. For three years, the widowed Amelia and Bevvy try to stay on and work the farm. The boy whom Jimmy had befriended, Doll, wants to help them; but Amelia does not want a sawmill child around.

Finally, Amelia admits defeat and sells the farm. She and Bevvy prepare to leave. Secretly Doll tells Bevvy he will follow them someday. Amelia and Bevvy set out for Anchor House, where Amelia hopes that Randall Gray will have pity and take them in.

After days of traveling, they reach Anchor House to find that Randall Gray has died, as well as his son Rand Gray. Only the grandson, Randall Gray, remains in the house. He is annoyed that they have come but realizes that Amelia is ill and consents to their staying the night. However, Amelia has a stroke; after that, he cannot turn them out. He assigns Bevvy (now a sixteen-year-old) and her helpless mother to one wing of the house and promises to supply food. Otherwise, Bevvy is to remain out of his sight, he says.

Bevvy watches Randall leave the house each morning. She assumes he is supervising the farmworkers at the edge of the plantation lands. She wants to be useful to him: she tends a little flower garden and cleans up the family grave plot. She begins to long for the sight of him coming home—she likes the straight carriage of this twenty-some-year-old man. She cooks his evening meal and leaves it at his place at the table. She keeps out of sight. Nothing is said.

One day Bevvy sees clothes hanging on a line to air and she recognizes one dress: it belonged to Miss Rosemary, who wears it in the portrait prominently displayed in the house. All her life Miss Rosemary had been her idol because of the stories Amelia told her. On impulse, Bevvy takes the dress from the line and tries it on. When she looks in the mirror, she realizes that she resembles Miss Rosemary. Randall comes in and is startled to see the familiar dress, now worn by Bevvy, who has the same mist of black hair, the same grey-blue eyes, and the same white face as his mother. He orders Bevvy to take the dress off.

After eight months, Amelia has a final stroke and dies. Bevvy tells Randall that she must go, that she will get work. She is nearly seventeen now. He asks what she wants to do, and she replies that she wants to be a teacher like Miss Rosemary. He offers to tutor her, and so they meet in the evenings at his mother's schoolhouse. Someone stealthily skirts the grounds. Bevvy is afraid it is Doll, who has followed the sawmill crew to the mill near Anchor House. One night she wakes to an eerie dawn light and soon realizes it is not dawn but a fire. The schoolhouse is burning.

Soon afterwards, visitors appear at the door and announce that they are Raife Hardy and his wife Evelina, that they are Amelia Hardy Lamm's cousins and therefore Bevvy's cousins. It is not right, they say, for a single man and a single woman to live in a house together. The Hardys cannot let someone in their family risk dishonor. In panic at the thought of leaving Randall, Bevvy runs to him and tells him she wants to stay with him. She asks him what he wants. He tells her he wants her to go with her cousins.

Raife and Evelina take Bevvy to their home and try to be kind. Bevvy meets others in the family, including Norman Hardy, whom she knows intuitively to be a troubled, wild young man. With the Hardys, Bevvy learns more about the feud between the Hardys and the Grays. A dispute about a boundary between lands is not all the trouble: Randall Gray's son Rand made Nolia Hardy pregnant. For this crime the Hardys caught him and emasculated him. Now Bevvy realizes that

Norman Hardy is the bastard son of Rand Gray. But who is the father of the present Randall Gray? When she asks, the reply is always, "Sin casts long shadows." She knows only that she longs for Randall: "There were times she felt impelled to cry out like a child that she had gone as long without sight of him as she could" (f162, p. 190).

In her contacts with Norman it becomes clear that he hates Randall, that he knows everything about what goes on at Anchor House. When Bevvy thinks about his words, she becomes aware that he lets slip indications that he enjoys destroying by fire. He tells her that she is his. He takes her on a carriage ride so fast and so dangerous that she is afraid she will be killed. He tells her that the ride is his present to her.

Bevvy, now eighteen, wants to make a living on her own, but the Hardy clan will not hear of it. They decide she will spend time in each Hardy home. She finds herself drawn into the emotional struggles of each household just as she once was torn between loyalty to her father and loyalty to her mother in their struggles. She is not sure who she is or where she belongs or what she should be doing. She stays as long as she is told and moves on when she is told.

In the last household, she resides with the thirteen-year-old Lillie Mae, who is caring for an elderly, dying husband, Ed Hardy. Lillie Mae and her younger brother have little food in the house; Lillie Mae has been trying to make money by going out each day to cook for the sawmill workers. When Ed dies, Lillie Mae's relatives come and carry her and her brother away. Bevvy goes to the sawmill to take Lillie Mae's place as the cook. There she meets Doll again.

Bevvy realizes the sawmill workers are illiterate. Shunned by the landowners and taken advantage of by all, they are in need of education just to know how to protect themselves. She befriends a sawmill hand's wife, Mecie, who is dying of tuberculosis. Mecie asks Bevvy to go with her to the doctor, but the doctor turns out to be a witch doctor, who attributes tuberculosis to breathing graveyard dust. The witch doctor takes a week's pay and assures Mecie that she is not dying, since she has not breathed in the dust. Bevvy and Mecie start out for the sawmill.

> When Bevvy turned to leave her she said involuntarily, "Mecie, don't
> believe it."
> "Not believe it?" Mecie challenged. "Why, she told me I haven't

breathed in death. It wasn't no graveyard dust! I'm fixed up now for spring!" As she swung her hips toward the cypresses, she added over her shoulder, "And for love!" (F162, no page number)

Doll, now a member of the sawmill crew, shows Bevvy the house he is building for her: "It's yourn," he said. "I aimed it for you, case you ran out of homes in this strange country." He asks only to be her servant and to live nearby. She knows this structure can never be her house, but his selfless love for her touches her.

> She looked at Doll. He was waitman standing there, asking nothing. Hadn't he always been so? All he had ever asked, except to cut her wood and draw her water and shrub her new ground, was that she 'learn' him to draw letters. Hadn't she been running from that plea ever since? (F162, p. 310)

Bevvy begins to teach. Once more Raife and Evelina come to get her—they will not have a member of their family cooking for sawmill workers. Bevvy defies them and stays. But she feels a desperate need for her own place. Bevvy tries to find her great-grandfather's house in the deep woods, the Caleb Hardy house, long since abandoned. She does find the old house, and she has a sense of contentment as she rests there on the plain board floor of the main room.

Norman tracks her down. He is in a rage: it's his house, he says, but the Hardys will not let him have it. At one point he comes close to raping Bevvy but lets her go. Running away from Norman, she hides until she is sure he has gone and then finds her way back through a rainstorm to the Caleb Hardy house. She stays there during the rains that pour for days. Word gets around that she is missing.

Actually, she is in danger from the rising water of the creek. Randall, who has heard that she is lost and has been searching for her, finds her at the Caleb Hardy place. She remembers that the Hardys might also look for her there, but she is so glad to see him, she goes with him to his carriage.

> For all the breathless speed and dreamlike suddenness of the ride, Bevvy for the moment felt no fear or reservation. Elijah would have had no sense of need to hold on to the chariot sides to keep from falling out, and she did not. There was only the warning sense that she would presently wake up out of her dream and start falling to earth.
>
> "I'm going to take you across," he said as they moved through the dimness of the woods.

"Oh." She fell to earth enough to think of the group waiting her return at the Caleb Hardy place. "But—"

"Lift your feet to the dashboard," he ordered. "And hold on. There's still high water."

She heard the splash, felt themselves sinking into water that seemed at first to weight them down. Then there was a feeling of buoyancy, as though they were floating. The chariot had become a boat, and they were riding the waves, and there was no bottom. Her feet even above the dashboard were splashed.

Then they were climbing out of water, tugging at the muddy slope, touching earth again.

After the buoyant smoothness just experienced she found herself holding on intensely, gasping for breath as the wild ride over the rough and uneven path continued.

"Where," she finally managed to say, as though out of a trance, "are we?"

"I'm taking you home," Randall said tersely and again lapsed into silence. (F162, pp. 321–322)

They have crossed the creek that divides Hardy land from Gray land. He takes her to Anchor House. She feels glad to be back there, and they both admit their love. He wants her to marry him.

Randall tells her that he has sold a strip of his land to the Hardys because they want to own it so they can tear down the sawmill workers' shanties. This will force the sawmill workers out of the neighborhood. He will use the money to rebuild his mother's schoolhouse, he says. But Bevvy realizes it is a schoolhouse that will never be a haven for the workers' children. She begs him to use the money to do something that will reconcile the Hardys and Grays. She passionately wants to stop the hatred that has lasted so many generations and poisoned their lives. She asks him to build a bridge over the creek between their landholdings as a gesture of reconciliation. He is shocked. She decides she wants him to take her back to the Hardys.

Unknown to her, Norman has observed her meeting with Randall. One night Doll comes to see Bevvy to tell her she is in danger. When Doll is returning through the pitch-black woods to the sawmill, Norman mistakes him for Randall and beats him senseless. He drags Doll back to the sawmill, where either he throws Doll against the saw or Doll falls on it accidentally—no one knows which—and Doll is killed. The Hardys—who suspect Norman is implicated—insist on the story that Doll's death was accidental. Norman runs away.

Bevvy, appalled at this slaughter, begs the Hardys to build a bridge, to heal the wounds in the community. But they use whatever money they can scrape up to refurbish the church where they worship in their closed group. Bevvy tries to find her own direction:

> After her impassioned plea for a bridge to the marsh was made to seem foolish, she turned her mind to bridging other chasms still deeper than the creek, the chasm of ignorance and superstition and illiteracy that were constant floodwaters. She was beginning to relate herself to this flood, wondering if she might not herself become at least a little footlog across it. (F162, p. 330)

Bevvy knows by now that Randall is Miss Rosemary's son by the mill owner Forrest. And she realizes that Randall has no farmworkers or crops in the field; with almost no money, he went each day, not to supervise his plantation workers, but to cut down trees to sell to the mill so that he could buy food for her and her mother.

When Randall comes to tell her that he is leaving the area, he explains that he must find out who he is. Bevvy lets him go even though she loves him. For her, romantic love has been overshadowed by her need to dispel the hate between families and to teach the sawmill people. She feels connected to the small farmers struggling with their burden of hatred; she feels connected to the illiterate workers struggling to bring some quality into their lives. Harris summarized the meaning of the novel in a letter to her mentor, J. O. Bailey: "Bevvy Lamm is concerned with the impact of people on one who has not known people except from the outside."[23]

Now that Bevvy is clear about her purpose, has chosen a role in the community, she knows for the first time who she is. She rejects her mother's distinctions between landed and landless—but perpetuates her mother's love of learning. She makes it clear to Randall that she is not like his mother either: she will not be a teacher for the privileged few. Bevvy's way is her own.

She goes back to her great-grandfather's abandoned house and convinces the Hardys that she should have the house as her mother's part of the family inheritance. No longer will she be a boarder in someone else's house: she will have her own home. Her mother, Amelia, identified with Anchor House and with a lifestyle that was not hers—even naming her home after someone else's place. Bevvy identifies with her house because it was her great-grandfather's and hers by inheritance, but even more important to her, she knows it is the means by which she can be independent, can be truly herself. Clearly possession of the house is a metaphor for owning the self. When Bevvy wanders through the deep woods to find the house, she is struggling to possess understanding of herself.

Randall takes her through the water, and she experiences the buoyant feeling of romantic love. But the landing on the other side brings clarity about what this romantic love costs. Bevvy is beginning to know intuitively that she will not give up her life's purpose to have his love.

Harris does not deny the possibility of Randall's coming back but makes it clear that he, too—stripped of his identity as a Gray—must come to understand who he is. At the end of the novel, Randall is willing to stop looking back, to relinquish his dream of reconstructing a past that both he and Bevvy realize was faulty at best. But only when he also comes to know and accept himself can he be a partner to Bevvy. Then he will be able to respect her purpose.

Once again, Harris treats the theme of autonomy versus connection. In this resolution, the character comes to know who she is through defining her purpose in the community; and the self-direction she acquires becomes more important even than belonging in a union of romantic love. Bevvy could leave her community, could go with Randall, but she would have to give up her dreams of a better future for the community she has made her own. To go with Randall on his journey of self-discovery would be to deny her own: she stays. In this novel the main character finds autonomy within connection—the connection is to a community, not to a lover—but the chief gain is autonomy.

Harris identified with Bevvy: the description of Bevvy's mist of black hair, smoke blue eyes, and white face is that of the young Bernice Kelly. Bevvy's love of teaching she felt herself: it was her conviction that to have the words to express experience gives power as well as beauty to one's life. And certainly, Harris feared the hatred of one group of people toward another. The class antagonism which she had observed and felt since childhood and which she treated consistently in her novels is an integral part of "Bevvy Lamm."

There are situations reminiscent of earlier work: Bevvy's little graveyards of wildflowers under glass can be found in the earlier *Sage Quarter*. Two ancient ladies keep captive a fifty-year-old niece who wants to marry, as in Harris's play of the thirties, *Judgment Comes to Dan'l*. The family tries to force Bevvy to be the dependent unmarried woman living in relatives' homes as Tiny was forced to be in *Sage Quarter*.

Harris's writing style in "Bevvy Lamm" is also like her writing in earlier works: the beauty of the words precisely chosen, the expert presentation of regional speech, the natural feeling, yet tension, in the dialogue, the impact achieved by the structuring of the sentences, the incisive rendering of elusive psychological states. A critic said there is a "thunderstorm atmosphere brewing" in *Sweet Beulah Land*;[24] the sense of impending danger is felt even more strongly here.

Indeed, the feeling in the novel is dark and brooding. People's actions are furtive. Questions go unanswered. And always the sawmill bell reminds people that there stands ready the saw's teeth mindlessly cutting: it is symbolic of the way their mindless hating cuts into them, diminishing them and eventually annihilating them. The alternative is to turn away from hatred to face the community's problems.[25]

Ever aware that humans live in a symbolic universe, Harris characteristically delineates the symbolic action which shows the reader that some psychological change is occurring. The person is deliberating and taking a decisive step, although on the surface she seems to be doing something ordinary. At the end of *Purslane*, Dele mends the hole in her son's boyhood sailor suit before she gives him up to death. It is Dele's way of making herself know that she has taken care of his homely needs all his life and now in defining a last task she accepts the end of his life. Tiny defies the last authority in her life, Aunt Cherry, when she opens the door to help the drunk Jim Balk. She signals that she takes power to decide how she will behave in the world as a mature woman. Bevvy Lamm tries on Randall Gray's mother's dress, showing her desire to be like her. But at the end of the novel, she rejects Randall's plans for her to teach in his mother's schoolhouse and simply asks him to take her back across the swollen creek's waters to her own family. Bevvy's action in this reveals her first inkling that romantic love may not solve all, that she must find her own life work and meaning.

Unfortunately, only fragments of the manuscript of this novel remain among Harris's papers. From these, it is possible to reconstruct major portions of the novel, but putting the fragments together probably does not produce the final draft actually sent off. Harris mailed

"Bevvy Lamm" to her agent Diarmuid Russell, who liked it. He sent it on to Miss Claasen, who liked it.[26] The manuscript was not published. Any further mention of it ceased, and there are no records or memories of living persons to indicate what happened. Possibly Doubleday did not want to take a chance on another moderate-selling novel; the company might have been seeking a novel sure to be a best-seller. There is no evidence that her agent Diarmuid Russell submitted it to other publishing houses.[27]

In 1955, Bernice sent her manuscript "Seven Angry Men," whose title she had changed to "Seven Men of Eagleton," to Dick Walser. His reaction was something new to her:

> After several interruptions punctuated by two long weekends out of town, I settled down last night—it was raining and thus a good evening for reading—and went straight through *Seven Men of Eagleton*. Every half hour I had to stop and light a cigarette and assure myself that this was really written by Bernice Kelly Harris. It is very unlike your previous books and only a capitalized abstract or other minor Harris touch gives you away.
>
> Let me be candid: The novel has pace and suspense—salable commodities in this year 1955—and I can't see a publisher turning it down. It's a natural for the paperback reprints, or for the original paperbacks, if you need several thousand dollars right away. The best writing, to me, concerned the seven men during the 24 hours after the trip to the jail. In fact, those sections are so suspenseful that the courthouse scene and the last section seem to me (let me be candid!) somewhat slow.
>
> I hate for the story to slide to a stop. You must be true to your intent, of course: but this novel, when it is published, can't escape comparison with W. V. T. Clark's *The Ox-Bow Incident*, a mob story too. . . . Your seven Eagleton men must go free, sure, but is there sufficient retribution? The reader senses that there has been, but this seeming is a bit unfocused, vague. More details are needed. . . .
>
> [He continues to write about how hard it is for the reader to keep all the characters in mind.]
>
> What I'm trying to say is that this is a great story—one that needed to be written and needs to be read. Your point of "community solidarity" ought to be known to Northern editorialists and everybody else. I don't know how the widow story or the other one is progressing, but I do believe they can wait till Seven Men gets your final going-over. It's contemporary and it's *now*![28]

Of course, she needed several thousand dollars, but she was not going to be content with writing that was second-rate, as he knew.

The story in brief is an account of seven men in a small town who become convinced that a black man has attempted to molest a white woman; they decide to lynch him.[29] One of the problems with this novel is that the motivation of the men is not convincing. Possibly, Harris, who was so often able to put herself in another's head, whether human or a "book person," was not able to really understand individuals' reasons for lynching. Actually, the intended victim gets away so that Harris does not have to see a lynching even in imagination. But her usual shrewd understanding is evidenced in the way each community member is touched by this defiance of law. And the myth of pure, white, southern womanhood that must be protected is effectively demonstrated to be far from reality. Walser said the men had not been punished enough: they were let off on the basis of insufficient evidence. But what mattered to Harris was the way such a deed affected forever the individuals involved and the community as well. Community members lied to protect their own, but they never felt the same about the seven men again, nor did they feel the same about themselves.

This is a study of a community, but a novelist needs at least one main character who is the fulcrum for the plot—preferably a character the reader can identify with. The novel required further work.

In the spring of 1956, she had not finished the revision of "Seven Men." She was already working on another project. Walser advised her to keep working on the Eagleton story.[30]

But Walser's letter reached her just after the next family crisis had begun. In 1956, Bernice's father was ninety-seven years old. She dearly loved him and dreaded the time when he would not be with his family. She had visited him often all through the years, and she had always managed to see him at Christmas. For the last four years, she had spent time with him nearly every month. She wrote Mebane, anticipating the Christmas coming up at the end of 1955: "I'll spend the holidays in Wake County. My father is very feeble. Christmas at its brightest has its tinge of wistfulness, for we must always be remembering one Christmas ago, two Christmases, three or four—and thinking one Christmas from now, two Christmases, three or four."[31]

One Sunday afternoon in May 1956, as Bernice, William Olive, Mary, Gordon, and Alice Jo drove up to the farmhouse in Wake County, they saw Bill Kelly sitting on the edge of the porch, his feet dangling, waving his cane to attract the attention of passersby. They took one look at his wife, Miss Myrtle, lying on the porch, and they realized she had died. They had been aware for some time of her heart problems. Now the question was, "Can this man in his nineties live alone?" They thought not and insisted he live with a son or daughter—he obliged them but at every place he felt acute homesickness. He could not live away from his farm, and so they tried hiring families to live in the farmhouse and care for him. Nothing seemed to work.[32]

Bill Kelly's and Miss Myrtle's son, Haywood, and his family lived nearby and helped him. But Bernice and her brothers and their nieces and nephews agreed to take turns being with him, two weeks at a time. (Her sister Pearl was bed-ridden, by choice.) This totally disrupted any writing, as she explained to Mebane, "A whole week has elapsed since I had [a] chance to do a line of work. I was interrupted Tuesday, of course, and then on Thursday I had to go to Wake County."[33] When Mebane did get over to see Bernice, Mebane was shocked at how thin she had become.

Bernice was afraid to stay in the farmhouse alone with just her aged father; Miss Myrtle's youngest sister came out nights to stay with her, but the care of her father still was not easy. Sometimes he would have what she called a "talking-out-of-his head spell." When he had one during the night, there was no sleep. His children tried to impose a regimen of baths and a healthy diet. At such times, their father used language they had no idea he even knew; the worst term they had ever heard him use before was "confound," which he had said once to a mule. When Bernice made a custard for him and insisted it was good for him and that he would have to eat it, he said, "No, I don't either!" He did not eat it. She said, "He had become Papa again, and no girl-child was going to tell him what he had to eat."[34]

He tried to supervise the farming operation from his front porch. His tenant of thirty years, Russell Smith, did the farming and also helped to bathe and dress him. (In his will, Bill Kelly left Smith, an African American, part of his land.)

He died at age ninety-seven on November 28, 1956. Bernice was in Seaboard that day; William Olive came to drive her to their father's house. When Bernice came out of Mt. Moriah Church after the funeral service, it was Mebane's face she saw and remembered: "Your expressive face has been constantly in my mental view—the way you looked as you approached the entrance of Mt. Moriah Church, as you spoke to me at the cemetery, as you greeted me the Friday morning you came out of your way to give me a ride to Raleigh. The kindness and under-standing that radiate from your face remain a beautiful image." She added that the kindness of her friends around her in Seaboard also sustained her. "People move close when there is need," she said. "The sense of bond is infinitely precious."[35]

Bernice was at first disconsolate, then she tried to bring her father back, in a way, through writing. She had modeled characters on her father in *Purslane* and *Wild Cherry Tree Road*. In the June following his death, she published her essay about him as an article in the Father's Day edition of the *News and Observer*, calling it "Father's Second Sip of Life." She noted at the beginning of the article that it was a "Postscript to Purslane." In it, she recounted his last months, remembering the ways he insisted on being head of his house even after he grew feeble, and the strange and troubling feelings his children had as they watched his decline: "We older children remembered how Father had once set the pace in living around him, had dominated the conversation and activities, had directed hospitality, had run the farm with rigorous efficiency, had unequivocally handled his business. Until comparatively recently he had declared himself still in his eighties birthday after birthday, refusing to leave the decade."[36]

In December after her father's death, she prepared to go to Raleigh to spend Christmas with William Olive and Mary. It was the experience of the first Christmas without her father that she had anticipated and dreaded, as she had written in her letter to Mebane. In October the next year, the family gathered for the first family reunion without him: they tried to tell his stories and laugh again, but they were "very conscious of the last reunion with Papa" and time passing, taking them farther from him.[37]

16

Looking Back at a Good Decade to Live In

Fortunately, for once, demands on Bernice came at the right time. That January after her father's death George Harris appeared at her door, asking her to write a play for him to direct. He said he and a group of local people just wanted to get up a play for the fun of it. The Woman's Club in Seaboard would produce it—this was to be their money-raiser for their civic projects.

Bernice had been in George Harris's company but did not know him well; he was a second cousin to Herbert, and he was her close friend Elizabeth Harris's bridge partner. He had studied play production at the University of North Carolina, taught high school English, and directed plays. But the main point for her was that he had been the Seaboard citizen who had bought all her books.

Bernice immersed herself in the writing: within a month, she created a three-act play from the plot and characters in *Hearthstones*. Although the writing seemed to require only a short time, she had been thinking about how she would write a play based on this story for nearly a year. She took the title from the original version, the short story "Yellow Color Suit."

In February 1957, George Harris, as director, and she, as playwright, sat down to read the manuscript with the cast they had chosen. She was intensely engaged with it, as she told William Olive and Mary: "After the reading Monday night I worked till one o'clock, changing things that occurred to me. Yesterday I worked five hours straight. George has it now and is taking it to Ahoskie to get copies printed."[1]

She soon found that the process would require "diplomacy and efficiency and grace."[2] The little girl who lived across the street, Betsey Bradley, an actor in the play, said that George Harris would shout at an actor, "NO! NO!" He permitted Bernice to come to one rehearsal only. Betsey Bradley said the day Miss Kelly came to rehearsal, she sat calm and still, seeming to be at ease, smiling whenever she could.[3]

George Harris organized the community into committees responsible for different aspects of the production. After working at their jobs all day, her neighbors built the set. One afternoon Bernice slipped into the high school auditorium uninvited and saw the president of the Farmers Bank deep in paste and wallpaper. A local store supplied the contemporary costumes. Other costumes were historical, and histories of costume were consulted before patterns were made. People gave up from their own homes heirlooms, such as a little trunk; and molded high-top shoes that had been gathering dust on shelves of a long-ago closed country store were pressed into service. Other furniture traveled from people's living rooms to the stage to form the set—something the set designer had learned to rely on in the thirties. The character Lollie took lessons on how to card the batts of cotton. The costume committee found the right rinse to give the soldier "yellow color hair." Bernice said, "It became the town's project."

Reece Bullock, then an official with the county health department, was master electrician and lighting designer—"a real artist with lighting effects," Bernice said. Three of the players had acted in her plays in the 1930s and had been good friends since then. Her close friend in Seaboard, Elizabeth Harris, was wardrobe mistress and the outside footsteps in the play.[4] Being involved again in writing and producing plays, Bernice told Charlotte Hilton Green, "makes me feel young again—in spirit."[5] For a little supper before opening night in the middle of March Bernice had invited friends—probably more than her house could hold. Bernadette Hoyle (whom Thad Stem had called "photographer extraordinaire") came with her camera, ready to write an article for the *News and Observer*. Margarette Smethurst, Charlotte Hilton Green, Ovid Pierce, Thad and Marguerite Stem, Mebane and John Burgwyn, Grace and Gilbert Stephenson, and her family, William Olive, Mary and Alice Jo, were there with her. There were two rows at the front of the auditorium marked with white ribbons for

Bernice's guests. It was an exciting time she remembered for the rest of her life: "It was a heart-warming experience to have my family near, to have such staunch and loved friends around me, to be in the midst of my town and county, to look down the ribboned row and see Margarette and Mebane and Charlotte and Grace and Gilbert and Mary and Alice Jo and Olive. They were all liking me, whatever the play turned out to be. And they were soon liking the play."[6] When she told Ovid Pierce she had been nervous, he said he had been nervous, too.[7]

"Yellow Color Suit" was so successful that the cast traveled with it to Chowan College in Murfreesboro. Soon after, the Carolina Playmakers asked Bernice and George Harris to bring the play to Chapel Hill to present at the annual festival as a special guest production.

Community solidarity pleased Bernice Harris immensely. She was elated, as she wrote Walser:

> It was a wonderful thing here. It was amazing. I have been misty-eyed, amused, thrilled over the community creation. The reaction to the play was the most amazing thing of all. Even the youngsters were held spell-bound. One child said to Henny (Rebie Long), "Aunt Rebie, I couldn't keep from crying when the soldier left, but I tried to be quiet so it wouldn't bother anybody." Little Mack Harris who adores Lollie (Bickley Bullock) got so mad with her "for being mean to her sisters" that he wouldn't speak to her a while afterwards. People have picked up lines that did not seem quotable when I wrote them. When I commended David Gay (one of the town men who helped make the set), he said, "Miss Kelly, we needed this." That to me was it—the emotional impact, the need of a community to make something beyond zippers and skirts in factories. . . . It is still playing in the consciousness of people here.[8]

NBC televised it on the matinee series on September 26, 1957. Bernice received a contract awarding her $500 (less the agent's fee).[9] Bernice wrote Walser, "Those Southern accents next Thursday—! I don't care what they do. I am at this point thrilled."[10]

For the people who had seen the production in Seaboard, watching on a tiny black-and-white screen was disappointing.[11] Bernice's niece Rosalie Upchurch wrote to her, "Yours were better in real life," and added tactfully, "but these did a good job."[12] Bernice saw the flaws; the worst was that the meaning was changed. In her story, the ancient sisters rehabilitate the deserter; in the televised play, the girl does. And there were attempts to make the play folksy. Bernice told William

Olive and Mary, "But while ham hock is what Phil Harris likes about the South, it surely is not what I use as food in my books." She added, "All right, just the same I was mightily pleased."[13]

She had already begun work on the next play, "Kalline," taking the story from *Wild Cherry Tree Road*. In October 1957, she told William Olive and Mary that it was shaping up.[14] It was produced and directed by George Harris in Seaboard in March 1958 as "Pate's Siding." The next month, Clifton Britton, a director who wanted to stage the play in Goldsboro, North Carolina, rewrote a part of it without her permission. He told her that he had taken some privileges with the script.[15] But he did not tell her just how much he had rewritten and added. She found out opening night.

Her original three-act play opens with Aunt Martha getting Hannah Gowen, Sim Gowen, their married daughter Lucy, and ten-year-old daughter Neva to prepare for George's wedding to Daphne. While the family and Martha are out and George is alone, agonizing over a marriage he does not want, Kalline sneaks Penny into the house. George and Penny have a chance to talk alone and decide to elope. Martha makes sure Kalline is punished by sending her away to the poorhouse.

In the last act, Kalline returns by invitation. Martha has decided to marry her off to the loafer Cousin Sell. George has even built a little house for them. The family and Martha think she ought to be grateful; of course, Kalline fools them all by refusing the deal—"I got to get back home, much obliged," she says. George explains to the enraged family that she has real friends in the poorhouse: "A roof is not all of it, Aunt Martha." He clinches the meaning of the play, referring to her friends in the county home, staff and residents: "She's got somebody to miss her now, to care whether she goes or stays."[16]

When Bernice saw the Goldsboro production, she was sick at heart. In her original play, the main story is Kalline's; Britton made it a simple love story—boy (George) wins girl (Penny). Then he added a dream scene with Penny's dead mother returning.[17]

That Kalline was the main character in the play was important to Harris. In the play of the thirties based on this person from her childhood, *Ca'Line: A Country Comedy*,[18] the theme is the independence of this woman whom everybody wants to control. In the play in the sixties, Kalline's motivation is more complex and clearer. It is her sense of belonging to the people in the county home that makes her want to go back.

Bernice wrote another three-act play, "The Forever House," which was based on the twin sisters' relationship in *Sage Quarter*. It was presented in the Seaboard High School auditorium on March 20, 1959.[19] (The typescript no longer exists.) Some people in the audience thought it was her best play yet. Grace Stephenson said she wanted to speak to Bernice after the play but that Bernice was surrounded by people congratulating her.[20] The players took it to other towns in the area.

Her last play, "Beulah Land," based on the novel *Sweet Beulah Land*, was produced the first of April, 1960.[21] By this time, the usual actors were tired from the effort play production required, and new players were solicited. She told Bailey, "Miss Partheny, the lead, had never been in a play before. It had become a matter of who would be in the play, not of who could." She added, "The triumph of it was that raw recruits *would*."[22] Just the same, this time she did not invite her friends to come to Seaboard to see it.

Even before "Yellow Color Suit" played, she was thinking about reviving the playwriting group.[23] She started organizing it, and during the late fifties, she had people in a playwriting class meeting in her living room. Bernice's friends Elizabeth Harris, Maria Bradley, and Marian Hall wrote one-act plays that were produced. The Seaboard Woman's Club was thus provided with plays for their annual festival, gathering in money for their civic projects. Betsey Bradley, who acted in the plays, remarked about Bernice's role in these events: "She was always trying to give everyone a moment in the limelight."[24] Marian Hall wrote Bernice to thank her, "for the recognition I received in writing the play and all of the hard work and long hours that you spent helping me."[25]

Money made from the plays was usually put into improving educational facilities or adding to teachers' salaries. One year, the Woman's Club decided to spend proceeds from the play festival to design street signs and have them manufactured. The town council balked: Seaboard did not need street signs. Couldn't any fool see the street with the railroad running down the middle was Railroad Street? That the street with the church on it was Church Street? The town council was all male; the women began to see this as male sensibility against female. Bernice wrote an article, partly humorous, for the *News and Observer* about the confrontation, the article ending with her observation that the club women began to acquire an identity with universal womanhood.[26] But the outcome put a damper on the club members' enthusiasm about making the town a better place to live; they lost heart and therefore interest in raising money through play production.

In addition, a very poor year for the peanut crop cast a pall over the town, as she wrote William Olive and Mary, "People are so blue over the peanut situation that they have no heart to play at anything."[27] And energies were lagging anyway so interest in the annual festival of plays began to wane at the end of the fifties; the last one (featuring the three one-act plays by Seaboard women) was in 1961.

Writing plays and the playwriting classes had interrupted other writing, and when she had a chance to return to these earlier works, probably the energy she would have needed to finish them had been drained. She made no further effort to publish "Bevy Lamm," and she did not return to revising "Seven Men of Eagleton." But even at the beginning of the decade, when she was working on these two manuscripts, she had been thinking seriously about writing an autobiography. First she disguised herself and others in her life by writing her life story as fiction. (Scattered pages of this novel remain, shuffled into folders randomly.) She confided to Dick Walser, "The thing I've worked on this winter has been such an autobiographical novel that I have about concluded to make it straight autobiography, to be used posthumously if any publisher might be interested in bringing out a story that certainly has its points of interest."[28] Finally, she began to form her thoughts about autobiography. She wrote to J. O. Bailey:

> In my study I should be willing to "tell all" to a certain extent—a contradictory idea, I realize. I should like to tell something about my experience with editors, specifically with the Doubleday editor who signed me up and then came down on an Easter week-end later on to talk to me about moving to Harcourt-Brace with him. There are things to tell about publishers and their wooing after *Purslane*, about business dealings and the loss of royalties after Herbert's death. There are the writers whose manuscripts I have read, as you suggested. Some have been good enough to be published, and others were so bad I suffered over having to tell the truth.[29]

She was not about to "tell all," however. She destroyed Herbert's love letters to her—Dick Walser was aghast and lectured her on preserving her papers (as he felt he should, since he was her literary executor).[30] Later, in the sixties, she made other choices and threw away letters she did not think important or letters that were disagreeable, such as complaints about her not saying much about the race of characters in *Janey Jeems*. Perhaps rejection letters were also tossed out.[31] Near the end of 1955, she could see that the first draft of the autobiography was close to being finished. In 1956 Bernice sent Clara Claasen at Doubleday some chapters from the autobiography she was working on—Claasen told her to send the rest of the manuscript.[32] Bernice asked Walser's advice and added: "Don't I have a literary executor?"[33] She received a prompt reply from Walser: "You do have a lit. ex. and he directs you to finish that auto. for Claasen, to have the play produced, and to pull out that Eagle and let him fly."[34]

She put final touches on the autobiography and sent it to her agent, Diarmuid Russell. His reaction astounded her. She wrote Claasen July 31, 1957:

> Sometime ago I wrote you about Mr. Russell's (Russell & Volkening) reaction to my personal experience story. At my request he returned the manuscript to me without submitting it to a publisher. There has been further revision and a critical reading by Richard Walser, Professor of English at State College, biographer of Thomas Wolfe (Harper) and other North Carolina writers, including me, and a valued mentor. Mr. Russell seemed unsure that parts of the material would "come through" for northern readers, and he mentioned a University Press as a likely publisher. Mr. Walser respects that opinion, but he is not in agreement. He has assigned certain revisions, though he prefers that you give editorial advice about its present form and its possibilities for Doubleday. He stated that it is a *must* now and should not be filed away for a literary executor.
>
> My own judgment is that if PURSLANE came through, this book should also. It is a sort of digest of the PURSLANE story, which was autobiographical, a distillation of the writing experience as well as living by an author who continues to regard both with respect and awe.
>
> From what you know of it, Miss Claasen, will you tell me frankly if it seems suitable for the Doubleday list or if it would be better for me to try a new and fresh point of view elsewhere?[35]

She began to doubt the worth of it and sent J. O. Bailey an extract from the manuscript (which she now called "Bookwriter"). He replied,

> Now, I turn to the extract from your *Bookwriter.* . . . You wonder whether there is anything in the book to "justify the writing of mem-

oirs," and you think of a "certain sociological importance." In my idea of this question, I do not know enough about the rest of the book to judge sociological importance—reflections, I presume, upon presented scenes of life in Eastern North Carolina. But the sample suggests another more important importance—human interest, a perceptive and personal view of life in a somewhat sequestered area, that none the less parallels certain basic features of life anywhere.[36]

He then addressed certain parts of the autobiography in manuscript, dealing with her qualms about putting in the personal problem of Herbert's refusal to let her have a child:

Perhaps some people might think the passage indelicate, a too-frank discussion for a "biography"; but others might see in it, as I believe I do, the transfiguration of a personal experience into art, into, that is, a subject for universal contemplation. . . . I don't know that it's a puzzle, but it's certainly a theme of constant interest: the way women and men differ about the question of having a child. I think I know all the biological answers, and even some of the philosophical ones: but I, as male, do not feel about children as a woman does. (That is, I think I understand Herbert perfectly.)[37]

She continued to work on the autobiography. Some parts were published as articles in the *News and Observer*, such as the story of the peddlers who came to her mother's house and the story about Melissa Lowery's keeping their chickens during World War II. What Bernice chose to reveal and what to leave out is indicative of her judgments about her life and also about artful writing. She admitted her fears that Seaboard would not like her for what she had indicated about this small town in *Portulaca*. She discussed Herbert's decision that they would have no children, but shortened the story. She described in detail the terrible time in her life when Herbert had his first stroke. But she omitted material that might have caused offense to living persons. She chose to leave out the Harris family's taking the largest portion of Herbert's and her property after his death; only two brief paragraphs treat the problem of a husband dying without a will. She praised individuals in the Writers Conference, but declined to say anything negative about any writer. She decided not to elaborate on the description of her college years, explaining that they were not important in her evolution as a writer.[38]

The autobiography ends with the death of her father; she chose not to discuss her own family's problems over his will. In the will, Haywood Kelly had received his deceased mother's portion as well as his own, as one of the siblings. This gave him much more of the land than anyone else: Bernice and William Olive objected, but a compromise was reached and a court case averted.

Apparently Claasen questioned having so much discussion on Bernice's relationship to editors, and Bernice reduced that section. The assistant editor at the University of North Carolina Press shortened a section on the distillation of experience into writing.[39]

Doubleday eventually turned it down. Harris decided to send it to the University of North Carolina Press with the title *Southern Savory*.

When Thad Stem read the manuscript, the letter he wrote to her must have impressed her with its understanding:

> There is hardly anyone else who could write such a book as SAVORY. It always requires a genius and a certain, sure, and eloquent hand to give the proper dramatic intensity to the little things. But most of our great literature isn't about something big, something luminous, or portentous. I love people such as you, Robert Frost, Marjorie Rawlings, Elizabeth Roberts, James Stephens, [Ovid] Pierce, Sara Orne Jewett, and Siegfried Sassoon who see the vast world through the eye of a needle or through a small telescope that keeps expanding in its own magnificent way, without shoving, pushing, or forcing.
>
> For instance, you didn't say a lot about your honeymoon, but good readers see a whole saga. In a few sentences you create a great dramatic story in your description of the return to Seaboard. And Herbert isn't just mankind in his normal sense of preoccupation with the worldly; for, you, the unseen sharer, are simultaneously a tragic and beautiful heroine of a ruthless system, but also a poem that is about to occur, or, perhaps, a fine and poignant song that is sung inaudibly, but all the same with enduring tenderness and bitter-sweetness.[40]

While she awaited the university press's verdict on publication, she was working on other writing projects. One involved a proposed novel to be written with Harry Golden on the Jewish peddler. He had been impressed with the way she wrote about the "Dutch" peddler in *Purslane*, he said. He told her that the immigrant Jewish traders who went from house to house on foot were called "Dutch," whether they were from Germany or not, because they spoke German.[41] In the fall of 1957, he wrote, "I've been waiting for you to ask me to collaborate on a book."[42] Ten days later Harris wrote to him that Lois Cole, an editor at his publishing company, G. P. Putnam's, had contacted her. Cole was interested in whatever book Harris and Golden would write together. Harris told Golden, "You furnish the brains and knowledge, and I'll contribute something of plot and story."[43]

But the proposed novel never happened. The reasons they did not work together are unknown; perhaps Harry Golden was much involved in his own writing and publishing—he was very prolific at the time. Collaboration on a work in creative writing demands a high level of trust, and Bernice may have felt they needed a "session" face-to-face to talk through the novel and to build trust. He kept promising to come to Seaboard but did not come. There is no evidence that he sent the notes he promised. As early as February 1958, Harris had doubts about whether the book would materialize. She wrote to William Olive and Mary, saying that they were going to start the novel in March, but added "never really."[44] At the end of 1958, Golden was still writing her such things as, "It would be worthwhile for us both to work up an outline and it may also be a good point from which to eventually work up a novel."[45]

Harris published an essay on the peddler in the *News and Observer* on November 16, 1959. In 1962, Golden asked her for information on the peddler he might quote in a book for young people.[46] He published the book as *Forgotten Pioneer* in 1963[47]—she congratulated him sincerely, saying he had "done a fine service in preserving this American for us."[48]

Elmer Oettinger at the radio station connected with the University of North Carolina asked her to write a radio play. She did, it was called "A Voting Man." Oettinger liked it, but of the original radio plays he solicited, he produced only a few before the series ended. Among those he did not get around to producing were plays by Paul Green and Bernice Harris.[49]

Although these important writing enterprises fizzled out, her short story "The Lace Cloth" was published by the University of North Carolina Press in 1959 in Richard Walser's edited collection *Short Stories from the Old North State.*

And honors came to her. In 1958 the Carolina Dramatic Association wound up its thirty-fifth annual drama festival by giving Bernice Harris a citation for "unusual contributions to drama" in North Carolina. At the end of the decade, Wake Forest University awarded Bernice Harris an honorary doctorate. The next year, 1960, Woman's

College of the University of North Carolina also gave her a doctorate. Dick Walser wrote her from Europe that he wanted to be the first person in Denmark to congratulate the new Dr. Harris. One of her students at South Forks Institute at Maiden, North Carolina, during the First World War, wrote her that he was pleased about her honor but that she would always be Miss Kelly to him.[50] And that was true for her, too. For her, an important occasion was her speech to Meredith College on the occasion of her niece Alice Jo Kelley's graduation in 1959. She worried for weeks before the graduation that she would not be good enough as a speaker, that somehow she would disappoint Alice Jo. (Alice Jo Kelley, nervous herself about things she had to do at the graduation, was nevertheless extremely proud of her aunt— Bernice could not have disappointed her.)[51]

One thing Bernice especially treasured was a letter from Adlai Stevenson. Not directly involved in party politics herself, she followed political developments and was greatly disappointed when he lost the election in 1956. She wrote Stevenson, "I would rather have lost supporting a candidate of your stature than for my vote to have helped win the Presidency for a lesser man." He sent her a gracious reply.[52]

Looking back, she summed up the ten years since Herbert's death: "The decade has been lively. Since 1950 there have been other losses. There has been stress. I have had to adjust to living alone. Through it I have remained a family. It has become natural to tell friends to come to see us. I am we. . . . It has been a good decade to live in. Life has been rewarding."[53] Possibly she meant that living alone in a house does not mean that one is always alone: she was aware of two communities around her—both the townspeople and the writers. Or, possibly she meant that she had opened her home to others; it was hardly ever "unpeopled." But there is a sense of wholeness—just by herself—in this statement.

And yet, the disappointment over two novels that were never published she alluded to in another account of the decade. She stated simply, "Circumstances during the 1950s have not allowed me to make affirmation in books."[54] She referred then to William Faulkner's saying that writing is a ruthless art, but said she could not be ruthless and refuse to care for her aged father. She accepted that it was right for her that she spent years caring for Herbert and then five years interrupting her writing time to go to Wake County to look after her father.

And yet, despite interruptions, she had published an autobiography and articles and had plays produced—anyone else would have been most satisfied with these accomplishments. But these published works were not the novels that she had delved into her psyche to create: these were not the characters (her "book people," she called them) who lived in her head for months during the writing process and then traveled with her through life after the novel was finished. Nor was she expressing the stories in her mind as real and compelling to her as the ones going on outside of her. At one point she must have asked Dick Walser if she should spend her time on the plays. Walser told her,

> More important [than Britton's rewriting her play] is whether all this adaptation is worth it. "Am I justified?" you ask. Well, yes and no. You love these people, you do not want to have them die, you must see to it that they continue to live. But, you see, they are not dead. Maybe we could spend our energies to more profit by getting the books back in print. Maybe you could write other stories continuing their story.
>
> But now I must be harsh. For, the particular brand of Koch folkwriting is past. It was already fading when Koch died, and with his death there was an end. While there will never be an end of people and character, and a great writer can imprint his genius on any generation and on any trend of writing, the fact remains that the silly old world has moved on. The beauty of your people remains, and always will, though maybe they will have to wait a while for their genuine quality to become perceptive to blind eyes. So: yes, you are justified.
>
> You are not justified, however, if you do not push ahead. To remain static is to wither. You surely knew this was my reason for pushing the autobiographical account, and the mob story. At least they were departures, they were moving ahead. You can't go home again.
>
> So, you must write these plays, and you must write the radio things, but there must be new ideas, too. . . .
>
> I must stop, for I haven't written you a letter like this in my life, and I feel terrible about it. But you know how much I admire you and love your writings, and you asked the questions, and I am getting too old to be much more than frank with my friends. . . .
>
> Bless you, Pate's Siding was a fine play (how could it be anything else?), but it *was* a returning, a looking back. Even Kalline got so she didn't do that.[55]

He was right to chide her. She was making plays derivative of earlier novels when she should have been producing original work. And yet what someone else can point out, and what you know on one level is right, is not always felt on another level. Possibly the deaths of her husband and father meant not just interruptions and physical exhaustion but such emotional trauma that she was left depleted of the courage and ability to delve deep.

Writing is an endeavor best carried out in solitude, but she needed the company and support of others to survive. She may have turned to writing plays because play production requires the involvement of others. By the time the trauma of her husband's and father's deaths had somewhat subsided, the original impulse to work on "Seven Angry Men" had seeped away and she did not have the hope necessary to pursue publication of "Bevvy Lamm." By the second half of the fifties, the period of great creativity expressed in novel writing was over for her.

Still, she felt that some good had come of all this living through a decade. She said, "Although the 1950s have not been a writing decade, they have brought the richness of new friendships and the deepening of old. They have renewed my respect for the human spirit."[56]

17

Miss Kelly, Teacher Again

In 1960, Bernice Kelly Harris was sixty-nine years old—and very young. She was playing with her great-niece and -nephew as usual when a mishap occurred: "I was helping my little four-year-old namesake dramatize the story of the hare and tortoise. Her eight-year old brother unexpectedly assumed the role of a frisky rabbit and knocked the old mama turtle down."[1] She had a lot of back pain for several weeks but still thought the incident was funny.

She had written a story for children and their parents—a story to be read aloud at the Christmas season—and published it in the *News and Observer* on December 20, 1959, as "The Very Real Truth About Christmas." It is based on the family's story about her sister Rachel Floyd's young daughter, Rosalie, protecting her little brother, Carey, from learning the facts about Santa Claus.[2] Bernice had used the story in "Bevvy Lamm" to show Bevvy's gaining realizations about her family, but undoubtedly Bernice despaired of publishing the novel and extracted the story alone for publication.

In "The Very Real Truth About Christmas," Jimmy, nine years old, tells his older sister Jane he heard big boys at school saying there is no Santa Claus. When their parents leave to take food to a sick neighbor, the children search the house to find hidden Christmas presents—proof that Santa Claus does not bring the presents. They do find an old tintype of their mother when she was young. Jane becomes aware of how constant hard work has changed her mother. Jimmy demands that she climb the stepladder to the attic to find out if there are presents there. She does so and sees the wrapped presents, but she tells Jimmy that there is nothing in the attic except spider webs.

> Jane climbed down off the stepladder. She had implied that which was not-so. Yet she was glimpsing something important that was so. It was so that her mother was wearing old shoes in order that her child might have toy music. It was so that her father had refused to buy himself a new hat so that Jimmy might have a checked cap and an air rifle and trinkets. It was so, the wonder and goodness of Christmas. . . .
> "I am satisfied," she said resolutely. "I know there is a Santa Claus."
> "You do?" Jimmy's face brightened.
> She nodded. Jimmy was not even nine yet.[3]

This is a coming-of-age story for a girl. She has before her the model of a mother and father who can sacrifice to make sure their children have a happy Christmas. She does not want to lie to Jimmy but perceives there is a higher truth to be served. She protects her mother and father's secret—the hidden presents—thereby supporting the wish they have that Jimmy have the fun of the game of Santa Claus one more year.

J. O. Bailey suggested that Harris send the story to Doubleday.[4] Claasen was pleased with it: Doubleday published it in 1961, with reprints for several years following.

Bernice was feeling optimistic and told Bailey that she had a collection of short stories she would like for him to edit. Three had been published: others were stories she had written over decades; some were new.[5] He gladly agreed to work with her.[6]

And so, the 1960s started off well. In the fifties, Bernice had often gone to visit her favorite teacher in the Mt. Moriah school, Nina Brown, who had become Mrs. Thomas Elliot. She now lived on the coast in Edenton; and Bernice, with Elizabeth Harris, continued to visit her in the sixties. Bernice had made another friend in Ina Forbus, a writer of children's books. Ina Forbus lived just outside of Durham on a farm with her husband, Sample Forbus; they had converted its old gristmill into a home with a stream and pond. There the Scottish-born, blond, blue-eyed Ina welcomed visits from Bernice and Elizabeth Harris. Occasionally, in the sixties Ina and Bernice would be joined in sessions on writing by journalists Bernadette Hoyle and Betty Hodges.

Bernadette Hoyle organized the Writers' Roundtable, which met in Raleigh and featured introductory addresses by North Carolina writers. Bernice often attended those and was the featured speaker from time to time. In 1939, through the Strugglers, she had met children's book author Julia Street; they had remained good friends, and Bernice often arranged to see her when she was in the Raleigh area for those meetings. With all of these friends, she carried on a lively correspondence and telephone conversations.

There were losses, too. Margarette Smethurst died at the beginning of the sixties. And Bernice saw Mebane Burgwyn less often than she wished. After her children grew up, Mebane worked as a counselor in the county school system and soon became director of counseling services for Northampton County. She also served on the executive committee of the University of North Carolina's board of trustees from 1955 to 1971 and later on the board of governors of the consolidated university. Bernice understood the value of Mebane's work but greatly missed the time they had spent together earlier, and she regretted that Mebane neglected her writing now. In a letter in 1966, Bernice wrote: "Let's have some sessions together as in the good days. I miss our talks, our sharing of ideas and plans. It is not the will of either of us, I know, that we should not be together more, and I say let's defeat the circumstances and meet and talk and talk and talk."[7]

Often they had just brief conversations by telephone—the long, beautiful letters became scarce. In 1968, after a rare visit, Mebane wrote, "It was so good to see you last week. Really—the realization of a dream I'd had more than once. I know I stayed much too long."[8]

It is interesting that Bernice's close women friends were of all types: housewives in Seaboard, writers in all parts of the state, politicians, college professors. Several of her novels have as the central character a woman who realizes her potential. Bernice had said that the controversy over street signs would result in Seaboard's women identifying with "universal womanhood."[9] Nevertheless, Bernice distrusted the women's movement because she thought feminists denigrated the homely tasks women had always done—the things she enjoyed doing. She told Walser, "That Feminine Mystique female on TV last night made me sick with her jazz about women fulfilling themselves outside the home. Peas and watermelon pickle are fulfilling!"[10] She was not thinking about issues of equality in work or freedom to choose one's work, nor was she confronting problems of the conventional marriage structure in which male authority was expected to be unquestioned. And yet, in the early days of the women's movement, the media emphasized not the research being done on these subjects but the sensational aspects of the women's movement. Usually well-read and an astute social critic, Harris may not have had access to the solid research already known in academic circles.

A good example of her acumen in analyzing contemporary culture can be seen in a major speech. In November 1960, Bernice Harris was elected president of the North Carolina Literary and Historical Association—probably the most prestigious cultural organization in the state.[11] The next December she gave her presidential address, which she called, "A Land More Large Than Earth," quoting Thomas Wolfe. Harris began by reminding her audience that on May 5, 1961, Alan Shepard had declared, "What a beautiful view," as he looked back on Earth—just as he was leaving it. She asserted, "The intimations of cosmic vastness command wonder and awe and quest. But man remains a frontier, a cosmos to explore, 'a land more large than earth' in his spiritual potentialities. To break the barriers that keep him from realizing his identity and from understanding and respecting identities of persons on this planet is comparable in its urgency to breaking the sound barrier."[12]

The poet and the space-explorer, or any of us, could find much ugliness if we looked closely at our earth, she said. Much of our life today is packaged under shopworn labels and slogans. Much is obscured by this packaging. "Political candidates and commercial products likewise are often sold on the images they present rather than on their record," she explained. The results of this packaged culture are insecurity, futility, and stultifying uniformity.[13]

She argued that the real challenge is to cut through the shallowness and massive deception in our contemporary culture and find the values we have obscured. We can then affirm the inherent dignity of each individual. She declared, "Within the framework of cultural continuity there is the responsibility individually and in mass to stem the current tendency of presenting life in packages, of selling fun and good living and intrinsic values by creating images rather than by projecting reality."[14] She concluded that to find a land more large than earth is to demand the truth about the human experience without caricature or distortion of propaganda.[15]

At the reception afterwards, a man in the audience said he had never heard some of the words she used. She replied that she hadn't either until she wrote the speech—she had to look them up. She stood in the receiving line with the governor and his wife. That was exciting; still she was glad to get home again, she told William Olive and Mary.[16]

But the joy of the early sixties turned to sorrow abruptly. In May 1961, William Olive had a heart attack. Bernice went to Raleigh and stayed in the hospital during the long days with Mary, Alice Jo, and Gordon. Bernice was frightened: she told several friends that William Olive was the anchor for the family, that he was her rock—to be without him was unthinkable.

Her brother recovered from this one, but the final attack came in April 1962. She was able to get through the funeral and to stay a while to help her sister-in-law Mary.[17]

When Bernice reached home again, she saw that Magdeline Faison had cleaned the house and planted the garden.[18] When Faison's youngest daughter finished school in Seaboard, however, Faison was able to move the family to New York, where there were better opportunities for employment for herself and her grown children. Bernice tried to get used to a new housekeeper.

Friends came to visit. Still, Bernice told Mebane that it was unreal to think that William Olive was not there. She added that she would try to overcome the sense of floundering by the therapy of work.[19] Without William Olive, her rock, the one she counted on most, she felt she was expected to go on, and she tried.

Time passed but did not heal all things, as she was assured it would. Finally, she became extremely depressed. Perhaps this was the period in her life when she was so distraught that her close friends in the neighborhood held whispered conversations on what to do about Miss Kelly.[20] At some point in her life—it is not clear when—she was hospitalized a second time, now in Raleigh, for depression. This may have been the occasion.[21]

Bernice wrote to Dick Walser to thank him for his letter about her brother's death:

> Thank you so much for writing. Your words were meaningful and comforting because they were written by an old and dear friend and because they gave the consolation of a faith in my ability to produce further work. . . .

I do have two things I want to do, and I shall go back home and try to make a start. W. O. was the anchor. He was home. And so there is a sense of floundering a bit. But I wrote *Janey Jeems* after an experience like this.[22]

She was comparing her feelings now to her earlier bout with serious depression.

Bravely she wrote to Mary in May 1962, "For everything—and for being my sister—I am thankful." At the end of the letter, she declared, "I'll be seeing you soon whether I'm needed or not."[23] The emotional bond between the two can be glimpsed from this letter to Mary that Bernice wrote in September 1963: "One of the nicest things I've ever had said by the family was what you wrote. 'We do not think of you as a visitor,' you said. 'You are a part of our family away from home too much.' That's a wonderful way to put it, wonderfully reassuring and needed. I feel that way. How good it is to hear it stated."[24]

By the end of summer, Bernice had not recovered from the loss of William Olive, but she went to the Writers Conference with Mebane. Thad Stem observed to Harry Golden, "I see Bernice Harris fairly often. I regret that she seems depressed." Stem thought her depression came from disappointments about her writing. He told Golden, "She would not be aware that she is weary of the fulsome encomiums cast so indiscriminately at every johnny-come-lately, but, subconsciously, she evidently feels the critics have buried her. It's too goddam bad, Harry. The lady is still the tops."[25] Usually Bernice was good at disguising her low feelings. And Stem's assumption implies that she had not discussed anything about the cause, not even with him.

Actually she was having some success with things she had written earlier. Having had such a positive reception for her first Christmas book, Harris had worked on another, *The Santa on the Mantel.* It was a situation similar to a true story she had recorded for the Federal Writers' Project at the end of the thirties: the child was told at school that if Santa sees his statue anywhere, he will exit immediately without leaving presents. At home the little girl demanded that her mother take the small statue of Santa from the mantel where it stayed year round. The mother did as the child directed, but later put it back because there were no presents to place there during the night. She decided to bear the child's anger rather than extinguish all faith that some good might come another year.

In Harris's story, Lala, the mother, remembers the Christmas before when her husband was alive. He had brought home to her the title to their farm, having made the last payment on it. It was a happy Christmas, and he had splurged with the little money left and bought her four yards of blue silk for a dress. She had so treasured this symbol of their happiness that she had saved the silk. But this Christmas, he was dead.

There is not a penny in the house. Lala tries to think of some way to explain to her child, Birdie. How can she tell her the real facts about Santa Claus? During the night, Lala hides in the shadows near the doorway of the living room and watches Birdie take the Santa from the mantel. Lala is desperate to put something in the stocking; suddenly she remembers the blue silk and decides to tell Birdie that Santa left the silk to make a dress and matching coat set for her.

In the morning, the child wakes her mother crying, "Mommie, Santa Claus has been." She points to the stool she had arranged for Santa to sit on.

> "He come to see you, too!" she cried. "I fixed a place for Santa to leave you something, Mommie. And he did. Look!"
>
> A length of blue silk to make a blouse lay on the stool. "A waist for you and a dress for me!" Birdie cried happily.
>
> The scissors lay on the floor near the Christmas stocking.[26]

Claasen at Doubleday thought the story charming and published it in 1964. Harris dedicated it to her friend the poet Sam Ragan.

And other good news came: Lambert Davis, editor at the University of North Carolina Press, told her at the beginning of 1963 that he wanted to publish her autobiography, *Southern Savory*.[27] She dedicated the book to "William Olive, In Memory." It was published in 1964; reviews of the autobiography were positive. The reviewer for the *South Atlantic Quarterly* said, "It may be that these family-reunion front-piazza stories have a particular appeal for Southern readers; but the best of them deserve a larger audience, combining as they do, Mrs. Harris' fine sense of humor, her faculty for precise observation, with her affectionate and generous attitude toward the people and events she describes."[28] Especially pleased was she about her mentors' reactions, both J. O. Bailey and Dick Walser. Walser wrote her, "While reading SS, I kept wondering if you and Wolfe aren't the finest stylists old North Carolina has produced. . . . SS is so beautiful, so

marvelously different and improved from the manuscript I read in Seaboard once on your front porch—particularly one Sunday morning
while you were at church. Well, it's something!"[29]

The reviewer for the *North Carolina Historical Review*, Mary
Lynch Johnson, made some comparisons, placing it in a literary tradition:

> Because she has Wordsworth's "exquisite regard for common
> things," Mrs. Harris does not find life in a small town flat, stale and un-
> profitable; nor is it tainted with the dregs of evil. Her Seaboard is not
> *Main Street* or *Peyton Place*. Rather, she sees it as Edgar Lee Masters
> when he wrote:
>> Life all around me here in the village:
>> Tragedy, comedy, valor, and truth,
>> Courage, constancy, heroism, failure—
>> All in the loom, and oh what patterns![30]

All this helped, but Bernice was right when she said that work was
the best tonic for her. Possibly what happened that enabled her to
want to continue living was an offer in January 1963 to teach creative
writing at Chowan College in Murfreesboro, North Carolina (about
twenty miles from Seaboard).[31] It was to be a non-credit course and
paid only a little over a hundred dollars a month (raised in 1972 to
$150), plus $25 for transportation costs—Bernice gladly accepted. She
began teaching in February 1963.

She was in her element on Tuesday nights in that classroom in Murfreesboro. There was a mixture of students: there were some under-
graduates, but many were long out of college. Over the nearly ten
years she taught the course, there were such people in the class as an
optometrist, a florist, a dentist, an insurance agent, two ministers, a retired missionary to the Eskimos, a wildlife management expert, several
housewives, several teachers, a librarian, an antique dealer, an artist,
and a retired opera singer. And she found out from student writings
there were also a woman who had been in a mental institution, an ex-
convict, and a clairvoyant. The students drove from miles around to
attend the class; some had to spend the night each Tuesday because it
was too far to go and come home in one day. One woman had her son
fly her into Murfreesboro every week.[32]

James Ellis, a sixty-year-old man who operated the ferry which
crossed the Meherrin River nearby and who confessed to her that he

had gone through only seven grades of school, asked her if she thought he belonged in a college creative writing class. She told him that if he did not come into the class voluntarily, she would draft him.[33] He was soon publishing articles.

Letters from Bernice's students abound; they give an idea of her way of encouraging her students to write. James Ellis described this process: "She would correct me so gently I found myself looking forward to her next correction. She can encourage a student to where he wants to go on and on."[34] And another said, "Perhaps the greatest joy of all is completely being free to express myself to you because I'm so confident of your trust and love in me that every expression of mine is unafraid."[35] A housewife wrote an account of how the class had changed her world:

> The Creative Writing Class has meant to me education, recreation and relaxion [*sic*], as well as hurried suppers for my family—sometimes none at all for me. My husband was never able to understand my enthusiasm for attending, and my reluctance at missing a class; nor could I understand his love for riding around at night to spot deer eyes and listen to dogs bark. So we developed a mutual acceptance that each should "do his own thing."[36]

The students called the Tuesday night session the "Happy Hour." Usually, it ran over the allotted one and a half hours; and still, after the class was over, they would go out for coffee so they could keep talking about writing.

Harris was sure that every person had a story to tell: she saw in each student a potential great writer. She described her passion for discovering writers:

> Put into words, my wish to discover a writer sounds bold, perhaps even pretentiously noble. Writers, I am well aware, will be born or not without any midwifery from me. Certainly it has never occurred to me that there is any nobility in the wish. I do not deny that there has been a kind of impelling toward discovery. . . .
>
> It may be based in the instinct to experience that "rage of recognition," the poet writes of. "Always we walk through unknown people, guessing them," he says, "knowing that those guessed are somewhere ourselves." . . .
>
> The urge to discover a writer is inexplicable. But after a writing career, not yet ended, I am still looking for a writer. There have been intimations of the "rage of recognition."[37]

And yet, she got to the "bare bones" of the experience when she told Dick Walser: "It is not the merit of work turned in at the workshop that provides so much pleasure for me Tuesday evenings. There is some merit in some of the writing, and I search for it eagerly. But it is the people in the group that are as interesting as anything they hand in to read."[38]

Jane Gregory, a student in her class, wrote to her, "You have made us all more aware of the drama of everyday."[39] Harris tried to persuade her students to keep a writer's notebook. Her approach was to inspire her students to look at the goings-on around them and read widely, collect myths and legends, and search for old diaries, letters, and even canceled checks and address books. They were to describe these in the notebooks, then scrutinize the words they had used. They should ask, "Is there something here that awakens feelings in me?" She told her students,

> Some certain perception of character, some depth in an unlettered person, some intimation of beauty in ghettos, some odd warmth, some quirk like that of the woman who lost a fortune rather than confirm her age to acquire it, as well as that of the woman who made a career of finding out ages; some rascality, some search for identity on the part of one who has always been just Kalline; gullible, secretive, disturbing elements, colorful, quaint, a bit of excellence—all are in people you have known or know.[40]

The writer must then assign motivation. The "why" and its answer is given in the narration. Harris told her students, "You perceive people, illuminate the facts about them, tell the truth about them more exactly than facts ever tell the truth."[41]

After the semester was under way, class sessions would begin with news of what had happened publication-wise with student work; then the class would listen to someone's story and critique it. Harris would take the manuscript home, reread it, and make suggestions for revision. She had a hard time liking the stories that used profanity liberally, but even these she felt had to be accepted.

Harris made sure that her students published their work. Sometimes she even typed the final copy, after pointing out the needed corrections. Local newspapers started a column, "Fragile Bits and Pieces," in which her students' articles appeared. One student, Nancie Allen, had her one-act play produced at the 1964 drama festival in

Chapel Hill and won first place. Another, Virginia Harding, wrote a novel that was published as *The White Trumpet*.[42] Still others, such as Ann Basnight, had plays produced at Chowan College. Harris sent her students' best poems to Sam Ragan for his comments; he published the poems in the *News and Observer*. She encouraged still others to send articles to magazines, such as *The State*, and they often were accepted. (If the class was not in session at the time, students would write her to tell her about the publication and how much money they had received.) She wrote her editor at Doubleday about student work that should be considered for Doubleday's publishing lists.[43]

Harris puzzled over other means to make sure her students got their work published. She came up with an idea: everybody knew stories told for generations in their families, and their writing them down could be a way to preserve aspects of southern folklore. By writing these beliefs and practices as stories, the students could get valuable experience with publishing. She set as the first topic healing practices outside the usual realm of organized medicine. Members of the class (most took the course semester after semester) polished their stories with great enthusiasm. Bernice sought other accounts from her writer friends. *Southern Home Remedies* was published in Murfreesboro by Johnson Publishing Company at the end of 1968. Today medical researchers are now looking seriously at "folk medicine" for information about "new" drugs and procedures, but Harris may have been further advanced in her thinking about home remedies than many in the medical profession in the sixties. The reviewer for the *News and Observer* in January 1969 said: "*Southern Home Remedies* . . . has the charm of an intimate diary and the fascination of a good serial story."[44]

By the time *Southern Home Remedies* was published, the class had already begun working on a new anthology—this time, of ghost stories. These accounts of supernatural events, of happenings that cannot be explained, were published as *Strange Things Happen* in 1971, again by Johnson Publishing Company in Murfreesboro, North Carolina. The reviewer for *The State* wrote, "This . . . is the natural result of a fruitful rapport which exists among members of the creative writers group directed by Bernice Kelly Harris at Chowan College." He said the book of "strange" happenings could be enjoyed in small bites or devoured at a single meal—they would "fascinate almost everybody at almost any time."[45] The *Norfolk Virginian-Pilot* reviewer George

Tucker called it a "spine-tingling collection of ghostly goings on" (14 June 1971). The reviewer for *North Carolina Folklore* said the stories made his hair "stand straight up on his bristling scalp."[46]

Harris kept in close contact with other creative writing teachers. Occasionally, Ralph Hardee Rives, who taught at East Carolina University, would bring his creative writing students to Murfreesboro to join Harris's class for a session. Sam Ragan would also try once a semester to bring his writing class at North Carolina State University over for a joint session with Harris's class, and she visited his class.[47]

Each year's end brought a celebration that students called "Commencement." At someone's house, there would be a huge potluck picnic on the lawn, followed by readings and sometimes a one-act play. Harris would invite writers she knew—Betty Hodges, Ina Forbus, Sam Ragan, Thad Stem, and Ralph Hardee Rives—as well as the president of Chowan College, Bruce Whitaker. Betty Hodges described an evening in May 1967:

> Some forty-eight people sat in a large circle in the brick walled garden of Mrs. Ida Hayward Vick on East Fourth Street in Weldon the other Thursday night to take part in some rare "commencement exercises." . . .
>
> Occasionally there was an unplanned pause as an Atlantic Coastline train whistled through town to drown out a speech, and during the evening a friendly collie wandered from guest to guest in quiet greeting and Mrs. Vick's independent tom cat Daniel Boone searched the corners for a possible chicken bone.
>
> The class numbered 21 in all, and all but two were present. The students themselves remarked the varied character of the class, composed of writing aspirants ranging from an 83–year-old college professor to a ferryman who came seeking "something I didn't have a knowledge of—writing." . . .
>
> Minister, optometrist, musician, genealogist, artist, librarian, nurse, ferryman, they spoke with one voice in their devotion and gratitude to "Miss Kelly," who one said had touched them all "with a magic wand."[48]

Sam Ragan said that the students had through writing discovered things about themselves. "But perhaps of even more importance they had found a kinship with other people, for the bond that had developed among these fellow travelers on the journey of discovery was quite apparent." He summed up his feelings about the evening with its unhurried, stimulating talk about writing, "From it we felt that Bernice Kelly Harris, who has been the gentle interpreter of the land and its people, has now as teacher given a new dimension to the life of the region."[49]

In spite of all her efforts to make the class special and to encourage each student, Harris sometimes felt a failure. A student responded to her: "While driving home from class last night and thinking about you saying you felt you had failed to do your best with the writing class, I knew I would have to write and say you were wrong. I can only speak for myself, but I know what you have done for me. I think this is something I had wanted to try for a long time and you have given me enough confidence to try."[50]

Bernice's self-doubts were nearly always there, but her pleasure in teaching the class showed. Betsey Bradley Merritt, now grown up and married, would come back to Seaboard to visit her family, and Bernice would come to dinner. She said that Bernice talked happily about the class—she was more talkative about what she was doing than Betsey remembered her being earlier.[51] Dick Walser said, "Your letter was such a happy one: your pleasure in the students in your class, their admirable qualities, and their occasional perseverance."[52]

The Chowan College class presented her with a challenge: hers was one of the first classes to be integrated. During the fifties she, like others in her generation, had been presented with the possibility of a drastic change in the traditional way of life. Many feared this, even to the point of hysteria at times. In 1950, Frank Porter Graham, the state's champion of progress and equal rights, lost a bitterly contested primary election for the United States Senate because his opponent charged he was a "nigger lover." Dr. Graham replied that he was. Other elections were lost in the same way throughout the fifties and sixties—just a charge of advocating an integrated society was enough to cause defeat. But in 1954, in *Brown* v. *Board of Education,* the Supreme Court ruled that racially segregated schools were unconstitutional, and so North Carolina's schools were being integrated in the 1960s and 1970s. And even that old institution the Woolworth's lunch counter was integrated in Greensboro, North Carolina, in 1960.

Like everyone else Harris tried to understand what this new social order might portend. In 1957, Harris had been worried that African Americans were going to try to gain admittance to the high school auditorium where her play was to be given.[53] Many southerners of her generation—black and white—wanted "separate but equal." She thought that was what she wanted. Charlotte Hilton Green, Margarette Smethurst, and Harris stayed up all night several times hotly debating this issue. Harris received letters from writer friends violently opposed to integration, and she well knew the stance in favor of integration taken by other writers, especially her friends Paul Green, John Ehle, and Harry Golden.[54]

Like many whites and African Americans, integration frightened Bernice because she expected violence and loss of human life in the conflicts that would result. In her unpublished novel "Seven Men of Eagleton," she had explored mob violence, the way ordinary men can be led into "lawlessness strange to them."[55] The repercussions of their deed affected them and their community from then on.

Harris deplored the disorder integration had caused in the public schools in Northampton County.[56] This attitude was typical for segments of both black and white citizens at the time, but for different reasons. Whites thought that black students would not be up to whites' standards. Many African American parents were worried about what would happen to their children in the new integrated schools: they would lose their own schools—centers for the community—and teachers whom they knew and who knew their children. There is specific information for Hyde County, near Seaboard, where black educators were not consulted about arrangements for integration. African American parents participated in protest marches and a school boycott and finally were able to keep their two main schools open, with student assignment on basis of locality.[57] It was difficult for many living through those turbulent times to look decades into the future; in the immediate situation there was distrust and sometimes brutality by organized groups such as the Ku Klux Klan.

Harris was afraid of this kind of violence, but also she feared that culture as she had known it would be irrevocably changed, as she explained in an earlier letter to William Olive and Mary, referring to "the Arkansas tragedy" and Orval Faubus's stand (1957): "It's another civil war, and the Federals are winning. At least it's a similar situation that precipitated the Ft. Sumter business. We'll not fight this time, except in isolated instances. Our feelings and rights are not in the consideration. The steam-roller is too powerful. Our little Anglo-Saxon beach-head is doomed. We'll become Anglo-Africans, and that's the civilization we'll have. It's another kind of atomic bomb."[58]

It seems bizarre that Bernice Kelly Harris, who had written an entire novel about African American family life with its vividly and sympathetically portrayed black heroine, could take this stance. Describing her method in *Janey Jeems*, she said,

> First, I have treated colored people as human beings, with dignity. They are not copy. In order to have the reader accept my people as human beings, and not members of a minority group, I have carefully deleted any reference to color and presented their joys and sorrows, their loves and hates without bias either way, as Shakespeare did Othello. There are definite clues along, but the revelation does not come until near the end. Then the reader is supposed to sit up with a sudden start (if he's still awake) and say, "Why, of course!" and to feel rather resentful at the way color finally obtrudes.[59]

How could she oppose integration when she had written this, when she had worked side by side with black women in her house and garden, slept in the same room, shared her joys, worries, even intimate details of her life, and wept over their sorrows? Only by looking at the context of her life can an answer to this bifurcation of reality be understood: Bernice Harris was born in 1891 and came of age in the early part of the century; her rural, religious, southern upbringing remained always with her. Disfranchisement of African American voters had occurred at the turn of the century, and she, like everybody else, had heard over and over again speeches from revered leaders about the necessity to keep the races separate—even though the two races interacted constantly. The dominant rhetoric asserted that whites were different from, indeed superior to, blacks. But on some level, as *Janey Jeems* shows, Bernice Harris was not convinced of the superiority part. And she saw universality in experiences and emotions. Still, she did see differences in culture.

Two of the things she had learned as a child in her own family were to treat every person with respect and fairness and to keep the traditional ways. The implication of this is that any drastic social change will always be dangerous. In the past individuals from the two races had often been emotionally—indeed, sexually—together, but socially segregated, and so it should remain lest change cause an outcome they could not manage. Bernice reflected on her emotional reaction to the prospect of changes in the culture she had known. She was remarkable in her ability to stand outside of herself and observe her thinking and feeling processes and figure out what was going on. Her usual way to work out an emotional problem was to write fiction in which she identified with a character and placed herself in imagination in that character's situation. Now she imagined a story in which a young black college student, Jeems West, is the protagonist. Jeems is the grandson of another favorite "book person," Janey West, in *Janey Jeems*—that is, the grandson of Lucy Ivory, to whom Bernice had felt so drawn when she interviewed Mrs. Ivory for the Federal Writers' Project. It is significant that she did not choose just any young black male, but a man she would feel close to from the start.

In the story "Christmas Chimney," Jeems is in a sit-down strike at a lunch counter and is knocked unconscious. He and his fellow students had expected to have a peaceful demonstration, but jeers and physical shoving by onlookers had resulted in a fight that police broke up. Jeems, thrown by a blow under a counter, is not noticed when the police lock up the store.

When Jeems recovers consciousness during the night, he finds that somewhere in the darkness there is another person lying on the floor, injured. The man tells Jeems that he is a janitor who just came in to buy day-old sandwiches at half price to take out to eat as he usually did and he had been mistaken for a demonstrator. When Jeems asked why he took the sandwiches out, the janitor said the management would not let him sit at the counter. Jeems is reminded of his grandfather, who was a janitor at the white school in the last years of his life. Jeems tries to stand up and move around so that he can bring a cup of coffee to the injured man, whom he now identifies with his grandfather. With a little light from outside coming through the store window, he does manage to find the man. When he hands him the coffee, Jeems realizes that the hands that reach for the cup are white. The man calls him "Buddy." Jeems speaks gently to him.[60]

Harris makes clear the injustice that both white man and black man have suffered in being prevented from simply eating where they bought the food because they did not look just "right." She also seeks to awaken in the reader the realization that black and white can help each other, that the struggle for fair treatment is a common struggle.

Harris expressed concern about whether churches could be integrated.[61] In another story about the student Jeems West, she explores this issue. The story is based on an incident at Duke University's Gothic chapel, she said.[62] Jeems, as a college senior, has been studying church architecture for an art course. He keeps coming back to stare at a Gothic chapel at a university for whites.

> For several days at his off hours he had stood before it, at sunrise or noon or sunset. Each time he had felt a need to pray under the lofty spire reaching so high toward heaven. He had grown up a praying kind of boy, always "at a famish for good religion," as his grandmother had expressed it. The very structure of the Chapel had roused the worship in him. The clerestory and the piers, the flying buttresses, the pointed arches, the vaulting and the spire seemed to symbolize something of the aspiration Jeems had come to live by.[63]

Jeems and other students from his college decide to ask for admittance so that they can worship in this beautiful place. When the group of black students arrives at the chapel door, uncertain about what might happen and afraid, their leader asks the usher, "Where may we sit?" The usher replies, "Anywhere you like."

Jeems decides to bring to the chapel his grandmother, Janey, who had seen only the little white steeple she and his grandfather Jeems had erected on their country church. He wants her to experience the beauty of this Gothic chapel and to give her "a glimpse of the new day dawning for their people."[64]

Thus, through her fiction, Harris put herself in imagination into the very scenes painted ugly by others—sit-down strikes in restaurants, integration of public places—and explored a different way of looking at them. She relies on two of her strengths, imagination and compassion, to create in herself understanding and acceptance. Two ways of thinking derived from her upbringing were operating, but fear of social disorder gave way before her more heartfelt values—fairness and respect for every person.

The challenge to Harris's work on her own feelings about living in an integrated society came in the person of Eunice Brown. Brown, a teacher herself, was a graduate of Howard University. She was living in Winton, near Murfreesboro, when she read a notice in her local newspaper at the beginning of 1964 about a creative writing class at Chowan College. She had read *Purslane* and knew who the instructor was. Brown was pretty certain that Chowan College had not had black students before, and she was ready to integrate the college alone, if necessary. She went over to register for the course; the registrar hesitated a moment, then signed her up. The first night of the class, Harris "looked around nervously," then studied the class roster, trying to connect names and faces. After the class, Harris said to Eunice Brown, "I understood you were black." Brown, who is light in skin color, replied, "I am."[65]

In class Harris seemed apprehensive at first. But as soon as she realized Eunice Brown felt comfortable, she relaxed, too. One of the students deliberately talked to Brown before and after the class; soon all the students were accepting of each other. In later years, Harris wrote glowing recommendations for Brown to go to an institute at Columbia University and later to study journalism at the University of North Carolina. "She was lovely," Brown said.[66]

Harris was pleased to report to J. O. Bailey about the class, "A Negro teacher has been a part of it, here in eastern North Carolina, and an Irish Catholic is a present member among Baptists of Baptists."[67] He replied that for eastern North Carolina, her class composition was "truly remarkable."[68]

She had done an excellent job of teaching writing. She had faced a direct challenge to her habitual way of thinking about separation of the races, subjected it to close scrutiny, and changed. But she worried, even when she was doing an extraordinary job, that she was not as good as she should be. She had told Walser that she did not understand how he who knew her so well could write a positive biography. "I know so much that is uncomplimentary," she said, "but I try to keep it hidden as best I can."[69]

At night, her imagination conjured up unformed terror. She admitted to her friend Holley Bell that she was afraid to stay at home alone at night. When he asked her what she was afraid of, she could not say what that was exactly.[70]

Where did these fears and self-doubts come from? From her childhood, when she internalized her parents' high standards of conduct? From her church's castigation of the weakness in those who indulged in pleasure, the "fleshpots of Egypt"? From a culture which dictated such a strict behavioral code for women that few could fulfill its expectations of self-denial? From Herbert, who was critical and berating? These can only be speculations: certainly, because of any one of these influences, it would be hard to feel "good" enough. But the high level of generalized anxiety she suffered became evident only after her marriage to Herbert. Within a few years of her marriage, she began taking medication for "nervousness" and took something the rest of her life.

Several friends remarked about Bernice's appearance of sadness when she was not conscious of being observed.[71] It is possible that besides the two episodes of major depression, she experienced mild depression off and on during her adult life. Undoubtedly, the constant feeling of not being good enough was related to the depression; probably, the anxiety she felt in living with Herbert contributed as well.

Of course, she was not a plaster saint; she had her moments of feeling piqued, of complaining about someone, but this was not her usual state. Ironically, Bernice Harris, who saw herself as seriously flawed, was seen by others as a compassionate and generous person of great integrity.

18

The Last Garden

Teaching, attending to church work, writing, dining with friends, and sometimes attending a grand occasion—this was the way life for Bernice Kelly Harris seemed to the observer to go in the late 1960s and early 1970s. The grandest occasion occurred in 1966, when Bernice Harris was given the North Carolina Award (known as the Governor's Award) for "Great Distinction in Literature." On May 31, she attended the banquet and ceremony at the Hotel Sir Walter in Raleigh. Dick Walser escorted her to the speaker's platform and introduced her. She had bought a blue dress for the event and borrowed her friend Elizabeth Harris's white evening bag. By everyone's account, she looked beautiful. Awards were given to others at the same time, and so Bernice stood in the receiving line to shake hands with 450 people—many of them her own, because her family, friends, and even her students at Chowan College had come.

Telegrams and letters of congratulations poured in. Her friend from the thirties on through the decades, Paul Green, wrote to send her "love and good greetings" and to tell her of his "feelings of pride" in her award.[1] Her Doubleday editor, Clara Claasen, said she was happy about this honor because "few can write with such love and passion."[2] There were televised interviews and columns in newspapers about her. Then in 1968 she won the Carnegie Award for Women for contributions to North Carolina's literature. In 1971 she was named by Melrose Press of London as one of *Two Thousand Women of Achievement*: she was described as having made significant contributions to English literature.[3]

It was a heady time in her life, but also a lonely time. Her last living brother, Darwin, died four months after she received the Governor's Award. She told Dick Walser that she felt desolate because out of her original family of eight, she was the only one left.[4]

In Seaboard, she was still Miss Kelly, someone to turn to if there was a need for a good listener. Walter Moose, the pastor at her church, a learned man whose knowledge of history impressed her, was often a guest at dinner at Bernice's house with his wife Jessie Moose and Elizabeth Harris. He wrote an observation of her life in Seaboard in the sixties: The paper boy stopped at her house, on pretext of collecting for the paper, and played chess. Another little boy came by to show her the different colors he had discovered by crushing flower petals and weeds. Two little girls, twins, rang her bell to get her to hunt bird nests with them.[5]

Bernice still coached the neighborhood children in an annual outdoor play (often about cowboys and Indians with live ponies as props). One June day in 1967 she was moving chairs from her house to the back yard for the play when she felt a sudden, stabbing pain below her neckline. Then the pain shot down her arms. She managed to get to the telephone to call Dr. Parker. Immediately he knew—and she knew—that she had had a heart attack.[6]

The long stay in the hospital in Roanoke Rapids, North Carolina, with nurses around the clock, depleted the rest of her financial resources. Her niece Rosalie Upchurch, now a teacher and school principal, came to spend several weeks with her, staying by her side in the hospital every day. Rosalie wrote letters to Bernice's friends to keep her aunt from exerting herself too much, but often Bernice added a long postscript in a shaky hand.

Bernice's nurse, Mrs. Pat Kelley (no relation), came in one morning exclaiming, "It's the kind of day you can hear violets coming up!" Bernice told her nurse that she liked that. "You said it in *Sage Quarter*," Kelley replied.[7]

Magdeline Faison took the train from New York to see Bernice in the hospital. Bernice had just about convinced her doctor that she could go home, and she begged Faison to stay with her. When she realized that Faison could not stay, Bernice asked her to find a woman to be her helper whom Faison would judge right. Faison chose Annie Newsome, an African American townswoman in Seaboard.[8] Bernice stayed with Mary Kelley in Raleigh for six months—a "blessing," Bernice told Dick Walser. When Bernice returned home, Annie Newsome came and was with her until nearly the end of Bernice's life.

In the fall of 1968, Bernice was once again traveling to Murfreesboro to teach her creative writing students at Chowan College. Her hand shook when she tried to hold a pen, but she kept writing her students thorough critiques and words of encouragement. In the end-of-the-semester celebration, a student offered a toast: "To Dr. Bernice, Although there may be snow on the roof, there is fire in that furnace."[9]

One summer's evening in 1971, Bernice's friend Roy Parker Jr. (then Washington correspondent for the *News and Observer*) brought his wife Marie and their children to visit his mother Louise Parker and his aunt Elizabeth Howell in Seaboard. Both Louise and Elizabeth were old friends of Bernice. Elizabeth Howell was a newspaperwoman, an editor for the *Northampton County News* and the *Ahoskie Herald*, for whom Bernice had once written local news stories. They called to ask if she would walk over to be with them, and she was delighted. Now eighty years old, Bernice sat under a tree with them and drank beer (although she was not usually a beer drinker) and swapped stories. Both Louise Buffaloe Parker and her sister Elizabeth Buffaloe Howell were raconteurs. Louise could "break Bernice up, talking about people," Parker said. "She could talk about the food at funerals; Bernice thought it was hilarious. Louise and Elizabeth Howell were uncontrollable comics. When they got into a story, they would laugh and fall all over. Miss Kelly loved to listen."[10]

Bernice was still having a good time gardening, also. She had someone come in to plow, harrow, and help her plant: what she enjoyed most was seeing growing plants and gathering the harvest. As early as the mid-1960s, when she was seventy-four, she heard that the neighbors were concerned that she was out in the garden puttering about and digging. She never stopped, but she began to "garden on the sly, to rise at dawn on summer mornings so as not to be observed." In a little essay on her "last garden," she addressed the reader, "In every sly walk to the garden there was a wisp of joyous abandon, of knowing you could and would, even in your decade." She described the experience:

So, it is the last garden. You gather vegetables with a difference. Each handful of green hulls, plump with unblemished white beans, is dropped with care into the pail. Ridged okra, so magically matured right out of flower; peppers, paprika red among their green leaves; corn in ear below the brown silks, the graceful long-necked squash all contribute their final succulence and beauty.

The pedicels of purslane, salvaged in early summer from the hoe of the garden man, flourish in the row of cucumbers. Weed to the garden man, purslane is a symbol of the life-spirit in creation. Chopped up and left to die, it grows in vigor everywhere.

The grass, bladed and lush, no longer challenges as in early summer when it crowded young plants. It grew in sun and shower in your last garden, and it evokes a special tolerance now. Even the bugs that survived the dustings, the little yellow embryos on fading leaves, arouse little antagonism. Here on these butterbean vines they are having their final sustenance. They will mature on other ground, but this is their last garden here. Goodbye, little weevils.

Suddenly you glance at the bottom of the vines. Plump tan hulls show among the leaves, crisp and harvest-ripe. Inside there are unblemished dry beans, the token of continuity extending beyond decades.[11]

Bernice was gracious and welcoming when J. O. Bailey sent his graduate student Erma Glover to interview her in preparation for her doctoral thesis on the novels of Bernice Kelly Harris. The work was begun in 1967, and Mrs. Glover made several visits over the next few years. In the seventies, Bernice would occasionally lie down to rest while they were talking. One day Glover was startled when Bernice mused out loud, "Why did I become a writer?" Glover realized that Harris asked the question of herself. "I don't know, but when I get a pencil in my hand, something comes over me." An expression appeared on her face "which for a few seconds set her apart in a world of her own—but beyond self," Glover said.[12]

Harris continued to publish articles and book reviews in newspapers and magazines, but she was not having luck with her collection of short stories. The late sixties were a time of retrenchment for her publishers as far as fiction was concerned. Publishers became more attentive to money-making projects such as cookbooks.

Dick Walser had read and critiqued the stories in 1966; he thought they were good and should be published.[13] Bernice revised according to Walser's suggestions and sent the stories to Claasen early in 1967. Claasen wrote that she was very pleased with the collection.[14] For months Bernice heard nothing from Doubleday.[15] Then Claasen was transferred to the cookbook department,[16] and Doubleday said no to publishing Bernice's collection of short stories. Later in 1967, Bernice sent the stories to the University of North Carolina Press.[17] But she felt discouraged. Julia Street wrote her at the beginning of 1968, "You're so right, yours and my kind of writing doesn't seem to be 'in' at this time."[18]

In spring 1968, when J. O. Bailey asked the university press what had happened to Harris's stories, he was told that the press probably would not publish the book.[19] Leslie Phillabaum, who had taken over the editorship at the press, remembered that the press had stopped publishing original fiction at that time, that the quality of the stories and novels they received had no bearing on the matter.[20]

Bailey gave the stories a thorough critique.[21] Bernice continued to work on revisions of them.[22] Finally even she felt discouraged; she wrote Bailey in 1970: "It seems according to other writers as well as to my agent in New York that short stories are as dead as the novel was supposed to be only a short time ago. I wish you would scold me about not getting my hand back into writing."[23]

In September, she told him again,

> I have practically nothing to report. I revised one story and then kept fiddling with it until I could not decide which revision is best. I do want to write one more book. There are two unfinished manuscripts (Novels) that I want to look at again when I have the opportunity. One is out, since it is based on the Northampton mob that tried to lynch a black man in the late 1940s. There are some fairly good characterizations in this one, but the lynching will not do. I am not sure about any value in the other novel, since I have not looked at it since the early 1950s. Perhaps the silverfish have settled the question about any further work on it. I suppose I am writing through the work of members of the creative writing group.[24]

The one the silverfish might have gotten must be "Bevvy Lamm." The "one more book" may refer to a projected novel about Uncle Wes, a sympathetic character in *Purslane*. She wanted it to be about "a design for adjustment" to the problems and passions of middle age. She commented on her "book people," saying, "Uncle Wes, in DESIGN FOR NOON, seeing it all clearly and seeing it whole, seeing death as truly as birth a design for living."[25]

In 1968 and 1969, Harris and Sam Ragan were thinking about editing a book about teaching creative writing, using their stories, and their students' stories, as examples.[26] When Bernice asked Claasen's opinion about this, she gave no encouragement, saying that Doubleday had done several books in this field but they had not been more than moderately successful.[27] In the end, nothing came of their efforts.

The worry over money was a constant agony. The small inheritance of a few thousand dollars from her father had long since been used up.[28] Payment for articles, royalties on the two Christmas books, and her teaching salary for one course, once or twice a year, could hardly sustain her. Once, when she was worrying about back taxes, she told her sister-in-law Mary that maybe the government would put her in jail—it would be cheaper to live and she could get some writing done.[29]

Some income came in all through the sixties from having teachers living with her during the school semesters. She got so she enjoyed having them. However, when they were not there, she could invite her friends to dinner. Neighbor Betsey Bradley Merritt remembered going into Bernice's kitchen when there was a dinner for friends and seeing dishes on the work table, waiting to be served guests, but not much in the refrigerator for the next week.[30] Bernice made sure the profits from *Southern Home Remedies* and *Strange Things Happen* went to Chowan College; they amounted to several thousand dollars.[31] But meanwhile, she had to borrow $2,000 on her house in Seaboard.[32]

She had considerable medical expense: in 1967 she was taking librium for nervousness and anxiety, as well as several drugs for heart problems, and sleeping pills.[33] In 1971, she had a fall and was hospitalized, and there were office visits and medicines to buy in connection with this mishap.

Reece Bullock and other friends came over to do small repairs on the house, but major work was needed. Holes in the roof caused water damage—and worst of all, squirrels gained access to the house, enlarged the holes, tore off the porch roof shingles, ran around inside, and confronted her on the stairs. They knocked on the windowpane when she was trying to type and made so much noise at night that she could not sleep. Finally, she appealed to the town council for permission to poison them.[34] She also wrote a humorous essay about the squirrels, "Wild Life Came to Town."[35]

But few knew about her financial problems—she did not want to talk about them or ask for help. She liked it that a fellow writer said she had "guts overlaid with gentle courtesy."[36] However, Elizabeth Harris and Lib and Reece Bullock, who saw her frequently, understood what was happening. They discreetly contacted her close friends, such as Reece's brothers Alva and Welford Bullock and Elizabeth Harris's brother, Henry Russell Harris, and a few fellow church members: the group made up a sum that was sent monthly to Bernice from an unknown "Patron of the Arts."[37]

In spite of her worries about finances and house repair, in the early 1970s, although she had entered her eighties, Bernice continued to be active in state and community life. She still taught Sunday school and participated in the Woman's Missionary Society as she had when she first came to Seaboard in 1917. She gave a talk to the Writers' Roundtable on how to plot the novel in 1972.[38] "You were simply great at the Roundtable," Bernadette Hoyle said.[39] Bernice attended meetings of the Roanoke-Chowan Group each summer and went to the Writers Conference in 1971 and 1972, although she stayed only one day each time. And in spite of getting tired, she traveled to speak to women's book clubs, as she had always done.[40] In an effort to reduce some commitments, she resigned from the state library commission, which she had served on during the sixties.

In 1972 she was in Raleigh for the Christmas holidays with Mary Kelley as usual. She saw all the family, and on Christmas day she went to the home of Alice Jo and her husband, Hal Burrows, for dinner. Bernice thought it was "one of the most pleasurable Christmases" she had had in many years.[41]

On a spring day, April 13, 1973, she spent the morning sorting her correspondence and clippings to pack in boxes to send to the University of North Carolina library's Manuscripts Department and to Chowan College. Just before noon, she decided to lie down a few minutes before lunch while she listened to the television news broadcast. When Annie Newsome came in with a tray so that Bernice could sit by the upstairs window to have lunch, Bernice found she could not move off the bed—her left side was paralyzed. Dr. Parker had one word: "Hospital."[42]

The Rescue Squad took her to a local hospital, but it was clear that she needed special care: the stroke had left her so weakened on the left side that she could not walk. However, there was no money for rehabilitation services. She asked Lib Bullock to call Herbert's sister Zenobia to inquire if she would help financially—Bernice must have felt absolutely desperate. Lib did so, but Zenobia and her sister Anna said, "Well, we have a hard time getting along ourselves." They would not help.[43] Zenobia died in 1991 at well over a hundred years old—a very rich woman, alone as she had chosen to be, or perhaps as her father had chosen for her.

Reece and Lib Bullock went to the county social services officer, and he suggested that Bernice go to a convalescent center in Durham, North Carolina. She had to be declared a ward of the county so that costs could be paid by Northampton County.[44]

Reece persuaded a local undertaker to drive her to Durham in his hearse. Reece rode with her to Durham, holding her hand. She looked out the hearse's window and saw the blue sky and bright April sunshine; but she thought, "Having been treated for two nervous breakdowns in Norfolk and in Raleigh, and been given prescriptions for nervous disorder by Dr. Orgin at Duke, I was well aware that the breaking point had been reached."[45] In the convalescent home, she took Dr. Parker's sleeping pills, as usual, and closed her eyes; but this time, she "wanted not to wake up."[46]

While a southern lady was expected to be courteous and self-effacing, she was also expected to be a stoic about hardship and pain. Bernice Harris worked with a physical therapist and practiced walking every day. When the staff was not around, she tried to walk by herself and fell so often she jokingly referred to herself as "a fallen woman."[47]

Soon Bernice was making friends with staff and patients; her nurse liked her so much she became very protective of her. Bernice managed to get to arts and crafts and charmed the teacher there, too. She engaged the janitor in telling her his life story.[48] In fact, she listened to everybody's story and observed all the dramas taking place in the hall. She wrote about the life around her—probably not for publication but for the comfort and validation it gave her to write. And she wrote letters for other patients. She asked Lib and Reece Bullock to bring her typewriter when they came next time: "I wrote a letter for a Gumberry man (black) this morning. He expects to get a wooden leg this week."[49]

When Reece and Lib came one day just a few months after she was admitted, she said, "Lib and Reece, I want you to see what I can do." She walked down the hall and back again. She was proud and pleased.[50]

She had her hair done once a week, and she dressed each day in street clothes, hose, and shoes and sat up in her room. Family members came to visit on the weekends—one Sunday she recorded visits from nieces and nephews from fifty miles around, Garner, Clayton, Durham, and Raleigh, as well as friends from Ahoskie, Murfreesboro, and Winston-Salem.[51] She told her nephew Carey Coats that she had some more writing to do.[52]

When friends came from Seaboard, she wanted to know all the gossip—she seemed hungry to know what was going on. One sunny afternoon, she sat with Elizabeth Harris on the porch at the center and discussed in detail all the events and people they knew.[53]

She wanted to go home to Seaboard, but there was no money to pay for full-time care in her house. In any case, Annie Newsome, her housekeeper, was in a hospital in Roanoke Rapids, being treated for a malignancy. Mary Kelley, Alice Jo Burrows, and Gordon Kelley kept hoping the physical therapy which the center offered would help her to regain strength, that she would be able to walk safely again to the extent that she could stay by herself some of the time, so she could be in Raleigh with Mary.

Elizabeth Harris wrote letters and paid bills until Bernice was able to take over. During the week, the children's book author Ina Forbus came every day to see her. Soon the patients looked for Ina, too, because she took on the job of cheering up everybody. Smells in the building were not savory; Ina filled Bernice's room with little pots of mint and basil. She made sure Bernice had stationery and stamps and a bedside lamp so she could see to write.[54]

Ina Forbus belonged to a group that played recorders, and she brought her group to the center to play for the patients. One recorder player, an architect named George Pyne, was also an amateur photographer, and he would bring his slides of nature to Bernice's room. She especially enjoyed the slide show on the evolution of a monarch butterfly—a series of images that ended with the butterfly's first flight one late afternoon.[55]

George Pyne and his wife Mary would go to the convalescent center to get Bernice and take her to their home for dinner. He said, "She was a wonderful guest. She enjoyed everything. The minute she came in, the whole spirit of the house changed. She was a joyful, clever, very vivacious person."[56]

She was also invited to dinner occasionally by writers in the area. In

September she went to dinner at the home of Porter Cowles, an assistant director and business manager at the University of North Carolina Press. There she met William Couch, the editor who had published *Purslane* and given her the job interviewing for the Federal Writers' Project. She thought it was "wonderful to see him again."[57]

But these were brief excursions outside the center. That August of 1973 there was no possibility of her going to the Writers Conference. Ina Forbus, who would have gone, stayed with her in Durham instead. The writers at the conference sent her a huge card with their good wishes. Writers at the Roundtable also sent her a card with their greetings.

Writer friends, among them Thad and Marguerite Stem, Bernadette Hoyle, Betty Hodges, Sam and Marjorie Ragan, and Mary and J. O. Bailey, visited her. She told Dick Walser that because of the company of her writer friends, she was not lonely: "I have named these visits the Writers Conference."[58]

Walser, who had come to see her whenever he could, arrived one day in August. She did not bother to take his outstretched hand but shoved him out of the door, following on his heels, so eager was she to leave the center. He took her for an afternoon drive to Chapel Hill, ten miles away. They observed the crowd swinging along in the sunshine on Franklin Street—the street where University of North Carolina students and townspeople took their promenade. Her letter to him afterwards had a bittersweet tone of finality; she ended it by thanking him "most of all for being an understanding forever friend."[59]

On September 13, 1973, anticipating her eighty-second birthday coming up in October, Bernice was sitting up in bed, writing to her dear friends in Seaboard, Lib and Reece Bullock. She requested their advice and help with a letter she had received asking her for information about her life. She then began, in brief, to tell them some facts she thought they would need:

> In the 1930's I had groups meeting in my home to study the writing of community plays. From this project came production of plays for the benefit of the community.
> In the 1940's I nursed an invalid husband who died in 1950. In the middle 1950's I helped take care of[60]

The writing stopped there.

* * *

At the funeral service in the Seaboard Baptist Church two days later, her family members and friends listened to Chowan College president Bruce Whitaker say the words of tribute: "She was a great human being, a real humanist in the best sense of the word. She had a genuine interest in persons—whether of high or low estate, rich or poor, black or white. She looked upon all as persons, in her words, 'to be treated with dignity.' "[61] The choir sang her favorite hymn, "Faith of Our Fathers." The trumpets sounded.

Her body was placed beside Herbert's in the plot she had purchased at Herbert's death; it is, as he would have wished, in the corner of the church cemetery where the Harris family members lie. The stone simply bears the dates of her birth and death. She wears, according to *her* wish, the blue dress she wore in 1966 to receive the Governor's Award for Great Distinction in Literature.

What is Bernice Kelly Harris's *lasting* place in literature? Certainly there were critics in her era who recognized the strengths of her work. August Derleth asserted that her novels have universal meaning, that they are not just commentary on a region. Poet Sam Ragan testified to the honesty in every line of her writing; Caroline Gordon, to the imaginative quality and freshness of perception.[62]

Harris stands alone in the particular characteristics of her style and in her vision. She excelled in her ability to reproduce regional dialect and to choose the words and speech rhythms unique to the character. The dialogue, which sounds so natural, is carefully structured to achieve dramatic tension. With a few deft touches, a phrase of two or three words, she captures the essence of a scene or a character. She can use an everyday event to signal a turning point in a character's understanding and will to take action. She can insinuate into the most seemingly innocent occurrence or remark a depth of psychological distress. But she can also see and convey the magic in an ordinary moment.

Harris belongs in the tradition of women writers who present woman to the world as hero. Gender is all-important in the writings of women novelists contemporary with Harris such as Ellen Glasgow, Frances Newman, and Elizabeth Madox Roberts. Their female characters can maneuver only within narrow societal boundaries. A central aspect of this is the presentation of women's relationships to men. Harris treats from different angles a woman's need for freedom within the relationship with a man versus the need for complete, intimate union. But she widens this need for connection to the other to include connection to the human group, as well. She asks, How much and what do we give up to the community so that we can belong? What do we owe ourselves so that we remain honest with ourselves? And even more basic, Can there be any definition of self without belonging? The questions are as relevant to men as to women. The consistent confrontation with these questions sets her apart.

But at the time of her death, her novels had long been out of print, and she was not known outside of North Carolina. In well-known histories of southern literature, such as Richard H. King's *A Southern Renaissance: The Cultural Awakening of the American South, 1930–1955*,[63] her name does not appear. Nor is there any mention of her work in standard texts such as *Literary History of the United States* or anthologies like *Literature of the South*.[64] In *The History of Southern Literature*, edited by Louis D. Rubin Jr., the 588 pages have one paragraph on Bernice Kelly Harris, written by Anne Goodwyn Jones in a chapter called "*Gone With the Wind* and Others: Popular Fiction, 1920–1950."[65]

It is instructive to compare her career with the careers of other women writers coming to prominence in the thirties and forties. Eudora Welty and Bernice Harris had the same agent, Diarmuid Russell, and the same editor, John Woodburn. In some ways, Harris's situation was similar to Eudora Welty's: both were self-taught; they wrote often about the same subject, the southern family; they lived in small southern towns. However, Welty was eighteen years Harris's junior, and eighteen years of history between them made a difference in what a young woman would be allowed to do. Welty went to the University of Wisconsin the last two years of her college education and then attended graduate school at Columbia University. When she was at Columbia, she took advantage of the cultural opportunities New York offered. Harris was not able to leave North Carolina until she was nearly sixty, except for the brief honeymoon trip to Washington.

And while Harris grew up in a farm family, Welty grew up in an urban, middle-class family. Welty had enough financial security to give up the idea of a job early in her life and devote her time to writing. Harris had to be self-supporting and chose to be a teacher, a profession that left little time for anything else. She had to wait until she was forty-eight to publish her first novel: she was hardly the ingenue whom an older writer might take under her wing.

Welty traveled to New York in 1940 to meet Russell and Woodburn. Russell wrote Welty how glad he was that she had come; he declared, "Not only is our seal of approval upon your writing but also on the person so that all the furious energy we have will be bent on making the miserable crew of editors around the country recognize your worth."[66] Harris did not go to New York until 1953, after the last novel was published.

From the 1940 trip on, Welty went to New York regularly. Russell and Woodburn alike became Welty's good friends. Russell wrote to Welty in 1940, "John Woodburn . . . is evidently trying to fix up some plot to get the higher-ups interested in you and your career."[67] Woodburn was very much interested in advancing Harris's writing and begged her to go to Harcourt, Brace with him, but she stayed with Doubleday—there was no one to advise her otherwise. Richard Walser and James Ostler Bailey, both college professors, were astute critics and supportive mentors, but their expertise was not the informal workings of the national literary marketplace.

Russell was always Welty's first reader and she gratefully acknowledged his help: "If you keep telling me when what I write is clear and unobscured and when it is not, as it appears to you, then I will have something so new to me and of such value, a way to know a few bearings."[68]

Russell was untiring in his advocacy for Welty in the literary world, his assurance to her that her work was brilliant, and his efforts to get her work published.[69] Publishers looked for novels, and so it was no small feat to get her short stories published: Russell kept urging Welty to write a novel until she finally agreed to do it. But Russell did not know Bernice Harris, and he did not have to do much to help her, since Doubleday automatically published her next six novels after *Purslane*; he could just forward each manuscript to Doubleday and then look over the contract that Doubleday inevitably sent to him. When, in the 1950s, Doubleday rejected Harris's manuscripts, he seems to have been ineffectual in advising her about other publishers and advocating for her. In 1970 he simply told her that publishers were not interested in short stories.

Early in her career, in the thirties, Welty sent stories to the *Southern Review*, where editors Robert Penn Warren and Cleanth Brooks eventually became her supporters.[70] Although they turned down some stories at first, Brooks and Warren included two of Welty's stories in their popular text *Understanding Fiction*, published in 1943, which made her work widely known.

Welty was free to travel, not homebound early in her career because of an ailing husband, as Harris was. (Later Welty would be caring for her ailing mother and then her two brothers, but by then her career was well established.) Welty stayed at Bread Loaf, a writers' residence, where she became friends with Katherine Anne Porter. Porter wrote the glowing preface to Welty's first collection of short stories, *A Curtain of Green and Other Stories* (1941).[71] Welty visited Porter in Baton Rouge, and Porter stayed with Welty in Jackson. Elizabeth Bowen reviewed Welty's novel *Delta Wedding* for the *Tatler* in 1946, praising it highly and thereby assuring its fame in Britain. When Welty won a second Guggenheim Fellowship in 1949, she traveled on the Continent and to Britain and Ireland. In Dublin, she made it a point to meet Bowen, who also became a good friend.[72]

It was not that Welty's purpose was to influence the "right people." She was focused on writing and she enjoyed talking with writers. She was appreciative of people who liked her work, and she would go out of her way to see them. She gained knowledge about the literary world and such things as fellowships through Diarmuid Russell. Critic Michael Kreyling said that there was no way a writer outside the circle could know "the rituals by which literary business was conducted" unless an insider like Russell showed her.[73]

Other southern women writers, contemporaries of Harris, were differently situated from Harris, as well. Frances Newman was born into a wealthy, well-educated urban family in 1883. She worked as a librarian in Tallahassee, Florida, at the Florida State College for Women, then went to Atlanta to the Carnegie Library, and ended her library career at the Georgia Institute of Technology. She traveled widely, often to New York but to Europe too. In 1926, she chose New York City as her residence, but she also spent two summers at the MacDowell Colony in Peterborough, New Hampshire. James Branch Cabell and H. L. Mencken were her friends and mentors. Not widely known now, she had two novels acclaimed in her time: *The Hard-Boiled Virgin* (1926) and *Dead Lovers Are Faithful Lovers* (1928). Her death in 1928 cut short her career.[74]

Caroline Gordon, just four years younger than Harris, was a journalist, critic, and novelist. Gordon was married to the poet Allen Tate, who had an important role among the Agrarians and a national reputation as a man of letters. The couple regularly traveled around the country and to Europe. Among their close friends were the famous writers of the day, including the outstanding British author Ford Madox Ford. It was Allen Tate and Ford Madox Ford who urged Gordon to write her first novel, *Penhally* (published in 1931).[75]

Katherine Anne Porter, a year older than Bernice Harris, married in her early teens, but chose not to stay with her husband in a marriage that was unhappy. Referring to her first marriage, she told an interviewer, "I have no *hidden* marriages, they just sort of slip my mind."[76] She also chose not to stay with any husband or lover thereafter if life did not go well. She started writing for newspapers in Texas but left Texas for New York. She began writing short stories while she was still writing nonfiction for publications like the *Century* and soon acquired a reputation as a master of the short story form. All her life she traveled widely, sometimes living in New York, sometimes at Bread Loaf or Yaddo, sometimes in Washington, D.C., sometimes in Mexico. Everywhere she went, she made friends among influential writers like Tate, with whom she had a brief love affair and a long-term friendship. Editor and literary historian Matthew Josephson was her lover for a time and her mentor. Porter was dogged by money worries and sometimes had to borrow from friends; however, she was also awarded lucrative fellowships and teaching positions, as well as advances on promised books. There were periods when financial troubles were at bay and she had the time to concentrate on writing.

Many of Harris's fellow writers lived in small towns, but their contacts in the literary world were not restricted. For example, Jackson, Mississippi, was a home base from which Eudora Welty ventured into the wider world. But circumstances conspired to make Seaboard, North Carolina, not a place to start from, but a confining, isolating place in terms of Harris's career. If Harris had received advice and advocacy from a literary sophisticate with influence on the national level, it might have been different. Still, the joy of writing was hers. And the challenge of not "making a mess of living or dying" she took on like a champion.

NOTES

1. Bernice Kelly Harris, "From the Complex," folder 94, Bernice Kelly Harris Papers, no. 3804, Manuscripts Department, Southern Historical Collection, Louis Round Wilson Library, University of North Carolina, Chapel Hill, N.C. (Hereafter cited as BKH, UNC, with "f" for folder.)

2. Bernice Kelly Harris, *Southern Savory* (Chapel Hill: University of North Carolina Press, 1964), 33.

3. Research on Kelly land ownership was undertaken by attorney Gordon Kelley [*sic*], Bill Kelly's grandson, who handled family legal matters. Wake County, North Carolina, Clerk of Court, Register of Deeds, Deed Book 128, p. 52 (1894); Deed Book 135, p. 280 (1897); Deed Book 140, p. 162 (1897); Deed Book 140, p. 298 (1897); Deed Book 155, p. 337 (1896), a bequest from Calvin Kelly to his son shortly before his death; Deed Book 157, p. 11 (1899); Deed Book 162, p. 334 (1901); Deed Book 298, p. 27 (1910). After 1914, Bill Kelly started giving land to his children, such as a grant to his daughter Rachel Floyd and her husband, W. H. Coats, and so his acreage diminished as his children married.

Statistics on crops and land ownership are based on information in Bureau of the Census, *Thirteenth Census of the United States Taken in the Year 1910*, Vol. 7, *Agriculture, 1909 and 1910* (Washington, D.C.: Government Printing Office, 1913), 245. Out of the 6,137 farms in Wake County, only 42 had more than 500 acres. However, the census might be misleading in that an owner might have had additional farms in another part of the state.

4. Bureau of the Census, *Thirteenth Census*, Vol. 7, *Agriculture, 1909 and 1910*, p. 245. For a discussion on rise in prices of crops from 1899 to 1909, see pp. 229 and 230. See also Pete Daniel, *Breaking the Land: The Transformation of Cotton, Tobacco, and Rice Cultures Since 1880* (Urbana: University of Illinois Press, 1985). Daniel discusses fluctuation in prices of both cotton, which rose generally but had bad years in 1914 and 1920 (p. 18) and tobacco, which rose dramatically from 1911 to 1920, when there was a sharp fall (p. 35).

5. Gordon Kelley, oral history interview recorded by author, Chapel Hill, N.C., 26 June 1995, side 1, tape counter number 025, BKH, UNC. Subse-

quent citations of oral history tape recordings give the number of the tape side, followed by a colon and by the tape counter number.

6. Alice Jo Kelley Burrows, oral history interview recorded by author, Raleigh, N.C., 14 July 1996, 1:352, BKH, UNC.

7. Harris, *Southern Savory*, 34.

8. Ibid.

9. Ibid., 35.

10. Ibid., 31.

11. Ibid., 32.

12. Ibid., 33.

13. Ibid., 32.

14. F170, p. 292, BKH, UNC.

15. Harris, *Southern Savory*, 34.

16. Ibid., 32.

17. Ibid., 60–61.

18. Richard Walser, *Bernice Kelly Harris: Storyteller of Eastern Carolina* (Chapel Hill: University of North Carolina Library, 1955), 7.

19. Bernice Kelly Harris, "The Academy I Love the Best," Raleigh *News and Observer*, 28 May 1961.

20. Walser, *Bernice Kelly Harris*, 8.

21. Harris, *Southern Savory*, 55.

22. Ibid., 54–57.

23. Alice Jo Kelley Burrows, communication to author, 8 May 1997.

24. Harris, *Southern Savory*, 84.

25. Ibid., 92.

26. Ibid., 94.

27. Ibid., 95–97.

28. Ibid., 7.

29. Ibid., 6.

30. Ibid., 77–78.

31. Ibid., 7.

32. Burrows, oral history, 2:653.

33. Harris, *Southern Savory*, 34–35.

34. Ibid., 23–24.

35. Ibid., 21–22. For a discussion of the role of the peddler in the lives of rural southern women, see Lu Ann Jones, "Re-visioning the Countryside: Southern Women, Rural Reform, and the Farm Economy in the Twentieth Century South" (Ph.D. diss., University of North Carolina, Chapel Hill, 1996). Chapter 2, "Linking the Remote Countryside with Marts of Trade: Shrewd Farm Women and Itinerant Merchants," treats both peddlers and agents of companies.

36. Harris, *Southern Savory*, 15–17.

37. Paul D. Escott, *Many Excellent People: Power and Privilege in North Carolina, 1850–1900* (Chapel Hill: University of North Carolina Press, 1985), 148–149.

38. Harris, *Southern Savory*, 69.

39. Ibid.

40. Ibid., 69–70.

41. Ibid., 70.

42. Ibid., 26.

43. Ibid., 68. F93, p. 69, BKH, UNC. See f189 for a fragment of the novel "The Gypsy's Warning" in a child's handwriting.

44. Carol Gilligan, Nona Lyons, and Trudi Hammer, eds., *Making Connections: The Relational Worlds of Adolescent Girls at Emma Willard School* (Cambridge: Harvard University Press, 1990).

45. Harris, *Southern Savory*, 69.

46. Lucy Brashear, "The Novels of Mary Jane Holmes," in *Nineteenth-Century Women Writers of the English-Speaking World*, Rhoda B. Nathan, ed. (Westport, Conn.: Greenwood Press, 1986), 19–25; see p. 19.

47. Harris, *Southern Savory*, 35.

48. James L. Leloudis, *Schooling the New South: Pedagogy, Self, and Society in North Carolina, 1880–1920* (Chapel Hill: University of North Carolina Press, 1996), 74. Leloudis describes and ties together these strands in the movement toward change in education that resulted in an increasing number of women teaching; see chapters 3, 4, and 5 especially.

49. Walser, *Bernice Kelly Harris*, 9.

50. Leloudis, *Schooling the New South*, 115.

51. Harris, *Southern Savory*, 10.

52. Ibid., 110–111.

53. Lacy K. Ford Jr., in a preface to Ben Robertson's memoir, presents this quotation from Robertson, *Red Hills and Cotton* (1942; rpr. Columbia: University of South Carolina Press, 1960).

2   NO FLOWERY BED OF EASE

1. F151, p. 106, BKH, UNC.

2. F178, p. 13, BKH, UNC.

3. F178, p. 12, BKH, UNC.

4. Richard Walser, *Bernice Kelly Harris: Storyteller of Eastern Carolina* (Chapel Hill: University of North Carolina Library, 1955), 11.

5. F151, p. 106, BKH, UNC.

6. F178, p. 14, BKH, UNC.

7. F178, p. 15, BKH, UNC.

8. F178, p. 16, BKH, UNC.

9. F151, p. 106, BKH, UNC.

10. F178, pp. 17–18, BKH, UNC.

11. Elizabeth Bullock, oral history interview recorded by author, Seaboard, North Carolina, 19 June 1996, 1:065, BKH, UNC.

12. F178, p. 18, BKH, UNC.

13. F178, p. beginning "Put into words . . . ," BKH, UNC.

14. F178, p. 20, BKH, UNC.

15. Frederick Koch Correspondence, Introduction, Series 1, no. 4124, Frederick Koch Papers, Manuscripts Dept., Southern Historical Collection, Louis Round Wilson Library, University of North Carolina, Chapel Hill, N.C. See also Walter Spearman, *The Carolina Playmakers* (Chapel Hill: University of North Carolina Press, 1970); and Felix Sper, *From Native Roots: A Panorama of Our Regional Drama* (Caldwell, Idaho: Caxton Printers, 1948), 21 (for definition of folk drama), 22, 37, 38, 117 (on Koch), and 121 and 123 (on Bernice Kelly Harris).

16. F178, p. 20, BKH, UNC.

17. William Ivey Long, tape-recorded communication to author, Rock Hill, S.C., 17 May 1996. Private archives of author.

18. F178, pp. 124–126, BKH, UNC.

19. F178, p. 22, BKH, UNC.

20. F178, p. 23, BKH, UNC.

21. F178, p. 22, BKH, UNC.

22. F178, p. 23, BKH, UNC.

23. F178, p. 21, BKH, UNC.

24. F169, p. 130, BKH, UNC.

25. F178, p. 19, BKH, UNC.

26. F185, p. 134, BKH, UNC.

27. F185, p. 134, BKH, UNC.

28. F185, p. 134, BKH, UNC.

29. F148, one page labeled 24 and 142, BKH, UNC.

30. F185, p. 138, BKH, UNC.

31. F148, p. beginning "and sound . . . ," BKH, UNC.

32. F185, p. 137, BKH, UNC.

33. F185, p. 123, BKH, UNC.

34. F185, p. 123, BKH, UNC.

35. F185, p. beginning "I did not aim . . . ," BKH, UNC.

36. F185, p. 23, BKH, UNC.

37. Walser, *Bernice Kelly Harris*, 15.

38. Bernice Kelly Harris, *Southern Savory* (Chapel Hill: University of North Carolina Press, 1964), 116–117.

39. Bernice Kelly Harris, ed., *Strange Things Happen* (Murfreesboro, N.C.: Johnson Publishing, 1971), 130–132.

40. F94, "Notes from the Nursing Home," BKH, UNC.

41. F149, p. 119, BKH, UNC.

42. F178, p. 151, BKH, UNC.

43. F165, unpublished pages from the autobiography, BKH, UNC. See also Sandra Upchurch Poindexter, oral history interview recorded by author, Chapel Hill, N.C., 18 March 1997, 1:282.

44. Bernice Kelly Harris to Richard Walser, 14 June 1967, Richard Gaultier Walser Papers, no. 4168, Manuscripts Dept., Southern Historical Collection, Louis Round Wilson Library, University of North Carolina, Chapel Hill, N.C. (Hereafter cited as Walser, UNC, with "f" for folder).

45. F256, page fragment, Walser, UNC.

46. F185, p. 23, BKH, UNC.

47. F178, page labeled 26 and 154, BKH, UNC.

3   SHAMELESSLY JUST MARRIED BEFORE THE WORLD

1. F156, p. 152, BKH, UNC. Since much of Harris's writing about Herbert and his family was omitted from the published autobiography, I rely chiefly on these archival materials for this chapter.

2. Ibid.

3. Ibid.

4. Bernice Kelly Harris, *Southern Savory* (Chapel Hill: University of North Carolina Press, 1964), 137.

5. Bureau of the Census, *Fifteenth Census of the United States, Taken in the Year 1930*, vol. 3 (Washington, D.C.: U.S. Government Printing Office, 1932), 396. I give here an estimate for 1926, based on the population in the census for Seaboard Township of 2,772 in 1930 (see Table 21: Population by Sex, Color, Age, Etc., for Counties by Minor Civil Divisions: 1930).

6. Ibid., 250 (see County Table III: Value of Farm Products Sold, Traded, or Used by Operators).

7. Bureau of the Census, *Fourteenth Census of the United States, Taken in the Year 1920*, vol. 6 (Washington, D.C.: U.S. Government Printing Office, 1922), 298 (see County Table I: Farms and Farm Property, 1920, with Selected Items for 1910 and 1900).

8. Ibid. Farms with 20 to 49 acres numbered 1,646; there were 817 moderate-sized farms of 50 to 99 acres. Those with over 100 acres numbered 547. Of these large farms, 10 farms had over 1,000 acres.

9. Bureau of the Census, *Fourteenth Census of the United States*, vol. 3, p. 741 (see Table 9: Composition and Characteristics of the Population, for Counties: 1920).

10. Bureau of the Census, *Fourteenth Census of the United States*, vol. 6,

p. 298 (see County Table I: Farms and Farm Property, 1920, with Selected Items for 1910 and 1900). Whites owned 946 farms; blacks, 459.

11. Pete Daniel, *Breaking the Land: The Transformation of Cotton, Tobacco, and Rice Cultures Since 1880* (Urbana: University of Illinois Press, 1985), especially pp. 3–6. W. E. B. Du Bois, "The Black Codes," in *Justice Denied: The Black Man in White America*, ed. William Chase and Peter Collier (New York: Harcourt, Brace and World, 1970): see pages 166–167 for a discussion on laws used to control the black labor force. See also William Cohen, "Negro Involuntary Servitude in the South, 1865–1940," *Journal of Southern History* 42 (February 1976): 33–35. The activities and influence of the Ku Klux Klan are discussed in John Hope Franklin, *Reconstruction After the Civil War*, 2nd ed. (Chicago: University of Chicago Press, 1994); see especially the chapter "Counter Reconstruction," pp. 151–169.

12. Roy Parker Jr., oral history interview recorded by author, Fayetteville, N.C., January 31, 1996, 1:222, BKH, UNC.

13. Parker, oral history, 1:351.

14. Parker, oral history, 1:207.

15. Elizabeth Harris, oral history interview recorded by author, Seaboard, N.C., April 5, 1996, 1:533, BKH, UNC.

16. Parker, oral history, 1:289.

17. Harris, *Southern Savory*, 124–125.

18. Ibid., 130.

19. Ibid.

20. Ibid., 131.

21. F148, p. 184, BKH, UNC.

22. F148, p. beginning "lovely setting for our home," BKH, UNC.

23. F178, one page labeled 26 and 154, BKH, UNC.

24. F96, p. 168, BKH, UNC.

25. F96, p. 168, BKH, UNC.

26. F96, p. 168, BKH, UNC.

27. F169, p. 174, BKH, UNC.

28. E. Harris, oral history, 2:153.

29. F96, p. 169, BKH, UNC.

30. F96, p. 170, BKH, UNC.

31. F96, p. 170, BKH, UNC.

32. F185, p. 137, BKH, UNC.

33. F96, p. 170, BKH, UNC.

34. F147, p. 204, BKH, UNC.

35. F96, pp. 190–191, BKH, UNC.

36. F95, p. 209, BKH, UNC.

37. F96, p.209, BKH, UNC.

38. Bernice Kelly Harris to Gordon Kelley, 30 May 1964, private archives of Gordon Kelley.

39. Ed Hodges, conversation with author, Durham, N.C., 2 April 1997.

40. Jonathan Carey Coats (son of Bernice's sister Rachel Floyd Kelly Coats) and Patricia Coats Kube, oral history interview recorded by author, Clayton, N.C., 9 March 1997, 1:103, private archives of Jonathan Carey Coats. These patterns of visiting were typical of the southern family at the time. See a discussion of the structure of the southern family by sociologist Rupert Vance in the 1940s, "Regional Family Patterns: The Southern Family," *American Journal of Sociology* 52 (May 1948), 426–429.

41. E. Harris, oral history, 2:439.

42. F148, p. beginning "lovely setting for our home," BKH, UNC.

43. F170, p. 178, BKH, UNC.

44. F170, p. 178, BKH, UNC.

45. F156, p. 184, BKH, UNC.

46. F156, p. 184, BKH, UNC.

47. Parker, oral history, 1:572.

48. F158, p. 220, BKH, UNC.

49. F158, p. 220, BKH, UNC.

50. Richard Walser, *Bernice Kelly Harris: Storyteller of Eastern Carolina* (Chapel Hill: University of North Carolina Library, 1955), 19.

51. Harris, *Southern Savory,* 177.

52. F157, pp. 202–203, BKH, UNC.

53. F156, p. beginning "Each year at Christmas . . . ," BKH, UNC.

54. F158, one page labeled 230 and 34, BKH, UNC.

55. "Bantie Woman," *Saturday Evening Post* 213 (22 March 1941), 24–25, 122–125. This story was later published in Richard Walser, ed., *North Carolina in the Short Story* (Chapel Hill: University of North Carolina Press, 1948).

56. F158, p. 230, BKH, UNC.

57. Harris, *Southern Savory,* 205.

58. Joan Givner, *Katherine Anne Porter: A Life* (New York: Simon and Schuster, 1982), 96.

59. Anne Goodwyn Jones, *Tomorrow Is Another Day: The Woman Writer in the South, 1859–1936* (Baton Rouge: Louisiana State University Press, 1981), 256.

60. Ibid., 136.

61. Ibid. Jones refers to a critic's describing the subject of Kate Chopin's novel *The Awakening* (1899) as the "life behind the mask." C. L. Deyo's review of *The Awakening* appeared in the St. Louis *Post-Dispatch,* 20 May 1899, and is quoted in Kate Chopin, *The Awakening: An Authoritative Text, Contexts, Criticism,* ed. Margaret Culley (New York: Norton, 1976).

4   NORTHAMPTON COUNTY PRODUCES COTTON, PEANUTS, AND PLAYS

1. F158, p. 214, BKH, UNC.
2. Ibid.
3. F158, p. 196, BKH, UNC.
4. F158, p. beginning "for community drama . . . ," BKH, UNC.
5. F158, p. 196, BKH, UNC.
6. F147, p. beginning "to own tuxedos . . . ," BKH, UNC.
7. F147, p. beginning "the following direct quote . . . ," BKH, UNC. See also Federal Writers' Project Papers, no. 3709, "Ruth Vick Everett Speaking," p. 4, folder 495, Manuscripts Dept., Southern Historical Collection, Louis Round Wilson Library, University of North Carolina, Chapel Hill, N.C. (Hereafter cited as FWP, UNC, with "f" for folder number.)
8. F495, FWP, UNC. See also Bernice Kelly Harris, "In the 30's, the Play Was Really the Thing," Raleigh *News and Observer*, 2 March 1962.
9. F158, one page labeled 34 and 289, BKH, UNC.
10. F495, pp. 4–5, FWP, UNC.
11. Bernice Kelly Harris, *Folk Plays of Eastern Carolina*, ed. and with an introduction by Frederick Koch (Chapel Hill: University of North Carolina Press, 1940), 75–107.
12. Ibid., 231–268; see p. 266.
13. Ibid., 41–74.
14. Ibid., 1–39; see p. 33.
15. Ibid., pp. 33, 39.
16. Ibid., 198–230; see pp. 218–219.
17. Ibid., 18.
18. Ibid., 159–195.
19. Ibid., Introduction, "Plays of a Country Neighborhood," by Frederick Koch, xiv.
20. Ibid., 109–158; see p. 158.
21. Ibid., 1–39; see p. 22.
22. Ibid., 231–268; see p. 238.
23. Ibid.
24. Ibid., 246.
25. Ibid., 70.
26. Ibid., Introduction by Koch, vi–vi.
27. Ibid., xvii.
28. Ibid., v.

5   FARM GIRL COMPELLED TO WRITE

1. F146, p. 246, BKH, UNC.
2. Ibid. and f158, p. 214, BKH, UNC.

3. Bernice Kelly Harris, *Southern Savory* (Chapel Hill: University of North Carolina Press, 1964), 155.

4. Ibid.

5. Ibid., 154.

6. Bernice Kelly Harris, *Purslane* (Chapel Hill: University of North Carolina Press, 1939), 1. (Hereafter cited in the text by page number only.)

7. *Pusley* is a common variant of the word *purslane*.

8. Harris, *Southern Savory*, 205.

9. Jonathan Daniels, "Roots of the Tarheels," *Saturday Review of Literature*, 13 May 1939, p. 5.

10. Bernice Kelly Harris to J. O. Bailey, 20 May 1939, f1, BKH, UNC.

11. Sam Ragan, oral history interview recorded by author, Southern Pines, N.C., 31 January 1996, 1:272, BKH, UNC.

12. Mabel E. Gassian to Bernice Kelly Harris, November 1939, f2, BKH, UNC.

13. Clifton Fadiman, "Books," *New Yorker* 15 (13 May 1939), 78.

14. Gerald Johnson, "Hilarity Among the Share Croppers," *New York Herald Tribune*, 14 May 1939, p. 2 of Book Section.

15. Caroline Gordon, "Carolina in the Morning," *New Republic* 99 (12 July 1939): 286.

16. Paul Jordan-Smith, "What I Liked Last Week," *Los Angeles Times*, 7 May 1939, Part III, p. 6.

17. Harris, *Southern Savory*, 156.

18. Twelve Southerners, *I'll Take My Stand: The South and the Agrarian Tradition* (New York: Harper and Brothers, 1930).

19. Louis D. Rubin Jr., introduction to *I'll Take My Stand: The South and the Agrarian Tradition* (New York: Harper Torchbook, 1962), xiii–xiv; Richard King, *A Southern Renaissance: The Cultural Awakening of the American South, 1930–1955* (New York: Oxford University Press, 1980), 55.

20. Caroline Gordon, *Penhally* (New York: Charles Scribner's Sons, 1931).

21. Elizabeth Madox Roberts, *The Time of Man* (New York: Viking, 1926); Ellen Glasgow, *Barren Ground* (New York: Harcourt, Brace, 1925). See also Louis D. Rubin Jr., *No Place on Earth: Ellen Glasgow, James Branch Cabell, and Richmond-in-Virginia* (Austin: University of Texas Press, 1959), 16, 18, 26.

22. King, *A Southern Renaissance*, 7. King, looking back from the vantage point of fifty years later, summed up the period by saying that novelists had to "come to terms not only with the inherited values of the Southern tradition but also with a certain way of perceiving and dealing with the past." It was important, he said, "for them to decide whether the past was of any use at all in the present; and if so, in what ways?" In this broad view, Harris's *Purslane* was part of the dialogue of the times.

23. Harris, *Southern Savory*, 159.

24. F150, p. beginning "Yet the subtle suggestion . . . ," BKH, UNC.

25. Ibid.

26. F92, p. 227, BKH, UNC.

27. Richard Walser, *Bernice Kelly Harris: Storyteller of Eastern Carolina* (Chapel Hill: University of North Carolina Library, 1955), 21.

28. BKH to Betty Hodges, Notes for a Biographical Speech, Private Archives of Betty Hodges, Durham, N.C.

29. Walser, *Bernice Kelly Harris*, 20–21.

30. Harris, *Southern Savory*, 167.

31. Walser, *Bernice Kelly Harris*, 2.

6 HAUNTING WORK

1. Erskine Caldwell, *Tobacco Road* (New York: Charles Scribner's Sons, 1932); Erskine Caldwell, *God's Little Acre* (New York: Viking, 1933).

2. For a discussion of the downturn in market prices of cotton and tobacco, see Pete Daniel, *Breaking the Land: The Transformation of Cotton, Tobacco, and Rice Cultures Since 1880* (Urbana: University of Illinois Press, 1985), 18–22, 32–38. For a discussion of the definitions of tenant farmer and sharecropper, see Gilbert C. Fite, *Cotton Fields No More: Southern Agriculture, 1865–1980* (Lexington: University of Kentucky Press, 1984), 3–5; and Jack Temple Kirby, *Rural Worlds Lost: The American South, 1920–1960* (Baton Rouge: Louisiana State University Press, 1987), 140.

3. Dan B. Miller, *Erskine Caldwell: The Journey from Tobacco Road* (New York: Alfred A. Knopf, 1995), 37, 43–45.

4. Margaret Jarman Hagood, *Mothers of the South: Portraiture of the White Tenant Farm Woman* (1939; rpr. New York: Greenwood Press, 1969), 39.

5. Quoted in Jerre Mangione, *The Dream and the Deal: The Federal Writers' Project, 1935–1943* (Boston: Little, Brown, 1972), 4.

6. William Terry Couch, "Landlord and Tenant," *Virginia Quarterly Review* 14 (1938): 311. *Tobacco Road* is cited in note 1; Erskine Caldwell and Margaret Bourke-White, *You Have Seen Their Faces* (New York: Modern Age Books, 1937).

7. Tom Terrill and Jerrold Hirsch, "Conceptualization and Implementation: Some Thoughts on Reading the Federal Writers' Project Southern Life Histories," *Southern Studies*, fall 1979: 352–353.

8. Jerrold M. Hirsch, "Portrait of America: The Federal Writers' Project in an Intellectual and Cultural Context" (Ph.D. diss., University of North Carolina at Chapel Hill, 1984), 15, 17.

9. Ibid., 16.

10. Mangione, *The Dream and the Deal,* 46.

11. William Terry Couch, Papers of Regional Director William Terry Couch, Federal Writers' Project Records, 1936–1940, no. 3709, folder 38, Manuscripts Dept., Southern Historical Collection, Louis Round Wilson Library, University of North Carolina, Chapel Hill, N.C.

12. Richard Walser, *Bernice Kelly Harris: Storyteller of Eastern Carolina* (Chapel Hill: University of North Carolina Library, 1955), 22.

13. Federal Writers' Project, *These Are Our Lives: As Told by the People and Written by Members of the Federal Writers' Project of the Works Progress Administration in North Carolina, Tennessee, and Georgia* (Chapel Hill: University of North Carolina Press, 1939), 420–421.

14. Ibid., 417.

15. Leonard Rapport, "How Valid Are the Federal Writers' Project Life Stories? An Iconoclast Among the True Believers," *Oral History Review* (1979): 6–17.

16. Ibid., 7.

17. Valerie Raleigh Yow, *Recording Oral History: A Practical Guide for Social Scientists* (Thousand Oaks, Calif.: Sage Publications, 1994), 221–222.

18. David E. Faris, "Narrative Form and Oral History: Some Problems and Possibilities," *Oral History Review* 1, no. 3 (1980): 161–163.

19. Rapport, "How Valid Are the Federal Writers' Project Life Stories?" 15. Tom Terrill and Jerrold Hirsch, "Replies to Leonard Rapport's 'How Valid Are the Federal Writers' Project Life Stories? An Iconoclast Among the True Believers,' " *Oral History Review* 1, no. 3 (1980): 84.

20. Bernice Kelly Harris, *Southern Savory* (Chapel Hill: University of North Carolina Press, 1964), 182.

21. Federal Writers' Project Records, 1936–1940, no. 3709, folder 440, Manuscripts Dept., Southern Historical Collection, Louis Round Wilson Library, University of North Carolina, Chapel Hill, N.C. Nine hundred life histories are contained in this collection. Life histories written by Bernice Kelly Harris are in folders 416–480. (Hereafter cited in the text as FWP with "f" to indicate folder number.)

Other life histories are in the National Archives and in regional archives—see the bibliographical essay in Tom Terrill and Jerrold Hirsch, eds., *Such As Us: Southern Voices of the Thirties* (Chapel Hill: University of North Carolina Press, 1978). Only 65 stories of the more than 1,000 have been published: Couch published some of the stories in *These Are Our Lives* in 1939, and Terrill and Hirsch published others in *Such As Us.* Names and identifying characteristics were changed to protect the anonymity of the narrators both in the unpublished and published life histories.

22. Harris, *Southern Savory,* 185.

23. Ibid., 185–186.

24. Ibid., 182.
25. Ibid., 184.
26. Terrill and Hirsch, eds., *Such As Us*, 262.
27. Ibid., 277.
28. Harris, *Southern Savory*, 184.
29. Ibid., 186.
30. Ibid., 187.
31. Terrill and Hirsch, eds., *Such As Us*, 29.
32. Bernice Kelly Harris, *Sweet Beulah Land* (New York: Doubleday, 1943), 260.
33. Bernice Kelly Harris, *Sage Quarter* (New York: Doubleday, 1945).
34. Harris, *Southern Savory*, 202.
35. Bernice Kelly Harris, *Janey Jeems* (New York: Doubleday, 1946), 28.
36. Harris, *Southern Savory*, 189–191; see also f469, FWP.
37. Harris, *Southern Savory*, 179.
38. Ibid., 177–178.

7 TAKING RISKS

1. Bernice Kelly Harris, *Portulaca* (New York: Doubleday, 1941), 44–46. (Hereafter this novel is cited in the text by page number only.)
2. Sheila Rowbotham, *Women's Consciousness, Man's World* (Middlesex, England: Penguin Books, 1973), 27, 29, 31.
3. Bernice Kelly Harris, *Southern Savory* (Chapel Hill: University of North Carolina Press, 1964), 163.
4. Robert Penn Warren, "The Love and the Separateness in Miss Welty," *Kenyon Review* 6 (spring 1944): 246–259. Warren writes, "To begin with, almost all of the stories deal with people who, in one way or another, are cut off, alienated, isolated from the world." See pp. 249–251 for his brief discussion. Warren does not develop this analysis. Warren Akin IV, in *The Heart's Separateness and Love: Psychological Themes in Eudora Welty's Fiction* (Baton Rouge, La., 1986), presents a Freudian analysis, stressing incomplete resolution of aggressive and sexual desires as motivating Welty's characters in her early stories. Love, for Akin, means the attachment to mother that the maturing child must diminish in order to have a separate and mature sexual existence. I use instead the concept of connection developed by psychologist Carol Gilligan in *In a Different Voice: Psychological Theory and Women's Development* (Cambridge, Mass.: Harvard University Press, 1982).
5. Harris, *Southern Savory* 160; William Terry Couch to BKH, 30 September 1940, f3, BKH, UNC.
6. Harris, *Southern Savory*, 159–160; William Terry Couch to BKH, 30 September 1940, f3, BKH, UNC.

7. Harris, *Southern Savory*, 161.

8. Ibid. See original letter (W. T. Couch to BKH, 6 November 1940) in f3, BKH, UNC.

9. Herschel Brickell, *New York Times Book Review*, 4 May 1941, p. 7.

10. *Milwaukee (Wisc.) Journal*, 3 June 1941; clipping in f40, BKH, UNC.

11. Frank Smethurst, "Small Town Perspective," Raleigh *News and Observer*, 11 May 1941.

12. Ibid.

13. Sinclair Lewis, *Main Street* (New York: Harcourt, Brace, 1921).

14. Sam Ragan, conversation with author, 31 January 1996, Southern Pines, N.C.

15. Harris, *Southern Savory*, 160.

16. F96, p. 238, BKH, UNC. Folder 96 contains loose pages she did not use in her published autobiography.

17. Harris, *Southern Savory*, 162.

18. F96, p. 238, BKH, UNC.

19. Letter of Huntington to BKH, 5 May 1941, f4, BKH, UNC.

20. Harris, *Southern Savory*, 163.

21. Ibid.

22. Ibid.

23. Ibid., 164.

24. Elizabeth Harris, oral history interview recorded by author, Seaboard, N.C., 5 April 1996, 2:005.

25. Harris, *Southern Savory*, 164.

26. Betsey Bradley Merritt, oral history interview recorded by author, Roanoke Rapids, N.C., 5 April 1996, 2:202.

27. F96, p. unclear, may be 225, begins "and a few men read the book . . . ," BKH, UNC.

28. Women's clubs in North Carolina existed early in the nineteenth century but multiplied fast in the first three decades of the twentieth century. See Anastatia Sims, "Feminism and Femininity in the New South: White Women's Organizations in North Carolina, 1823–1930" (Ph.D. diss., Department of History, University of North Carolina, Chapel Hill, 1985), 91. See especially Chapter 3, "A Power for Good."

29. Walter Spearman to BKH, 15 July 1941, f4, BKH, UNC.

30. Ibid.

31. Anne Jackson to BKH, 27 November 1941, f4, BKH, UNC.

32. Harris, *Southern Savory*, 164.

8   FRIENDSHIPS AND *SWEET BEULAH LAND*

1. Bernice Kelly Harris, *Southern Savory* (Chapel Hill: University of North Carolina Press, 1964), 65.

2. F157, p. titled "Pig and Honey," BKH, UNC.

3. For an overview of the situation of black domestic workers in the South early in the century, see Elizabeth Clark-Lewis, "God and They People: The Rural South," chap. 1 in *Living In, Living Out: African American Domestics in Washington, D.C., 1910–1940* (Washington, D.C.: Smithsonian Institution Press, 1994), 9–49. Susan Tucker, in her book *Telling Memories Among Southern Women: Domestic Workers and Their Employers in the Segregated South* (Baton Rouge: Louisiana State University Press, 1988), presents oral histories by both white employers and black domestic workers which articulate different kinds of relationships. Tucker states that at the basis of these relationships was the fact that white women's "standard of living rested upon the cheap labor of all blacks, male and female" (32).

4. Magdeline Faison, oral history interview recorded by author, Roxboro, N.C., 28 August 1996, 1:597.

5. Ibid.

6. F475, "Ethel Vassar, Cook," FWP, UNC.

7. Harris, *Southern Savory*, 139.

8. Ibid.

9. Ibid., 141.

10. Ibid., 138.

11. Ibid., 142.

12. F157, "Pig and Honey," BKH, UNC.

13. Harris, *Southern Savory*, 143.

14. Ibid., 146.

15. F157, p. 278, BKH, UNC.

16. Harris, *Southern Savory*, 147.

17. Ibid., 149.

18. Ibid., 148–149.

19. Ibid., 148.

20. F157, pp. 280–281, BKH, UNC.

21. Bernice Kelly Harris, " 'The Essential Northampton'—A Portrait Drawn in Affection," Raleigh *News and Observer*, 27 July 1947, Sec. IV. The caption for the photo of Melissa Lowery, which does not come out of Harris's writing, was probably written by the editor, as journalist Betty Hodges pointed out to me: "Like an increasing number of her race, Melissa Lowery brings a background of education to her domestic service." It is the kind of subtle condescension that Harris tried to avoid.

22. F183, p. 287, BKH, UNC.

23. F183, p. 189, BKH, UNC.

24. Ibid.

25. F157, p. 286, BKH, UNC.

26. F186, p. 44, BKH, UNC.

27. F183, p. 295, BKH, UNC.

28. F178, p. 288, BKH, UNC.

29. F183, p. 293, BKH, UNC.

30. F183, p. 286, BKH, UNC.

31. Bernice Kelly Harris to Richard Walser, 31 August 1939, f255, Walser, UNC.

32. Bernice Kelly Harris to Richard Walser, 20 October 1939, f255, Walser, UNC.

33. John Woodburn to Bernice Kelly Harris, 15 October 1940, f3, BKH, UNC.

34. Frederick Wight, "Sweet Beulah Land," *New York Herald Tribune Weekly Book Review*, 21 February 1943.

35. Eudora Welty, "Plantation Country," *New York Times Book Review* 7 March 1943, p. 9. Reprinted in Eudora Welty, *A Writer's Eye: Collected Book Reviews*, ed. Pearl Amelia McHaney (Jackson: University Press of Mississippi, 1994), 6–7.

36. Harris, *Southern Savory*, 184.

37. Bernice Kelly Harris, *Sweet Beulah Land* (New York: Doubleday, 1943), 26.

38. "Change Inevitable: But Tar Heels Hold Fast," *Greensboro Daily News*, 28 February 1943, Sec. 1, p. 14.

39. Harris, *Sweet Beulah Land*, 260.

40. Ibid., 263; see also f430, FWP, UNC. The oral history is published as "No Stick Leg" in Tom Terrill and Jerrold Hirsch, eds., *Such As Us: Southern Voices of the Thirties* (Chapel Hill: University of North Carolina Press, 1978), 29–37.

41. Harris, *Southern Savory*, 197. See also Harris, *Sweet Beulah Land*, 117–118.

42. Gilbert C. Fite, *Cotton Fields No More: Southern Agriculture, 1865–1980* (Lexington: University of Kentucky Press, 1984), 180–189.

43. Jack Temple Kirby, *Rural Worlds Lost: The American South, 1920–1960* (Baton Rouge: Louisiana State University Press, 1987), 54. See also Pete Daniel, *Breaking the Land: The Transformation of Cotton, Tobacco, and Rice Cultures Since 1880* (Urbana: University of Illinois Press, 1985), 251.

44. Wight, "Sweet Beulah Land."

45. "Change Inevitable," *Greensboro Daily News*, 28 February 1943, Sec. 1, p. 14.

46. John Woodburn to Bernice Kelly Harris, 23 June 1942, f4, BKH, UNC.

47. Harris, *Sweet Beulah Land*, 343.

48. Mrs. H. R. Harris, September 1939, a tribute to Bernice Kelly Harris, "Sometimes in your eyes we find a wistful look / We know right then you are writing a book," f1, BKH, UNC.

9 WARTIME AND PEACH TREES IN BLOOM

1. Bernice Kelly Harris, *Southern Savory* (Chapel Hill: University of North Carolina Press, 1964), 190.

2. F469, "Tank Valentine Daughtry," FWP, UNC.

3. Bernice Kelly Harris, *Sage Quarter* (New York: Doubleday, Doran, 1945), 30. (Hereafter cited within the text by page number only.)

4. Jonathan Carey Coates, conversation with author, the Kelly homeplace, Clayton, N.C., 9 March 1997.

5. Elizabeth Watts, *Boston Globe*, 18 April 1945, p. 19.

6. Mary Ross, *New York Herald Tribune Weekly Book Review*, 13 May 1945, p. 10.

7. Andrea Parke, *New York Times Book Review*, 22 April 1945, p. 25.

8. Sandra M. Gilbert and Susan Gubar, "A Dialogue of Self and Soul: Plain Jane's Progress," in *The Madwoman in the Attic: The Woman Writer and the Nineteenth Century Literary Imagination* (New Haven: Yale University Press, 1984), 371.

9. Richard Walser, *Bernice Kelly Harris: Storyteller of Eastern Carolina* (Chapel Hill: University of North Carolina Library, 1955), 49.

10. John Woodburn to BKH, 4 May 1943, f5, BKH, UNC.

11. Vaughn Holoman to BKH, undated, f31, BKH, UNC.

12. F158, p. 231, BKH, UNC. The letter is quoted in the unpublished portions of the manuscript for Harris's autobiography.

13. John Woodburn to BKH, 30 July 1943, f5, BKH, UNC. See also Woodburn's letters to her 9 April 1943 and 23 July 1943, in the same folder. See also manuscript page 234, beginning "M. McK. Woodburn," f150, BKH, UNC.

14. William Terry Couch to BKH, 30 September 1940; John M. McK. Woodburn to BKH, 30 October 1940; William Terry Couch to BKH, 6 November 1940: f3, BKH, UNC.

15. Clara Claasen to BKH, undated, f31, BKH, UNC.

16. F157, p. beginning "During World War II . . . ," BKH, UNC.

17. Ibid.

18. F157, p. beginning "their assigned hours . . . ," BKH, UNC.

19. Army Air Forces I Fighter Command Aircraft Warning Service Certificate of Honorable Service to Mrs. Herbert Kavanaugh Harris, 29 May 1944, f5, BKH, UNC.

20. Harris, *Southern Savory*, 144.

21. Ibid., 145.

22. Ibid.

23. Dick Walser to BKH, 8 February 1943, f5, BKH, UNC.

24. J. O. Bailey to BKH, 13 March 1943, f5, BKH, UNC.

25. Frederick Koch to BKH, 19 March 1943, f5, BKH, UNC.

26. Harris, *Southern Savory*, 172. See also original letter of Dick Walser to Bernice Kelly Harris, 12 December 1943, f5, BKH, UNC.

27. Harris, *Southern Savory*, 172. See also original letter of George Butler to Bernice Kelly Harris, 7 October 1943, f5, BKH, UNC.

28. Elizabeth Bullock, oral history interview recorded by author, Seaboard, N.C., 19 June 1996, 1:292.

29. F157, p. beginning "I had forty dollars . . . ," BKH, UNC.

30. F183, p. 293, BKH, UNC.

10 AGAINST THE GRAIN

1. F183, p. 293, BKH, UNC.

2. *Diagnostic and Statistical Manual of Mental Disorders*, 4th ed. (Washington, D.C.: American Psychiatric Association, 1994): see especially pages 320–327 and 340–342 for discussion of psychosocial stressors followed by episodes of major depressive disorder.

3. See also the discussion by novelist Lee Smith on the ban in southern families against public acknowledgment of mental illness: she quotes from her short story "Tongues of Fire," in which the mother—a traditional southern woman—says, "The family should keep up appearances at all costs. *Nobody should know.*" "Southern Voices," speech delivered to the North Carolina Literary and Historical Association, 17 November 1995, Raleigh, N.C.

4. F183, p. 295, BKH, UNC.

5. Dick Walser to Bernice Kelly Harris, 2 May 1962, f255, Walser, UNC.

6. Bernice Kelly Harris, *Southern Savory* (Chapel Hill: University of North Carolina Press, 1964), 200.

7. Ibid.

8. Ibid., 201.

9. Ibid., 202.

10. Ibid., 203.

11. F469, FWP, UNC.

12. Bernice Kelly Harris, *Janey Jeems* (Garden City, N.Y.: Doubleday, 1946), 277.

13. Ibid., 297.

14. Harris, *Southern Savory*, 176.

15. Vashti Crutcher Lewis, "The Mulatto Woman as Major Female Character in Novels by Black Women, 1892–1937" (Ph.D. diss., University of Iowa, 1981).

16. Ann Petry, *The Street* (Boston: Beacon Press, 1946).

17. Zora Neale Hurston, *Their Eyes Were Watching God* (New York: J. B. Lippincott, 1937).

18. Ovid Pierce, "Dark Mixture of Religion, Superstition," *Dallas Times Herald*, 1 September 1946.

19. Ibid.

20. F438, p. 5631, FWP, UNC.

21. Langston Hughes and Arna Bontemps, *The Book of Negro Folklore* (New York: Dodd, Mead, 1958). See also Zora Neale Hurston, *Of Mules and Men* (1935; rpr. Bloomington: Indiana University Press, 1979); Newbell Niles Puckett, *Folk Beliefs of the Southern Negro* (Chapel Hill: University of North Carolina Press, 1926).

22. F469, pp. 19–20, FWP, UNC.

23. F467, p. 6053, FWP, UNC.

24. F469, pp. 21–22, FWP, UNC.

25. For a bibliography of works on African American folklore, see John F. Szwed and Roger D. Abrahams, Part I: North America, *Afro-American Folk Culture: An Annotated Bibliography of Materials from North, Central, and South America and the West Indies* (Philadelphia: Institute for the Study of Human Issues, 1978). A more recent general bibliography that has some information on African American folklore is Susan Steinfirst, *Folklore and Folk Life: A Guide to English-Language Reference Sources* (New York: Garland Publishing, 1992). Two collections to consult are J. Mason Brewer, *American Negro Folklore* (Chicago: Quadrangle Books, 1968), and Harold Courlander, *A Treasury of Afro-American Folklore* (New York: Crown Publishers, 1976). Richard Dorson, *Folklore and Folklife: An Introduction* (Chicago: University of Chicago Press, 1972), puts beliefs in a worldwide perspective. For a compendium of specific beliefs, practices, and sayings, see Wayland D. Hand, Anna Casetta, and Sondra B. Thiederman, eds., *Popular Beliefs and Superstitions: A Compendium of American Folklore* (Boston: G. K. Hall, 1981).

26. F438, p. 5630, FWP, UNC.

27. F475, p. 5, FWP, UNC.

28. F438, pp. 5630–5631, FWP, UNC.

29. Nash Burger, *New York Times*, 11 August 1946, book review section, p. 5.

30. *Quincy (Mass.) Patriot Ledger*, 26 September 1946, in f41, BKH, UNC.

31. Harris, *Janey Jeems*, 42.

32. Harris, *Southern Savory*, 205.

33. Diane LeBow, "Selfhood in Free Fall: Novels by Black and White American Women" (Ph.D. diss., University of California at Santa Cruz, 1985).

34. Harris, *Southern Savory*, 174–175.

35. F94, "Untitled Notes," BKH, UNC.

36. Lillian Smith, *Strange Fruit* (New York: Raynal and Hitchcock, 1944).

37. Smith is quoted in Anne C. Loveland, *Lillian Smith: A Southerner Confronting the South* (Baton Rouge: Louisiana State University Press, 1986), 66.

38. Ibid., 66. Loveland states, "Perhaps she thought the novel would induce the psychological change she believed was a prerequisite for the elimination of segregation."

39. Julia Peterkin, *Scarlet Sister Mary* (Indianapolis: Bobbs Merrill, 1928).

40. Susan Millar Williams, *A Devil and a Good Woman, Too: The Lives of Julia Peterkin* (Athens: University of Georgia Press, 1997), xiii.

41. Bernice Kelly Harris, untitled notes for a speech, Bernice Kelly Harris Papers, Whittaker Library, Chowan College, Murfreesboro, N.C. (This collection is cited hereafter as BKH, Chowan.)

11 COMMUNITY DENIED

1. F435, FWP, UNC.

2. Alice Jo Kelley Burrows, oral history interview recorded by author, 14 July 1996, Raleigh, N.C., 1:062–084.

3. Ibid.

4. F33, p. beginning "Dear, dear: How is it with you?", BKH, UNC.

5. F33, p. beginning "Dear Mrs. Holoman," BKH, UNC.

6. E. S. Morgan to BKH, undated, f36, BKH, UNC. This letter was written after *Hearthstones* was televised as a play, "Yellow Color Suit," and shown on NBC in 1957.

7. Thomas Daniel Young, *The Past in the Present: A Thematic Study of Modern Southern Fiction* (Baton Rouge: Louisiana State University Press, 1981), 18. Young refers to John Crowe Ransom's exposition in *The World's Body* (Baton Rouge: Louisiana State University Press, 1968), 30–35.

8. Elizabeth Harris, oral history interview recorded by author, Seaboard, N.C., 19 June 1996, 1:061.

9. F33, p. beginning "Dear, dear: How is it with you?" BKH, UNC.

10. Elizabeth Harris, oral history interview recorded by author, 5 April 1996, Seaboard, N.C., 1:246, 2:057.

11. Ann Bradley Ford, oral history interview recorded by author, 19 June 1996, Seaboard, N.C., 1:030–056.

12. *Colliers Magazine* 113 (3 June 1944): 23, 71–72, 74.

13. F92, BKH, UNC.

14. Bernice Kelly Harris, *Hearthstones* (New York: Doubleday, 1948), 1. (Hereafter cited in the text by page number only.)

15. John Pilkington, "The Memory of the War," in *The History of Southern Literature*, ed. Louis D. Rubin Jr. (Baton Rouge: Louisiana State University Press, 1985), 356–362; see especially p. 358.

16. Nash Burger, "Manor House vs. Cabin," *New York Times Book Review*, 3 October 1948, p. 27.

17. Coleman Rosenberger, "*Hearthstones*: A Novel of the Roanoke River Country in North Carolina," *New York Herald Tribune Weekly Book Review* 25 (26 September 1948), p. 2.

18. Margarette Smethurst, "Tar Heel Novel of the Roanoke Country," Raleigh *News and Observer*, 12 September 1948, sec. 4, p. 5.

19. Ibid.

12   THE TROUBLED LATE 1940S

1. Bernice Kelly Harris, *Southern Savory* (Chapel Hill: University of North Carolina Press, 1964), 223.

2. Ibid.

3. Ibid., 224–225.

4. Ibid., 224–226.

5. Ibid., 228.

6. Ibid., 230.

7. BKH to Mary and William Olive, 25 June 1949, f8, BKH, UNC.

8. George Butler to BKH, 27 February 1947, f7 BKH, UNC.

9. J. O. Bailey to BKH, 24 December 1947, f7, BKH, UNC. Bailey quotes from her letter to him of 12 September 1947.

10. BKH to Mebane Burgwyn, 18 June 1947, private archives of Stephen White Burgwyn (Mebane Burgwyn's son), Jackson, N.C. (Hereafter cited as Burgwyn archives.)

11. J. O. Bailey to BKH, 24 December 1947, f7, BKH, UNC. Bailey quotes from her letter to him of 12 September 1947.

12. Charlotte Hilton Green to BKH, 6 February 1948, f7, BKH, UNC.

13. Richard Walser, ed., *North Carolina in the Short Story* (Chapel Hill: University of North Carolina Press, 1948).

14. Richard Walser to BKH, 26 March 1948, f7, BKH, UNC.

15. BKH to Mebane Burgwyn, 28 November (no year given but sense indicates 1950), Burgwyn archives.

16. BKH to William Olive and Mary, 27 September 1948, f7, BKH, UNC.

17. Mebane Burgwyn to BKH, 2 February 1948, f7, BKH, UNC.

18. Mebane Burgwyn to BKH, 17 March 1948, f7, BKH, UNC.

19. BKH to Mebane, n.d. (letter is headed "Friday night"), Burgwyn archives.

20. BKH to Mebane, n.d. (letter is headed "Saturday," letter begins "Thank you for your kind note"), Burgwyn archives.

21. BKH to William Olive and Mary, 17 November 1948, f7, BKH, UNC.

22. BKH to Alice Jo Kelley, n.d. (letter begins "Dear Alice"), f7, BKH, UNC.

23. Alice Jo Kelley Burrows, oral history interview recorded by author, 14 July 1996, Raleigh, N.C., 2:619.

24. BKH to Alice Jo Kelley, 19 November 1948, f7, BKH, UNC.

25. Jonathan Carey Coats and Patricia Coats Kube, oral history interview recorded by author, Clayton, N.C., 9 March 1997, 1:388.

26. BKH to William Olive and Mary, fall 1948, f7, BKH, UNC.

27. BKH to William Olive and Mary, 1949, f8, BKH, UNC.

28. BKH to William Olive and Mary, 17 January 1949, f8, BKH, UNC.

29. Ibid.

30. BKH to William Olive and Mary, Thursday, 1949, f8, BKH, UNC.

31. BKH to William Olive and Mary, 13 June 1949, f8, BKH, UNC.

32. BKH to William Olive and Mary, 17 January 1949, f8, BKH, UNC.

33. Harris, *Southern Savory*, 234.

34. BKH to Mebane Burgwyn, 1948 ("If I had written you as often as I wanted"), Burgwyn archives.

35. BKH to Mebane Burgwyn, 4 January (no year given; sense indicates 1950), Burgwyn archives.

36. Ibid.

37. BKH to William Olive and Mary, f9, BKH, UNC. The letter has been dated incorrectly as 18 September 1950; Herbert is referred to as still living but he died 13 July 1950, so the letter was written before July 1950.

38. BKH to J. O. Bailey, September 1951, f8, BKH, UNC.

39. F96, "It seemed odd . . . ," BKH, UNC.

40. Harris, *Southern Savory*, 234.

13   A SOLITARY LIFE

1. F96, pp. beginning "It seemed odd . . . ," BKH, UNC. This chapter is largely based on unpublished pages from drafts of the autobiography; these were scattered among different folders when they were deposited in the Southern Historical Collection at the University of North Carolina after Harris's death.

2. Magdeline Faison, with her daughter Shirley Trotter, oral history interview recorded by author, Roxboro, N.C., 28 August 1996, 1:048.

3. Bernice Kelly Harris, *Southern Savory* (Chapel Hill: University of North Carolina Press, 1964), 234–235.

4. F96, "in this present void," BKH, UNC.

5. F147, BKH, UNC.

6. F96, "We left . . . ," BKH, UNC.

7. F148, p. 283, BKH, UNC.

8. F96, "We left . . . ," BKH, UNC.

9. F157, p. 305, f168, p. 306, BKH, UNC.

10. General Statutes of North Carolina, Containing General Laws of North Carolina Through the Legislative Session of 1949, vol. 2A, Division VI, Decedents' Estates, Chapter 30, Widows, Article 2, Dower, Section 30-4, p. 120.

11. F168, p. 306, BKH, UNC.

12. F95, p. 302, BKH, UNC.

13. F157, p. 305, BKH, UNC.

14. BKH to William Olive and Mary, 3 November 1950, f8, BKH, UNC.

15. North Carolina, Northampton County, In the Superior Court Before the Clerk. Inventory. In Re: Mrs. Bernice Kelly Harris, Administratrix, and J. J. Harris, Administrator, of the Estate of Herbert K. Harris, Deceased. November 27, 1950.

16. Ibid.; f168, p. 306, and f157, p. labeled both 305 and 44, BKH, UNC.

17. F168, "served the afternoon," BKH, UNC.

18. Northampton County. Inventory. Estate of Herbert K. Harris.

19. Gordon Kelley, oral history interview recorded by author, 26 June 1995, Chapel Hill, N.C., 2:425.

20. F148, "and sound," BKH, UNC.

21. F96, "one Sunday," BKH, UNC.

22. F96, "be forever spiritual," BKH, UNC.

23. Ibid.

24. Harris, *Southern Savory*, 234.

25. F95, "legal percentages," BKH, UNC.

26. F96, "be forever spiritual," BKH, UNC.

27. F147, p. 301, f96, p. 301, BKH, UNC.

28. F148, "beyond their money," BKH, UNC.

29. F148, "sound and neat," BKH, UNC.

30. F148, "fires beyond," BKH, UNC.

31. F148, "Had love served . . . ," BKH, UNC.

32. Harris, *Southern Savory*, 234.

33. F96, "be forever spiritual," BKH, UNC.

34. Alice Jo Kelley Burrows, oral history interview recorded by author, 14 July 1996, Raleigh, N.C., 2:142.

35. Gordon Kelley, conversation with author, 26 June 1995, Chapel Hill, N.C.

36. Betsey Bradley Merritt, oral history interview recorded by author, 5 April 1996, Roanoke Rapids, N.C., 1:594.

37. F96, "be forever spiritual," BKH, UNC.

38. BKH to Mebane Burgwyn, 8 August 1950, Burgwyn archives.

39. BKH to Mebane Burgwyn, 27 September (no year but sense indicates 1950), Burgwyn archives.

40. F95, BKH, UNC.

41. Bernice Kelly Harris, *Wild Cherry Tree Road* (New York: Doubleday, 1951), 39. (Hereafter cited in the text by page number only.)

42. BKH to J. O. Bailey, 17 September 1951, f8, BKH, UNC.

43. Leo Marx, *The Machine in the Garden: Technology and the Pastoral Ideal in America* (New York: Oxford University Press, 1964), 99. Marx discusses works that idealize a pastoral way of life, works that blur the lines between the farmer who does the work and the gentleman "who enjoys rural ease." He suggests that American writers responded to industrialization and urbanization by arguing that the pastoral way of life was superior to an urban, manufacturing life.

44. August Derleth, "A Satisfying Novel of a Border Region," *Chicago Sunday Tribune,* 14 October 1951, book review section, p. 13.

45. "Hardyesque Gem," *Greensboro Daily News,* 21 October 1951.

46. BKH to Mebane Burgwyn, 25 October 1952, Burgwyn archives.

47. BKH to Mebane Burgwyn, 15 November 1952, Burgwyn archives.

48. BKH to Mebane Burgwyn, 25 July 1952, Burgwyn archives.

49. BKH to Mebane Burgwyn, 29 September 1952, Burgwyn archives.

50. Bernadette Hoyle, *Tar Heel Writers I Know* (Winston-Salem: John F. Blair, 1956), 66–69.

51. Nell Battle Lewis, Raleigh *News and Observer,* 11 February 1951 (clipping in the file on North Carolina history in the North Carolina Collection, Louis Round Wilson Library, University of North Carolina, Chapel Hill, N.C.).

52. Charlotte Hilton Green to BKH, n.d., Burgwyn archives. Probably Harris, wanting to share the letter with Mebane Burgwyn, sent it to her, and Burgwyn kept it with her other letters from Harris.

53. Margarette Wood Smethurst to BKH, n.d., f35, BKH, UNC.

54. Sandra Upchurch Poindexter, conversation with author, Chapel Hill, N.C., 18 March 1997.

55. Jonathan Carey Coats and Patricia Coats Kube, oral history interview recorded by author, Clayton, N.C., March 9, 1997, 1:060.

56. Ibid., 1:145.

57. Burrows, oral history, 1:062–084.

58. BKH to J. O. and Mary Bailey, 14 December 1953, f9, BKH, UNC.

59. F96, single page labeled 316 and 236, BKH, UNC.

60. BKH to Mebane Burgwyn, n.d., Burgwyn archives.

61. BKH to J. O. and Mary Bailey, 14 December 1953, f9, BKH, UNC.

62. Burrows, oral history, 2:021.

63. Ann Bradley Ford, oral history interview recorded by author, Seaboard, N.C., 19 June 1996, 1:371.

64. Ibid., 1:308.

65. Alice Jo Kelley Burrows, telephone conversation with author, 2 February 1997.

66. Merritt, oral history, 1:175–191.

67. Ibid., 1:487.

68. Ford, oral history, 1:097.

69. Ann Bradley Ford, conversation with author, 5 April 1996, Seaboard, N.C.

70. Ford, oral history, 1:182; Merritt, oral history, 2:063, 2:093.

71. BKH to Mebane Burgwyn, 20 August 1951, Burgwyn archives.

14   A WRITERS' COMMUNITY

1. BKH to Mebane Burgwyn, 2 October (no year), Burgwyn archives.

2. Bernadette Hoyle, *Tar Heel Writers I Know* (Winston-Salem: John F. Blair, 1956), 1.

3. Ibid., "A Few Introductory Words."

4. BKH to Dick Walser, n.d., f255, Walser, UNC.

5. F94, untitled notes on the Writers Conference, BKH, UNC.

6. Hoyle, *Tar Heel Writers I Know*, 194.

7. F147, "journalism at the university," BKH, UNC.

8. Frank Borden Hanes, oral history interview recorded by author, Winston-Salem, N.C., 30 July 1996, 1:051.

9. Ibid., 1:051.

10. F94, notes for speech, "Out of this apparent chaos," BKH, UNC.

11. F145, "Communal wakes over the dead," BKH, UNC.

12. F94, untitled notes on the Writers Conference, BKH, UNC.

13. BKH to Inglis Fletcher, Inglis Fletcher Papers, East Carolina Manuscript Collection, 21.19.e, East Carolina University, Greenville, N.C.

14. Sam Ragan to BKH, 14 December 1965, f20, BKH, UNC.

15. Sam Ragan, oral history interview recorded by author, Southern Pines, N.C., 31 January 1996, 1:190.

16. Ibid., 1:280.

17. Roy Parker Jr., oral history interview recorded by author, Fayetteville, N.C., 19 March 1996, 3:009.

18. Hoyle, *Tar Heel Writers I Know*, 183.

19. Betty Hodges, conversation with author, 31 January 1996, Southern Pines, N.C.; Parker, oral history, 2:445.

20. Thad Stem to BKH, n.d., Box 4, BKH, Chowan.

21. Thad Stem to BKH, 22 June 1959, f14, BKH, UNC.

22. Thad Stem to BKH, 23 September 1960, f15, BKH, UNC.

23. F150, handwritten notes on the Writers Conference, BKH, UNC; see also Chalmers Davidson to BKH, 29 August 1960, f15, BKH, UNC.

24. F150, handwritten notes on the Writers Conference, and f182, untitled pages on the Writers Conference, BKH, UNC.

25. Dick Walser to BKH, 3 September 1953, f10, BKH, UNC.

26. Parker, oral history, 2:408.

27. "Tar Heel Writers Meet: Northampton Authors Lead Conclave," unidentified clipping, private archives of Roy Parker Jr. Probably this article was written by Parker and published in the *Bertie Ledger-Advance* in 1957.

28. BKH to William Olive and Mary, 29 July 1957, f11, BKH, UNC.

29. Frank Borden Hanes to BKH, 10 October 1957, f12, BKH, UNC.

30. Bernadette Hoyle to BKH, n.d. (letter begins "Am enclosing chapter"), f37, BKH, UNC.

31. John Ehle, oral history interview recorded by author, Winston-Salem, N.C., 30 July 1996, 1:031; John Ehle, letter to author, 21 July 1997, private archives of author.

32. Ehle, oral history, 1:320; John Ehle, letter to author, 13 June 1997, private archives of author.

33. Ragan, oral history, 1:570.

34. Ehle, oral history, 1:133.

35. Thad Stem to BKH, n.d. (first page missing), f35, BKH, UNC.

36. F95, "Sam Ragan, executive editor," BKH, UNC.

37. Ehle, oral history, 1:133.

38. Betty Hodges, telephone conversation with author, 14 February 1997.

39. F94, handwritten notes on the Writers Conference, BKH, UNC.

40. Hanes, oral history, 1:056.

41. Bernadette Hoyle, "Seaboard Author: Writing Has Its Rewards," Raleigh *News and Observer*, 29 August 1954.

42. Ibid.

43. Hanes, oral history, 1:151.

44. Ragan, oral history, 1:245.

45. Parker, oral history, 1:572.

46. F94, untitled notes, "Put into words, my wish," BKH, UNC.

47. BKH to Mebane Burgwyn, 12 January 1953, Burgwyn archives.

48. BKH to Mebane Burgwyn, n.d. ("Friday morning"), Burgwyn archives.

49. BKH to Thad Stem Jr., 9 November (no year), private archives of Marguerite Stem.

50. BKH to Harry Golden, n.d. (fragment of a letter), f36, BKH, UNC.

51. BKH to Harry Golden, 23 June 1958, Harry Golden Collection, J. Murrey Atkins Library, University of North Carolina, Charlotte, N.C. (Hereafter cited as Golden, UNC Charlotte.)

52. BKH to Frank Borden Hanes, note attached to a copy of her review of his book, n.d. (sense indicates 1961), private archives of Frank Borden Hanes.

53. Parker, oral history, 2:505.

54. Bernadette Hoyle to BKH, n.d. (letter begins "Am enclosing chapter"), f37, BKH, UNC.

55. Ovid Pierce to BKH, 5 February 1956, f10, BKH, UNC. See also Ovid Pierce to BKH, 1 July 1969, f26, BKH, UNC.

56. Minutes of the North Carolina Literary and Historical Association, 5 June 1952, f9, BKH, UNC.

57. Christopher Crittenden (president of the North Carolina Literary and Historical Association), to BKH, 19 July 1961, f16, BKH, UNC.

58. BKH to Mebane Burgwyn, n.d. (letter is headed "Tuesday morning"; sense indicates fall 1952), Burgwyn archives.

59. Hanes, oral history, 1:109.

60. Margarette Wood Smethurst, "In My Opinion," Raleigh *News and Observer*, 17 September 1957.

61. John Ehle to Miss Lucille Sullivan, 25 April 1957, f11, BKH, UNC. Sullivan was employed at Annie Laurie Williams, Inc.

62. Hoyle, *Tar Heel Writers I Know*, 93.

63. BKH to J. O. Bailey, n.d. (letter is headed "Seaboard, Tuesday a. m."; sense indicates 1955), f32, BKH, UNC.

64. Richard Walser, *Bernice Kelly Harris: Storyteller of Eastern Carolina* (Chapel Hill: University of North Carolina Library, 1955), preface.

65. BKH to Mebane, n.d. (letter begins "I hope all is well with you"), Burgwyn archives.

66. F94, untitled notes on the Writers Conference and her illness, BKH, UNC.

67. Walser, *Bernice Kelly Harris*, preface.

68. Ibid.

69. Dick Walser to BKH, 23 June 1954, f9, BKH, UNC.

70. Dick Walser to BKH, 5 November 1962, f17, BKH, UNC.

71. BKH to Mebane Burgwyn, n.d. (letter is headed "Tuesday morning"; sense indicates 1956), Burgwyn archives.

72. BKH to Dick Walser, 2 November (no year; sense indicates 1962), f255, Walser, UNC.

73. Dick Walser to BKH, 21 April 1959, f14, BKH, UNC.

74. BKH to J. O. Bailey, n.d. (someone has put in the date "1955"), f32, BKH, UNC.

75. BKH to Dick Walser, 14 July 1954, f255, Walser, UNC.

76. J. O. Bailey to BKH, 18 July 1955, f10, BKH, UNC.

77. BKH to Mebane Burgwyn, n.d. (letter is headed "Friday morning"; sense indicates 1954), Burgwyn archives.

78. Mebane Burgwyn to BKH, 30 August 1954, Burgwyn archives.

79. Mebane Burgwyn to BKH, n.d., Burgwyn archives.

80. Holley Mack Bell to BKH, 28 November 1955, f10, BKH, UNC.

81. Mebane Burgwyn to BKH, 28 January 1957, f11, BKH, UNC.

82. BKH to Harry Golden, n.d. (fragment of a letter), f36, BKH, UNC.

15 STRUGGLING TO BE BOTH WRITER
AND PERSON

1. BKH to J. O. Bailey, 9 April 1952, f9, BKH, UNC.

2. BKH to Mebane Burgwyn, 29 September 1952, Burgwyn archives.

3. The description of "Bevvy Lamm" is in f180, BKH, UNC. See letter of BKH to Mebane Burgwyn, 15 November 1952, Burgwyn archives.

4. BKH to Mebane Burgwyn, n.d. ("Tuesday morning"), Burgwyn archives.

5. BKH to Mebane Burgwyn, n.d. ("Monday morning"), Burgwyn archives.

6. "Tar Heel of the Week," Raleigh *News and Observer,* clipping in Box 3: Harris, Bernice Kelly—Clippings, Personal Correspondence, PC 1773, Bernadette Hoyle Papers, Special Collections, Division of Archives and History, Raleigh, N.C.

7. BKH to Chalmers Davidson, 28 November 1960, f7, BKH, UNC.

8. Ann Bradley Ford, oral history interview recorded by author, Seaboard, N.C., 19 June 1996, 1:151.

9. Clara Booth Byrd to BKH, 2 February 1959, f14, BKH, UNC.

10. Bernadette Hoyle, "Seaboard Author: Writing Has Its Rewards," Raleigh *News and Observer,* 29 August 1954, clipping in f253, Walser, UNC.

11. Frank Parker to BKH, 10 July 1955, f10, BKH, UNC.

12. Frank Parker to BKH, 6 August 1955, f10, BKH, UNC.

13. Frank Parker to BKH, 13 August (no year), f30, BKH, UNC.

14. Alice Jo Kelley Burrows, telephone conversation with author, 2 February 1997.

15. BKH to Mebane, n.d., Burgwyn archives.

16. Mebane Burgwyn to BKH, 28 September 1955, f10, BKH, UNC.

17. Frank Parker to BKH, 21 January 1956, f10, BKH, UNC.

18. BKH to Dick Walser, 4 July 1955, f255, Walser, UNC.

19. BKH to William Olive and Mary, n.d., f35, BKH, UNC.

20. BKH to William Olive and Mary, 14 January 1956, f10, BKH, UNC.

21. Elizabeth Harris to BKH, n.d., f35, BKH, UNC.

22. F146 and f162, BKH, UNC. The pages of this novel that remain were scattered. When they were deposited in the Louis Round Wilson Library's Southern Historical Collection, Manuscript Department, at the University of North Carolina, number 3804, they were placed in different folders. I extracted pages positioned among other papers in about a dozen folders and put them together consecutively to get an idea of the quality of the writing and the plot of "Bevvy Lam." I have gathered and arranged the pages and placed them in folders 146 and 162; although some pages are missing and multiple revisions make it difficult occasionally to place pages consecutively, the main

thrust of the novel can be discerned. Hereafter the folder number and page are cited within the text.

23. BKH to J. O. Bailey, n.d. (letter is headed "Christmas"; sense indicates December 1952), f32, BKH, UNC.

24. Frederick Wight, "Sweet Beulah Land," *New York Herald Tribune Weekly Book Review,* 21 February 1943.

25. Leo Marx in *The Machine in the Garden: Technology and the Pastoral Ideal in America* (New York: Oxford University Press, 1964) discusses the susceptibility of some writers to idealize the rural way of life and to see technology as evil. Harris, however, sees evil in the way men think technology can save them without realizing that the minds of men direct technology; she is critical of the assumption that all progress comes through technology, but she also rejects notions about an ideal pastoral society.

26. BKH to William Olive and Mary, 14 May 1953, f10, BKH, UNC.

27. In replying to the author's inquiry, both Doubleday and Russell and Volkening wrote that they could not be of assistance; historical archives were not kept in either company.

28. Note attached to letter from BKH to Dick Walser, which she dated "July 4," with his penciled year "1955," f255, Walser, UNC.

29. Pages of the manuscript "Seven Men of Eagleton" I have arranged in numerical order and placed in folders 167 and 172. There are gaps; there are also several versions of the same page. F167 and f172, BKH, UNC.

30. Dick Walser to BKH, 11 May 1956, f10, BKH, UNC.

31. BKH to Mebane, n.d. ("Everyday I have been appreciating"), Burgwyn archives.

32. Bernice Kelly Harris, *Southern Savory* (Chapel Hill: University of North Carolina Press, 1964), 240–242.

33. BKH to Mebane Burgwyn, n.d. (sense indicates November 1956), Burgwyn archives.

34. Harris, *Southern Savory,* 245.

35. BKH to Mebane Burgwyn, 13 December (no year, sense indicates 1956), Burgwyn archives.

36. Bernice Kelly Harris, "Father's Second Sip of Life," Raleigh *News and Observer,* 16 June 1957.

37. BKH to William Olive and Mary, 13 February 1957, f11, BKH, UNC.

16   LOOKING BACK AT A GOOD DECADE TO LIVE IN

1. BKH to William Olive and Mary, 13 February 1957, f11, BKH, UNC.

2. F257, "A Peep Behind the Scenes," Walser, UNC.

3. Betsey Bradley Merritt, oral history interview recorded by author, Roanoke Rapids, N.C., 5 April 1996, 1:059.

4. BKH to Dick Walser, 1 March [1957] (letter is headed "Seaboard"), f255, Walser, UNC.

5. BKH to Charlotte Hilton Green, 15 February 1957, Personal Correspondence, PC 1661, Charlotte Hilton Green Papers, Special Collections, Division of Archives and History, Raleigh, N.C. (Hereafter cited as Green, N.C. State Archives.)

6. BKH to Dick Walser, n.d., f257, Walser, UNC.

7. F184, "my guests," BKH, UNC.

8. BKH to Dick Walser, 3 April 1957, f255, Walser, UNC.

9. Lucille Sullivan to BKH, 14 August 1957, f12, BKH, UNC.

10. BKH to Dick Walser, 19 September [1957], f255, Walser, UNC.

11. Merritt, oral history, 2:162.

12. Rosalie [Upchurch] to "Dearest Aunt Bernice," n.d, f37, BKH, UNC.

13. BKH to William Olive and Mary (letter has penciled date 27 September 1957), f12, BKH, UNC.

14. BKH to William Olive and Mary, 4 October 1957, f12, BKH, UNC.

15. Clifton Britton to BKH, 10 April 1958, f13, BKH, UNC.

16. Bernice Kelly Harris, "Pate's Siding," typescript, North Carolina Collection, Louis Round Wilson Library, University of North Carolina, Chapel Hill, N.C.

17. BKH to Walser, n.d. (letter is headed "Monday"), f255, Walser, UNC.

18. Bernice Kelly Harris, *Folk Plays of Eastern Carolina*, ed. and with an introduction by Frederick Koch (Chapel Hill: University of North Carolina Press, 1940), 103.

19. Clipping from a newspaper, unidentified, in f253, Walser, UNC, and " 'The Forever House': Seaboard Sets Play Date," Raleigh *News and Observer*, 6 March 1959.

20. Ruth Vick Everett O'Brien (a local director) to BKH, 26 March 1959, and Grace Stephenson to BKH, 21 April 1959, f14, BKH, UNC.

21. The typescript for "Beulah Land" is no longer extant. Both Clara Claasen and J. O. Bailey thanked BKH for "Beulah Land" programs she sent them: Claasen to BKH, 26 April 1960, Bailey to BKH, 12 May 1960, f15, BKH, UNC.

22. BKH to J. O. Bailey, 4 April 1960, f15, BKH, UNC.

23. BKH to Charlotte Hilton Green, 15 February 1957, PC 1661, Green, N.C. State Archives.

24. Merritt, oral history, 1:191.

25. Marian Hall to BKH, 12 April 1961, f16, BKH, UNC.

26. Bernice Kelly Harris, "Blend Women, Men and Signposts and the Mixture Equals Trouble," Raleigh *News and Observer*, 16 September 1962, clipping in f257, Walser, UNC.

27. BKH to William Olive and Mary, 13 January 1958, f13, BKH, UNC.

28. BKH to Dick Walser, 13 April (no year), f255, Walser, UNC.

29. BKH to J. O. Bailey, n.d. (letter is headed "Seaboard, Tuesday A.M.";
sense indicates that the date was soon after Walser's biography of her was
published in 1955), f32, BKH, UNC.

30. BKH to Dick Walser, 22 September 1965, f256, Walser, UNC.

31. BKH to Dick Walser, 2 November (no year, sense indicates 1962),
f255, Walser, UNC.

32. BKH to Dick Walser, September 1957, f255, Walser, UNC.

33. BKH to Dick Walser, 27 April 27 [1956], f255, Walser, UNC.

34. Dick Walser to BKH, 11 May 1956, f10, BKH, UNC.

35. BKH to Clara Claasen, 31 July 1957, f255, Walser, UNC.

36. J. O. Bailey to BKH, 20 December 1957, f12, BKH, UNC.

37. Ibid.

38. BKH to Clara Claasen, 16 November 1956, f95, BKH, UNC.

39. Leslie E. Phillabaum to BKH, 20 March 1964, f19, BKH, UNC.

40. Thad Stem Jr. to BKH, n.d., f38, BKH, UNC.

41. Harry Golden to BKH, 16 February 1955, f10, BKH, UNC.

42. Harry Golden to BKH, 11 October 1957, f12, BKH, UNC.

43. BKH to Harry Golden, 21 October 1957, Harry Golden Collection, J.
Murrey Atkins Library, University of North Carolina, Charlotte, N.C. (Hereafter cited as Golden, UNC Charlotte.)

44. BKH to William Olive and Mary, 20 February 1958, f13, BKH, UNC.

45. Harry Golden to BKH, 24 December 1958, f13, BKH, UNC.

46. Harry Golden to BKH, 12 February 1962, f17, BKH, UNC.

47. Harry Golden, *Forgotten Pioneer* (Cleveland: World Publishing,
1963).

48. BKH to Harry Golden, 17 June 1963, Golden, UNC Charlotte.

49. Elmer Oettinger, telephone conversation with author, 1 March 1997.
Mr. Oettinger could not remember why the production schedule ended sooner
than planned, and for this era files at the radio station of the University of
North Carolina are no longer extant.

50. Dennis Cooke to BKH, 8 June 1959, f14, BKH, UNC.

51. Alice Jo Kelley Burrows, communication to author, 9 May 1997.

52. F163, p. labeled 3, beginning "Herald Tribune," BKH, UNC.

53. F96, p. labeled 315 and 235 and 47, beginning "Prototypes," BKH,
UNC.

54. F95, p. with title "Afterword," BKH, UNC.

55. Walser to BKH, 25 April 1958, f13, BKH, UNC.

56. F95, p. with title "Afterword," BKH, UNC.

17   MISS KELLY, TEACHER AGAIN

1. BKH to J. O. Bailey, 14 December 1960, f15, BKH, UNC.

2. Carey Coats and Patricia Coats Kube, conversation with author, Clayton, N.C., at homeplace of Bernice Kelly Harris, 9 March 1997.

3. Bernice Kelly Harris, *The Very Real Truth About Christmas* (New York: Doubleday, 1961).

4. BKH to J. O. Bailey, 4 April 1960, f15, BKH, UNC.

5. Ibid.

6. J. O. Bailey to BKH, 12 May 1960, f15, BKH, UNC.

7. BKH to Mebane Burgwyn, 7 June (no year, sense indicates 1966), Burgwyn archives.

8. Mebane Burgwyn to BKH, 20 August 1968, f25, BKH, UNC.

9. Bernice Kelly Harris, "Blend Women, Men and Signposts and the Mixture Equals Trouble," Raleigh *News and Observer,* 16 September 1962, clipping in f257, Walser, UNC.

10. BKH to Dick Walser, [15 August 1963], f255, Walser, UNC.

11. Dick Walser to BKH, 21 November 1960, f15, BKH, UNC.

12. Bernice Kelly Harris, "A Land More Large Than Earth," *North Carolina Historical Review,* spring 1962: 178.

13. Ibid., 177.

14. Ibid., 176.

15. Ibid., 178.

16. BKH to William Olive and Mary, 4 December 1961, f16, BKH, UNC.

17. BKH to Mary Kelley, May 1962, f17, BKH, UNC.

18. Elizabeth Harris to BKH, 17 April 1962, f14, BKH, UNC.

19. BKH to Mebane Burgwyn, 2 May 1962, Burgwyn archives.

20. Ann Bradley Ford, oral history interview recorded by author, Seaboard, N.C., 19 June 1996.

21. F94, untitled notes beginning "I never thought possible . . . ," BKH, UNC.

22. BKH to Dick Walser, 2 May 1962, f255, Walser, UNC.

23. BKH to Mary Kelley, n.d. ("5/62" is the date BKH had jotted down on the top of the page), f17, BKH, UNC.

24. BKH to Mary Kelley, 16 September 1963, f18, BKH, UNC.

25. Thad Stem Jr. to Harry Golden, 29 August 1962, Box 18—Correspondence with Thad Stem, Golden, UNC Charlotte. I am indebted to archivist Robin Brabham for pointing out this letter to me.

26. Bernice Kelly Harris, "Santa on the Mantel," manuscript in the North Carolina Collection, Louis Round Wilson Library, University of North Carolina, Raleigh, N.C.

27. Lambert Davis to BKH, February 19, 1963, f18, BKH, UNC.

28. Louise Abbot, review of *Southern Savory, South Atlantic Quarterly* 64 (spring 1965): 274–275.

29. Dick Walser to BKH, 27 September 1964, f19, BKH, UNC.

30. Mary Lynch Johnson, review of *Southern Savory, North Carolina Historical Review* 42, no. 2 (April 1965): 232–233.

31. Charley L. Sandifer to Dr. Bernice Kelly Harris, 12 January 1963, BKH, Chowan.

32. "Column: 'Fragile Bits and Pieces,' Who Made Up the Group?" BKH, Chowan.

33. F169, pp. 2 and 3, beginning "two being across the Cashie River," BKH, UNC. See also tribute she paid to Ellis shortly after his death: "A Most Unusual Ferryman," *The State,* 15 August 1972, pp. 14–15.

34. J. A. Ellis to Rosa, 20 September 1967, packet 4, BKH, Chowan. Rosa was Harris's housekeeper after her heart attack.

35. M.L.L. to BKH, 12 March 1965, packet 4, BKH, Chowan.

36. Wilma Wynns, "Drink deep, or taste not the Pierian Spring," single sheet, f94, BKH, UNC.

37. F94, pages beginning "Put into words . . . ," pp. 1 and 2, BKH, UNC.

38. BKH to Dick Walser, 3 March 1966 (stamped on envelope), f256, Walser, UNC.

39. Jane Gregory to BKH, n.d., packet 1, BKH, Chowan.

40. Bernice Kelly Harris, Notes for class, BKH, Chowan.

41. Ibid.

42. Virginia Harding, *The White Trumpet* (Verona, Va.: McClure Press, 1972).

43. Clara Claasen to BKH, 16 July 1969, f26, BKH, UNC.

44. Review of *Southern Home Remedies,* edited by Bernice Kelly Harris, Raleigh *News and Observer,* 6 January 1969.

45. Review of *Strange Things Happen: A Collection of 68 Stories Relating to Ghosts, ESP, Reincarnation, Coincidences, Providences, Illusions,* edited by Bernice Kelly Harris, *The State,* 15 July 1971.

46. Review of *Strange Things Happen: A Collection of 68 Stories Relating to Ghosts, ESP, Reincarnation, Coincidences, Providences, Illusions,* edited by Bernice Kelly Harris, *North Carolina Folklore* 19 (November 1971): 200.

47. Ralph Hardee Rives to BKH, 11 April 1966 and 8 June 1966, f21, BKH, UNC; Sam Ragan to BKH, 23 November 1966, f22, BKH, UNC.

48. Betty Hodges, "Book Nook," *Durham Morning Herald,* 28 May 1967, p. 5D.

49. Sam Ragan, "Southern Accent," Raleigh *News and Observer,* 28 May 1967, Sec. III, p. 3.

50. Jeannette to BKH, 26 April 1972, BKH, Chowan.

51. Betsey Bradley Merritt, oral history recorded by author, Roanoke Rapids, N.C., 5 April 1996, 2:180.

52. Dick Walser to BKH, n.d., BKH, Chowan.

53. BKH to William Olive and Mary, 11 March 1957, f11, BKH, UNC.

54. Harry Golden discusses his own position and his respect for Frank Porter Graham in his autobiography, *The Right Time: An Autobiography* (New York: G. P. Putnam, 1969), 265–273.

55. BKH to J. O. Bailey, 9 April 1952, f9, BKH, UNC.

56. BKH to J. O. Bailey, 25 November 1970, f27, BKH, UNC.

57. Recent research published by historian David Cecelski documents these struggles in Hyde County. Once it was accepted that all three schools would remain open and students would be assigned on the basis of geographical proximity, planning committees of black and white students in each school figured out ways to ease the transition to integration. David S. Cecelski, *Along Freedom Road: Hyde County, North Carolina, and the Fate of Black Schools in the South* (Chapel Hill: University of North Carolina Press, 1994).

58. BKH to William Olive and Mary, 12 September 1957, f12, BKH, UNC.

59. Bernice Kelly Harris, notes for a speech, BKH, Chowan.

60. Bernice Kelly Harris, "Christmas Chimney" (17 pages), f102, BKH, UNC. Harris was writing this story in 1960. In April 1960, she wrote Dick Walser that she was working on a piece about a current sit-down strike, temporarily titled "The Other Side of the Counter." F255, Walser, UNC. She wrote Thad Stem, "I want very much to talk to you about a work that I am mulling over, since it is connected with Janey Jeems. I am thinking of a young Jeems. But I am afraid I do not know the young Jeems well enough, as some of my liberal friends recently suggested." BKH to Thad Stem, n.d., private archives of Marguerite Stem.

61. BKH to Mary, 28 February 1966, f21, BKH, UNC.

62. BKH to Jim Chaney, n.d., f137, BKH, UNC. (The letter is attached to the story "The Spire.") Howard C. Wilkinson said that when he went to Duke as chaplain in July 1957, he told all the student ushers to admit all comers, without regard to race. The Duke graduate school admitted black students in 1961; the undergraduate school, in 1962. Although he does not remember a specific incident, he said black students started coming to the Duke chapel several years before the institution was integrated. Howard C. Wilkinson, in Greensboro, N.C., telephone conversation with author in Chapel Hill, 28 May 1997. The story is not dated, but it was published in the Raleigh *News and Observer,* December 25, 1960, Sec. III, p. 1, as "Little White Steeples in the Vision of Her Faith." It was probably written just before or just after the other Jeems story, which she was working on in spring 1960.

63. Bernice Kelly Harris, "The Spire," f137, BKH, UNC.

64. Ibid.

65. Eunice Brown, in Winton, N.C., telephone conversation with author in Chapel Hill, 9 March 1997.

66. Ibid.

67. BKH to J. O. Bailey, 21 November 1964, f19, BKH, UNC.

68. J. O. Bailey to BKH, 10 December 1964, f19, BKH, UNC.

69. BKH to Dick Walser, 14 July 1954, f255, Walser, UNC.

70. Clara Bond Bell and Holley Bell, oral history interview recorded by

author, Raleigh, N.C., 24 April 1997, 1:572. See also Magdeline Faison, oral history interview recorded by author, Roxboro, N.C., 28 August 1996, 1:168.

71. Marguerite Stem, oral history interview recorded by author, 9 May 1996, Raleigh, N.C., 1:254, 2:002. Frank Borden Hanes, oral history interview recorded by author, Winston-Salem, N.C., 30 July 1996, 1:151. Faison, oral history, 2:133. Needless to say, the wide range of medications available now to treat depression and anxiety were not in use then, and Harris did not have access to psychological counseling; there probably was never available an effective means of treating her mild depression, if indeed she experienced those symptoms.

18 THE LAST GARDEN

1. Paul Green to BKH, 20 June 1966, f18, BKH, UNC.

2. Clara Claasen to BKH, 1 July 1966, f21, BKH, UNC.

3. Southern Pines (N.C.) *Pilot,* 26 January 1972, clipping in BKH, Chowan.

4. BKH to Walser, 20 October 1966, f256, Walser, UNC.

5. Walter Moose, "At Home, She's Miss Kelly," private archives of Mrs. Jessie Stanley (Jessie Moose).

6. Bernice Kelly Harris, "Thank God for My Heart Attack," p. 1, f94, BKH, UNC. The title was meant to be ironic. See also Thomas L. Umphlet, M.D., to Dr. John Wesley Parker, 11 April 1968, f25, BKH, UNC, for a medical report.

7. F256, Walser, UNC. Sam Ragan recounted Harris's letter to him, quoting her in "Southern Accent," Raleigh *News and Observer,* 13 August 1967.

8. Magdeline Faison, oral history interview recorded by author, Roxboro, N.C., 28 August 1996, 1:386.

9. BKH to Mary, December 1971, f28, BKH, UNC.

10. Roy Parker Jr., oral history interview recorded by author, Fayetteville, N.C., 31 January 1966, 2:359.

11. F159, 2 pages on her garden, BKH, UNC. The essay was published in expanded, finished form as "Face It, This Year's Garden Is Your Last One" in the Raleigh *News and Observer,* 26 September 1965, sec. III, p. 9. It ends with the gardener choosing seeds for the next year's planting.

12. Erma Glover, telephone conversation with author, Chapel Hill, N.C., 22 March 1997. See also Erma W. Glover, "Salt of the Earth: Plain People in the Novels of Bernice Kelly Harris" (Ph.D. diss., University of North Carolina—Chapel Hill, 1977), 179.

13. Dick Walser to BKH, 9 June 1966, f21, BKH, UNC.

14. BKH to Mebane Burgwyn, 15 January 1967, Burgwyn archives.

15. BKH to Dick Walser, 10 May 1967, f256, Walser, UNC.

16. BKH to Dick Walser, 25 May 1967, f256, Walser, UNC.

17. Lambert Davis to BKH, 11 August 1967, f24, BKH, UNC.

18. Julia Street to BKH, 28 January 1968, f25, BKH, UNC.

19. J. O. Bailey to BKH, 24 April 1968, f25, BKH, UNC.

20. Leslie Phillabaum, letter to author, 7 March 1997, private archives of author.

21. J. O. Bailey to BKH, 12 May 1968, f25, BKH, UNC.

22. J. O. Bailey to BKH, 3 February 1969, f26, BKH, UNC.

23. BKH to J. O. Bailey, 25 March 1970, f27, BKH, UNC.

24. BKH to J. O. Bailey, 24 September 1970, f27, BKH, UNC. F98–f142 contains stories, many unpublished, as well as articles and speeches.

25. F172, 2 pages titled "Postscript Fictional," BKH, UNC. On the first page, "Fictional" is crossed out and "Apocryphal" is written above it.

26. Ragan to BKH, 26 July 1968, f25, Ragan to BKH, 24 April 1969, f26; Ragan to BKH, 29 May 1969, f26, BKH, UNC.

27. Claasen to BKH, 25 February 1969, f26, BKH, UNC.

28. Gordon Kelley, Raleigh, N.C., telephone conversation with author, Chapel Hill, N.C., 24 July 1997. Mr. Kelley read from Bill Kelly's will of 1952.

29. BKH to Mary Kelley (see postscript), 9 May 1966, f21, BKH, UNC.

30. Betsey Bradley Merritt, conversation with author, Roanoke Rapids, N.C., 5 April 1996.

31. President Whitaker to BKH, 5 December 1968 and 5 May 1971, BKH, Chowan.

32. F29, bank loan statement, 22 February 1972, BKH, UNC.

33. Thomas L. Umphlet, M.D., to Dr. John Wesley Parker, 11 April 1968, f25, BKH, UNC.

34. BKH to the Seaboard Town Commission, undated, f35, BKH, UNC.

35. F90, BKH, UNC.

36. BKH to Dick Walser, 2 May 1967, f256, Walser, UNC.

37. Elizabeth Bullock, oral history interview recorded by author, Seaboard, N.C., 19 June 1996, 1:047; Elizabeth Harris, oral history interview recorded by author, Seaboard, N.C., 19 June 1996, 1:107.

38. Bernice Kelly Harris, "To Plot a Story," f152, BKH, UNC.

39. Bernadette Hoyle to BKH, 25 August 1972, f29, BKH, UNC.

40. Bernice Kelly Harris, "Observations on Trends in Current Books," BKH, Chowan.

41. BKH to Alice Jo and Hal Burrows, 3 January 1973, private archives of Alice Jo Burrows.

42. F94, untitled pages, BKH, UNC.

43. Bullock, oral history, 1:378.

44. Ibid., 1:103, 1:149.

45. F94, untitled notes beginning "I never thought possible . . . ," p. 5, BKH, UNC.

46. Ibid.

47. Ibid., p. 6.

48. F95, pages titled "Mr. Simmons," BKH, UNC.

49. BKH to Lib and Reece Bullock, 18 September [1973], private archives of Mrs. Reece Bullock.

50. Bullock, oral history, 1:180.

51. F94, single page labeled "Leaf from the Diary of Bernice Kelly Harris," BKH, UNC.

52. Jonathan Carey Coats and Patricia Coats Kube, oral history interview recorded by author, Clayton, N.C., 9 March 1997, 1:614.

53. E. Harris, oral history, 1:553.

54. F91, pages titled "Thank God for My Heart Attack," BKH, UNC.

55. George Pyne, oral history interview recorded by author, Durham, N.C., 26 February 1996, 1:022. See also f94, untitled pages containing descriptions of fellow patients and events at the convalescent center, BKH, UNC.

56. Pyne, oral history, 1:033.

57. BKH to J. O. and Mary Bailey, 10 September 1973, f29, BKH, UNC.

58. BKH to Dick Walser, postcard, July 1973, f256, Walser, UNC.

59. BKH to Dick Walser, 23 August [1973], f256, Walser, UNC. The letter bears the incorrect year—1972—penciled in in brackets. It was August 1973 that Harris was in the nursing home. The letter also bears, in Walser's hand, the notation "Her last letter to me."

60. BKH to Lib and Reece Bullock, 13 September [1973], BKH, UNC. This letter was recently deposited in the Bernice Kelly Harris Papers at the University of North Carolina, Chapel Hill, by Elizabeth Bullock.

61. Bruce Whitaker, "Tribute to Bernice Kelly Harris, Funeral Remarks, 15 September 1973," BKH, Chowan.

62. Sam Ragan, oral history interview recorded by author, Southern Pines, N.C., 31 January 1996, 1:272; August Derleth, review of *Wild Cherry Tree Road*, *Chicago Tribune*, 14 October 1951, p. 13; Caroline Gordon, "Carolina in the Morning," *New Republic* 99 (12 July 1939): 286.

63. Richard H. King, *A Southern Renaissance: The Cultural Awakening of the American South, 1930–1955* (New York: Oxford University Press, 1980).

64. *Literary History of the United States*, rev. ed., vol. entitled *History* (New York: Macmillan, 1974); Thomas Daniel Young, Floyd C. Watkins, and Richmond Croom Beatty, eds., *The Literature of the South*, rev. ed. (Atlanta: Scott, Foresman, 1968).

65. Anne Goodwyn Jones, "*Gone with the Wind* and Others: Popular Fic-

tion, 1920–1950," in *The History of Southern Literature*, ed. Louis D. Rubin Jr. (Baton Rouge: Louisiana State University Press, 1985), 371.

66. Michael Kreyling, *Author and Agent: Eudora Welty and Diarmuid Russell* (New York: Farrar, Straus, Giroux, 1991), 39. Russell gave Welty her letters to him shortly before he died and she had kept several hundred of his letters to her; she turned over the correspondence to Kreyling. (See pp. 3–4.) When I wrote to Russell and Volkening to ask about Diarmuid Russell's correspondence with Bernice Kelly Harris, the reply was that the company had no archives and could offer no help. Letters from him in Harris's collection are impersonal and brief.

67. Ibid., 51.

68. Ibid., 49.

69. Ibid., 117.

70. Peggy Whitman Prenshaw, ed., *Conversations with Eudora Welty* (Jackson: University Press of Mississippi, 1984), 23.

71. Katherine Anne Porter, preface to *A Curtain of Green and Other Stories*, by Eudora Welty (New York: Doubleday, 1941). See also Eudora Welty, *One Writer's Beginnings* (Cambridge, Mass.: Harvard University Press, 1984), 96–97; Ruth M. Vande Kieft, *Eudora Welty*, rev. ed. (Boston: Twayne Publishers, 1987), 11; Louise Westling, *Eudora Welty* (Totowa, N.J.: Barnes and Noble, 1989), 19, 30–31; Joan Givner, *Katherine Anne Porter: A Life* (New York: Simon and Schuster, 1982), 483, 510.

72. Prenshaw, ed., *Conversations with Eudora Welty*, 32, 196, 231; Westling, *Eudora Welty*, 30–31.

73. Kreyling, *Author and Agent*, 14.

74. Anne Goodwyn Jones, "Frances Newman: The World's Lessons," in *Tomorrow Is Another Day: The Woman Writer in the South, 1859–1936* (Baton Rouge: Louisiana State University Press, 1981), 271–312. See also Anne Firor Scott's foreword to the 1980 reprint of Newman's novel, *The Hard-Boiled Virgin* (Athens: University of Georgia Press, 1980), v–xix.

75. Rose Ann C. Fraistat, *Caroline Gordon as Novelist and Woman of Letters* (Baton Rouge: Louisiana State University Press, 1984).

76. Joan Givner, *Katherine Anne Porter*, 86.

Index